DEATH
AND
SOCIETY

A Book of Readings and Sources

DEATH
AND
SOCIETY

A Book of
Readings and Sources

James P. Carse
New York University

Arlene B. Dallery
La Salle College

Harcourt Brace Jovanovich, Inc.
New York   Chicago   San Francisco   Atlanta

© 1977 by Harcourt Brace Jovanovich, Inc.

ISBN: 0-15-517211-5

Library of Congress Catalog Card Number: 7659627

Printed in the United States of America

Acknowledgments appear on page 470, which is a continuation
of the acknowledgments page.

PREFACE

"Death," Melville wrote in *Moby Dick,* "is only a launching into the region of the strange Untried; it is but the first salutation to the possibilities of the immense Remote, the Wild, the Unshored." Traditionally, discussion about death has been concerned chiefly with that "region of the strange Untried." What characterizes the present interest in death is an abrupt shift of focus from the point of arrival to the point of departure. The primary concern in the current literature is not with the fate of the dead but with the process or the experience of dying.

In the most recent books and articles we can, rather generally, identify two major emphases. There has been, on the one hand, great popular interest in the personal experience of dying. A number of deeply moving accounts by and about persons with mortal illnesses, as well as Kübler-Ross's famous study of dying patients, *On Death and Dying,* fall into this category. On the other hand, there is an increasing interest in the social context of dying. What social factors influence the way in which persons die? What impact does death have on the social fabric? What special responsibilities does society have with respect to death?

This book is concerned with the latter category: the shared, or social, meaning of death. It is impossible to make the distinction between social and personal aspects of death absolute, of course, and we do not presume to do so. The essays included here are not insensitive to the personal character of death. But primarily, and in a wide variety of ways, they challenge existing social attitudes and social practices concerning death. We have selected essays in which the challenge is intelligent and relevant enough so that we have been constrained to clarify our own thinking on each of the issues. Indeed, this volume may be taken as a tribute to the intelligent and courageous efforts of scholarly and professional men and women to provoke public consideration of issues we should carefully examine but often prefer to avoid.

We would like to thank a number of persons for invaluable critical and editorial assistance. Chief among them is C. Richard Roelofs, formerly a professor of philosophy at Kirkland College and currently Philosopher-Resident at Montefiore Hospital in New York City. Roelofs's knowledge of the literature and his keen critical abilities have significantly improved this volume. Professor Robert Fogelin of Yale University and Professor John McDermott of Queens College, both philosophers, have made vivid and useful judgments on the material included. To collect under one cover essays from such diverse origins and authors as are represented here inevitably brings with it an accumulation of editorial and textual difficulties. We have been enormously assisted in solving these by the patient attention to detail of Nancy Sebastiani, our editor, and Anne Boynton and Alexandra Roosevelt of the Harcourt Brace Jovanovich staff. Certainly the foresight and persistent encouragement of William Pullin, the supervising editor, have been indispensable. Alisa and Jamie Carse served enthusiastically as research assistants.

CONTENTS

Section Three   Suicide

Section Four   Death and the Law

Section Five   Death and Aging

Section Six   Death and the Caring Institutions

INTRODUCTION

This book is offered as a provocation for further reflection on the problem of death. Its design is to provide not conclusions but goads to further thought. Where conclusions do occur in the following essays, they were selected because they are certain to arouse more deliberation than they will quiet.

The selection of the pieces gathered in this volume was guided by three philosophical convictions. It is well that these be fully exposed at the outset.

The first conviction is that the discussion of the issues addressed by the authors of the following pages is inherently resistant to conclusions. It would be alarming if we came to suppose that we had done all the thinking necessary to arrive at a permanent settlement of even one of the questions considered here. If anyone should come to believe that the issue of euthanasia, or abortion, or capital punishment has been *forever settled,* we can be certain that he or she has presumed more knowledge and wisdom than is available to the human intelligence.

This is not to suggest, however, that these issues remain so ambiguous that they are beyond even preliminary resolution. We must remind ourselves that, for one thing, the issues do not wait until we are ready to act. They are issues precisely because we *must* act on them, whether or not we have the sufficient wisdom. Therefore, our choice is either to meet them blindly or to come to them as deliberately as possible without losing a sense of humility and modesty appropriate to matters of life and death.

The second philosophical conviction guiding the selection of material for this book is more complicated, although in its simplest statement it appears to be something of a truism: it is not possible to speak of death without speaking of life. This apparent commonplace cuts in two directions. To begin with, it implies that death in itself is not a subject available to investigation. To look directly at death is, in a strict sense, to look at nothing at all. It is true enough that death is a word of very frequent use, and a concept found everywhere in both high and low literature. But what is it a concept *about?* What does the word *mean?*

Death never presents itself to us in the abstracted form of a word or a concept; there is no such thing as death in general; neither is death simply a condition in which certain kinds of objects are to be found. Death is always the death *of something.*

Consider for a moment several of the ways in which we ordinarily use the word "dead." We would say that a mummy is dead, but we would not say that a stone is dead. The mummy was once alive, the stone never was. In this case, "dead" refers to the absence of life, and although the mummy has no more life in it than a stone it powerfully reminds us of a life now forever ended. In a somewhat different way we might, on the other hand, use the word "dead" for objects that were never alive. We say that a radio has gone dead, or that we have brought the car to a dead stop. This way of using the word does not imply a prior state of life, but has rather the sense of a definitive conclusion. When the radio goes dead it is not that the sound has gone too low to hear; when the car is brought to a dead stop it has not merely slowed. Here dead means complete disfunction, an absolute end.

It is instructive to note what these uses of the word "dead" have in common. They refer to a prior state, but a state that has utterly ceased to exist. They do not, it should be emphasized, indicate in any way a continuing state. When the radio has gone dead we do not say that the radio is in a state of death. And when we say of the mummy that it is dead it is very different from saying that the mummy now lies in the realm of death—as though death was a kind of place or a condition that continues from the end of life. Something is dead because it has come to a perfect end; it continues to exist or to function in no way whatsoever.

When we examine the ordinary uses of "dead" and "death" it is clear that we have moved into a slightly murky terminological region. We are tempted into some curious inconsistencies and therewith into confusion, which in some cases can have unfortunate consequences. In the example of the mummy, for instance, we are likely to say that although the mummy is dead *it* once was alive. It is not the mummy that once lived, however; it is a person whose body is now this mummy. This is not to say that the mummy somehow survived death in the way that the person did not; the mummy is profound evidence that a *person* has come to an end without remainder. The possible confusion in this rises in the thought that something *both* comes to an end *and* continues.

There is something in this terminology that roughly resembles a question like "Where does the light go when the candle has been put out?" The question as phrased seems to demand as an answer that there is a place to which the light has gone after leaving the wick of the candle. We can see easily in the case of the candle that such thinking is nonsensical, but in the case of the death of a person it seems to make more sense. "Where does a person go after he or she has died?" It is easier to think of a realm of extinguished persons than a realm of extinguished candle flames. But it makes no more sense. If a person "goes somewhere" after death, then the person has not died; the person has not come to an end without remainder, has not ceased utterly to exist. A person cannot *both* die *and* continue to exist.

The reader should be careful to note that we are only clarifying our terminology and not making claims about the nature of death itself. It may well be that persons *do* go somewhere after they have apparently died, but if they do we are constrained by the consistency of our discourse to say that the death of persons can only be "apparent."

This brief look at our use of the words "dead" and "death" has been offered only in the interest of clarifying the second philosophical conviction guiding the editorial judgments in this book, that is, that it is not possible to speak of death without speaking of life. When we talk about death we cannot talk about a *state* or a *condition,* but only about that which has come to an end without remainder. In this book we speak about death in a special sense: we are not simply noting that life has here and there come to an end, we are asking why and how life came to an end in these ways for these persons, and whether that must be so. In other words, we are examining death as though it were an issue, but an issue that can be resolved only within the context of life.

It was asserted earlier that the commonplace—one cannot speak of death without speaking of life—cuts in two directions. Here is the other side of it: when we see that death is always the death *of something,* we see just as clearly that life, too, is always the life *of something.* Life does not present itself from this perspective as an abstract force somehow separate from living entities. In truth, we do not see life as it is in itself at all; we see only living beings.

To be sure, we must have some way of knowing whether this entity or that is in fact alive. There are assorted attempts to develop definitions of life that will remove whatever confusion we might have in this matter, but in our ordinary going and coming we are rarely confused, even if we are fully ignorant of the scientific definitions of life. When we regard something as alive we seem at least to be granting it the qualities of spontaneity and unpredictability and ascribing to it a range of still unrealized possibility. When we say that something is alive we are saying that to some degree its future is still open and the possibilities that lie before it are a function of its own momentum forward in time. We are especially attentive to the vitality of something—usually another person—when we can see that his or her future is likely to have a strong influence on our own. We mean at least this, and no doubt much more, when we ascribe life to other beings.

This observation is not offered as a novelty, and certainly not as an invention of the present writer, for it is ancient wisdom indeed. We might put it all in another way: when we reflect on the fact that life is in every case the life of something, or of someone, life appears to us in its limitless variety, its dazzling manifold. This has the consequence of sharpening the awareness of one's own engagement with the world of living beings.

But when we see life in its endless variability it wears another, darker aspect. It appears exceedingly fragile and vulnerable. When we see life as the life of something we are not deceived by the numerical vastness of life. The fact that a city is teeming with life may not replace the fact that the mass is composed only of single individuals for whom the question of life and death is particular and absolute. The life of a group, or a nation, or a species is never exchangeable with the life of an individual. Therefore, where we see variety we see fragility; more than that—we see intricate patterns of interdependence. This brings us to the third philosophical conviction around which the essays and readings in this volume have been organized.

The brutish fact that life is not an abstract force separate from the concrete manifold draws attention to the radical dependency of all living creatures on their environment and on each other. Life can neither originate nor continue in a social or physical vacuum. Nothing has life entirely of itself. It does not give birth to itself, nor can anything sustain its life without recourse to a community of living beings.

This is even more obviously true when we inquire into the nature of human existence. It is impossible to imagine how personhood can generate *ex nihilo,* without, that is, a quite specific physical environment. If, however, we see personhood only in terms of its physical origin and composition we might know *what* a person is, but not *who* he or she is. And unless we can know *who* someone is, we cannot know him or her as a person. Personhood cannot develop in a social vacuum, but must always develop in relation with others as persons. To ask who a person is we must ask *with whom* he or she is in relation.

If I should learn, for example, that this person is an artist, and that person is a weightlifter, I might know in a superficial sense what they are, by knowing the characteristics generally shared by all artists and by all weightlifters. But I am still far from knowing *who* these two persons are, for I do not know for whom and with whom they pursue their labors; I do not know what their dreams are, or their disappointments. However, even when I have learned all this about them, I still will not have learned *who* they are until I relate to them myself, and they to me, as persons.

There is an enchanting paradox that makes its appearance at this point. According to this line of thinking personhood arises in a context of social interdependence, but at the same time each person is utterly distinct from all others. Personhood is socially derived, yet existentially unique. To be a person one must exist in a public medium, but to be a person is simultaneously to be irreducibly private.

What does this third conviction—the interdependence of life

and particularly personal life—have to do with death? It means that, at the human level, death always shows itself as the death of a person—a unique and irreducibly private person. When we reflect on the death of persons we must therefore consider death an event that occurs within the deepest secrecy of one's own internality, and at the same time an event that occurs within the patterns of interdependence in the social fabric.

In a community of persons it is essential to remember that dependence is reciprocal, that persons are *inter*dependent on each other. There are few events, if any, more revealing of interdependence than death. Consider, as an example, the death of a child. It is obvious enough that the child is dependent for its well-being, and often its life, on a circle of adults. What is less obvious is that there is also a circle of persons who depend on the well-being of the child. The child's death is certain to compel the attending physicians, the parents, and others close to the child to revise the way they understand themselves and subsequently each other.

In an acute sense every death is testimony to the limitations of support any community can provide; and just as acutely each death tears at the structure of relations by which persons have arrived at their own identities. The surgeon whose patient dies in the course of an operation, the mother whose child is killed crossing a street, even the person who has lost a parent at an advanced age, must, to some degree, re-examine the images and roles by which they understand themselves.

There is a subtle issue in the question of the limitations of support available to each of us from our several communities. Is death *in every case* attributable to the inability of others to provide support? It might well be argued that some deaths are natural, others fitting, and still others deserved—and therefore have nothing to do with the dependence of the dying person on others. Indeed, some of the following essays argue for the appropriateness of death on both social and personal grounds. But beneath the matter of appropriateness there is a persistent question: even in those cases where disease has become so painful and destructive that death is a kind of blessing, is there not still some sense in which we have failed? We have failed to eliminate the disease, or to protect the healthy from disease. This question persists equally in the issue of the "natural" death of the aged, or the imposed death of the criminal.

The force of this line of reflection lies not in the vision of an indefinitely prolonged life, but in the perceived difficulty of marking that point at which the struggle against death should be abandoned. It is the point at which the community of caring persons must acknowledge its limitations in sustaining life. It is also the point at which another issue emerges: having accepted the fact that we do not have the resources, skill, or ability to keep a person alive, what may we do to make life richer and more meaningful. The inevitable failure of the caring community to keep death from the door makes "the quality of life" question inescapable. This, too, is what is comprehended in the term interdependence.

It is the interdependence of human society—as it is exposed by the phenomenon of death—which each of the essays in this book addresses. What has been omitted has been any literature primarily concerned with death as it was faced and experienced subjectively by separate individuals. This is by no means to make the judgment that such literature is unworthy of thoughtful consideration; on the contrary, one's reflection on the nature of death is most incomplete without it. It is only to acknowledge that that literature is too vast to be adequately represented here. It is the impression of the present editors that there has been a far deeper interest in the private, existential anguish of the dying and the bereaved, than in the societal implications of death. This book is therefore a modest attempt to stimulate the discussion and the exploration of the latter.

The essays selected in this volume are in almost every case taken from scholarly and legal journals, and are not, therefore, easily available to the general reader. It will be immediately apparent that they are addressed to both learned and personal interests. The topics and the controversies they have traced out and examined are persistent, potentially dangerous, and exceedingly timely. Moreover, they are matters on which each one of us, given the interdependence of our relation to our own society, must take some part in resolving. Even our inaction will, in each of these issues, count as an action. It is therefore the design of this volume to prepare the reader for this reflection with some of the best material available.

DEATH
AND
SOCIETY
A Book of Readings and Sources

section

ABORTION

When it is raised as an issue abortion presents several unique characteristics in the general subject of death and society. It shares with other types of death—notably suicide, homicide, and euthanasia—the fact that it is a *death by choice,* but the nature and terms of that choice are quite unique to abortion.

Certainly, in one sense, abortion *is* homicide. It is the willful ending of a life. But in another sense it is useful for the sake of discussing the issues to make a distinction between abortion and murder, if by "murder" we mean not only the willful, but also the illegal and immoral, termination of one person's life by another person. Abortion is an issue because there are many who do not consider it murder, and some who do not even consider it homicide —views deeply offensive to many others.

There are superficial differences between abortion and murder that should not distract our attention from the weightier issues. In the great majority of cases, for example, abortion is performed by a highly trained clinician in a medically controlled setting at the conscious request of an adult woman in good physical and mental health. Murder, on the other hand, is almost always performed by a person whose motives arise from irrational passions, who has given very little, if any, thought to the act and its consequences. To be sure, there are murders committed by coolly deliberate, or even professional, killers, and there are abortions performed by desparate amateurs with serious potential complications for the pregnant woman. But, in either case, we should not be misled into thinking that the abortion issue is resolved because nearly all abortions are now performed by competent medical personnel who have driven the incompetent amateurs out of business. The question of the legality and the morality of abortion remains regardless of the medical skill and competence of the abortionist.

We might note that euthanasia shares with abortion a particularly deliberative character. It is a kind of death that requires a willful act, and, inasmuch as the act is willful, presupposes a reasoning process. But the reasoning appropriate to euthansia is quite distinct from that involved in abortion. The question concerns not the meaning of a life as yet unlived, but the meaning of a life with great suffering or permanent impairment of personality.

By what paths of deliberation, then, does one determine whether abortion is legal and/or moral? For the most part, the abortion debate has centered on a relatively few questions: At what point in the development of a fetus can we say it has become a *person?* What is the status of a fetus's or infant's *right to life?* What are the *social factors* that make abortion desirable, or abhorrent? What is the proper role of the *courts and legislatures* in the abortion issue? That is, is the decision to abort a fetus a matter to be resolved by the pregnant woman in the *privacy* of her own conscience, or is it a matter to be resolved through the legal institutions representative of the society at large?

It can be seen in these questions that one of the most provocative features of the abortion debate is the way in which it joins matters of public policy with matters of privacy. Many persons are apalled by the decisions of (mostly male) judges and legislators concerning how much control a woman should have over her own body. At the same time, a large segment of the population vividly expresses its shock at what appears to be the blithe capacity of a growing number of young women and their physicians to execute the innocent unborn.

Given the long history of abortion and its almost universal practice in the modern world, it is certain that it will not go away by itself. For that reason there is no way of avoiding the development of public policy concerning abortion. Not to have a social policy is, in effect, to have one, for to have no laws forbidding or regulating it would allow abortion to flourish—and, in the opinion of many, allow a particularly dreadful crime to abound. On the other hand, to have a restrictive public policy is viewed as repugnant by many others. It violates their own moral or philosophical views, or it is seen as the cause of widespread illegal and therefore often medically dangerous practice of abortion.

What hope is there for a public policy that can reconcile all parties to the issue? Is there even a way of bringing clarity into the discussion through careful exploration of the issues?

It is prudent, of course, to acknowledge that attitudes toward the question of abortion are affected by social and personal factors that have little to do with rational deliberation. If recent studies of some of the measurable social factors show any general agreement, it is that religious affiliation exerts a greater influence on attitudes toward abortion than such other factors as age, political affiliation, geographical location, income, and educational level. Studies of the latter factors are inconsistent in assessing their influence.

One recent survey of the attitudes of nurses and social workers toward abortion* shows that while younger persons tended more frequently to approve of abortion, it was religion that had the greatest influence. Forty-two percent of the conservative Christians polled approved of abortion, whereas 74 percent of the liberal Christians polled approved. ("Approval" of abortion in this study includes approval under any one of the following conditions: endangered health of the mother, expected deformity of the fetus, rape, pregnancy out of wedlock, economic hardship, and the desire to have no more children.)

One provocative finding of this study is that frequency of church attendance was more important than actual affiliation in determining attitudes. Among both conservatives and liberals infrequent church attendance was associated with proabortion attitudes. Fifty-six percent of the conservatives who occasionally or never attend church approve abortion, while 83 percent of the poorly attending liberals approve. The reasons for the association

---

* Bradley Hertel, Gerry E. Hendershot, James W. Grimm, "Religion and Attitudes Toward Abortion: A Study of Nurses and Social Workers," *Journal for the Scientific Study of Religion,* vol. 13, no. 1, March, 1974, pp. 23–34. This article contains a useful bibliography for the student interested in coordinating the social factors involved in abortion.

between attitudes on this question and church attendance are left open by the authors, though they suggest that "the most obvious interpretation is that in the course of attending worship services the memberships of conservative as well as liberal denominations find reinforcement for conservative attitudes toward abortion."†

If the rational development of a public policy concerning abortion must take into account religious affiliation as an influence on individual attitudes, it must also take notice of economic factors. There is certainly no way in which the value of a human life can be measured in dollars, but there are economic realities that will have some effect on the public response to abortion legislation.

It has been well-documented that in states where abortion is prohibited except for narrowly specified medical or psychiatric reasons, the frequency of abortion is directly related to the woman's economic status. In these states costly medical examination, or travel to another state or country, may be necessary.‡

There are less obvious but equally significant economic and social factors involved in the abortion issue. When an unwanted pregnancy forces the marriage of the teenage father and mother, for example, they tend to terminate their education much earlier than their peers, thereby sharply reducing their expected life earnings. Such marriages are less stable, lead to a higher percentage of mental illness, and, due to poor prenatal medical care, have a greater chance of producing mentally retarded offspring.

Unwanted births within even a stable marriage can be economically and socially costly to the entire family. Mothers with young children are very frequently required to interrupt or cease their employment altogether, with the ironic effect that the family's income is reduced at a time when its expenses are increased. Some studies indicate that there may be more than 1,000,000 unwanted births a year. It is further relevant to note the fact that poverty and family size are positively related. It is difficult to say, of course, whether it is poverty that causes an increase in the number of children, or family size that depresses the family's economic status, but the association of these factors should not be ignored—particu-

† Ibid, p. 31.
‡ The relevant studies are cited by Charlotte Muller, "Socioeconomic Out-moomes of Restricted Access to Abortion," *American Journal of Public Health,* vol. 61, no. 6, June, 1971, pp. 1110–1118.

larly in light of the studies indicating that the desired size of poor and nonpoor families is about the same.§

In sum, there is compelling evidence that unwanted pregnancy and birth can not only reduce a family's economic viability but can also retard or prevent its achievement of economic viability, with serious consequences to the psychological and physical health of its members.

It is important to keep in mind that the socioeconomic factors are not in themselves arguments for liberal abortion legislation. They constitute evidence that may be used for such arguments. But the same data might be used by opponents of liberal legislation as a guide to the formulation of social policy. Abortion, after all, is not the only way of preventing an unwanted pregnancy from being an economic or psychological hardship to a person or a family.

In 1973 the Supreme Court handed down two decisions relating directly to the abortion issue, *Roe* v. *Wade,* 410 U.S. 113 (1973) and *Doe* v. *Bolton,* 410 U.S. 179 (1973). (The names used in these cases, Jane Roe and Jane Doe, are fictitious—to protect the anonymity of the two women involved.) While these two decisions have by no means settled the question, they have had the effect of establishing public policy on the question of abortion, causing a profound change in medical practice. The first selection in this section summarizes the two abortion decisions, sets them in their legal context, and indicates the likely areas of controversy.

Since the Supreme Court deliberately left unanswered the question as to whether the fetus is a *person,* there is certain to be a continuing objection to the decisions around the question of the personhood of the unborn. The second selection in this section is an article written by Eugene F. Diamond, a pediatrician, who insists that personhood begins with conception and that abortion is therefore to be regarded as homicide. Diamond's article was written before the decision, but it forcefully states the position many have taken in opposition to the Court.

It may be thought that Diamond's position is typical of the attitude most members of the Catholic church have toward abortion. That not all thoughtful Catholics take this position is evident in the

§ For more detailed discussion and documentation of these issues see Muller, op. cit.

third selection, "A Liberal Catholic's View," by J. F. Donceel. Following an unusual line of argument Donceel says that the soul of a person does not come into existence at the moment of conception and concludes that abortion in the early months of pregnancy is therefore permissable.

The fourth selection, "Abortion: Parameters for Decision," by R. J. Gerber, carefully examines the basic distinction involved in the discussion of the personhood issue. One may consider the nature of the unborn fetus either from a genetic perspective, or from an interpersonal perspective. In the genetic view the fetus is regarded primarily in relation to itself; that is, it is already genetically complete, it is biologically unique, and, while it cannot exist independently of the mother, it cannot be considered a "part" of the mother, for it has a number of physical characteristics quite distinct from her. In the interpersonal view the fetus is regarded primarily in relation to others. It must therefore be seen as incomplete in itself until it has entered into the postnatal world of social relations in which its personhood begins to develop. Gerber pays his respects to both views, but gives his concluding support to the former.

In Judith Thomson's "A Defense of Abortion," the next article in this section, the question of the personhood of the fetus is set aside. Thomson's rather surprising and novel approach to the abortion question is to examine the fetus's "right to life," which is claimed for it by most who are antiabortion. Thomson's article occasioned a vigorous response, to which reference will be made later as a guide to those readers who would wish to follow out the lines of this argument.

Another aspect of the right-to-life question is considered by Michael Tooley, in his "Abortion and Infanticide," where he takes what could be called the extreme liberal position, arguing that an organism has a right to life only when it is a person in the interpersonal sense mentioned above. This has the surprising consequence of a limited approval of infanticide, and in rare instances a disapproval of the killing of animals.

The final essay in this section moves just beyond the edge of abortion proper and addresses the question of infanticide itself. Phillip Resnick's study of neonaticide is a grim reminder of one of the consequences at stake in the larger question of abortion. Lacking the technical knowledge, perhaps also the courage, mothers desiring to abort their children may wait until they are born before they destroy them. The practice is common enough so that it would be irresponsible to omit this from one's final view of abortion. Of course, the specter of neonaticide may support either side of the abortion issue: for supporters of liberal legislation it is one more reminder of the need for early and medically supervised abortion; for antiabortion views it is one more social phenomenon to be addressed by individuals and institutions committed to caring for unwanted pregnancies and unwanted births.

THE SUPREME COURT
DECISIONS ON ABORTION

James P. Carse

*In two of the most controversial and emotion-laden cases ever
to have come before the Supreme Court, a majority of justices
concurred in decisions allowing abortion to be performed by
licensed physicians with only limited interference from the state.
The decisions were bold and sweeping, and though they did little
to settle the controversy, they have done much to define its major
issues.*

James P. Carse is an editor of the present volume.

The Supreme Court decisions on abortion came in companion cases,
Roe v. *Wade* and *Doe* v. *Bolton,* on January 22, 1973. The Court
heard these cases in the midst of considerable public controversy
and against a murky and confused legal background. The controversy has not been ended by the decisions in *Wade* and *Bolton;*
indeed, in some respects it may have been refueled. It does seem
evident, however, that the Court's approach to the issue in its majority decision has had a broad impact on the shape of the discussion.
Involved in the Court's deliberations were the notions of the mother's
right to privacy, the personhood of the fetus, and the health of
the mother.

In *Wade* the Court heard the case of a single woman (referred
to anonymously as "Jane Roe") who, in March of 1970, had challenged a Texas criminal statute permitting abortion only when the
life of the mother was at stake. Ms. Roe sought to have her pregnancy terminated by a licensed physician under medically safe
circumstances and was prevented by the District Attorney of Dallas
County. She then sought, and received, a court's permission to have
the abortion performed by a physician. Roe's physician had already

been arrested for two illegally performed abortions, and he eventually joined his patient in the case that went before the Supreme Court.

The Court concluded that the statute was unconstitutional, chiefly on the grounds that the mother's right to privacy, as guaranteed by the due process clause of the Fourteenth Amendment, was being violated.

By appealing to the right to privacy the Court raised the question of abortion in its most acute form. Justice Blackmun, writing the majority opinion, notes that the right to privacy is nowhere mentioned in the constitution, but that there is a long list of Court decisions in which such a right is inferred from the constitution as intended by its framers. A right to privacy, so inferred, "is broad enough to encompass a woman's decision whether or not to terminate her pregnancy."[1]

But what is the basis of this right, and exactly how broad is it? On the face of it, we might assume that the reason the Court included abortion under the right to privacy is that such a right allows one to do with one's body whatever one wishes, without the intervention or approval of another. When such a right is introduced into the abortion discussion it brings with it the assumption that the fetus is just as much a part of the mother's body as her appendix or tonsils, and may therefore be removed upon request.

When the right to privacy is appealed to in this way it would seem to be absolute in the question of abortion. Certainly one way in which the absolute exercise of that right could be challenged is to argue that the fetus is, in fact, not a part of the mother's body in the way her appendix is a part; that the fetus is a person in its own right. This point is not lost on the Court, for they admit that if the fetus is a person then Jane Roe's case "of course, collapses, for the fetus's right to life would then be guaranteed specifically by the [Fourteenth] Amendment."[2]

This point constrains the Court to inquire into the possibility that the fetus is a person. Two remarks are made concerning the personhood of the fetus, each of them confusing and controversial.

---

[1] All quotations in this article come from *The Supreme Court Reporter,* vol. 93, pp. 727–36.
[2] Ibid., p. 728.

The first is that "no case could be cited that holds that a fetus is a person within the meaning of the Fourteenth Amendment."[3] Nowhere does the constitution seem to regard the fetus as a person "in the whole sense." Unborn children, for example, have no property rights. They must be born alive to be considered heirs. This remark seems to have the effect of removing any challenge to the mother's right to privacy.

The second observation on the personhood of the fetus comes in the Court's admission that there is considerable dispute on this question and that it may be unanswerable:

> We need not resolve the difficult question of when life begins. When those trained in the respective disciplines of medicine, philosophy and theology are unable to arrive at any consensus, the judiciary, at this point in the development of man's knowledge, is not in a position to speculate as to the answer.[4]

There are serious difficulties with both of these remarks. The fact that the law does not recognize the fetus as a person does not have as a logical consequence that one can therefore do with the fetus whatever one wishes. Dogs and cats are also not recognized as persons by the law; though the state is presumed to have the right to limit the amount of physical harm done to such creatures.

The fact that it cannot be determined whether a fetus is a person, beyond the appeal to legal precedent, does not mean that we can then approve legislation that assumes the fetus is *not* a person, as the Court seems to do—at least, the fetus is not considered a person during the first two trimesters, or six months, of pregnancy.

So far it would appear that the Court is giving the mother an absolute right to privacy, including a decision to terminate her pregnancy whenever she wishes. The Court, however, refuses to give her this right without limitation. The right to privacy is not "absolute" Justice Blackmun has written.

> The Court's decisions recognizing a right of privacy also acknowledge that some state regulation in areas protected by that right is appropriate."[5]

[3] Ibid., pp. 728f.
[4] Ibid., p. 730.
[5] Ibid., p. 727.

For example, the state may pass legislation having regulatory effect "in safeguarding health, in maintaining medical standards, and in protecting potential life."[6]

The Court then concluded that, when considering the mother's right to privacy along with the state's right to protect the mother's health, there should be no interference from the state during the first trimester of pregnancy. The Court cited evidence that mortality rates for abortion during the first trimester are lower than for delivery at full term, therefore abortion in that period is in the interest of the mother's health.

The Court then went on to say that since the danger to the mother's health increases in abortions performed during the second trimester, the state may enact such legislation as will protect the mother's health in this period and to that degree may interfere with the practice of abortion. Critics have been quick to point out that this prescription of the Court is extremely vague, leaving unresolved precisely what legislation would be appropriate.

There is another limitation to the right to privacy: it is limited not only by the state's legitimate concern for the mother's health, but also by what the Court refers to as the "viability" of the fetus. The Court means by its use of the term viability, that the fetus "has the capability of meaningful life outside the mother's womb."[7] The Court ascertained from medical evidence that viability begins with the third trimester, or at the end of the sixth month. From that point on states may enact legislation that protects the "potential life" of the fetus, allowing abortion only when the mother's "health or life" are at stake. This provision is also quite vague, but it clearly permits the states to enact stronger regulatory legislation than seems to be acceptable for the second trimester.

In the second case before the Court, *Doe* v. *Bolton,* ("Jane Doe" is also a pseudonym) the opinions were somewhat less controversial, but nonetheless significant in their social consequences. In *Bolton* the Court declared unconstitutional a number of procedural requirements established by law in the state of Georgia. The Court struck down the requirement that the hospital in which the abortion was performed be accredited by the Joint Committee on Accreditation of Hospitals. The Court determined that abortions could be performed in clinics or other facilities that were properly

[6] Ibid., p. 727.
[7] Ibid., p. 732.

equipped for such services. The requirement that a woman must be a resident of the state was voided on the ground that the same requirement does not apply to other kinds of medical treatment. Much the same reasoning was used in striking down a provision that called for the concurrence of two other physicians in the decision to abort.

The effect of these requirements, and others similar to them was plainly to make the practice of abortion much more inconvenient for the pregnant woman. The Court's action therefore had the consequence of increasing the availability of abortions, and, incidentally, decreasing their cost. It was a decision that dramatically expanded the use of abortion for reasons that are as much personal and social as they are medical.

It is appropriate to note here that it may well be that among the consequences of this action of the Court is the establishment of abortion as a remedy so extensive in use that the public will begin to consider it a permanent ingredient in medical care, making it all the more difficult to pass legislation restricting the availability of abortion. In other words, however one feels about the legality or morality of abortion, this action of the Court has gone far in affecting actual social practice.

This latter point is all the more notable for the fact that in a dissenting opinion Mr. Justice White wrote that this action was "an improvident and extravagant exercise of the power of judicial review," insisting that this is the sort of matter that "should be left with the people and to the political processes."[8] It may be that following *Wade* and *Bolton* the general political climate concerning abortion is strongly inclined toward liberal legislation. Justice Rehnquist had also expressed his doubt, in a dissenting opinion, that the public actually intends to deprive the fetus of its right to life. This is also the sort of sentiment that can be profoundly altered by the widespread practice of abortion. It may seem much less abhorrent as the act becomes more common.

It was observed above that while the Supreme Court's decisions clarified the murky legal status of abortion as it was addressed in a number of state statutes, other questions of a significant legal nature were raised. A number of critics of the Court's action on abortion, including the dissenting justices, have pointed out that the majority

[8] Ibid., p. 736.

opinion had too much the character of *making* law, and did little by way of *interpreting* the law. It is certainly the case that the Supreme Court must infer from the constitution many points of law not directly specified there, but it is widely felt that, particularly in *Roe* v. *Wade,* the Court inferred points of law, and perhaps also points of value, that have no basis in the constitution. How much weight was the Court giving to the constitution, or at least the intentions of the constitution, and how much to prevailing social and medical thought?

It is evident that the Court, in reaching its conclusions, made use of medical opinion, especially in the matter of the viability of the fetus, and in the question of the health of the mother. This has the effect of the Court deciding which medical opinions to accept, thereby raising the question as to why it should be the Court and not the state legislatures that should be dealing with such points of substance. Is there a special wisdom inherent in the Justices of the Supreme Court but not found in the elected officials of the people? Are there not questions about the desires and beliefs of the public that only their elected representatives would be in a position to answer?

The difficulties become even subtler when we consider the shifting nature of medical knowledge and practice. What, for example, if it is learned that a fetus is viable much earlier than the final trimester? What if it is possible to eliminate all danger to the health of the mother during the second trimester? Which of these developments would have the greater weight? Does this mean that abortion should be restricted during the second trimester, or is it rather that it should be even less restricted than the Court specified in *Wade?*

These questions persist. The Court was under great pressure to act, and its decision to hear these cases may even have been courageous. At the very least it can be said that the medical and philosophical issues have been both intensified and sharpened by the Court's opinions, and that access to abortion has been enormously eased, with the likely consequence of giving greater strength to the social forces pressing for the further liberalization of abortion legislation.

THE HUMANITY OF THE UNBORN CHILD

Eugene F. Diamond, M.D.

Combining his experience and knowledge as a physician with a strong point of view, Dr. Diamond offers this essay as a statement on behalf of the unborn child and in opposition to the practice of abortion. "Ninety-two percent of abortions are performed for social reasons, not medical," he argues, and indicates that the medical necessity for abortion is often exaggerated.

Eugene F. Diamond is on the staff of the Department of Pediatrics, Loyola University Stritch School of Medicine.

This article is taken from the Catholic Lawyer, *Spring, 1971.*

My position is to speak for the fetus and to be his advocate. This is an appropriate assignment for a pediatrician and in keeping with the current trend in the relationship between obstetrician and pediatrician; the obstetrician now recognizes that he is responsible for two patients, the mother and her unborn child.

To consider the fetus not to be a separate person but merely a part of the mother has not been tenable since the sixteenth century when Arantius showed that the maternal and fetal circulations were separate—neither continuous nor contiguous. The genetic material of this separate human embryo is certainly unique, determinative and complete. It is certainly alive since it possesses that hallmark of life—the ability to reproduce dying cells. It can be distinguished at any stage of development from any other non-human species. Once implanted, it requires only time and nutrition. Only two possible futures are open to it. It can become a live human being or a dead human fetus.

An editorial in *California Medicine* poses the life and death issues of abortion in their proper perspective:

> Since the old ethic has not yet been fully displaced, it has been necessary to separate the idea of abortion from the idea of killing, which continues to be socially abhorrent. The result has been a curi-

ous avoidance of the scientific fact, which everyone really knows, that human life begins at conception and is continuous whether intra or extra-uterine until death. The very considerable semantic gymnastics which are required to rationalize abortion as anything but taking a human life would be ludicrous if they were not often put forth under socially impeccable circumstances.[1]

Let us trace the typical pregnancy as it relates to the question of abortion. The average woman will not suspect she is pregnant until her menstrual period is missed and overdue by about a week. By this time, she is three weeks pregnant and the embryo's heart is already beating. She can confirm her pregnancy after six weeks of gestation by a biological test. By six weeks, all organ systems are present and functioning in the unborn child. Most abortions are performed between the eighth and the twelfth week of pregnancy. At eight weeks of pregnancy, we have a functioning nervous system. If you stroke the upper lip of an eight week fetus, it will flex its neck. This is a confirmation of reflex activity and a functional nervous system. Furthermore, an electroencephalographic tracing done at eight weeks will show brain waves essentially the same as the newborn infant and not substantially different from the brain waves of a mature adult. By twelve weeks the fetus will squint, swallow and suck his thumb. More importantly, he will withdraw from a painful stimulus or, in other words, he perceives pain. When abortion is done at twelve weeks, it is done by the method of dilitation and curettage. That is, the neck of the womb is opened up and the fetus removed in pieces by a sharp curet. When such a procedure is done, there is little doubt that the fetus, in fact, feels what is done to it. Between the sixteenth and the twentieth week, the preferred abortion procedure would be hysterotomy. A small Caesarean section is done and the fetus removed intact. Such a procedure at this stage almost always results in a live birth by the criteria established internationally for the definition of a live birth. In New York, for example, when a hysterotomy is performed at twenty weeks, the law requires that the operating surgeon first fill out a birth certificate and *after all signs of life subside,* that he then fill out a death certificate. It is obviously ludicrous to suggest that life did not exist when a birth has been certified by a legal document and equally

---

[1] Editorial, *California Medicine.* 113:3 (1970).

ludicrous to suggest that abortion does not result in death when the State requires the confirmation of a death by a death certificate. The New York City Health Department does admit to the report of twenty-six such live births (as confirmed in a Chicago Tribune expose by Ron Kotulak). One of the live births actually survived and has survived and has now been adopted. Between twenty and twenty-four weeks gestation, the preferred method of abortion is by the saline amniocentesis or "salting out" method. This procedure is accompanied by a high risk of complications. The New York State Health Department reported complications as occurring in 30–33% of women who had abortions by salting-out during the first four months of the New York law. The procedure consists in the injection of a 20% salt solution into the womb. The purpose of this injection is to kill the baby. He usually has a few convulsive movements prior to death and labor occurs spontaneously a short time later with the expulsion of a dead fetus. One instance was reported in which the saline was injected into the amniotic sac of only one of a pair of fraternal twins (because the diagnosis of twins had not been made). When labor occurred, twins were born; one of which was dead and the other (uninjected) twin was alive. We have photographs of fetuses in various stages of development which further confirm the fact that abortion procedures are not performed on "amorphous cell masses" or "blobs of protoplasm" as some abortion lobbyists have suggested. No abortion in history has ever been performed on a "fertilized egg" because the woman does not even know she is pregnant at this point. What we as a society must really face up to, in the push toward abortion on demand, is the fact that developed, anthropomorphic human beings are to be sacrificed to achieve allegedly desirable societal goals. There is a serious question as to whether these goals are even achieved, but the means proposed for their achievement must be clearly understood. The public must comprehend that the real issue is whether any woman at any time, for any reason (or for no reason) should be allowed to terminate her pregnancy. Since the vast majority of Americans reject the principle abortion on demand (77% are opposed according to a recent study[2]); we can safely presume that they would reject any legislative proposal which was clearly recognizable as espousing demand abortion.

[2] Blake, *Abortion and Public Opinions,* The 1960–1970 Decade Science. 171:540 (1971).

The consensus of the American people regarding abortion for various medical indications is another matter. The principle of "therapeutic abortion" is not overwhelmingly rejected by the American people. In most instances, however, the portrayal of the true issues involved in therapeutic abortion has been distorted or oversimplified.

The incidence of abortions done in hospitals to preserve the mother's life, to preserve the mother's health, and for psychiatric indications have all decreased in the past twenty years. The only type of abortion which has increased during that time is the abortion done for the so-called "fetal indication." The use of this term is in itself a misnomer. One cannot justify an abortion on the basis of a fetal indication since no fetus has ever survived an abortion. The justification for such an abortion must then be either a form of euthanasia to spare the child a life with handicaps or for the purpose of saving the parents the happenstance of having an abnormal child, or to provide for the termination of an unwanted pregnancy.

There is no evidence to indicate that the infant with congenital anomalies would rather not be born, since he cannot be consulted and no one really represents him when the abortion decision is made. There is evidence that handicapped persons do value life after they are born, since the incidence of suicide among handicapped persons is apparently lower than that of the general population.

Fetal indications are more accurately parental indications, then, and are based on a reluctance on the part of parents to accept a certain mathematical risk that an infant will be abnormal. Every pregnancy, of course, carries with it the risk of the birth of an infant with congenital anomalies. The risk is never zero percent. It must be stated that the risk involved in *no* presently recognized maternal hazard would support a program of routine abortion. There is no accurate and safe method of recognizing the abnormal embryo in utero during the period when an abortion could be done. Trying to do a karyotype during the first trimester carries an excessive risk of terminating the pregnancy or producing fetal damage. Recognizing chromosomal sex·is not conclusive since the sex-linked disorders now recognized are principally sex-linked recessives. What, then, are the risks involved, and do they justify the consideration of termination of the life of the fetus? In the situation of maternal rubella during the first trimester, modern prospective, virologically controlled studies indicate that no more than 10–20% of infants will be at risk. Even a figure of 20% would have to include such anomalies as remediable cardiac defects, tonal hearing loss and intrauterine growth retardation. When one talks of severe life-blighting congenital anomalies due to German measles, he is talking about cataracts and mental retardation. The risk of an infant suffering one of these calamities is much less than 20%. In fact, an eleven year prospective follow-up of offspring born to mothers contracting German measles during the first sixteen weeks of pregnancy showed their intelligence distribution to be normal. The risk of an infant being born with any type of congenital anomaly is much less in any non-epidemic year than it is during a rubella epidemic. Since Mayer and Parkman, of the National Institute of Health, have already produced and marketed an effective and potent rubella vaccine, it is likely that we can use this vaccine to prevent the next rubella epidemic, since epidemics usually occur every five to seven years. The answer to the rubella dilemma lies in this vaccine and not in therapeutic abortion. Rh incompatibility, once one of the leading fetal indications for therapeutic abortion, is no longer mentioned. I predict that in 2–3 years rubella will go the same route as Rh disease.

The problem of teratogenic drug ingestion would also seem irrelevant in this context. Thalidomide was not on the American market. It is unlikely that a drug with such a teratogenic capability could pass the progeny study requirements now made mandatory by the Food and Drug Administration. Progeny studies require testing to provide a drug safe for pregnant women and their unborn children. Indeed, thalidomide progeny studies on the rat and more recently on the baboon have produced limb bud anomalies in animal fetuses almost identical to the phocomelia seen in human beings. Thus, if progeny studies had been required in Europe, the dangers of thalidomide could have been recognized before marketing the drug. The thalidomide tragedy was, in a sense, iatrogenic and, therefore, deserving of our profession's utmost concern and compassion. In keeping with noblest medical traditions is the work of Dr. Gustav Hauberg of the Anna Stift rehabilitation school in Hanover, Germany. In this institution, a team of orthopedists, social workers, and teachers has been engaged in the developing of abilities of thalidomide-damaged children so that, despite their heavy handicaps, they will still value life. Mental and psychological development has been normal, in most cases, and higher education potential is attributed to most. Thus even such a poignant situation as the birth of 7,000 phocomelics can have its positive aspect when medical resources are properly mobilized. The best preventative against the recurrence of such a tragedy is the basic reluctance of obstetricians to give any new drugs to pregnant women.

It is difficult to formulate a therapeutic principle which would apply to the various situations posed by exposure to drugs or disease. If the principle is that it is better for eight or nine normal babies to die than for one or two abnormal babies to be born, then I must say that I reject this principle as wasteful and unreasonable. It seems to me that this viewpoint derived from a cult of perfection which says that life is not worth living unless it is free of handicaps. That *vita* is not *vita* unless it is *La Dolce Vita*. Experience in working with handicapped children would suggest that human nature frequently rises above its impediments and that, in Shakespeare's words, "Best men are molded out of faults and, for the most, become much more the better for being a little bad."

Certainly the entire medical profession, not just abortion law revisionists, has compassion for victims of forcible rape and incest. There is a question, however, as to the true dimensions of this problem. Studies on human fertility would suggest that not too many pregnancies are likely to result from a single act of forcible rape. I am informed, by the Chicago state's attorney's office that their staff could not recall a single incident of such a pregnancy in an experience covering about nine years of prosecutions for rape. If such a pregnancy were to occur, there is no scientific evidence that psychological trauma would be prevented, unaffected, or intensified by compounding the shame of rape with the possible guilt of abortion. In the case of statutory rape, there is likewise a question as to the relevance of therapeutic abortion. These pregnancies are not the results of ignorance or contraceptive failure. According to a recent North Carolina study, 95% of pregnant unmarried teenagers know how to obtain and use contraceptives. Teenage girls who become pregnant are largely a group characterized by social isolation and alienation from their parents. Frequently, they look forward to the birth of the infant as a further loneliness compensation and, therefore, do not present themselves for therapeutic abortion consideration. Incestuous pregnancy is no less a difficult problem. Many such pregnancies are not recognized or admitted until physically obvious and beyond the time when abortion would be possible. Many cases of alleged incest will fail of recognition because the victim or her mother will shrink from the financial ruin involved in accusing the father or the social ruin involved in convicting a brother. In 1966, there were only twelve indictments for incest entered in Cook County and only a fraction of these involved pregnancies to which therapeutic abortion would have related under any law.

Much is made of the appeal to prevent the birth of unwanted children. It seems to me that there is a confusion involved here which results from the failure to distinguish between the unwanted child and the unwanted pregnancy. In fifteen years of experience with the parent-child relationship, I have very rarely encountered a mother who asked to be rid of her child once she had taken it home from the nursery. I have encountered many mothers, pregnant with their third or fourth child who undergo a kind of panic which requires the sympathetic support of their family doctor and their husbands. According to Hoerck, 75% of women who were refused abortion under the Swedish system, went on to have their babies and were happy with them.[3] According to Aren and Amark, more of these women have an improvement in their mental adjustment than a deterioration of mental health.[4] I wonder if we really want a situation like that in Denmark, for example, where the principal indications for abortion are: (1) the stress syndrome of housewives, (2) symptoms of insufficiency, and (3) impending exhaustion.

One of the uninsurable risks of medical practice is that we sometimes begin to believe in the fantasies of our patients. Patients may ascribe god-like qualities to us, but I doubt that they will approve of our acting them out. The notion that a physician should be allowed to perform any abortion he chooses within the framework of the physician-patient relationship is a unique and unprecedented request for any profession. Does the lawyer ask that since law is his specialty, laws should be left to his conscience? Does the educator suggest that his position as an educator entitles him to decide when prayer should occur in public schools? A doctor may know how to do an abortion; he does not necessarily know when it should be done, or if it should be done at all.

---

[3] Hoerck, *cited by* Asplund, *Discussion of Swedish Abortion Experience,* 11 Bull. Sloane Hosp. 77 (1965).
[4] Aren & Amark, *The Prognosis of Granted but not Performed Legal Abortions,* Acta Psych. Neur. Scandanavian Supp. 99 (1955).

Ninety-two percent of abortions are performed for social reasons, not medical. Physicians are not equipped by training to handle such requests. A large percentage of abortions in the United States are performed on women who are married, healthy, and living with their husbands. Ninety-five percent of the fetuses destroyed in these abortions would have been born normal, if allowed to go to term. If we accept the Kinsey statistics, 88–95% of abortions are performed by technically competent doctors of medicine. What do we expect to gain, then, from changing the law?

It seems to me that we have a good law in Illinois. When physicians throughout the state were asked, through the Illinois Medical Journal, to report cases where the present law had worked to the detriment of the physical or mental health of the mother by depriving her of a needed abortion, *no such cases were reported.* During the past five years, in Illinois, we have had five maternal deaths due to septic criminal abortion, an average of one a year. This must be close to an irreducible minimum. If the law is changed to allow for a vast increase in the number of abortions performed, there will be many more lives lost and these will be the lives of unborn children. The mortality is 100% for them. Most states recognize that the unborn child does have rights under the law. A mother may sue for the support of her unborn child or may hold a defendant liable for injuries sustained of her unborn child as a result of accident or assault. An unborn child may share in an inheritance or workmen's compensation benefits. A pregnant woman convicted of a capital crime may not be executed until after her baby is born. The Constitution, in the fifth amendment, provides that no person shall be deprived of life without due process of law. It is certainly a matter of pause for the medical profession to decide whether two doctors in agreement, or even an "Abortion Committee," constitutes due process.

It seems ironical that when we have established a National Institute of Child Health which specifically directs its attention to child development from the time of conception, and while tens of millions are being spent by various national foundations to improve the lot of the unborn, that we should see in this day a movement for more liberal "fetal indications" for abortion.

If you ask me, therefore, to speak for the fetus, then speak for him I will. I speak for him intact or deformed. I speak for him wanted or unwanted. Yes, and I speak for him be he illegitimate or high-born. I am for life and the preservation of life. I believe that any life is of infinite value and that this value is not significantly diminished by physical or mental defect or the circumstances of that life's beginning. I believe that this regard for the quantity, as well as the quality of life, is a cornerstone of Western culture. I believe our patients are served best by a medical ethic which also holds this principle sacred.

A LIBERAL CATHOLIC'S VIEW

Joseph F. Donceel

Contrary to popular characterization there is considerable debate within Catholicism over the church's proper position on the issue of abortion. As this essay makes clear there are grounds in Catholic tradition for supporting the limited practice of abortion.

Joseph F. Donceel is Professor Emeritus of Philosophy, Fordham University.

This article appeared in Abortion in a Changing World, *volume I, R. E. Hall, editor, Columbia University Press, 1970.*

I fully agree with the basic Catholic principle that we are never allowed to kill an innocent human being. Therefore, if there is a real human being from the moment of conception, abortion would have to be considered immoral at any stage of pregnancy. The majority Catholic opinion holds nowadays that there is indeed a real human being from the first moment of conception, or, at least, that we cannot be certain that such is not the case. But there is also a minority Catholic opinion, which has good standing in the church, which was the opinion of her greatest theologian, Thomas Aquinas,[1] and which is now slowly regaining favor among Catholic thinkers. This minority opinion holds that there is certainly no human being during the early stages of pregnancy. I would like to show you briefly why Thomas held this position, how it was given up by his successors on account of erroneous scientific theories, and how, even after these theories had been given up, the Catholic church did not return to her traditional view because of a philosophy which was at variance with her official doctrine of the nature of man.

---

[1] See *Summa contra Gentiles,* II, 88–89; *De Potentia,* Q. 3, Art. 9–12; *Summa Theological,* I, Q. 118, Art. 1–3.

Traditional Catholic philosophy holds that what makes an organism a human being is the spiritual soul and that this soul starts to exist at the moment of its "infusion" into the body. When is the human soul infused into the body? Nowadays the majority of Catholic thinkers would not hesitate to answer: at the moment of conception. This is known as the *theory of immediate animation*. However, during long centuries Catholic philosophy and theology held that the human soul was infused into the body only when the latter began to show a human shape or outline and possessed the basic human organs. Before this time, the embryo is alive, but in the way in which a plant or an animal is alive. It possesses, as the traditional terminology puts it, a vegetative or an animal soul, not yet a human soul. In more modern terms we might say that it has reached the physiological or the psychological, not yet the spiritual level of existence. It is not yet a human person; it is evolving, within the womb, toward hominization. This is the *theory of mediate or delayed* animation.

Why did Thomas and the great medieval thinkers favor this theory? Because they held the doctrine of hylomorphism, according to which the human soul is the substantial form of man, while the human body is the result of the union of this soul with materiality, with undetermined cosmic stuff, with what was then known as prime matter. Hylomorphism holds that the human soul is to the body somewhat as the shape of a statue is to the actual statue. The shape of a statue cannot exist before the statue exists. It is not something which the sculptor first makes and subsequently introduces into a block of marble. It can exist only in the completed statue. Hylomorphism holds that, in the same way, the human soul can exist only in a real human body.

Although Thomas knew nothing about chromosomes, genes, DNA, or the code of life, he knew that whatever was growing in the mother's womb was not yet, early in pregnancy, a real human body. Therefore he held that it could not be animated by a human soul, any more than a square block of marble can possess a human shape. The medieval thinkers knew very well that this growing organism would develop into a human body, that virtually, potentially, it was a human body. But they did not admit that an actual human soul could exist in a virtual human body. The Catholic church, which had officially adopted the hylomorphic conception of human nature at the Council of Vienne, in 1312, was so strongly convinced of this position that, for centuries, her law forbade the faithful to baptize and premature birth which did not show at least some human shape or outline.

Under the influence of erroneous scientific reports, however, Catholic thinkers gave up this traditional doctrine. In the early seventeenth century, as a result of a combination of poor microscopes and lively imaginations, some physicians saw in embryos which were only a few days old a tiny human being, a homunculus, with microscopic head, legs, and arms. This view of the fetus implied the *preformation theory,* which held that organic development simply consists of the gradual increase in size of organs and structures which are fully present from the very start. If there really were from the beginning a human body, be it ever so small, there might also from the start exist a human soul. Even a microscopic statue must have a shape. Granted the preformation theory, immediate animation was compatible with the hylomorphic conception of man.

The theory of preformation was eventually replaced by the *theory of epigenesis,* which maintains that the organism, far from being microscopically preformed from the start, develops its organs through a complex process of growth, cleavage, differentiation, and organization.

Why did the Christian thinkers not return to the delayed animation theory, which seems to be demanded by their hylomorphic theory of man? The main reason seems to have been the influence of Cartesian dualism. For Descartes, both man's soul and his body are each a complete substance. The soul is a thinking substance, the body an extended substance. This is no longer hylomorphism. To express it in nontechnical language, this is no longer a "shape in the statue" conception, but rather a "ghost in the machine" conception of the human soul. A full-fledged ghost can manage very well with a microscopic machine. If the soul is no longer the formal cause, the constitutive idea of the body, it might well become its efficient cause, that which produces the ovum's development from the start. Instead of being the idea incarnated in the body, it has turned into the architect and the builder of the body. Just as the architect exists before the first stone of the building is laid, so there can be a real human soul from the first moment of conception, before the emergence of a real human body.

This way of explaining embryogeny is not absurd. The Cartesian outlook, although quite unfashionable nowadays, has been held by many great thinkers. This kind of philosophy calls for immediate animation, which is clearly in conflict with the hylomorphic doctrine of man, solemnly endorsed by the Catholic church at the Council of Vienne.

There have been other influences which explain the shift in Catholic opinion. One of them may have been the long-standing opposition of the church to the idea of evolution. Thomas admitted some kind of evolution of the embryo and the fetus in the mother's womb. How could the church admit this evolution in the womb and reject it in the race? Since the Catholic church has finally come around to admitting the evolution of the human body, it might also be willing to return to Thomas's idea of evolution in the womb.

Moreover, once we give up the idea of immediate animation, we can no longer say when the human soul is infused, when the embryo or the fetus becomes a human person. That is why those who want to play it absolutely safe claim that the human soul is present from the moment of conception. They seem to take it for granted that, since we do not know when the human soul is present, we neither can know for sure when it is not yet present. This assumption is false. Let us consider another case, where we do not know when a certain factor is present, while knowing very well when it is not yet present. Nobody can tell with certitude when a child is capable of performing his first free moral choice, but all of us are quite certain that, during the first months or years of his life, a human baby is not yet a free moral agent. Likewise, I do not know when the human soul is infused, when the embryo becomes human. But I feel certain that there is no human soul, hence no human person, during the first few weeks of pregnancy, as long as the embryo remains in the vegetative stage of its development.

Some people make much of the following objection to my position. They say that from the very first the fertilized ovum possesses forty-six human chromosomes, all the human genes, its code of life —that it is a human embryo. This is undeniable. But it does not make it a human person. When a heart is transplanted, it is kept alive, for a short while, outside of the donor. It is a living being, a human heart, with the human chromosomes and genes. But it is not a human being; it is not a person.

The objection may be pressed. Not only does the fertilized human ovum possess the human chromosomes; unlike the heart, it will, if circumstances are normal, develop into a human being. It is virtually a human being. I admit this, but it does not affect my position. The fertilized human ovum, the early embryo, is virtually a human body, not actually. Correctly understood, the hylomorphic conception of human nature, the official Catholic doctrine, cannot admit the presence of an actual human soul in a virtual human body. Let me use a comparison again. A deflated rubber ball is virtually round; when inflated, it can assume no other shape than the spherical shape. Yet it does not actually possess any roundness or sphericity. In the same way, the early embryo does not actually possess a human soul; it is not a human person.

Experimental embryology tells us that every single cell of the early embryo, of the morula, is virtually a human body. It does not follow that each of these cells possesses a human soul. When embryologists carefully separate the cells of a morula in lower organisms, each one of these cells may develop into a complete organism. Starting with the pioneering attempts of Hans Driesch, such an experiment has been performed on many animal species. We do not see why it might not eventually succeed with the human embryo. As a matter of fact, nature frequently performs it on human ova. Identical twins derive from one ovum fertilized by one spermatozoon. This ovum splits into two at an early stage of pregnancy and gives rise to two human beings. In this case the defenders of immediate animation must admit that one person may be divided into two persons. This is a metaphysical impossibility.

Throughout my exposition I have taken for granted the hylomorphic conception of human nature. This is in line with the purpose of my essay, which is not only to present a liberal Catholic's view of fetal animation, but also to show that this view seems to be the only one which agrees with the official Catholic conception of human nature. In other words, I submit that Catholics should give up the immediate animation theory, because it implies a Cartesian, dualistic conception of man, which conflicts with the doctrine endorsed by the Council of Vienne.

In conclusion I would like to say a few words about the standing of hylomorphism among contemporary philosophers. Very few non-Catholic philosophers hold the doctrine of hylomorphism today. Even among Catholics it has fallen into disrepute, although personally I cannot see how one may avoid dualism without this theory or some theory which resembles it. Hylomorphism is radically opposed to dualism, to the doctrine which considers both the soul and the body as complete substances. Contemporary philosophy, as a rule, is also strongly opposed to this kind of dualism. In this sense, negatively, the doctrine I have defended continues to live; it is stronger than ever, although it may be known by other names.

Both linguistic analysis, the leading philosophy in the English-speaking countries, and existential phenomenology, which tends to dominate the field elsewhere, reject any form of Cartesian dualism. Gilbert Ryle, a leading British analyst, has strongly attacked what he calls "the dogma of the ghost in the machine." And Maurice Merleau-Ponty, possibly France's greatest phenomenologist, defended a doctrine which looks very much like an updated form of hylomorphism. For him there are three kinds of behavior: the syncretic, the amovable, and the symbolic. We might perhaps put it more simply and speak of three levels in man: the level of reflex activity and of instincts, the level of learning, and the level of symbolic thinking. Or again, the physiological, the psychic, and the spiritual level. Each lower level stands to the next higher one in the same relation as data stand to their meaning, as materiality stands to the idea embodied in it. The data are not data if they do not possess some meaning, and there can be no meaning which is not embedded in some data. Each higher level presupposes the lower one; there can be no mind before the organism is ready to carry one and no spirit before the mind is capable of receiving it. I submit that this clearly implies delayed animation.

In my opinion there is a great amount of agreement between the contemporary antidualistic trend of philosophy and the hylomorphic conception of man. It is wise therefore to return to this conception or, at least, to accept the conclusions which follow from it. One of these conclusions is that the embryo is certainly not a human person during the early stages of pregnancy, and that, consequently, it is not immoral to terminate pregnancy during this time, provided there are serious reasons for such an intervention.

Let me insist on this restriction: the opinion which I have defended may lead to abuses, to abortions performed under flimsy pretexts. I would be among the first to deplore and condemn such abuses. Although a prehuman embryo cannot demand from us the absolute respect which we owe to the human person, it deserves a very great consideration, because it is a living being, endowed with a human finality, on its way to hominization. Therefore it seems to me that only very serious reasons should allow us to terminate its existence. Excesses will unavoidably occur, but they should not induce us to overlook the instances where sufficiently serious reasons exist for performing an abortion during the early stages of pregnancy.

ABORTION: PARAMETERS FOR DECISION

R. J. Gerber

At the center of the abortion dispute lies the question of the personhood of the fetus. Gerber examines two views: that personhood is genetic and therefore the fetus is a person at the moment of conception, and that personhood is social and therefore the fetus is not a person until after birth.

At the time this essay was written Mr. Gerber was a member of the Department of Philosophy at Notre Dame University.

This article is taken from Ethics, *volume 82, number 2, January, 1972.*

"Babies," remarked Mrs. Jill Knight, a Conservative, Protestant member of Parliament during a debate in the House of Commons in 1966, "are not like bad teeth to be jerked out just because they cause suffering. An unborn baby is a baby nevertheless."

"There ought to be no special laws regulating abortion," wrote psychiatrist Thomas Szasz in the same year. "Such an operation should be available in the same way as, say, an operation for the beautification of a nose."[1]

Such dialectics mark the two issues central in the abortion debate now on appeal before the Supreme Court and before the entire nation. One view sees the unborn child possessing inviolable rights, including the right to life, from the moment life begins in the womb. The other view sees the unborn child as less than human, often as merely "a part of the mother's body," whose rights necessarily yield to the convenience of its parents and society at large.

---

[1] "The Ethics of Abortion," *Humanist,* July 22, 1966.

These contemporary attitudes on taking fetal life are organic developments of two fundamentally different legal mentalities, the Hellenistic-medieval, epitomized by Thomas Aquinas, and the modern, epitomized by Roscoe Pound, Ashley Montagu, and others. In the abortion debate, it is not merely two individuals facing each other; it is a confrontation between the world views of two fairly distinct cultures, one traditional and dated, the other new and untested.

The debate now centers on a practical legal question: should existing laws against abortion be relaxed to make abortions easier to obtain? Dr. Szasz states the issue clearly: "If abortion is murder . . . , it is an immoral act which the law must prohibit." On the other hand, if abortion is not murder, if it is nothing more serious than any other medical procedure, there is no reason why it should concern the law at all. In that case, "the proper remedy must be sought not in medically and psychiatrically 'liberal' abortion laws, but in the repeal of all such laws." Obviously, the law should not tolerate murder; but, by the same token, neither should the law show more alarm about the removal of a blob of nonhuman tissue from the womb than it shows about the removal of a sore tooth or the beautification of a nose.

Central to the abortion debate is the question: how define human value? The various answers to that question tend, in general, to pit individualist approaches against social criteria in ways reminiscent of not only Hans Driesch but also Herman Melville's and Thomas Mann's novels. For example, is humanity determined by structure or by function? By genetic code or by social interaction? By an a priori deduction or by an inference from social activity? In a larger context, is human value a metaphysical conclusion of an abstract system such as natural law, or is it attested only in the pragmatic, social interests emphasized by sociological jurisprudence?

Before we approach such large questions, much less answer them, some qualifications must be made about the convictions underlying the following pages. The first is that the abortion question is not primarily a religious issue. The debate is not furthered by quotations from the Bible or by edicts from Rome. It is a secular, moral matter best resolved by secular, moral arguments. The second conviction is that the abortion movement in the United States will almost certainly succeed within five years in realizing at least a modified form of abortion on demand. Such a result is not wholly bad: benefits will ensue from such liberalization, such as the emancipation of women, the elimination of illegal abortion rings, a possible reduction in population rate, and a decrease in unwanted children. While admitting such positive and realistic benefits, however, one can also be convinced that such liberalization will involve detriments beyond the loss of fetal life. Third, it is likely that abortion on demand will see its demise at some future date when the population rate has diminished, when contraceptives have become more commonplace, and when human consciousness belatedly extends ecological and environmental protection to the human womb. In light of these convictions, the following pages seek to balance the arguments on both sides of the issue with special reference to what abortion-liberalization arguments imply not only about the unborn but also about the born.

Parameters for Decision

From the foregoing, some conclusions can be drawn. In the first place, the abortion controversy involves two prime participants, the unborn child and the pregnant mother. Any argument that enters the lists on either side should acknowledge the arguments on the other side. Second, with the exception of the dubious privacy argument, it is apparent that the arguments on the side of the mother are primarily social in nature: population, woman's sexual freedom, quality of life, reduction of ADC* payments. Third, it is apparent that the arguments favoring the fetus are primarily individual-oriented and involve an incongruous interweaving of metaphysics and genetics. The metaphysical notion of human potentiality and the genetic DNA structure together suggest that the status of humanity fits the very early fetus but that his social value as a person has yet to be achieved.

In this light, any decision touching on abortion must take into account two values: first, the value of an isolated individual whose humanity is attested only by structure, not by function; second, the value of socially interacting human beings-ourselves—whose humanity is attested by social functions supportive of society at large. What this implies is that our criterion of humanity must embrace both structure and function, both genetics and sociology. To define

* ADC: Aid to Dependent Children.

human value exclusively by structure or by function is to court trouble. To deny the genetic structure as an index of humanity would be to limit humanity to social and technological functioning, a view against which Gabriel Marcel, Alfred North Whitehead, Charles Reich, and a host of modern authorities warn; for, as Nietzsche observes, an individual does remain human once his function ceases. On the other hand, to deny some potentiality for social functioning as an index of human value would involve a priori abstractions investing test-tube babies and genetic monsters with the values of an Aristotle, a Churchill, a Kennedy.

. The proabortionist is tempted to define human value in terms of adult achievements and to contrast achievements with the *tabula rasa* of the unborn child. Underlying this attempt is the conviction that human value is, in Ashley Montagu's words, "an achievement rather than an endowment," in the sense that no comparison exists between an adult who acts in the world and an unborn fetus who has months to travel before achieving his first social act at birth. At bottom, this kind of thinking puts the premium on activity; it judges value pragmatically by social consequences. In this view, human potentiality is prized only when it acts significantly. But the question then arises of how to explain the careful nurture, rearing, and education accorded a child in our society for the first ten or fifteen years of his life. Rarely, if ever, is such a child valued for his great achievements or his great contributions to society, or for his prowess in the lists of love or rationality; yet our society has always treated him as a human being of great value because of the untapped promise he holds for such functioning in the future. The careful education tendered the young in our society suggests that we do, in fact, prize human potential for what it may actually achieve in the distant future. The parallel between the child of three years and the fetus of three months should be obvious: their differing potentials are only matters of degree and of time.

If that parallel be considered a first touchstone in approaching the abortion dilemma, then a second principle would be this: nothing should be done arbitrarily to cut off human life as long as less drastic solutions exist. Is there a less drastic solution to the abortion dilemma on the side either of the fetus or of the mother? The fetus once conceived has no alternative but to continue to grow, just as he had no choice in his parents' engaging in sex or his becoming conceived or growing up blond or blue-eyed. The fetus is the *de trop* of the Sartrean enigma; he is without recourse and without remedy. The same cannot be said for the mother, who faces at least three alternatives to the abortion decision: initial will power, grossly out of fashion today; contraceptives, which deserve to be more grossly fahionable; and finally, the transfer of the unwanted, living infant to a Birthright Center after birth. While this view does not totally resolve the continuing confrontation of abortion, it does suggest that it is the fetus, not the mother, who is the ineluctable victim and that it is the mother, not the fetus, who controls the origins of life and should take the precautions necessary to avoid unthinking creation and destruction of it.

Finally, an ideal approach to abortion should be characterized by true liberality. One would suspect that a true liberal of the sort who would attack the senseless killing of peasants in Vietnam, of babes in arms at My Lai, of students at Kent State, would favor laws broadening life and oppose those limiting life to narrow, arbitrary classifications. A truly liberal law is one which seeks to enhance and preserve the most varied expression of life; a restrictive law is one which seeks to categorize who is and who is not human. While this principle does no more to lighten the individual burden of abortion, it does suggest that the self-styled liberals who would "liberalize" the abortion laws to the point of "destruction of life on demand" seek to impose on society an arbitrary definition of humanity inconsistent with values we already prize. Surprisingly, the humanity of the fetus is often too speculative an affair for many who pronounce with papal conviction on the immorality of war, the rights of conscientious objectors, the inhumanity of violence, and the cruelty and novelty of capital punishment by gas and electrocution, not to mention those who devote themselves to protecting oil-coated sea gulls and innocent seal pups. Yet to decide humanity on the basis of external signs leads to results whose awkward logic only history can dispel. Montesquieu once observed that there could be no humanity in the majestically passive people of black skin in Africa: "It is so natural," he said, "to think that it is color which constitutes humanity that the people of Asia always doggedly deny to the Blacks any rapport with us humans."

While "sanctity of life" is a term of impenetrable meaning, it is fleshed out somewhat by a famous passage by Albert Schweitzer, who spent his life enhancing the lives of those who did not function well on Wall Street standards: "Let a man once begin to think about the mystery of his life and the links which connect him with the life that fills the world and he cannot but bring to bear upon his own life and all the other life that comes within his reach the principle of reverence for life and manifest by this principle the ethical affirmation of life. Existence will thereby become harder for him in every respect than it would be if he lived for himself, but at the same time it will be richer, more beautiful, and happier."[2]

The central issue—whether there should be abortion laws—is still open, and it is worth recalling, again, that both good and evil will flow from either alternative. Yet it is worth noting that the moral aspirations of the law are minimal. Law seeks to establish and maintain only that minimum of actualized morality necessary for the healthy functioning of the social order. It enforces only what is minimally acceptable and in this sense socially necessary. Mindful of its nature, the law is required to be tolerant of many evils morality condemns. The question thus remains: is there any social necessity that the law adopt and protect minimal standards of what constitutes humanity?

For example, it is often suggested that legalization of abortion will merely put the law in a position of neutrality with respect to fetal life. Given the obvious effects of liberalization, a position of "neutrality" with respect to fetal life is hardly more tenable than to maintain that removal of civil rights laws would be "neutral" toward the lives of blacks. Removal of a law is tantamount to approving what the removal sanctions. Justice Brandeis's warning in a famous dissent is apposite: "Our Government is the potent, the omni-present teacher. For good or for ill, it teaches the whole people by its example. Crime is contagious."[3]

Whatever the answer to the legal question, it seems that the teaching function (as opposed to the coercive function) of the law should emphasize that our society does not exclude from its ranks the children and cripples and infirm whose endowment is human potential rather than human achievement. Herein lies a great danger in the abortion movement, a danger which does not touch the fetus as much as it does those already born. Well beyond the loss of fetal life there looms in nearly all abortion arguments an implication invidious to certain classes of extrauterine human beings.

The basic argument for relaxing the abortion laws essentially

[2] *Out of My Life and Thought* (New York: Macmillan Co., 1963), p. 179.
[3] Olmstead v. United States, 277 U.S. 438, 485 (Brandeis, J. dissenting).

relies on Ashley Montagu's notion that humanity is an "achievement" which results from social interaction. In this view, human rights are social in the sense that they derive from social interplay, not from a priori conditions either logically or chronologically precedent to such interplay. Where the philosophical wellsprings of this theory lie involves an exploratory task worthy of an inner-space program of the most ambitious sort, but the guess may be defended that the contemporary popularity of the "I-thou" interpersonal relationship has come home to roost with a vengeance—a vengeance touching those who, for varied reasons, cannot come up to the demands of instant intersubjectivity. Fertilized by some fifty years of the work of thinkers like Gabriel Marcel, Martin Buber, Emmanuel Levinas, Victor Frankl, Carl Rogers, and Harvey Cox, the mentality of the average Westerner of even modest intelligence is preoccupied if not obsessed with concern over his interpersonal rating chart. The ringing injunction to "make love not war" has spurred a secret war on those who cannot love: if they cannot love, one surmises, how can they be human? The cry for communal sharing of mountains, forests, and living quarters suggests the inhumanity of those who cannot share—those, for example, whose greatest curse is always to receive rather than to give: receive the care of a nurse, take food from a needle, accept welfare checks, take nourishment through an umbilical cord. The examples are as endless as they are intriguing and pathetic, but the fact seems clear: so obsessed is the average mind with the communal quest for interpersonal fulfillment that it has come to suspect any speculative thesis about human value that cannot be verified inductively in one's own intersubjective experience.

The concentration on shared experience, abstracted from the given structures making it possible, has forged new ethical patterns rooted largely in a shift from quantity to quality, from a structural to a functional humanism, from a natural law to a sociological jurisprudence, wherein people are not created equal but become equal through what Roscoe Pound calls the socialization of their interests. Isolated nature no longer is a finished vessel whose given nature one must respect in order to utilize. Nature is clay to be broken and remolded responsibly and creatively to one's Faustian desires. Such is the cyclopean view of the otherwise laudable "I—Thou" mentality: a resolute focusing on interpersonal dealings, a refusal to look to a priori considerations to downstage intersubjectivity, and a consequent sense of responsibility for humanizing to the utmost the pattern of interpersonal relations. Life is no longer merely *vita;* it must be *la dolce vita.*

Accordingly, while the modern mind reacts strongly to the experience of persons going to death in death row or undergoing harsh treatment in prisoner of war camps or suffering the shame of public poverty, this same mind sees little carry-over from those values to a fetus for whom there is no overt sign of interpersonal activity. After all, its existence is still shrouded in the dark waters of the womb, and its creative self-project will not begin for a long time even after birth. The implication is obvious: we are putting a premium on social utility. Speaking in favor of the euthanasia bill in England last year, Lord Dawson of Penn invoked the *dolce vita* argument: "This is a courageous age, but it has a different sense of values from the ages which have gone before. It looks upon life more from the point of view of quality than of quantity. It places less value in life *when its usefulness has come to an end.*"

Whether it be a heritage of existentialism, phenomenology, or humanist psychology, the interpersonal mentality lies at the heart of the "quality-of-life" arguments for abortion. Whether couched in terms of fetal dependency, deformity, inchoacy, nonviability, or uselessness, the basic argument implies that valuable human life is independent, viable, well-oiled, and capable of what Maslow and Rogers call those "self-actualizing" acts which lead to "peak experiences." It is a Nietzschean view, indeed, a view of man as a sociological superman. In his famous letter to the *New York Times,* Ashley Montagu contended: "The embryo, the fetus, and newborn of the human species, in point of fact, do not really become functionally human until humanized in the human socialization process. . . . Humanity is an achievement, not an endowment. The potentialities constitute the endowment, their fulfillment requires a humanizing environment."[4]

What that socialization argument does indeed suggest is precisely the difficulty with a haunting by-product of the abortion reform movement: humanity has been subtly redefined in terms of degrees of achieved social involvement. Man is not vested with human rights at creation or at birth or even as a "newborn" but

[4] Quoted in R. Ayd, "Voluntary Euthanasia: The Right to Be Killed," *Medical-Moral Newsletter* (January and February 1970), p. 17.

only much later when he contributes to the "quality" of life. As Montagu put it: "I consider it a crime against humanity to bring a child into the world whose fulfillment as a healthy human being is any way menaced or who itself menaces . . . the quality of the society into which it is born."[5]

Dr. Garret Hardin, in similar vein and with similar convictions, states: "If the total circumstances are such that the child born at a particular time and under particular circumstances will not receive a fair shake in life, then she (the mother) should know—she should feel in her bones—that she has no right to continue the pregnancy. . . . It may seem a rather coldhearted thing to say, but we should make abortions available to keep down our taxes. . . ."[6] The unfortunate corollary of those statements is that the quality of life and the rate of taxes are influenced less by the unborn and much more by many classes of persons already born. The day may come when coercive measures are taken to insure that some individuals do not threaten the "quality" of the rest of our lives. One need only recall one of the blacker marks on American jurisprudence, *Buck* v. *Bell,* wherein the Supreme Court in the person of Oliver Wendell Holmes sanctioned the compulsory sterilization of mental defectives. Bearing in mind current "scientific" claims that blacks are genetically inferior, one might anticipate an argument for compulsory abortion of the disadvantaged and compulsory elimination of nonquality individuals along the lines of the infamous argument in *Buck:* "We have seen more than once that the public welfare may call upon the best citizens for their lives. It would be strange if it could not call upon those who already sap the strength of the State for these lesser sacrifices, often not felt to be such by those concerned, *in order to prevent our being swamped with incompetence.*"[7]

The argument that social importance or societal "value" or "interaction" constitutes protected degrees of humanity offers no threat to the Nixons, Johnsons, Calleys, and J. Edgar Hoovers of this world of power. They all can point to their social involvements to assert their claim to a humanity supposedly engendered by those involvements. Such involvement, however, is no help to the unborn fetus who has yet to meet his mother, to the husband in a womb-

[5] Ibid.
[6] Address delivered at the Second Annual California Conference on Abortion, May 11, 1969, quoted in the *New York Times,* May 12, 1969, p. 66, col. 5.
[7] Buck v. Bell, 274 U.S. 200, 207 (1927).

like iron-lung, to the senile grandmother who will never again recognize a person. Neither is that argument much help to the Helen Kellers, Ludwig Beethovens, Friedrich Nietzsches, and Lord Byrons whose physical disabilities retard their social interactions and consequently diminish their social importance, while raising everyone else's taxes.

The New York abortion debate provides a case in point. The proposed bill would have permitted abortion "when there is medical evidence of a substantial risk that the foetus, if born, would be so grossly malformed, or would have such serious physical or mental abnormalities, as to be permanently incapable of caring for himself." In 1969, Martin Ginsberg, a New York State assemblyman who is crippled by polio incurred as an infant and who uses metal crutches and hand and leg braces to move, made the following observation to the Assembly: "What this bill says is that those who are malformed or abnormal have no reason to be part of our society. If we are prepared to say that a life should not come into this world malformed or abnormal, then tomorrow we should be prepared to say that a life already in this world which becomes malformed or abnormal should not be permitted to live."

The real effect of the abortion laws as they seem certain to appear in five years is not so much the loss of the unborn. We may survive that with calluses on top of our psychic scars. The real danger lies in the possible diminution of value and humanity accorded to the socially deprived among the born: the infant of six months, the spastic teenager, the adult in an iron lung, the woman in a wheelchair, the lunatic in an asylum, the convicted criminal, the recluse, the hermit. On the scales of social intercourse the humanity of each of these individuals either never appears or registers only at inferior levels. If a little legal logic goes a long way, it seems likely that the practical as well as the logical distinctions will shortly disappear among abortion, infanticide, and the various sociological conveniences called "mercy killing"—to the detriment of the extra—as well as of the intrauterine life. Once again, the English experience may become American precedent: those who pushed for a liberalized abortion law in Britain three years ago are now pushing for a euthanasia bill defeated in the House of Lords by only sixty-one votes to forty last year. The entire experience might suggest that there is no such stage as "just a little bit pregnant," or "a little less human," or a "little more equal," or a "little less constitutional."

The quantitative differentiations of the yardstick, the scales, the Gallup Polls, and the welfare and tax rolls are close cousins to a functional and technological assessment of humanity, the entirety of which may constitute a sociological disposal system, a *dolce vita* smoother and more antiseptic than ever devised by any tyrant or Führer.

A DEFENSE OF ABORTION

Judith Jarvis Thomson

In this essay Professor Thomson directly challenges that part of the position of antiabortionists usually thought unassailable: the "right to life." She argues that, even if we concede that the fetus is a person, there are still strong reasons why some abortions might be legitimate.

Judith Jarvis Thomson is a professor of philosophy at the Massachusetts Institute of Technology.

This article is taken from Philosophy and Public Affairs, *volume 1, number 1, Fall, 1971.*

Most opposition to abortion relies on the premise that the fetus is a human being, a person, from the moment of conception. The premise is argued for, but, as I think, not well. Take, for example, the most common argument. We are asked to notice that the development of a human being from conception through birth into childhood is continuous; then it is said that to draw a line, to choose a point in this development and say "before this point the thing is not a person, after this point it is a person" is to make an arbitrary choice, a choice for which in the nature of things no good reason can be given. It is concluded that the fetus is, or anyway that we had better say it is, a person from the moment of conception. But this conclusion does not follow. Similar things might be said about the development of an acorn into an oak tree, and it does not follow that acorns are oak trees or that we had better say they are. Arguments of this form are sometimes called "slippery slope arguments"—the phrase is perhaps self-explanatory—and it is dismaying that opponents of abortion rely on them so heavily and uncritically.

I am inclined to agree, however, that the prospects for "drawing a line" in the development of the fetus look dim. I am inclined to think also that we shall probably have to agree that the fetus has already become a human person well before birth. Indeed, it comes as a surprise when one first learns how early in its life it begins to acquire human characteristics. By the tenth week, for example, it already has a face, arms and legs, fingers and toes; it has internal organs, and brain activity is detectable. On the other hand, I think that the premise is false, that the fetus is not a person from the moment of conception. A newly fertilized ovum, a newly implanted clump of cells, is no more a person than an acorn is an oak tree. But I shall not discuss any of this. For it seems to me to be of great interest to ask what happens if, for the sake of argument, we allow the premise. How, precisely, are we supposed to get from there to the conclusion that abortion is morally impermissible? Opponents of abortion commonly spend most of their time establishing that the fetus is a person, and hardly any time explaining the step from there to the impermissibility of abortion. Perhaps they think the step too simple and obvious to require much comment. Or perhaps instead they are simply being economical in argument. Many of those who defend abortion rely on the premise that the fetus is not a person, but only a bit of tissue that will become a person at birth; and why pay out more arguments than you have to? Whatever the explanation, I suggest that the step they take is neither easy nor obvious, that it calls for closer examination than it is commonly given, and that when we do give it this closer examination we shall feel inclined to reject it.

I propose, then, that we grant that the fetus is a person from the moment of conception. How does the argument go from here? Something like this, I take it. Every person has a right to life. So the fetus has a right to life. No doubt the mother has a right to decide what shall happen in and to her body; everyone would grant that. But surely a person's right to life is stronger and more stringent than the mother's right to decide what happens in and to her body, and so outweighs it. So the fetus may not be killed; an abortion may not be performed.

It sounds plausible. But now let me ask you to imagine this. You wake up in the morning and find yourself back to back in bed with an unconscious violinist. A famous unconscious violinist. He has been found to have a fatal kidney ailment, and the Society of

Music Lovers has canvassed all the available medical records and found that you alone have the right blood type to help. They have therefore kidnapped you, and last night the violinist's circulatory system was plugged into yours, so that your kidneys can be used to extract poisons from his blood as well as your own. The director of the hospital now tells you, "Look, we're sorry the Society of Music Lovers did this to you—we would never have permitted it if we had known. But still, they did it, and the violinist now is plugged into you. To unplug you would be to kill him. But never mind, it's only for nine months. By then he will have recovered from his ailment, and can safely be unplugged from you." Is it morally incumbent on you to accede to this situation? No doubt it would be very nice of you if you did, a great kindness. But do you *have* to accede to it? What if it were not nine months, but nine years? Or longer still? What if the director of the hospital says, "Tough luck, I agree, but you've now got to stay in bed, with the violinist plugged into you, for the rest of your life. Because remember this. All persons have a right to life, and violinists are persons. Granted you have a right to decide what happens in and to your body, but a person's right to life outweighs your right to decide what happens in and to your body. So you cannot ever be unplugged from him." I imagine you would regard this as outrageous, which suggests that something really is wrong with that plausible-sounding argument I mentioned a moment ago.

In this case, of course, you were kidnapped; you didn't volunteer for the operation that plugged the violinist into your kidneys. Can those who oppose abortion on the ground I mentioned make an exception for a pregnancy due to rape? Certainly. They can say that persons have a right to life only if they didn't come into existence because of rape; or they can say that all persons have a right to life, but that some have less of a right to life than others, in particular, that those who came into existence because of rape have less. But these statements have a rather unpleasant sound. Surely the question of whether you have a right to life at all, or how much of it you have, shouldn't turn on the question of whether or not you are the product of a rape. And in fact the people who oppose abortion on the ground I mentioned do not make this distinction, and hence do not make an exception in case of rape.

Nor do they make an exception for a case in which the mother has to spend the nine months of her pregnancy in bed. They would agree that would be a great pity, and hard on the mother; but all the same all persons have a right to life, the fetus is a person, and so on. I suspect, in fact, that they would not make an exception for a case in which, miraculously enough, the pregnancy went on for nine years, or even the rest of the mother's life.

[Thomson argues next against what she refers to as the "extreme view," namely, that abortion is not permissible even when the mother's life is at stake. She concludes that, while people "do not have a right to do anything whatever to save their lives," abortion is certainly one action one does have the right to perform to save her life. She proceeds then to examine the notion of a "right to life."]

In some views having a right to life includes having a right to be given at least the bare minimum one needs for continued life. But suppose that what in fact *is* the bare minimum a man needs for continued life is something he has no right at all to be given? If I am sick unto death, and the only thing that will save my life is the touch of Henry Fonda's cool hand on my fevered brow, then all the same, I have no right to be given the touch of Henry Fonda's cool hand on my fevered brow. It would be frightfully nice of him to fly in from the West Coast to provide it. It would be less nice, though no doubt well meant, if my friends flew out to the West Coast and carried Henry Fonda back with them. But I have no right at all against anybody that he should do this for me. Or again, to return to the story I told earlier, the fact that for continued life that violinist needs the continued use of your kidneys does not establish that he has a right to be given the continued use of your kidneys. He certainly has no right against you that *you* should give him continued use of your kidneys. For nobody has any right to use your kidneys unless you give him such a right; and nobody has the right against you that you shall give him this right—if you do allow him to go on using your kidneys, this is a kindness on your part, and not something he can claim from you as his due. Nor has he any right against anybody else that *they* should give him continued use of your kidneys. Certainly he had no right against the Society of Music Lovers that they should plug him into you in the first place. And if you now start to unplug yourself, having learned that you will otherwise have to spend nine years in bed with him, there is nobody in the world who must try to prevent you, in order to see to it that he is given something he has a right to be given.

Some people are rather stricter about the right to life. In their view, it does not include the right to be given anything, but amounts to, and only to, the right not to be killed by anybody. But here a related difficulty arises. If everybody is to refrain from killing that violinist then everybody must refrain from doing a great many different sorts of things. Everybody must refrain from slitting his throat, everybody must refrain from shooting him—and everybody must refrain from unplugging you from him. But does he have a right against everybody that they shall refrain from unplugging you from him? To refrain from doing this is to allow him to continue to use your kidneys. It could be argued that he has a right against us that *we* should allow him to continue to use your kidneys. That is, while he had no right against us that we should give him the use of your kidneys, it might be argued that he anyway has a right against us that we shall not now intervene and deprive him of the use of your kidneys. I shall come back to third-party interventions later. But certainly the violinist has no right against you that *you* shall allow him to continue to use your kidneys. As I said, if you do allow him to use them, it is a kindness on your part, and not something you owe him.

The difficulty I point to here is not peculiar to the right to life. It reappears in connection with all the other natural rights; and it is something which an adequate account of rights must deal with. For present purposes it is enough just to draw attention to it. But I would stress that I am not arguing that people do not have a right to life—quite to the contrary, it seems to me that the primary control we must place on the acceptability of an account of rights is that it should turn out in that account to be a truth that all persons have a right to life. I am arguing only that having a right to life does not guarantee having either a right to be given the use of or a right to be allowed continued use of another person's body—even if one needs it for life itself. So the right to life will not serve the opponents of abortion in the very simple and clear way in which they seem to have thought it would.

There is another way to bring out the difficulty. In the most ordinary sort of case, to deprive someone of what he has a right to is to treat him unjustly. Suppose a boy and his small brother are jointly given a box of chocolates for Christmas. If the older boy takes the box and refuses to give his brother any of the chocolates, he is unjust to him, for the brother has been given a right to half of them. But suppose that, having learned that otherwise it means nine years in bed with that violinist, you unplug yourself from him. You surely are not being unjust to him, for you gave him no right to use your kidneys, and no one else can have given him any such right. But we have to notice that in unplugging yourself, you are killing him; and violinists, like everybody else, have a right to life, and thus in the view we were considering just now, the right not to be killed. So here you do what he supposedly has a right you shall not do, but you do not act unjustly to him in doing it.

The emendation which may be made at this point is this: the right to life consists not in the right not to be killed, but rather in the right not to be killed unjustly. This runs a risk of circularity, but never mind: it would enable us to square the fact that the violinist has a right to life with the fact that you do not act unjustly toward him in unplugging yourself, thereby killing him. For if you do not kill him unjustly, you do not violate his right to life, and so it is no wonder you do him no injustice.

But if this emendation is accepted, the gap in the argument against abortion stares us plainly in the face: it is by no means enough to show that the fetus is a person, and to remind us that all persons have a right to life—we need to be shown also that killing the fetus violates its right to life, i.e., that abortion is unjust killing. And is it?

I suppose we may take it as a datum that in a case of pregnancy due to rape the mother has not given the unborn person a right to the use of her body for food and shelter. Indeed, in what pregnancy could it be supposed that the mother has given the unborn person such a right? It is not as if there were unborn persons drifting about the world, to whom a woman who wants a child says "I invite you in."

But it might be argued that there are other ways one can have acquired a right to the use of another person's body than by having been invited to use it by that person. Suppose a woman voluntarily indulges in intercourse, knowing of the chance it will issue in pregnancy, and then she does become pregnant; is she not in part responsible for the presence, in fact the very existence, of the unborn person inside her? No doubt she did not invite it in. But doesn't her partial responsibility for its being there itself give it a right to the use of her body? If so, then her aborting it would be more like the boy's taking away the chocolates, and less like your unplugging yourself from the violinist—doing so would be depriving it of what it does have a right to, and thus would be doing it an injustice.

And then, too, it might be asked whether or not she can kill it even to save her own life: If she voluntarily called it into existence, how can she now kill it, even in self-defense?

The first thing to be said about this is that it is something new. Opponents of abortion have been so concerned to make out the independence of the fetus, in order to establish that it has a right to life, just as its mother does, that they have tended to overlook the possible support they might gain from making out that the fetus is *dependent* on the mother, in order to establish that she has a special kind of responsibility for it, a responsibility that gives it rights against her which are not possessed by any independent person—such as an ailing violinist who is a stranger to her.

On the other hand, this argument would give the unborn person a right to its mother's body only if her pregnancy resulted from a voluntary act, undertaken in full knowledge of the chance a pregnancy might result from it. It would leave out entirely the unborn person whose existence is due to rape. Pending the availability of some further argument, then, we would be left with the conclusion that unborn persons whose existence is due to rape have no right to the use of their mother's bodies, and thus that aborting them is not depriving them of anything they have a right to and hence is not unjust killing.

And we should also notice that it is not at all plain that this argument really does go even as far as it purports to. For there are cases and cases, and the details make a difference. If the room is stuffy, and I therefore open a window to air it, and a burglar climbs in, it would be absurd to say, "Ah, now he can stay, she's given him a right to the use of her house—for she is partially responsible for his presence there, having voluntarily done what enabled him to get in, in full knowledge that there are such things as burglars, and that burglars burgle." It would be still more absurd to say this if I had had bars installed outside my windows, precisely to prevent burglars from getting in, and a burglar got in only because of a defect in the bars. It remains equally absurd if we imagine it is not a burglar who climbs in, but an innocent person who blunders or falls in. Again, suppose it were like this: people-seeds drift about in the air like pollen, and if you open your windows, one may drift in and take root in your carpets or upholstery. You don't want children, so you fix up your windows with fine mesh screens, the very best you can buy. As can happen, however, and on very, very rare occasions does happen, one of the screens is defective; and a seed drifts in and takes root. Does the person-plant who now develops have a right to the use of your house? Surely not—despite the fact that you voluntarily opened your windows, you knowingly kept carpets and upholstered furniture, and you knew that screens were sometimes defective. Someone may argue that you are responsible for its rooting, that it does have a right to your house, because after all you *could* have lived out your life with bare floors and furniture, or with sealed windows and doors. But this won't do—for by the same token anyone can avoid a pregnancy due to rape by having a hysterectomy, or anyway by never leaving home without a (reliable!) army.

It seems to me that the argument we are looking at can establish at most that there are *some* cases in which the unborn person has a right to the use of its mother's body, and therefore *some* cases in which abortion is unjust killing. There is room for much discussion and argument as to precisely which, if any. But I think we should sidestep this issue and leave it open, for at any rate the argument certainly does not establish that all abortion is unjust killing.

There is room for yet another argument here, however. We surely must all grant that there may be cases in which it would be morally indecent to detach a person from your body at the cost of his life. Suppose you learn that what the violinist needs is not nine years of your life, but only one hour: all you need do to save his life is to spend one hour in that bed with him. Suppose also that letting him use your kidneys for that one hour would not affect your health in the slightest. Admittedly you were kidnapped. Admittedly you did not give anyone permission to plug him into you. Nevertheless it seems to me plain you *ought* to allow him to use your kidneys for that hour—it would be indecent to refuse.

Again, suppose pregnancy lasted only an hour, and constituted no threat to life or health. And suppose that a woman becomes pregnant as a result of rape. Admittedly she did not voluntarily do anything to bring about the existence of a child. Admittedly she did nothing at all which would give the unborn person a right to the use of her body. All the same it might well be said, as in the newly emended violinist story, that she *ought* to allow it to remain for that hour—that it would be indecent in her to refuse.

Now some people are inclined to use the term "right" in such a way that it follows from the fact that you ought to allow a person to use your body for the hour he needs, that he has a right to use your body for the hour he needs, even though he has not been given that right by any person or act. They may say that it follows also that if you refuse, you act unjustly toward him. This use of the term is perhaps so common that it cannot be called wrong; nevertheless it seems to me to be an unfortunate loosening of what we would do better to keep a tight rein on. Suppose that box of chocolates I mentioned earlier had not been given to both boys jointly, but was given only to the older boy. There he sits, stolidly eating his way through the box, his small brother watching enviously. Here we are likely to say "You ought not to be so mean. You ought to give your brother some of those chocolates." My own view is that it just does not follow from the truth of this that the brother has any right to any of the chocolates. If the boy refuses to give his brother any, he is greedy, stingy, callous—but not unjust. I suppose that the people I have in mind will say it does follow that the brother has a right to some of the chocolates, and thus that the boy does act unjustly if he refuses to give his brother any. But the effect of saying this is to obscure what we should keep distinct, namely the difference between the boy's refusal in this case and the boy's refusal in the earlier case, in which the box was given to both boys jointly, and in which the small brother thus had what was from any point of view a clear title to half.

A further objection to so using the term "right" that from the fact that A ought to do a thing for B, it follows that B has a right against A that A do it for him, is that it is going to make the question of whether or not a man has a right to a thing turn on how easy it is to provide him with it; and this seems not merely unfortunate, but morally unacceptable. Take the case of Henry Fonda again. I said earlier that I had no right to the touch of his cool hand on my fevered brow, even though I needed it to save my life. I said it would be frightfully nice of him to fly in from the West Coast to provide me with it, but that I had no right against him that he should do so. But suppose he isn't on the West Coast. Suppose he has only to walk across the room, place a hand briefly on my brow—and lo, my life is saved. Then surely he ought to do it, it would be indecent to refuse. Is it to be said "Ah, well, it follows that in this case she has a right to the touch of his hand on her brow, and so it would be an injustice in him to refuse"? So that I have a right to it when it is easy for him to provide it, though no right when it's hard? It's rather a shocking idea that anyone's rights should fade away and disappear as it gets harder and harder to accord them to him.

So my own view is that even though you ought to let the violinist use your kidneys for the one hour he needs, we should not conclude that he has a right to do so—we should say that if you refuse, you are, like the boy who owns all the chocolates and will give none away, self-centered and callous, indecent in fact, but not unjust. And similarly, that even supposing a case in which a woman pregnant due to rape ought to allow the unborn person to use her body for the hour he needs, we should not conclude that he has a right to do so; we should conclude that she is self-centered, callous, indecent, but not unjust, if she refuses. The complaints are no less grave; they are just different. However, there is no need to insist on this point. If anyone does wish to deduce "he has a right" from "you ought," then all the same he must surely grant that there are cases in which it is not morally required of you that you allow that violinist to use your kidneys, and in which he does not have a right to use them, and in which you do not do him an injustice if you refuse. And so also for mother and unborn child. Except in such cases as the unborn person has a right to demand it—and we were leaving open the possibility that there may be such cases—nobody is morally *required* to make large sacrifices, of health, of all other interests and concerns, of all other duties and commitments, for nine years, or even for nine months, in order to keep another person alive.

We have in fact to distinguish between two kinds of Samaritan: the Good Samaritan and what we might call the Minimally Decent Samaritan. The story of the Good Samaritan, you will remember, goes like this:

> A certain man went down from Jerusalem to Jericho, and fell among thieves, which stripped him of his raiment, and wounded him, and departed, leaving him half dead.
> And by chance there came down a certain priest that way; and when he saw him, he passed by on the other side.

> And likewise a Levite, when he was at the place, came and looked on him, and passed by on the other side.
> But a certain Samaritan, as he journeyed, came where he was; and when he saw him he had compassion on him.
> And went to him, and bound up his wounds, pouring in oil and wine, and set him on his own beast, and brought him to an inn, and took care of him.
> And on the morrow, when he departed, he took out two pence, and gave them to the host, and said unto him. "Take care of him; and whatsoever thou spendest more, when I come again, I will repay thee."

> (Luke 10:30–35)

The Good Samaritan went out of his way, at some cost to himself, to help one in need of it. We are not told what the options were, that is, whether or not the priest and the Levite could have helped by doing less than the Good Samaritan did, but assuming they could have, then the fact they did nothing at all shows they were not even Minimally Decent Samaritans, not because they were not Samaritans, but because they were not even minimally decent.

These things are a matter of degree, of course, but there is a difference, and it comes out perhaps most clearly in the story of Kitty Genovese, who, as you will remember, was murdered while thirty-eight people watched or listened, and did nothing at all to help her. A Good Samaritan would have rushed out to give direct assistance against the murderer. Or perhaps we had better allow that it would have been a Splendid Samaritan who did this, on the ground that it would have involved a risk of death for himself. But the thirty-eight not only did not do this, they did not even trouble to pick up a phone to call the police. Minimally Decent Samaritanism would call for doing at least that, and their not having done it was monstrous.

After telling the story of the Good Samaritan, Jesus said "Go, and do thou likewise." Perhaps he meant that we are morally required to act as the Good Samaritan did. Perhaps he was urging people to do more than is morally required of them. At all events it seems plain that it was not morally required of any of the thirty-eight that he rush out to give direct assistance at the risk of his own life, and that it is not morally required of anyone that he give long stretches of his life—nine years or nine months—to sustaining the life of a person who has no special right (we were leaving open the possibility of this) to demand it.

Indeed, with one rather striking class of exceptions, no one in any country in the world is *legally* required to do anywhere near as much as this for anyone else. The class of exception is obvious. My main concern here is not the state of the law in respect to abortion, but it is worth drawing attention to the fact that in no state in this country is any man compelled by law to be even a Minimally Decent Samaritan to any person; there is no law under which charges could be brought against the thirty-eight who stood by while Kitty Genovese died. By contrast, in most states in this country women are compelled by law to be not merely Minimally Decent Samaritans, but Good Samaritans to unborn persons inside them. This doesn't by itself settle anything one way or the other, because it may well be argued that there should be laws in this country—as there are in many European countries—compelling at least Minimally Decent Samaritanism. But it does show that there is a gross injustice in the existing state of the law. And it shows also that the groups currently working against liberalization of abortion laws, in fact working toward having it declared unconstitutional for a state to permit abortion, had better start working for the adoption of Good Samaritan laws generally, or earn the charge that they are acting in bad faith.

I should think, myself, that Minimally Decent Samaritan law would be one thing, Good Samaritan laws quite another, and in fact highly improper. But we are not here concerned with the law. What we should ask is not whether anybody should be compelled by law to be a Good Samaritan, but whether we must accede to a situation in which somebody is being compelled—by nature, perhaps—to be a Good Samaritan. We have, in other words, to look now at third-party interventions. I have been arguing that no person is morally required to make large sacrifices to sustain the life of another who has no right to demand them, and this even where the sacrifices do not include life itself; we are not morally required to be Good Samaritans or anyway Very Good Samaritans to one another. But what if a man cannot extricate himself from such a situation? What if he appeals to us to extricate him? It seems to me plain that there are cases in which we can, cases in which a Good Samaritan would extricate him. There you are, you were kidnapped, and nine years in bed with that violinist lie ahead of you. You have your own life to lead. You are sorry, but you simply cannot see giving up so much of your life to the sustaining of his. You cannot extricate yourself, and ask us to do so. I should have thought that—in light of his having no right to the use of your body—it was obvious that we do not have to accede to your being forced to give up so much. We can do what you ask. There is no injustice to the violinist in our doing so.

Following the lead of the opponents of abortion, I have throughout been speaking of the fetus merely as a person, and what I have been asking is whether or not the argument we began with, which proceeds only from the fetus' being a person, really does establish its conclusion. I have argued that it does not.

But of course there are arguments and arguments, and it may be said that I have simply fastened on the wrong one. It may be said that what is important is not merely the fact that the fetus is a person but that it is a person for whom the woman has a special kind of responsibility issuing from the fact that she is its mother. And it might be argued that all my analogies are therefore irrelevant—for you do not have that special kind of responsibility for that violinist, Henry Fonda does not have that special kind of responsibility for me. And our attention might be drawn to the fact that men and women both are compelled by law to provide support for their children.

I have in effect dealt (briefly) with this argument above; but a (still briefer) recapitulation now may be in order. Surely we do not have any such "special responsibility" for a person unless we have assumed it, explicitly or implicitly. If a set of parents do not try to prevent pregnancy, do not obtain an abortion, and then at the time of birth of the child do not put it out for adoption, but rather take it home with them, then they have assumed responsibility for it, they have given it rights, and they cannot *now* withdraw support from it at the cost of its life because they now find it difficult to go on providing for it. But if they have taken all reasonable precautions against having a child, they do not simply by virtue of their biological relationship to the child who comes into existence have a special responsibility for it. They may wish to assume responsibility for it, or they may not wish to. And I am suggesting that if assuming responsibility for it would require large sacrifices, then they may refuse. A Good Samaritan would not refuse—or anyway, a Splendid Samaritan, if the sacrifices that had to be made were enormous. But then so would a Good Samaritan assume responsibility for that violinist; so would Henry Fonda, if he is a Good Samaritan, fly in from the West Coast and assume responsibility for me.

My argument will be found unsatisfactory on two counts by many of those who want to regard abortion as morally permissible. First, while I do argue that abortion is not impermissible, I do not argue that it is always permissible. There may well be cases in which carrying the child to term requires only Minimally Decent Samaritanism of the mother, and this is a standard we must not fall below. I am inclined to think it a merit of my account precisely that it does *not* give a general yes or a general no. It allows for and supports our sense that, for example, a sick and desperately frightened fourteen-year-old schoolgirl, pregnant due to rape, may *of course* choose abortion, and that any law which rules this out is an insane law. And it also allows for and supports our sense that in other cases resort to abortion is even positively indecent. It would be indecent in the woman to request an abortion, and indecent in a doctor to perform it, if she is in her seventh month, and wants the abortion just to avoid the nuisance of postponing a trip abroad. The very fact that the arguments I have been drawing attention to treat all cases of abortion, or even all cases of abortion in which the mother's life is not at stake, as morally on a par ought to have made them suspect at the outset.

Secondly, while I am arguing for the permissibility of abortion in some cases, I am not arguing for the right to secure the death of the unborn child. It is easy to confuse these two things in that up to a certain point in the life of the fetus it is not able to survive outside the mother's body; hence removing it from her body guarantees its death. But they are importantly different. I have argued that you are not morally required to spend nine months in bed, sustaining the life of that violinist; but to say this is by no means to say that if, when you unplug yourself, there is a miracle and he survives, you then have a right to turn round and slit his throat. You may detach yourself even if this costs him his life; you have no right to be guaranteed his death by some other means, if unplugging yourself does not kill him. There are some people who will feel dissatisfied by this feature of my argument. A woman may be utterly devastated by the thought of a child a bit of herself, put out for adoption and never seen or heard of again. She may therefore want not merely that the child be detached from her, but more, that it die. Some opponents of abortion are inclined to regard this as beneath contempt—thereby showing insensitivity to what is surely a powerful source of despair. All the same, I agree that the desire for the child's death is not one which anybody may gratify should it turn out to be possible to detach the child alive.

At this place, however, it should be remembered that we have only been pretending throughout that the fetus is a human being from the moment of conception. A very early abortion is surely not the killing of a person, and so is not dealt with by anything I have said here.

[Thomson's article provoked a lively debate.* One of the most vigorous critical responses is John Finnis's "The Rights and Wrongs of Abortion," [ibid.] In his long, often technical, reply Finnis charges that Thomson's discussion of the "right to life" is a red herring. In the end, Finnis says, Thomson's argument rests not on the nature of the rights one has over others, or over oneself, but on the nature of the responsibility one has for others.

Finnis faults Thomson for confusing "special" responsibility with "ordinary" responsibility. "Special" responsibility depends on such prior acts as grants, concessions, and assumption. That is, unless one had conceded or assumed responsibility, one would not be responsible. "Ordinary" responsibility is not granted or assumed, but is the duty one always has to protect and to advance the welfare of one's neighbor. Chief among such ordinary responsibilities is protection of the neighbor's life. This is not a responsibility one may or may not accept; it is a responsibility one has by virtue of being human.

It is this latter responsibility Finnis thinks Thomson has overlooked when she claims a woman's "right" to abort. A pregnant woman has the unquestioned duty to do everything possible to preserve the life of the fetus, he argues. Does this mean she should willingly give her own life if it means saving the life of her unborn child? The answer to this question turns on the intention of the mother or the physician. It is permissible, Finnis claims, to remove a cancerous womb, even if the fetus is healthy and will be destroyed in the process, if the intention is to save the mother, and

---

* Thomson's complete article and some of the responses to it are published in *The Rights and Wrongs of Abortion,* edited by Marshall Cohen, Thomas Nagel, and Thomas Scanlon, Princeton University Press, Princeton, 1974.

not to kill the child. Finnis believes this is morally distinct from directly killing the child for the mother's convenience, or even for her health, when the intention is specifically to destroy the fetus.

In Finnis's judgment, abortion, as such, is never justified. The death of a fetus, however, may be the result of a justifiable medical act to save the mother's life. If it is the result of any measure short of saving the mother's life, it is not permissible for, in that case, abortion is plainly an act against life.

Thomson answers Finnis's objection by attacking his distinction between direct and indirect killing. She finds that the distinction is not convincing. The physician and the mother certainly know that the fetus will die if the cancer operation is performed. It is therefore improper to suggest that they do not intend the fetus's death. They do not intend only to kill the fetus, but then neither does the woman who seeks an abortion for reasons of psychiatric or economic hardship. Thomson admits that there might be a difference between direct and indirect killing but insists that Finnis has not shown it.

Thomson's point is that Finnis has not adequately demonstrated his thesis that abortion is murder except in those rare instances where the mother's life is at stake. Those, too, must be considered murder—and if they are, Finnis must either forbid abortion in every case because murder is to be forbidden, or specify those cases in which murder is acceptable. He seems to reject the complete prohibition of abortion; and to settle the problem of when murder is acceptable, he would have to debate the question with which Thomson dealt: what is the nature of the fetus's—and the mother's—right to life?]

ABORTION AND INFANTICIDE

Michael Tooley

This exerpt from a longer essay by Michael Tooley represents something of an extreme view in the current abortion debate. Following the editor's summary of the first part of the essay is Tooley's challenge to what he considers "the conservative position."

Michael Tooley is an assistant professor of philosophy at Stanford University.

This acticle is taken from Philosophy and Public Affairs, *volume 2, number 1, Fall, 1972*).

[Tooley approaches the right-to-life question from a perspective somewhat different from those of the previous authors and therefore with quite different conclusions. He does not, like Thomson, explore the notion of a right to life in itself; rather he asks which organisms have a right to life, and when they first have such a right. Do only human organisms have such a right, and do they have it from the moment of conception?

Tooley's answers to these questions carry him to what could be called the extreme liberal position. He concludes that abortion is permissible at anytime during pregnancy, and even infanticide may be permissible "during a time interval shortly after birth." He reaches that conclusion by arguing first that only *persons* have a right to life. But he is emphatic in keeping a clear distinction between "person" and "member of the species homo sapiens." It is unnecessary to assume that all human organisms are persons, or even that all persons must be human. (Tooley leaves the door open to the possibility that some animals may qualify as persons and therefore have an equal right to life.)

But what is a person? That is, which organisms have a serious right to life? His answer: "An organism possesses a serious right to life only if it possesses the concept of a self as a continuing subject of experiences and other mental states, and believes that it is itself such a continuing entity."* Plainly a fetus cannot be so described; neither can a newborn infant.

Tooley is aware that he opens himself to the conservative argument that, although the fetus is not a self-aware subject, it is potentially so in a way in which other organisms are not, therefore, to kill a potentially conscious person is quite as serious as killing an actually conscious person. In the final section of his paper, exerpted here, he speaks directly to what he takes to be the conservative position.]

Refutation of the conservative position

Many have felt that the conservative's position is more defensible than the liberal's because the conservative can point to the gradual and continuous development of an organism as it changes from a zygote to an adult human being. He is then in a position to argue that it is morally arbitrary for the liberal to draw a line at some point in this continuous process and to say that abortion is permissible before, but not after, that particular point. The liberal's reply would presumably be that the emphasis upon the continuity of the process is misleading. What the conservative is really doing is simply challenging the liberal to specify the properties a thing must have in order to be a person, and to show that the developing organism does acquire the properties at the point selected by the liberal. The liberal may then reply that the difficulty he has meeting this challenge should not be taken as grounds for rejecting his position. For the conservative cannot meet this challenge either; the conservative is equally unable to say what properties something must have if it is to have a right to life.

Although this rejoinder does not dispose of the conservative's argument, it is not without bite. For defenders of the view that abortion is always wrong have failed to face up to the question of the basic moral principles on which their position rests. They have been content to assert the wrongness of killing any organism, from a zygote on, if that organism is a member of the species Homo

* Cohen, Nagel, and Scanlon, *op. cit.,* p. 59.

sapiens. But they have overlooked the point that this cannot be an acceptable *basic* moral principle, since difference in species is not in itself a morally relevant difference. The conservative can reply, however, that it is possible to defend his position—but not the liberal's—*without* getting clear about the properties a thing must possess if it is to have a right to life. The conservative's defense will rest upon the following two claims: first, that there is a property, even if one is unable to specify what it is, that (i) is possessed by adult humans, and (ii) endows any organism possessing it with a serious right to life. Second, that if there are properties which satisfy (i) and (ii) above, at least one of those properties will be such that any organism potentially possessing that property has a serious right to life even now, simply by virtue of that potentiality, where an organism possesses a property potentially if it will come to have that property in the normal course of its development. The second claim—which I shall refer to as the potentiality principle—is critical to the conservative's defense. Because of it he is able to defend his position without deciding what properties a thing must possess in order to have a right to life. It is enough to know that adult members of Homo sapiens do have such a right. For then one can conclude that any organism which belongs to the species Homo sapiens, from a zygote on, must also have a right to life by virtue of the potentiality principle.

The liberal, by contrast, cannot mount a comparable argument. He cannot defend his position without offering at least a partial answer to the question of what properties a thing must possess in order to have a right to life.

The importance of the potentiality principle, however, goes beyond the fact that it provides support for the conservative's position. If the principle is unacceptable, then so is his position. For if the conservative cannot defend the view that an organism's having certain potentialities is sufficient grounds for ascribing to it a right to life, his claim that a fetus which is a member of Homo sapiens has a right to life can be attacked as follows. The reason an adult member of Homo sapiens has a right to life, but an infant ape does not, is that there are certain psychological properties which the former possesses and the latter lacks. Now, even if one is unsure exactly what these psychological properties are, it is clear that an organism in the early stages of development from a zygote into an adult member of Homo sapiens does not possess these properties.

One need merely compare a human fetus with an ape fetus. What mental states does the former enjoy that the latter does not? Surely it is reasonable to hold that there are no significant differences in their respective mental lives—assuming that one wishes to ascribe any mental states at all to such organisms. (Does a zygote have a mental life? Does it have experiences? Or beliefs? Or desires?) There are, of course, physiological differences, but these are not in themselves morally significant. *If* one held that potentialities were relevant to the ascription of a right to life, one could argue that the physiological differences, though not morally significant in themselves, are morally significant by virtue of their causal consequences: they will lead to later psychological differences that are morally relevant, and for this reason the physiological differences are themselves morally significant. But if the potentiality principle is not available, this line of argument cannot be used, and there will then be no differences between a human fetus and an ape fetus that the conservative can use as grounds for ascribing a serious right to life to the former but not to the latter.

It is therefore tempting to conclude that the conservative view of abortion is acceptable if and only if the potentiality principle is acceptable. But to say that the conservative position can be defended if the potentiality principle is acceptable is to assume that the argument is over once it is granted that the fetus has a right to life, and, as was noted above, Thomson has shown that there are serious grounds for questioning this assumption. In any case, the important point here is that the conservative position on abortion is acceptable *only if* the potentiality principle is sound.

One way to attack the potentiality principle is simply to argue in support of the self-consciousness requirement—the claim that only an organism that conceives of itself as a continuing subject of experiences has a right to life. For this requirement, when taken together with the claim that there is at least one property, possessed by adult humans, such that any organism possessing it has a serious right to life, entails the denial of the potentiality principle. Or at least this is so if we add the uncontroversial empirical claim that an organism that will in the normal course of events develop into an adult human does not from the very beginning of its existence possess a concept of a continuing subject of experiences together with a belief that it is itself such an entity.

I think it best, however, to scrutinize the potentiality principle itself, and not to base one's case against it simply on the self-consciousness requirement. Perhaps the first point to note is that the potentiality principle should not be confused with principles such as the following: the value of an object is related to the value of the things into which it can develop. This "valuation principle" is rather vague. There are ways of making it more precise, but we need not consider these here. Suppose now that one were to speak not of a right to life, but of the value of life. It would then be easy to make the mistake of thinking that the valuation principle was relevant to the potentiality principle—indeed, that it entailed it. But an individual's right to life is not based on the value of his life. To say that the world would be better off if it contained fewer people is not to say that it would be right to achieve such a better world by killing some of the present inhabitants. *If* having a right to life were a matter of a thing's value, then a thing's potentialities, being connected with its expected value, would clearly be relevant to the question of what rights it had. Conversely, once one realizes that a thing's rights are not a matter of its value, I think it becomes clear that an organism's potentialities are irrelevant to the question of whether it has a right to life.

But let us now turn to the task of finding a direct refutation of the potentiality principle. The basic issue is this. Is there any property J which satisfies the following conditions: (1) There is a property K such that any individual possessing property K has a right to life, and there is a scientific law L to the effect that any organism possessing property J will in the normal course of events come to possess property K at some later time. (2) Given the relationship between property J and property K just described, anything possessing property J has a right to life. (3) If property J were not related to property K in the way indicated, it would not be the case that anything possessing property J thereby had a right to life. In short, the question is whether there is a property J that bestows a right to life on an organism *only because* J stands in a certain causal relationship to a second property K, which is such that anything possessing that property ipso facto has a right to life.

My argument turns upon the following critical principle: Let C be a causal process that normally leads to outcome E. Let A be an action that initiates process C, and B be an action involving a minimal expenditure of energy that stops process C before outcome E occurs. Assume further that actions A and B do not have any other consequences, and that E is the only morally significant outcome of process C. Then there is no moral difference between intentionally performing action B and intentionally refraining from performing action A, assuming identical motivation in both cases. This principle, which I shall refer to as the moral symmetry principle with respect to action and inaction, would be rejected by some philosophers. They would argue that there is an important distinction to be drawn between "what we owe people in the form of aid and what we owe them in the way of non-interference,"[1] and that the latter, "negative duties," are duties that it is more serious to neglect than the former, "positive" ones. This view arises from an intuitive response to examples such as the following. Even if it is wrong not to send food to starving people in other parts of the world, it is more wrong still to kill someone. And isn't the conclusion, then, that one's obligation to refrain from killing someone is a more serious obligation than one's obligation to save lives?

I want to argue that this is not the correct conclusion. I think it is tempting to draw this conclusion if one fails to consider the motivation that is likely to be associated with the respective actions. If someone performs an action he knows will kill someone else, this will usually be grounds for concluding that he wanted to kill the person in question. In contrast, failing to help someone may indicate only apathy, laziness, selfishness, or an amoral outlook: the fact that a person knowingly allows another to die will not normally be grounds for concluding that he desired that person's death. Someone who knowingly kills another is more likely to be seriously defective from a moral point of view than someone who fails to save another's life.

If we are not to be led to false conclusions by our intuitions about certain cases, we must explicitly assume identical motivations in the two situations. Compare, for example, the following: (1) Jones sees that Smith will be killed by a bomb unless he warns him. Jones's reaction is: "How lucky, it will save me the trouble of killing Smith myself." So Jones allows Smith to be killed by the bomb, even though he could easily have warned him. (2) Jones wants Smith dead, and therefore shoots him. Is one to say there is a significant difference between the wrongness of Jones's behavior in these two cases? Surely not. This shows the mistake of drawing a distinction between positive duties and negative duties and holding

[1] Philippa Foot, "The Problem of Abortion and the Doctrine of the Double Effect," *The Oxford Review* 5 (1967): 5–15. See the discussion on pp. 11ff.

that the latter impose stricter obligations than the former. The difference in our intuitions about situations that involve giving aid to others and corresponding situations that involve not interfering with others is to be explained by reference to probable differences in the motivations operating in the two situations, and not by reference to a distinction between positive and negative duties. For once it is specified that the motivation is the same in the two situations, we realize that inaction is as wrong in the one case as action is in the other.

There is another point that may be relevant. Action involves effort, while inaction usually does not. It usually does not require any effort on my part to refrain from killing someone, but saving someone's life will require an expenditure of energy. One must then ask how large a sacrifice a person is morally required to make to save the life of another. If the sacrifice of time and energy is quite large it may be that one is not morally obliged to save the life of another in that situation. Superficial reflection upon such cases might easily lead us to introduce the distinction between positive and negative duties, but again it is clear that this would be a mistake. The point is not that one has a greater duty to refrain from killing others than to perform positive actions that will save them. It is rather that positive actions require effort, and this means that in deciding what to do a person has to take into account his own right to do what he wants with his life, and not only the other person's right to life. To avoid this confusion, we should confine ourselves to comparisons between situations in which the positive action involves minimal effort.

The moral symmetry principle, as formulated above, explicitly takes these two factors into account. It applies only to pairs of situations in which the motivations are identical and the positive action involves minimal effort. Without these restrictions, the principle would be open to serious objection; with them, it seems perfectly acceptable. For the central objection to it rests on the claim that we must distinguish positive from negative duties and recognize that negative duties impose stronger obligations than positive ones. I have tried to show how this claim derives from an unsound account of our moral intuitions about certain situations.

My argument against the potentiality principle can now be stated. Suppose at some future time a chemical were to be discovered which when injected into the brain of a kitten would cause the kitten to develop into a cat possessing a brain of the sort possessed by humans, and consequently into a cat having all the psychological capabilities characteristic of adult humans. Such cats would be able to think, to use language, and so on. Now it would surely be morally indefensible in such a situation to ascribe a serious right to life to members of the species Homo sapiens without also ascribing it to cats that have undergone such a process of development: there would be no morally significant differences.

Secondly, it would not be seriously wrong to refrain from injecting a newborn kitten with the special chemical, and to kill it instead. The fact that one could initiate a causal process that would transform a kitten into an entity that would eventually possess properties such that anything possessing them ipso facto has a serious right to life does not mean that the kitten has a serious right to life even before it has been subjected to the process of injection and transformation. The possibility of transforming kittens into persons will not make it any more wrong to kill newborn kittens than it is now.

Thirdly, in view of the symmetry principle, if it is not seriously wrong to refrain from initiating such a causal process, neither is it seriously wrong to interfere with such a process. Suppose a kitten is accidentally injected with the chemical. As long as it has not yet developed those properties that in themselves endow something with a right to life, there cannot be anything wrong with interfering with the causal process and preventing the development of the properties in question. Such interference might be accomplished either by injecting the kitten with some "neutralizing" chemical or simply by killing it.

But if it is not seriously wrong to destroy an injected kitten which will naturally develop the properties that bestow a right to life, neither can it be seriously wrong to destroy a member of Homo sapiens which lacks such properties, but will naturally come to have them. The potentialities are the same in both cases. The only difference is that in the case of a human fetus the potentialities have been present from the beginning of the organism's development, while in the case of the kitten they have been present only from the time it was injected with the special chemical. This difference in the time at which the potentialities were acquired is a morally irrelevant difference.

It should be emphasized that I am not here assuming that a

human fetus does not possess properties which in themselves, and irrespective of their causal relationships to other properties, provide grounds for ascribing a right to life to whatever possesses them. The point is merely that if it is seriously wrong to kill something, the reason cannot be that the thing will later acquire properties that in themselves provide something with a right to life.

Finally, it is reasonable to believe that there are properties possessed by adult members of Homo sapiens which establish their right to life, and also that any normal human fetus will come to possess those properties shared by adult humans. But it has just been shown that if it is wrong to kill a human fetus, it cannot be because of its potentialities. One is therefore forced to conclude that the conservative's potentiality principle is false.

In short, anyone who wants to defend the potentiality principle must either argue against the moral symmetry principle or hold that in a world in which kittens could be transformed into "rational animals" it would be seriously wrong to kill newborn kittens. It is hard to believe there is much to be said for the latter moral claim. Consequently one expects the conservative's rejoinder to be directed against the symmetry principle. While I have not attempted to provide a thorough defense of that principle, I have tried to show that what seems to be the most important objection to it—the one that appeals to a distinction between positive and negative duties—is based on a superficial analysis of our moral intuitions. I believe that a more thorough examination of the symmetry principle would show it to be sound. If so, we should reject the potentiality principle, and the conservative position on abortion as well.

Summary and Conclusions

Let us return now to my basic claim, the self-consciousness requirement: An organism possesses a serious right to life only if it possesses the concept of a self as a continuing subject of experiences and other mental states, and believes that it is itself such a continuing entity. My defense of this claim has been twofold. I have offered a direct argument in support of it, and I have tried to show that traditional conservative and liberal views on abortion and infanticide, which involve a rejection of it, are unsound. I now want to mention one final reason why my claim should be accepted. Consider the example mentioned in section II—that of killing, as opposed to torturing, newborn kittens. I suggested there that while in the case of adult humans most people would consider it worse to kill an individual than to torture him for an hour, we do not usually view the killing of a newborn kitten as morally outrageous, although we would regard someone who tortured a newborn kitten for an hour as heinously evil. I pointed out that a possible conclusion that might be drawn from this is that newborn kittens have a right not to be tortured, but do not have a serious right to life. If this is the correct conclusion, how is one to explain it? One merit of the self-consciousness requirement is that it provides an explanation of this situation. The reason a newborn kitten does not have a right to life is explained by the fact that it does not possess the concept of a self. But how is one to explain the kitten's having a right not to be tortured? The answer is that a desire not to suffer pain can be ascribed to something without assuming that it has any concept of a continuing self. For while something that lacks the concept of a self cannot desire that a self not suffer, it can desire that a given sensation not exist. The state desired—the absence of a particular sensation, or of sensations of a certain sort—can be described in a purely phenomenalistic language, and hence without the concept of a continuing self. So long as the newborn kitten possesses the relevant phenomenal concepts, it can truly be said to desire that a certain sensation not exist. So we can ascribe to it a right not to be tortured even though, since it lacks the concept of a continuing self, we cannot ascribe to it a right to life.

This completes my discussion of the basic moral principles involved in the issue of abortion and infanticide. But I want to comment upon an important factual question, namely, at what point an organism comes to possess the concept of a self as a continuing subject of experiences and other mental states, together with the belief that it is itself such a continuing entity. This is obviously a matter for detailed psychological investigation, but everyday observation makes it perfectly clear, I believe, that a newborn baby does not possess the concept of a continuing self, any more than a newborn kitten possesses such a concept. If so, infanticide during a time interval shortly after birth must be morally acceptable.

But where is the line to be drawn? What is the cutoff point? If one maintained, as some philosophers have, that an individual possesses concepts only if he can express these concepts in language, it would be a matter of everyday observation whether or not a given organism possessed the concept of a continuing self. Infanticide would then be permissible up to the time an organism learned how to use certain expressions. However, I think the claim that acquisition of concepts is dependent on acquisition of language is mistaken. For example, one wants to ascribe mental states of a conceptual sort—such as beliefs and desires—to organisms that are incapable of learning a language. This issue of prelinguistic understanding is clearly outside the scope of this discussion. My point is simply that *if* an organism can acquire concepts without thereby acquiring a way of expressing those concepts linguistically, the question of whether a given organism possesses the concept of a self as a continuing subject of experiences and other mental states, together with the belief that it is itself such a continuing entity, may be a question that requires fairly subtle experimental techniques to answer.

If this view of the matter is roughly correct, there are two worries one is left with at the level of practical moral decisions, one of which may turn out to be deeply disturbing. The lesser worry is where the line is to be drawn in the case of infanticide. It is not troubling because there is no serious need to know the exact point at which a human infant acquires a right to life. For in the vast majority of cases in which infanticide is desirable, its desirability will be apparent within a short time after birth. Since it is virtually certain that an infant at such a stage of its development does not possess the concept of a continuing self, and thus does not possess a serious right to life, there is excellent reason to believe that infanticide is morally permissible in most cases where it is otherwise desirable. The practical moral problem can thus be satisfactorily handled by choosing some period of time, such as a week after birth, as the interval during which infanticide will be permitted. This interval could then be modified once psychologists have established the point at which a human organism comes to believe that it is a continuing subject of experiences and other mental states.

The troubling worry is whether adult animals belonging to species other than Homo sapiens may not also possess a serious right to life. For once one says that an organism can possess the concept of a continuing self, together with the belief that it is itself such an entity, without having any way of expressing that concept and that belief linguistically, one has to face up to the question of whether animals may not possess properties that bestow a serious right to life upon them. The suggestion itself is a familiar one, and one that most of us are accustomed to dismiss very casually. The line of thought advanced here suggests that this attitude may turn out to be tragically mistaken. Once one reflects upon the question of the *basic* moral principles involved in the ascription of a right to life to organisms, one may find himself driven to conclude that our everyday treatment of animals is morally indefensible, and that we are in fact murdering innocent persons.

MURDER OF THE NEWBORN:
A PSYCHIATRIC VIEW
OF NEONATICIDE

Phillip J. Resnick, M.D.

In the opinion of many, abortion is the murder of the unborn and, as such, is not to be sharply distinguished from the murder of the newborn either as a psychological or a sociological phenomenon. Dr. Resnick examines some of the features of the poignant issue of neonaticide.

Phillip J. Resnick is an assistant professor of psychiatry, Case Western Reserve University School of Medicine.

This article is taken from the American Journal of Psychiatry, *June, 1970.*

> A simple child,
> That lightly draws its breath,
> And feels its life in every limb,
> What should it know of death?
> Wordsworth[1]

There is no crime more difficult to comprehend than the murder of a child by his own parents. Nevertheless, the killing of children goes back as far as recorded history. Reasons have included population control, illegitimacy, inability of the mother to care for the child, greed for power or money, superstition, congenital defects, and ritual sacrifice. The practice of stabilizing buildings by enclosing children in their foundations is still symbolically represented by our foundation stones.

---

[1] William Wordsworth, "We are Seven" in Stevenson, B. E. *The Home Book of Verse,* vol. 1. (New York: Holt, Rinehart and Winston), 1965, pp. 316–18.

There was an ancient concept that those who create may destroy that which they have created. Roman law formalized this concept under *patria potestas,* which recognized a father's right to murder his children. Among Mohave Indians, half-breeds were killed at birth. A merciless environment forced Eskimos to kill infants with congenital anomalies as well as one of most sets of twins. The killing of female infants was common in many cultures. In China this practice was widespread as late as the 1800s. Daughters were sacrificed because they were unable to transmit the family name and imposed the burden on their parents of paying their marriage portion. It is claimed that the widespread murder of children in ancient times was first stemmed by the influence of the Christian religion.

In the literature, all child murders by parents are usually lumped together under the term "infanticide." In the author's opinion, there are two distinct types of child murder. "Neonaticide" is defined as the killing of a neonate on the day of its birth. "Filicide" is operationally defined as the murder of a son or daughter older than 24 hours. The data for this paper were obtained by reviewing the world literature on child murder from 1751 to 1968; relevant articles were found in 13 languages. From these papers and three cases treated by the author, 168 case reports were collected. A previous publication described the 131 cases that fell into the filicide category. This paper will discuss the 37 neonaticides. The cases are reported in varying detail from mental hospitals, psychiatrists in practice, prison psychiatrists, and a coroner's office.

Since neonaticide is usually viewed in a sociologic context, it has received little attention in the psychiatric literature. The purpose of this paper is to draw together our psychiatric knowledge about this crime. Neonaticide will be shown to be a separate entity, differing from filicide in the diagnoses, motives, and disposition of the murderer. Legal considerations and the present status of neonaticide will be discussed.

Methods of Neonaticide

The method of neonaticide listed in order of greatest frequency are suffocation, strangulation, head trauma, drowning, exposure, and stabbing. Less common methods include dismemberment, burning, acid, lye, throwing to pigs, and burying alive. The need to stifle the baby's first cry makes suffocation the method of choice for mothers attempting to avoid detection. The drownings are most often accomplished in toilets. Case reports of up to 48 stab wounds or decapitation may reflect the bitterness of the abandoned girl, who sees the child in her lover's image. Some mothers use extreme cleverness to avoid discovery of their deed. In India these methods have included drowning in milk and poisoning by rubbing opium on the mother's nipples. Some midwives killed newborns by thrusting a needle under the eyelid or into the anterior fontane. A needle from one such successful attempt was found at autopsy in the brain of a 70-year-old man.

Description of the Murderers

The 37 neonaticides were committed by 34 mothers, two fathers, and in one case, both parents. In order to simplify the data, only the mothers who committed neonaticide will be compared to the mothers who committed filicide. The mothers in the neonaticide group (range 16 to 38 years) were significantly younger than the mothers in the filicide group (range 20 to 50 years). Whereas most (89 percent) of the neonaticide group were under 25 years old, the majority (77 percent) of the filicide group were over 25. While 88 percent of the filicide group were married, only 19 percent of the neonaticide group enjoyed that status.

Comparison of the diagnoses of the two groups suggests that neonaticide and filicide are committed by two different psychiatric populations. Only 17 percent of the women in the neonaticide group were psychotic, but psychosis was evident in two-thirds of the filicide group. A serious element of depression was found in only three of the neonaticide cases, compared to 71 percent of the filicide group. Finally, suicide attempts accompanied one-third of the filicides, but none occurred among the neonaticide cases.

MOTIVES

In order to provide a framework for viewing child murder, the killings are divided into five categories by apparent motive (table 1). This classification is based on the explanation given by the murderer and is independent of diagnoses. The "unwanted child" murders are committed because the victim was not desired or is no longer wanted

by his mother. The "acutely psychotic" murders are committed by
mothers under the influence of hallucinations, epilepsy, or de-
lirium. The "altruistic" murders are carried out to relieve the victim
of real or imagined suffering, or in association with suicide. "Accidental" murders, lacking in homicidal intent, are often the result
of a battered child syndrome. The "spouse revenge" murders result
from deliberate attempts to make the spouse suffer.

It is apparent from table 1 that the motives that cause a mother
to kill her newborn are considerably different from those that drive
a mother to murder an older offspring. Whereas the majority of
filicides are undertaken for an "altruistic" motive, the great bulk of
neonaticides are committed simply because the child is not wanted.

TABLE 1

Classification of child murder by apparent motive

CATEGORY	MATERNAL NEONATICIDE		MATERNAL FILICIDE	
	Number	Percent	Number	Percent
"Unwanted child" murder	29	83	10	11
"Acutely psychotic" murder	4	11	21	24
"Altruistic" murder	1	3	49	56
"Accidental" murder	1	3	6	7
"Spouse revenge" murder	0		2	2
Total	35	100	88	100

The most common reason for neonaticide among married
women is extramarital paternity. One example is a woman who
became impregnated by her brother-in-law while her husband was
in prison. After cool deliberation, she murdered her infant at birth
to avoid suspicion of her affair. It is commonplace for fathers to
show some jealousy of their newborn children. The one case in
which both the husband and wife were known to consciously plan
the murder of their expected infant is an extreme example of this.
The 28-year-old father and 17-year-old mother made no preparations for the birth of their baby except to dig a grave in the cellar.
Both parents had physical deformities and feelings of inferiority.
They were deeply in love and could not bear the thought of a third

party interfering in their relationship. The husband initially proposed the crime against the "annoying animal" that deformed his "beloved wife's virginal figure." He assisted in the delivery at home, strangled the infant, and buried it.

The stigma of having an illegitimate child is the primary reason for neonaticide in unmarried women today, as it has been through the centuries. In 1826 Scott wrote:

> A delicate female, knowing the value of a chaste reputation, and the infamy and disgrace attendant upon the loss of that indispensable character, and aware of the proverbial uncharitableness of her own sex, resolves in her distraction, rather than encounter the indifference of the world, and banishment from society, to sacrifice what on more fortunate occasions, it would have been her pride to cherish.[2]

Hirschmann and Schmitz[3] divided women who killed their illegitimate infants into two major groups. The women in the first group are said to have "a primary weakness of the characterological superstructure." In the second group are women with strong instinctual drives and little ethical restraint. All but a small minority of our 35 cases fall into the former group. These women are usually young, immature primiparas. They submit to sexual relations rather than initiate them. They have no previous criminal record and rarely attempt abortion.

Gummersbach[4] points out that passivity is the single personality factor that most clearly separates women who commit neonaticide from those who obtain abortions. Women who seek abortions are activists who recognize reality early and promptly attack the danger. In contrast, women who commit neonaticide often deny that they are pregnant or assume that the child will be stillborn. No advance preparations are made either for the care or the killing of the infant. When reality is thrust upon them by the infant's first cry, they respond by permanently silencing the intruder.

The women in the second group—those with strong instinctual drives and little ethical restraint—are more callous, egoistic, and in-

[2] D. Scott, "Case of Infanticide," *Edinburgh Medical and Surgical Journal,* 26:62–73, 1826.
[3] V. J. Hirschmann and E. Schmitz, "Structural Analysis of Female Infanticide," *Psychother,* 8;1–20, 1958.
[4] K. Gummersbach, "Die Kriminalpsychologische Persönlichkeit der Kindesmördernnen un ihre Wertung im Gerichtsinedizinischen Gutachten," Wien. Med. Wschr, 88:1151–1155, 1938.

telligent. They tend to be older, strong-willed, and often promiscuous. Their crime is usually premeditated and not out of keeping with their previous life style.

A prominent feature in several of the neonaticides was the inability of the unwed girl to reveal her pregnancy to her mother. This may be due to the girl's shame or to fear that her mother's response would be anger, punishment, or rejection. In addition, unresolved oedipal feelings may cause some of these girls to have the unconscious fantasy that their pregnancy is proof of incest. One case treated by the author will be presented as an example of this speculation.

CASE REPORT

Mrs. C., a 36-year-old married, childless secretary, committed neonaticide at age 17. However, she did not have her first psychiatric contract until she made a suicide attempt almost two decades later.

Four months before her suicide attempt, Mrs. C. found a letter indicating that her husband had been unfaithful. As with each previous adversity she had encountered, she felt that this was retribution for her killing. She became anorectic and lost 22 pounds over a four-month period. She developed insomnia, indecisiveness, and inability to concentrate on her work. She began to feel that others could read her mind and influence her through voodoo. She had frightening dreams and fantasies in which both she and her husband were beaten, murdered, and crucified. When she looked in the mirror she saw herself as a devil. She became totally preoccupied with how "evil" she was, especially because of her neonaticide. Feeling that she deserved to die, she drank a glass of corrosive liquid that caused esophageal stricture, eventually necessitating a colonesophageal transplant.

The patient was the third of four sisters. Mrs. C. described her father as a jolly, outgoing, talkative laborer who brought home his paycheck weekly, but who was more like a roomer than a husband. He "ran around," and the patient had often heard her mother speak of the "other woman." Her mother was described as a strong-willed, decisive, brusque woman who often hurt the patient's feelings. Even the tone of her voice could make the patient feel as if she were being hit. Mrs. C. was constantly seeking her mother's approval but never felt that she received it. Her first memory occurred at age three. Her father had taken her out in a new dress and showed her off to some men. They kidded him by saying that she was too cute to be his. The patient had a recurrent dream from age eight to eleven in which a terrifying monster came at her from behind but never quite reached her. As far back as Mrs. C. could remember, her parents had slept in separate bedrooms. When she was 15 her parents separated permanently. However, her father would come back and have the patient launder his shirts.

The patient dated the boy who impregnated her only a few times. She passively submitted to sexual relations to avoid his disapproval. She did not know what to do about her pregnancy, but she was quite certain she could never let her mother know. She corsetted herself and successfully concealed the pregnancy from her family. Fortuitously alone at home when she began labor, she gave birth in the bathroom to a male child. She strangled the infant with her hands and then hung it on a towel rack with a hanger until she had cleaned up. She wrapped the body in old clothes and put it in a dresser drawer overnight. The next day she put it in the rubbish, and her crime was never discovered. She was amazed at her own coolness. She claims she had no feeling of guilt at the time. "It was just something that had to be done."

However, since the killing she has tried to do good "to even things up." She felt it would be appropriate for her to die in childbirth as a final balancing of the scales. She had an extended affair with a narcotics addict that ended after he had served a prison sentence. She felt it was her "lot in life" to put up with this man even though he treated her badly. The man who subsequently became her husband was married when she met him. During their affair she was very conscious of being the "other woman" of whom she had so often heard her mother speak.

The final diagnosis was psychotic depression. The patient's psychotic thinking cleared early in her three-month hospital stay. After her discharge she was seen weekly for one year as an outpatient.

Whereas some neonaticides result from psychosis, this case may be looked upon as a psychosis resulting in part from a neonaticide. When Mrs. C. learned of her husband's infidelity she developed murderous impulses toward him. In view of her past murder in reality, it was difficult for her to experience these wishes at a conscious level. Instead they took the form of fears in her psychosis that both she and her husband would be murdered. It is noteworthy that as Mrs. C.'s neonaticide injured her infant's throat, so her method of suicide damaged her own throat.

Various elements in the patient's history suggest that unresolved oedipal feelings may have been instrumental in this neonaticide. Her first memory questions her blood relationship to her father. Throughout her childhood the patient was unable to feel close to her mother. During psychological testing her response to Rorschach Card IV was of particular interest. She appeared terrified, threw down the card, and cried for a long time. She said it was dreadful, like the monster in her repetitive dream. Several months later she admitted that her first thought upon seeing the card had been that of her mother in a fur coat. After her parents' separation Mrs. C. took over the rather intimate chore of doing her father's laundry. In spite of protesting, she proceeded to become the "other woman" in relation to her husband. The sum of these factors suggests that Mrs. C. may have failed to reveal her pregnancy to her mother because of the unconscious idea that it would be viewed as proof of incest.

Although there are no previous reports of neonaticide attributed to an oedipal issue, this phenomenon has been observed in other pathological mother-child interactions. There is one report in which a married woman had an abortion because she unconsciously felt that she was carrying her father's child. Zilboorg[5] recounts a case of depression in a mother in which the central theme was a wish to destroy her child because she viewed it as living testimony of her unconscious incestuous attitude toward her father.

PATERNAL NEONATICIDE

Although it is not uncommon for fathers to murder older children, it is rare for a father to kill a newborn infant. Fathers have neither the motive nor the opportunity of mothers. Only two case reports were found in which the father was the sole killer. One mentally deficient 32-year-old man poisoned his newborn child because he felt that his own poor health might result in his death,

[5] G. Zilboorg, "Sidelights on Parent-Child Antagonism," *American Journal of Orthopsychiatry*, 2: 35–43, 1932.

leaving no one to provide for his wife and child. The other father was a bright 26-year-old man who was forced into marriage by his wife's pregnancy. He saw the coming child as a bar to his ambition. On one occasion he put poison in his wife's soup in an attempt to cause the infant to be stillborn. He strangled the infant while delivering it himself. Although free of overt psychosis at the time, he developed a full-blown picture of schizophrenia three years later. Both fathers were sentenced to ten years in prison. Fathers appear to receive more severe sentences than mothers for neonaticide and for filicide.

Disposition

Mothers who commit neonaticide are more likely to be sentenced to prison or probation, whereas mothers who commit filicide are more likely to be hospitalized. This difference is in keeping with the lesser number of pychoses in the neonaticide group. Victoroff[6] notes that there is some appreciation that a mother who destroys her own child constructs enough guilt in this act to punish her sufficiently for the crime. Juries often find that the woman accused of neonaticide does not correspond to their imagination of a murderess. For no other crime is there such a lack of conviction. Even those who are convicted often receive only probation or minimal prison sentences.

The likelihood of a woman's killing a second newborn child after standing trial for neonaticide is very slim. There are a few reports in which a mother did kill two or three successive newborns. However, in all but one case the previous neonaticides had been undiscovered and unpunished. There is a greater chance of recidivism if the crime is consistent with the life style of the mother.

Legal Considerations

To understand the current legal status of infant murder, it is instructive to review the English law regarding this crime. In the reign of James I, the law presumed an illegitimate newborn found

6 V. M. Victoroff, "A Case of Infanticide Related to Psychomotor Automatism: Psychodynamic, Physiological, Forensic and Sociological Considerations," *Journal of Clinical Experimental Psychopathology,*" 16: 191–220, 1955.

dead to have been murdered by its mother unless she could prove by at least one witness that the child had been born dead. In 1803 the same rules of evidence and presumption became required as in other murders. Death sentences for this crime were almost invariably commuted. Juries hesitated to find a verdict of guilty and send the accused to the gallows. Abse states, "Those juries knew that at or about the time of birth, dogs, cats, and sows . . . sometimes killed their own young. They were not prepared to extend less compassion and concern to a mentally sick woman than they would to an excitable bitch."[7]

A desire to make the punishment more suitable to the crime led to the Infanticide Act of 1922. This act reduced the penalties to those of manslaughter for a woman who killed her newborn child while the "balance of her mind was disturbed from the effect of giving birth." Critics of this law suggest that if a woman were insane at the time of the crime she should not be held responsible, rather than be convicted of a lesser crime.

Several European countries provide lesser penalties for neonaticide than for adult murder. These universally apply only to the mother; if a father kills a newborn child he is charged with murder. In the United States there is no legal distinction between the murder of adults and the murder of newborn infants. Although it is a common occurrence to find dead newborn infants in sewers, alleys, and incinerators in any metropolitan community, convictions are rare because of the difficulty in proving the guilt of those responsible. Several states have passed laws against the more easily prosecuted offense of concealment of birth.

In order to convict an individual of neonaticide it must be proven that he killed the infant by a specific act of commission or omission. It must also be proven that the infant breathed and had a viable separate existence from the mother after being fully extruded from the birth canal. Proving live birth was made easier by Swammerdam's discovery in 1667 that fetal lungs would float on water if respiration had occurred. However, this test was found to be not infallible, and even careful microscopic examination of neonatal lungs today does not always reveal a definitive answer. The other vexing forensic problem is proving that the child was wholly born. It is theoretically possible for a woman to cut the throat of

[7] L. Abse, "Infanticide and British Law," *Clinical Pediatrics,* 6: 316–317, 1967.

her half-born infant, report the incident to the authorities, and therefore escape prosecution for either murder or concealment. Such cases have been reported.

PRESENT STATUS OF NEONATICIDE

It is extremely difficult to get accurate figures on the incidence of neonaticide because so many cases are never discovered. Published figures do suggest a decline in the last century. Several factors may have contributed to this. Effective birth control measures are now widely available. Since the advent of antibiotics, abortions are rarely life threatening. Homes for unwed mothers have become available as a shelter from the "scoff and scorn of a taunting world," and placement of unwanted children can often be arranged. Finally, welfare payments today have reduced a woman's prospect of being destitute. Yet in spite of these advances, hundreds and possibly thouands of neonaticides still occur in this country each year.

Psychiatric intervention to prevent neonaticide is extremely difficult. Unlike filicide, in which 40 percent of murdering mothers seek medical or psychiatric consultation shortly before their crime, it is rare for women who commit neonaticide to seek any type of prenatal care. One way to further reduce the incidence of neonaticide would be a liberalization of abortion laws. Although this approach is far from ideal, it would provide women a less cruel alternative than killing their newborn infant. Each neonaticide is tragic—not only for the infant but also for the continuing effect that the crime has on the life of the mother.

SUMMARY

This paper has attempted to show that the killing of a newborn infant is a separate entity from other filicides. Hence a new word, "neonaticide," is proposed for this phenomenon. When mothers who commit neonaticide are compared with mothers who kill older children, they are found to be younger, more often unmarried, and less frequently psychotic. Whereas the majority of filicides are committed for "altrustic" reasons, most neonaticides are carried out simply because the child is not wanted. Reasons for neonaticide include extramarital paternity, rape, and seeing the child as an obstacle to parental ambition. However, illegitimacy, with its social stigma, is the most common motive.

The unmarried murderesses fall into two groups. In the first group are young, immature, passive women who submit to, rather than initiate, sexual relations. They often deny their pregnancy, and premeditation is rare. The women in the second group have strong instinctual drives and little ethical restraint. They tend to be older, more callous, and are often promiscuous.

It is speculated that unresolved oedipal feelings may contribute to some neonaticides that have previously been attributed to entirely sociologic factors.

section 2

EUTHANASIA

The fact that euthanasia is now an area of often fierce controversy is ironic. The term euthanasia means simply "a good death." Its origin is quite modest: it lies in that ancient desire of the physician and the patient to reduce both the unnecessary pain of terminal illness and the unnecessary anguish of death. The stress here should be on the word "unnecessary." Pain and anguish are unnecessary when death is inevitable and cannot be avoided by the heroic efforts of either the physician or the patient. For centuries there has been an unquestioned agreement between all parties involved that once the patient's condition is hopeless the physician's task is to reduce the suffering.

The irony comes with the technological age and the extraordinary ability of the medical profession to challenge the inevitability of death. There is no question that the deep human desire for prolonging life has borne dramatic results through the use of sophisticated drugs and mechanical devices. But, as a number of widely publicized cases in the last few years have illustrated, prolongation is sometimes achieved at enormous personal and material costs.

It might be said that the pain and anguish of terminal illness is now often necessary if life has been prolonged artificially. Of course, it is rare that a person is required to endure great physical pain as he or she approaches death because of the great variety of drugs available. Therefore, the issue is not one of pain as much as it is one of "dignity," to use the current term. There is not much doubt when one is in pain, but when shall we say that a person's dignity has been lost? Pain is a phenomenon of consciousness. We *know* when we are in pain. The term dignity is used for persons regardless of whether they are conscious. It is frequently asserted that the dignity of human existence has been destroyed when a body is kept alive at a close to vegetative state. It is also argued that the deep psychic stress of an impending death, particularly where there has been a severe loss of normal human functioning, also costs a person his or her dignity.

It is self-evident that it is far more problematical to determine when a person's dignity has been damaged than when a person is in acute pain. How do we draw the line on this issue? How can we develop a clear definition of the term *dignity?* It is around these questions that much of the euthanasia debate revolves. Two of the following articles are addressed directly to this aspect of the debate. Eliot Slater's "The Case for Voluntary Euthanasia" offers a physician's view of the dilemma. As any physician knows, there are illnesses that can leave persons irretrievably comatose or miserable. Moreover, there is only too often a terrible price of indignity paid by the aged.

The philosopher Antony Flew in his essay, "The Principle of Euthanasia," examines the euthanasia issue from a different perspective. Flew begins by assuming a person's right to make a decision to end his or her own life, then systematically addresses the objections to the doctrine of voluntary euthanasia. Since euthanasia, as Flew takes the term, requires the conscious consent of the patient, it is similar to the issue of suicide. Flew includes in his essay argument for the moral justification of suicide.

One frequent distinction made in the discussion of euthanasia draws a sharp line between active and passive forms of the act. While this seems to have considerable appeal, particularly in a clinical setting where "allowing" someone to die is an alternative to actively "killing" that person, it is a philosophically unjustified distinction, according to James Rachels in his essay, "Active and Passive Euthanasia." Rachels adds the further specter that in some instances "passive" act of euthanasia could cause considerably more suffering than actively intervening to end the life of a person suffering from a hopelessly terminal illness.

In a hard-hitting article Paul Ramsey raises several objections to euthanasia—in any form—by attacking the notion of "death with dignity." Ramsey claims it is an inexcusable distortion of the issue to think that death could ever be dignified. Although he does not direct his fire at the whole battery of arguments offered by proponents of euthanasia, he does suggest one of the strongest reasons for rejecting euthanasia in every case, regardless of the psychic or material costs to patients and their families. It may sometimes be true that certain comatose conditions are irreversible, and that a patient will never regain those qualities of consciousness considered essential to personhood, but death is even more irreversible. As long as there is life there is hope; there is no hope when a patient has died. Even if the patient is capable of only the weakest gestures of biological existence, he or she is still not lost to the community of sharing and concern.

It is this view which lies behind much of the interest in establishing "hospices," institutions concerned exclusively with the care of the terminally ill. Such institutions express the conviction of some persons that "dignity" is never lost in human existence. Since dignity is a term that presupposes the attitudes of others toward oneself, to say that life has lost its dignity is to say that others have lost their concern. The mere existence of hospices is testimony to the fact that there are people who intend never to lose their attitude of concern for human life.

It is unrealistic to assume that this position will be convincing to everyone. It is particularly the case that there are many persons who have strong convictions concerning their own potential helplessness or misery in illness or old age. The popularity of such devices as "The Living Will" is evidence of a desire to avoid the costs of sharply reduced human functioning—particularly when it is the consequence of medical technology having "unnaturally" postponed the arrival of death.

It is an open and important question whether voluntary euthanasia is consistent with a full sense of the dignity of life. Assuming that it is, there remains a confusing question about the legality of euthanasia. Is it legally—and morally—possible for a doctor actively to take a person's life, even where that person has requested the action? The legal terrain that must be explored before adequate legislation can be enacted is described in Sander's essay, "Euthanasia: None Dare Call it Murder." Joseph Fletcher, in his "Ethics and Euthanasia," vigorously defends the morality of euthanasia.

While the articles by Sanders, Fletcher, and Flew seem to clear the ethical, legal, and philosophical ground for euthanasia, the final selection in this chapter, Anthony Shaw's "Dilemmas of 'Informed Consent' in Children" offers a vivid picture of the range of human judgment that will never be completely eliminated by any amount of legal and ethical clarity. Taking the life of another human being, regardless of the reasons and regardless of the circumstances, is a grave and dangerous act. It is the counsel of wisdom that we shall never have reflected on such an act sufficiently to enter into it with perfect certainty that it should be committed. Similarly, we can never decide with perfect certainty that there is no circumstance in which euthanasia is not acceptable.

THE CASE FOR VOLUNTARY EUTHANASIA

Eliot Slater

The appropriateness of having a part in the decision as to the timing of one's own death is explored in this essay by Dr. Eliot Slater, an English physician who has had a long career in medicine and an active role in debating the issues of euthanasia.

Eliot Slater, until his retirement in 1964, was active as a researcher and as a clinical psychiatrist. He is a member of the Committee of the Voluntary Euthanasia Society.

This article is taken from Contemporary Review, *August, 1971.*

Considering that we all have to die one day, it is surprising that we do not make more effort to choose a time to suit ourselves, rather than leave such an important matter to chance, or to exhausted nature, or to the decisions of others. There is an inertia in living, which tends to keep the life process going until the difficulties become insurmountable. Doctors know that most patients shy away from death and, however uncomfortable their life, would rather die tomorrow than today. Such is their respect for this primitive urge that doctors have now made an ethical principle out of it.

It was not always so. Medical ethics, despite the conservatism of the profession, change steadily with time; and they are different now in this respect from what they were when I was a young houseman, rather more than 40 years ago. Then there was not very much one could do to keep life going in the moribund patient; and it was considered wise and humane to let the dying patient slip away without trying to hold him back. Nowadays the profession has such powers to arrest the process of dying that it is difficult to leave them unused. In 1969 the Representative Body of the British Medical Association, in a strong condemnation of euthanasia, affirmed the 'fundamental objects of the medical profession as the relief of suffering and the preservation of life'. The preservation of life has, in fact, been made officially into a cardinal principle, although there is certainly a considerable number of doctors who would not agree with this unreservedly, and despite the many difficulties which this principle creates now that medicine has become what it is.

The official view gave the first priority to the prevention of suffering, but the order is frequently reversed. There are many conditions in which the preservation of life can only be bought by the prolongation of suffering. Doctors, especially the energetic teams of doctors and nurses in hospitals, can appreciate the preservation of life as a clear directive; and the measures it will call for will be plain enough. The prevention of suffering is a much more nebulous aim, and it is difficult to see how far one is successful in providing it. So the straightforward thing to do is to keep life going at any cost, and then do what one can to relieve the suffering entailed. The result is that there is a very great deal of most uncomfortable dying. Estimates by family doctors and other doctors of great experience vary between five and fifteen percent of cases in which there is serious or prolonged distress and suffering. It is possible to control pain in very painful conditions, but only by close and unremitting attention; injections, for instance, have to be repeated at short intervals. This is not generally a working practice in hospitals, except in special units; and it is rarely possible at home. But there are other distresses besides pain; and it is much more difficult to relieve nausea, difficulty in breathing, and the feeling of being wretchedly feeble and ill. It is quite common for circumstances to arise in which the doctor has to choose between the preservation of life and the relief of suffering, since the suffering can only end with the end of life. These are the situations in which, as some of us believe, it would be natural and right for the patient's own wishes to be consulted and obeyed.

Wherever they can, doctors avoid talking to their patients about their life expectation, or of death in any personal application. The subject lies under a kind of taboo. This is felt so much by patients that, when at last they become aware that they might be dying, they still feel it is impossible to ask their doctor whether this is so or not. If they are given the chance to talk about it, they will often seize it with gratitude and relief. Doctors then find, to their surprise, that there are many patients, particularly among the elderly, in whom the life-urge has burnt itself out, and who would be glad to die. In two combined National Opinion Polls, 1964 and 1965, each of 1,000 general practitioners taken at random from the Medical Register, nearly half (48.6 percent) of those who replied answered 'yes' to the question: 'Have you ever been asked by a dying patient to give him or her final release from suffering which was felt to be intolerable?' If the request were a legal one, would there be any humane grounds for refusing it? This is the direction in which lay, if not medical, opinion is tending to veer, for instance the informed and sensitive opinion of the priest. The Archbishop of Canterbury, Dr. Ramsay, when asked how he felt about euthanasia, said: 'We need some more Christian exploration on this. I would say that where a patient is lingering on in great distress, without any possibility of continuing life or happiness or purpose, it is not necessary for the doctor to continue keeping him alive.' (*The Times,* 3.5.71).

The preservation-of-life principle can be taken to lengths which are patently absurd. Two examples can be given of the many that might be thought of. One is provided by the young man who suffers a severe head injury in a road accident. He is taken into hospital unconscious, and remains unconscious though still not quite dead, since his heart is kept beating with electronic aid and he still breathes with assisted respiration. The brain is shocked to begin with, so that one cannot tell how much brain tissue has been destroyed and how much put temporarily out of action, leaving recovery still possible. The greater the amount of tissue destruction, the longer unconsciousness is likely to last; and one can argue back from the duration of unconsciousness to the degree of recovery that can be expected. More exact information is available in the electrical output of the brain, which is traced in wave form by the electroencephalograph. It is still possible, even after some weeks of unconsciousness, for a man to recover and after months of convalescence regain a fairly normal life, though there will be some personality changes. If unconsciousness persists longer and longer, the chance of worthwhile recovery recedes. The state becomes a vegetative one, keeping going without electronic aid or artificial feeding. The heart beats; the chest breathes; bladder and bowels automatically empty themselves from time to time; food carefully spooned into the mouth calls up the swallowing reflex. But the patient is in a deep sleep, from which he cannot be roused; great areas of the brain, on which awareness depends, have gone for ever. It is our practice to keep patients alive in this state for as long as we can, for five years, six years and more, in fact for years after the last hope has gone that they will ever be conscious again. No one supposes that the hospital is rendering any service to the unconscious man, for whom life and death have equally ceased to exist. Nor could one claim that any service is done to the family. Relatives, and parents especially, will go on hoping and hoping, however unreasonably, in a state so painful that, when death finally does come, it is felt as a relief. Least of all has any service been rendered to society. The burden on the community is quite a heavy one. The nursing of such an unconscious patient makes a considerable demand on the hospital's resources; and the consequence is that medical aid to other patients must be denied or delayed. The reason for so much care and devotion so uselessly expended is that any other course is felt to be morally indefensible. The spark of life needs constant support: the monitoring of vegetative functions, antibiotics, special feeding, cleaning, care, protection, etc. Withhold it, and it dies. To withdraw it, then, is to kill; and for those who have dedicated themselves to the preservation of life, killing is unthinkable.

At the other end of life doctors are faced with an equivalent dilemma, and one which is now becoming extremely common. This is the problem of the very old. People start to age not all at the same time, and not all at an equal rate. Different tissues of the body have their own times for getting old, so that muscles, bones and joints, the arteries and the heart, the eyes and the hearing and the nervous system are not equally old at the same time; and here too there are wide differences between individuals. As time goes on into the seventies and the eighties, small incapacities and disabilities gradually accumulate. Life becomes more and more restricted, and even the restricted life becomes more and more difficult. Very often there is very little money to spare, or even downright poverty. Still more often there is great loneliness. Nowadays old people are no longer part of the nuclear family. Their children, with husbands or wives and children of their own, have no room for them in their homes, or in their lives. The world moves on with bewildering rapidity, and every new social change comes as an added strain. Then perhaps comes illness or an accident; the old person is taken into hospital, and soon transferred to a geriatric ward. Here he gets the best attention, and what is possible is done to put him right and make him able to look after himself again; then he can go home, perhaps with yet another minor disability; or into an old persons' home; or into a chronic ward where he can wait for death. These old people are very tenacious of life, and often get a lot of enjoyment and interest out of pitifully limited existences. But even then, as doctors who work in geriatric wards know well, about one in five of these patients will tell you if you ask them—or even listen to them—that they would very much like to be dead and done with it all, if only that were possible.

The most pathetic state is that of the old person whose brain ages faster than the other organs, so that he or she (it is usually she, since women live longer than men) becomes mentally senile. Experts have estimated that, by the age of 80, about one in 40 people can expect the onset of senile dementia. This is a hateful condition, degrading and slow to kill. Thirty years ago or so, before the discovery of antibiotics, the senile patient usually died quickly, since his resistance was so low and he was very liable to infections which were deadly in that enfeebled state. Pneumonia was 'the old man's friend' and, once it came, snuffed out existence in a day or so. Now our drugs are so powerful that the old man's friend is kept from the door when he calls. Protected against accidents and all causes of quick death in a well-run hospital ward, the senile patient goes on into a state in which all mental faculties wither away, memory, intelligence, interest, understanding and judgment, love and affection, even the realisation of where one is, and the recollection of who one is. The final state is one of mindlessness. The shrivelled patient sits in bed with dull gaze and fingers plucking the bedclothes, unresponsive when spoken to, unnoticing of doctors, nurses, visitors, family, passively receiving the administration of food, the unremitting cleaning and care. An infection can run through such a ward like a Black Death, so that special precautions and the free use of antibiotics are needed; but with their aid these helpless bodies linger on for one year, two years and more. The excellent doctors and the devoted nurses (always too few for the great strain the work imposes) will say that this is right, and that this is not an undignified end. But surely there are few who would not dread it for themselves.

There are, of course, many last illnesses in which death can still come quickly and irresistibly; but the increasing powers of the doctors are closing these exits. More and more, patients are shown the way to a slower death, drifting downwards by infinitesimal stages into extreme debility, physical or mental or both. The long process is not easy, and often involves much suffering and distress. What we need is a means by which the private individual can exercise some self-determination. When the course is irretrievably downwards, the alternative to drifting is a quicker plunge, which must be by a voluntary act. What avenues are open today?

Since the Suicide Act of 1961, suicide in this country has not been an offence under the law. However, it is a long-standing and persistent medical tradition to regard it as abnormal, usually the act of a mentally sick man, indeed itself constituting strong *prima facie* evidence of mental illness. Doctors think it their duty to interrupt a suicide, at any moment however late before death; and then, after he has been resuscitated, to try to help the patient to solve his problems in other ways. Anyone who wishes to forestall the well-meant rescue would do well to draw up a solemn declaration of his intention, and formally forbid anyone to interfere with it or lay hands on his person while alive.

I do not know that this has ever been done. But it seems to be lawful, and it might become an accepted practice. If it did, it would solve only a part of the problem. Patients who are very ill and confined to bed are helplessly in the hands of others and have no easy means of suicide. Those who wished to die could perhaps be helped by an amendment to the Suicide Act, releasing from the general prohibition against aiding and abetting a suicide the registered medical practitioner acting *bona fide* in his professional relationship. A doctor, who would never consider being an 'executioner', might find it easier, if the law allowed, to place the means of death within the reach of his patient, for him to use if he wished of his own accord, neither encouraging nor preventing him.

This would still leave the cases of those who, without realising what has happened to them, lapse into a demented state in which volitional acts are no longer possible. Their predicament would call for a change in the law, to give effect to a declaration made in advance, asking that in such a state they should be allowed to die as soon as possible. This was the substance of a Euthanasia Bill presented in the Lords in 1969 by Lord Raglan, which was defeated, though against a substantial minority.

The present state of affairs in law and in practice is a patent absurdity. In the long run the human desire for comfort will find a way round the distresses and indignities of incurable illness or incapacity. Some time man's need for freedom and self-determination will win against the forces that keep him in the servitude of a life sentence without remission or parole.

THE PRINCIPLE OF
EUTHANASIA

Antony Flew

While much of the controversy concerning euthanasia focuses on legal matters, there remain important, distinct moral and philosophical questions that in some cases are prior to the legal resolution of the issue. In this essay Professor Flew presents a philosophical case for euthanasia, including a defense of the right to suicide.

Antony Flew is a professor of philosophy at the University of Keele, Staffordshire, England.

This essay appeared in Euthanasia and the Right to Die, *A. B. Downing, editor, published in London by Peter Owen, Ltd., 1969.*

1

My particular concern here is to deploy a general moral case for the establishment of a legal right to voluntary euthanasia. The first point to emphasize is that the argument is about *voluntary* euthanasia. Neither I nor any other contributor to the present volume advocates the euthanasia of either the incurably sick or the miserably senile except in so far as this is the strong, constant, and unequivocally expressed wish of the afflicted candidates themselves. Anyone, therefore, who dismisses what is in fact being contended on the gratuitously irrelevant grounds that he could not tolerate compulsory euthanasia, may very reasonably be construed as thereby tacitly admitting inability to meet and to overcome the case actually presented.

Second, my argument is an argument for the establishment of legal right. What I am urging is that any patient whose condition is hopeless and painful, who secures that it is duly and professionally certified as such, and who himself clearly and continuously desires to die should be enabled to do so: and that he should be enabled to do so without his incurring, or his family incurring, or those who provide or administer the means of death incurring, any legal penalty or stigma whatsoever. To advocate the establishment of such a legal right is not thereby to be committed even to saying that it would always be morally justifiable, much less that it would always be morally obligatory, for any patient to exercise this right if he found himself in a position so to do. For a legal right is not as such necessarily and always a moral right; and hence, *a fortiori*, it is not necessarily and always a moral duty to exercise whatever legal rights you may happen to possess.

This is a vital point. It was—to refer first to an issue now at last happily resolved—crucial to the question of the relegalization in Great Britain of homosexual relations between consenting male adults. Only when it was at last widely grasped, and grasped in its relation to this particular question, could we find the large majorities in both Houses of Parliament by which a liberalizing bill was passed into law. For presumably most members of those majorities not only found the idea of homosexual relations repugnant—as most of us do—but also believed such relations to be morally wrong—as I for one do not. Yet they brought themselves to recognize that neither the repugnance generally felt towards some practice, nor even its actual wrongness if it actually is wrong, by itself constitutes sufficient reason for making or keeping that practice illegal. By the same token it can in the present instance be entirely consistent to urge, both that there ought to be a legal right to voluntary euthanasia, and that it would sometimes or always be morally wrong to exercise that legal right.

Third, the case presented here is offered as a moral one. In developing and defending such a case I shall, of course, have to consider certain peculiarly religious claims. Such claims, however, become relevant here only in so far as they either constitute, or may be thought to constitute, or in so far as they warrant, or may be thought to warrant, conclusions incompatible with those which it is my primary and positive purpose to urge.

Fourth, and finally, this essay is concerned primarily with general principles, not with particular practicalities. I shall not here discuss or—except perhaps quite incidentally—touch upon any questions of comparative detail: questions, for instance, of how a Eu-

thanasia Act ought to be drafted; of what safeguards would need
to be incorporated to prevent abuse of the new legal possibilities by
those with disreputable reasons for wanting someone else dead; of
exactly what and how much should be taken as constituting an
unequivocal expression of a clear and constant wish; of the circumstances, if any, in which we ought to take earlier calculated expressions of a patient's desires as constituting still adequate grounds
for action when at some later time the patient has become himself
unable any longer to provide sufficiently sober, balanced, constant
and unequivocal expressions of his wishes; and so on.

I propose here as a matter of policy largely to ignore such particular and practical questions. This is not because I foolishly regard
them as unimportant, or irresponsibly dismiss them as dull. Obviously
they could become of the most urgent interest. Nor yet is it because
I believe that my philosophical cloth disqualifies me from contributing helpfully to any down-to-earth discussions. On the contrary, I happen to be one of those numerous academics who are
convinced, some of them correctly, that they are practical and busi-
nesslike men! The decisive reason for neglecting these vital questions of detail here in, and in favour of, a consideration of the
general principle of the legalization of voluntary euthanasia is that
they are all secondary to that primary issue. For no such subordinate
question can properly arise as relevantly practical until and unless
the general principle is conceded. Some of these practical considerations are in any event dealt with by other contributors to this volume.

2

So what can be said in favour of the principle? There are two
main, and to my mind decisive, moral reasons. But before deploy-
ing these it is worth pausing for a moment to indicate why the onus
of proof does not properly rest upon us. It may seem as if it does,
because we are proposing a change in the present order of things;
and it is up to the man who wants a change to produce the reasons for making whatever change he is proposing. This most rational
principle of conservatism is in general sound. But here it comes into
conflict with the overriding and fundamental liberal principle. It
is up to any person and any institution wanting to prevent anyone
from doing anything he wishes to do, or to compel anyone to do

anything he does not wish to do, to provide positive good reason to justify interference. The question should therefore be: *not* "Why should people be given this new legal right?"; *but* "Why should people in this mater be restrained by law from doing what they want?"

Yet even if this liberal perspective is accepted, as it too often is not, and even if we are able to dispose of any reasons offered in defence of the present legal prohibitions, still the question would arise, whether the present state of the law represents a merely tiresome departure from sound liberal principles of legislation, or whether it constitutes a really substantial evil. It is here that we have to offer out two main positive arguments.

(1) First, there are, and for the foreseeable future will be, people afflicted with incurable and painful diseases who urgently and fixedly want to die quickly. The first argument is that a law which tries to prevent such sufferers from achieving this quick death, and usually thereby forces other people who care for them to watch their pointless pain helplessly, is a very cruel law. It is because of this legal cruelty that advocates of euthanasia sometimes speak of euthanasia as "mercy-killing." In such cases the sufferer may be reduced to an obscene parody of a human being, a lump of suffering flesh eased only by intervals of drugged stupor. This, as things now stand, must persist until at last every device of medical skill fails to prolong the horror.

(2) Second, a law which insists that there must be no end to this process—terminated only by the overdue relief of "death by natural causes"—is a very degrading law. In the present context the full force of this second reason may not be appreciated immediately, if at all. We are so used to meeting appeals to "the absolute value of human personality," offered as the would-be knockdown objection to any proposal to legalize voluntary euthanasia, that it has become hard to realize that, in so far as we can attach some tolerably precise meaning to the key phrase, this consideration would seem to bear in the direction precisely opposite to that in which it is usually mistaken to point. For the agonies of prolonged terminal illness can be so terrible and so demoralizing that the person is blotted out in ungovernable nerve reactions. In such cases as this, to meet the patient's longing for death is a means of showing for human personality that respect which cannot tolerate any ghastly travesty of it. So our second main positive argument, attack-

ing the present state of the law as degrading, derives from a respect for the wishes of the individual person, a concern for human dignity, an unwillingness to let the animal pain disintegrate the man.

Our first main positive argument opposes the present state of the law, and of the public opinion which tolerates it, as cruel. Often and appositely this argument is supported by contrasting the tenderness which rightly insists that on occasion dogs and horses must be put out of their misery, with the stubborn refusal in any circumstances to permit one person to assist another in cutting short his suffering. The cry is raised, "But people are not animals!" Indeed they are not. Yet this is precisely not a ground for treating people worse than brute animals. Animals are like people, in that they too can suffer. It is for this reason that both can have a claim on our pity and our mercy.[1]

But people are also more than brute animals. They can talk and think and wish and plan. It is this that makes it possible to insist, as we do, that there must be no euthanasia unless it is the firm considered wish of the person concerned. People also can, and should, have dignity as human beings. That is precisely why we are urging that they should be helped and not hindered when they wish to avoid or cut short the often degrading miseries of incurable disease or, I would myself add, of advanced senile decay.

3

In the first section I explained the scope and limitations of the present chapter. In the second I offered—although only after suggesting that the onus of proof in this case does not really rest on the proposition—my two main positive reasons in favour of euthanasia. It is time now to begin to face, and to try to dispose of, objections. This is the most important phase in the whole exercise. For to anyone with any width of experience and any capacity for compassion the positive reasons must be both perfectly obivous and strongly felt. The crucial issue is whether or not there are decisive, overriding objections to these most pressing reasons of the heart.

---

[1] Thus Jeremy Bentham, urging that the legislator must not neglect animal sufferings, insists that the "question is not 'Can they *reason?*' nor 'Can they *talk?*' but 'Can they *suffer?*'" (*Principles of Morals and Legislation,* Chap. XVII, *n.*)

(1) Many of the objections commonly advanced, which are often mistaken to be fundamental, are really objections only to a possible specific manner of implementing the principle of voluntary euthanasia. Thus it is suggested that if the law permitted doctors on occasion to provide their patients with means of death, or where necessary to do the actual killing, and they did so, then the doctors who did either of these things would be violating the Hippocratic Oath, and the prestige of and public confidence in the medical profession would be undermined.

As to the Hippocratic Oath, this makes two demands which in the special circumstances we have in mind may become mutually contradictory. They cannot both be met at the same time. The relevant section reads: "I will use treatments to help the sick according to my ability and judgment, but never with a view to injury and wrong-doing. I will not give anyone a lethal dose if asked to do so, nor will I suggest such a course."[2] The fundamental undertaking "to help the sick according to my ability and judgment" may flatly conflict with the further promise not to "give anyone a lethal dose if asked to do so." To observe the basic undertaking a doctor may have to break the further promise. The moral would, therefore, appear to be: not that the Hippocratic Oath categorically and unambiguously demands that doctors must have no dealings with voluntary euthanasia; but rather that the possible incompatibility in such cases of the different directives generated by two of its logically independent clauses constitutes a reason for revising that Oath.

As to the supposed threat to the prestige of and to our confidence in the medical profession, I am myself inclined to think that the fears expressed are—in more than one dimension—disproportionate to the realities. But whatever the truth about this whole objection would bear only against proposals which permitted or required doctors to do, or directly to assist in, the actual killing. This is not something which is essential to the whole idea of voluntary euthanasia, and the British Euthanasia Society's present draft bill is so formulated as altogether to avoid this objection. It is precisely

[2] The Greek text is most easily found in *Hippocrates and the Fragments of Heracleitus,* ed. W. H. S. Jones and E. T. Withington for the Loeb series (Harvard Univ. Pr. and Heinemann), Vol. 1, p. 298. The translation in the present essay is mine.

such inessential objections as this which I have undertaken to eschew in this essay, in order to consider simply the general principle.

(2) The first two objections which do really bear on this form a pair. One consists in the contention that there is no need to be concerned about the issue, since in fact there are not any, or not many, patients who when it comes to the point want to die quickly. The other bases the same complacent conclusion on the claim that in fact, in the appropriate cases, doctors already mercifully take the law into their own hands. These two comfortable doctrines are, like many other similarly reassuring bromides, both entirely wrong and rather shabby.

(a) To the first the full reply would probably have to be made by a doctor, for a medical layman can scarcely be in a position to make an estimate of the number of patients who would apply and could qualify for euthanasia. But it is quite sufficient for our immediate purposes to say two things. First, there can be few who have reached middle life, and who have not chosen to shield their sensibilities with some impenetrable carapace of dogma, who cannot recall at least one case of an eager candidate for euthanasia from their own experience—even from their own peacetime experience only. If this statement is correct, as my own inquiries suggest that it is, then the total number of such eager candidates must be substantial. Second, though the need for enabling legalization becomes progressively more urgent the greater the numbers of people personally concerned, I wish for myself to insist that it still matters very much indeed if but one person who would have decided for a quick death is forced to undergo a protracted one.

(b) To the second objection, which admits that there are many cases where euthanasia is indicated, but is content to leave it to the doctors to defy the law, the answer is equally simple. First, it is manifestly not true that all doctors are willing on the appropriate occasions either to provide the means of death or to do the killing. Many, as they are Roman Catholics, are on religious grounds absolutely opposed to doing so. Many others are similarly opposed for other reasons, or by force of training and habit. And there is no reason to believe that among the rest the proportion of potential martyrs is greater than it is in any other secular occupational group. Second, it is entirely wrong to expect the members of one profession as a regular matter of course to jeopardize their whole careers by breaking the criminal law in order to save the rest of us the labour and embarrassment of changing that law.

Here I repeat two points made to me more than once by doctor friends. First, if a doctor were convinced he ought to provide euthanasia in spite of the law, it would often be far harder for him to do so undetected than many laymen think, especially in our hospitals. Second, the present attitude of the medical establishment is such that if a doctor did take the chance, was caught and brought to trial, and even if the jury, as they well might, refused to convict, still he must expect to face complete professional disaster.

(3) The next two objections, which in effect bear on the principle, again form a pair. The first pair had in common the claim that the facts were such that the question of legislative action need not arise. The second pair are alike in that whereas both might appear to be making contentions of fact, in reality we may have in each a piece of exhortation or of metaphysics masquerading as an empirical proposition.

(a) Of this second relevant pair the first suggests that there is no such thing as an incurable disease. This implausible thesis becomes more intelligible, though no more true, when we recall how medical ideologues sometimes make proclamations: "Modern medicine cannot recognize any such thing as a disease which is incurable"; and the like. Such pronouncements may sound like reports on the present state of the art. It is from this resemblance that they derive their peculiar idiomatic point. But the advance of medicine has not reached a stage where all diseases are curable. And no one seriously thinks that it has. At most this continuing advance has suggested that we need never despair of finding cures *some day*. But this is not at all the same thing as saying, what is simply not true, that *even now* there is no condition which is at any stage incurable. This medical ideologue's slogan has to be construed as a piece of exhortation disguised for greater effect as a paradoxical statement of purported fact. It may as such be instructively compared with certain favourite educationalists' paradoxes: "We do not teach subjects, we teach children!"; or "There are no bad children, only bad teachers!"

(b) The second objection of this pair is that no one can ever be certain that the condition of any particular patient is indeed hopeless. This is more tricky. For an objection of this form might be given two radically different sorts of content. Yet it would be easy and is common to slide from one interpretation to the other, and back again, entirely unwittingly.

Simply and straightforwardly, such an objection might be made by someone whose point was that judgments of incurability are, as a matter of purely contingent fact, so unreliable that no one has any business to be certain, or to claim to know, that anyone is suffering from an incurable affliction. This contention would relevantly be backed by appealing to the alleged fact that judgments that "this case is hopeless, *period*" are far more frequently proven to have been mistaken than judgments that, for instance, "this patient will recover fully, *provided that* he undergoes the appropriate operation." This naïve objector's point could be made out, or decisively refuted, only by reference to quantitative studies of the actual relative reliabilities and unreliabilities of different sorts of medical judgments. So unless and until such quantitative empirical studies are actually made, and unless and until their results are shown to bear upon the question of euthanasia in the way suggested, there is no grounded and categorical objection here to be met.

But besides this first and straightforwardly empirical interpretation there is a second interpretation of another quite different sort. Suppose someone points to an instance, as they certainly could and well might, where some patient whom all the doctors had pronounced to be beyond hope nevertheless recovers, either as the result of the application of new treatment derived from some swift and unforeseen advance in medical science, or just through nature taking its unexpected course. This happy but chastening outcome would certainly demonstrate that the doctors concerned had on this occasion been mistaken; and hence that, though they had sincerely claimed to know the patient's condition to have been incurable, they had not really known this. The temptation is to mistake it that such errors show that no one ever really knows. It is this perfectly general contention, applied to the particular present case of judgments of incurability, which constitutes the second objection in its second interpretation. The objector seizes upon the point that even the best medical opinion turns out sometimes to have been wrong (as here). He then urges, simply because doctors thus prove occasionally to have been mistaken (as here) and because it is always—theoretically if not practically—possible that they may be mistaken again the next time, that therefore none of them ever really knows (at least in such cases). Hence, he concludes, there is after all no purchase for the idea of voluntary euthanasia. For this notion presupposes that there are patients recognizably suffering from conditions known to be incurable.

The crux to grasp about this contention is that, notwithstanding that it may be presented and pressed as if it were somehow especially relevant to one particular class of judgments, in truth it applies—if it applies at all—absolutely generally. The issue is thus revealed as not medical but metaphysical. If it follows that if someone is ever mistaken then he never really knows, and still more if it follows that if it is even logically possible that he may be mistaken then he never really knows, then, surely, the consequence must be that none of us ever does know—not *really*. (When a metaphysician says that something is never really such and such, what he really means is that it very often is, *really*.) For it is of the very essence of our cognitive predicament that we do all sometimes make mistakes; while always it is at least theoretically possible that we may. Hence the argument, if it hold at all, must show that knowledge, *real* knowledge, is for all us mortal men forever unattainable.

What makes the second of the present pair of objections tricky to handle is that it is so easy to pass unwittingly from an empirical to a metaphysical interpretation. We may fail to notice, or noticing may fail convincingly to explain, how an empirical thesis has degenerated into metaphysics, or how metaphysical misconceptions have corrupted the medical judgment. Yet, once these utterly different interpretations have been adequately distinguished, two summary comments should be sufficient.

First, in so far as the objection is purely metaphysical, to the idea that *real* knowledge is possible, it applies absolutely generally; or not at all. It is arbitrary and irrational to restrict it to the examination of the principle of voluntary euthanasia. If doctors never really know, we presumably have no business to rely much upon any of their judgments. And if, for the same metaphysical reasons, there is no knowledge to be had anywhere, then we are all of us in the same case about everything. This may be as it may be, but it is nothing in particular to the practical business in hand.

Second, when the objection takes the form of a pretended refusal to take any decision in matters of life and death on the basis of a judgment which theoretically might turn out to have been mistaken, it is equally unrealistic and arbitrary. It is one thing to claim that judgments of incurability are peculiarly fallible: if that suggestion were to be proved to be correct. It is quite another to claim that it is improper to take vital decisions on the basis of sorts of judgment which either are in principle fallible, or even prove occasionally in fact to have been wrong. It is an inescapable feature of the human condition that no one is infallible about anything, and there is no sphere of life in which mistakes do not occur. Nevertheless we cannot as agents avoid, even in matters of life and death and more than life and death, making decisions to act or to abstain. It is only necessary and it is only possible to insist on ordinarily strict standards of warranted assertability, and on ordinarily exacting rather than obsessional criteria of what is beyond reasonable doubt.

Of course this means that mistakes will sometimes be made. This is in practice a corollary of the uncontested fact that infallibility is not an option. To try to ignore our fallibility is unrealistic, while to insist on remembering it only in the context of the question of voluntary euthanasia is arbitrary. Nor is it either realistic or honourable to attempt to offload the inescapable burdens of practical responsibility, by first claiming that we never really *know,* and then pretending that a decision not to act is somehow a decision which relieves us of all proper responsibility for the outcome.

(4) The two pairs of relevant objections so far considered have both been attempts in different ways to show that the issue does not, or at any rate need not, arise as a practical question. The next concedes that the question does arise and is important, but attempts to dispose of it with the argument that what we propose amounts to the legalization, in certain circumstances, of murder, or suicide, or both; and that this cannot be right because murder and suicide are both gravely wrong always. Now even if we were to concede all the rest it would still not follow, because something is gravely wrong in morals, that there ought to be a law against it; and that we are wrong to try to change the law as it now subsists. We have already urged that the onus of proof must always rest on the defenders of any restriction.

(a) In fact the rest will not do. In the first place, if the law were to be changed as we want, the present legal definition of "murder" would at the same time have to be so changed that it no longer covered the provision of euthanasia for a patient who had established that it was his legal right. "Does this mean," someone may indignantly protest, "that right and wrong are created by Acts of Parliament?" Emphatically, yes: and equally emphatically, no. Yes indeed, if what is intended is *legal* right and *legal* offence. What is meant by the qualification "legal" if it is not that these rights are the rights established and sanctioned by the law? Certainly not, if what is intended is *moral* right and *moral* wrong. Some moral rights happen to be at the same time legal rights, and some moral wrongs similarly also constitute offences against the law. But, notoriously, legislatures may persist in denying moral rights; while, as I insisted earlier, not every moral wrong either is or ought to be forbidden and penalized by law.

Well then, if the legal definition of "murder" can be changed by Act of Parliament, would euthanasia nevertheless be murder, morally speaking? This amounts to asking whether administering euthanasia legally to someone who is incurably ill, and who has continually wanted it, is in all relevant respects similar to, so to speak, a standard case of murder; and whether therefore it is to be regarded morally as murder. Once the structure of the question is in this way clearly displayed it becomes obvious that the cases are different in at least three important respects. First, whereas the murder victim is (typically) killed against his will, a patient would be given or assisted in obtaining euthanasia only if he steadily and strongly desired to die. Second, whereas the murderer kills his victim, treating him usually as a mere object for disposal, in euthanasia the object of the exercise would be to save someone, at his own request, from needless suffering, to prevent the degradation of a human person. Third, whereas the murderer by his action defies the law, the man performing euthanasia would be acting according to law, helping another man to secure what the law allowed him.

It may sound as if that third clause goes back on the earlier repudiation of the idea that moral right and wrong are created by Act of Parliament. That is not so. For we are not saying that this action would now be justifiable, or at least not murder morally, simply because it was now permitted by the law; but rather that the change in the law would remove one of possible reasons for moral objection. The point is this: that although the fact that something is enjoined, permitted, or forbidden by law does not necessarily make it right, justifiable, or wrong morally, nevertheless the fact that something is enjoyed or forbidden by a law laid down by established authority does constitute one moral reason for obedience. So a doctor who is convinced that the objects of the Euthanasia

Society are absolutely right should at least hesitate to take the law into his own hands, not only for prudential but also for moral reasons. For to defy the law is, as it were, to cast your vote against constitutional procedures and the rule of law, and these are the foundations and framework of any tolerable civilized society. (Consider here the injunction posted by some enlightened municipal authorities upon their public litter bins: "Cast your vote here for a tidy New York!"—or wherever it may be.)

Returning to the main point, the three differences which we have just noticed are surely sufficient to require us to refuse to assimilate legalized voluntary euthanasia to the immoral category of murder. But to insist on making a distinction between legalized voluntary euthanasia and murder is not the same thing as, nor does it by itself warrant, a refusal to accept that both are equally immoral. What an appreciation of these three differences, but crucially of the first, should do is to suggest that we ought to think of such euthanasia as a special case not of murder but of suicide. Let us therefore examine the second member of our third pair of relevant objections.

(b) This objection was that to legalize voluntary euthanasia would be to legalize, in certain conditions, the act of assisting suicide. The question therefore arises: "Is suicide always morally wrong?"

The purely secular considerations usually advanced and accepted are not very impressive. First, it is still sometimes urged that suicide is unnatural, in conflict with instinct, a breach of the putative law of self-preservation. All arguments of this sort, which attempt directly to deduce conclusions about what *ought* to be from premises stating, or mis-stating, only what *is* are—surely—unsound: they involve what philosophers label, appropriately, the "Naturalistic Fallacy." There is also a peculiar viciousness about appealing to what is supposed to be a descriptive law of nature to provide some justification for the prescription to obey that supposed law. For if the law really obtained as a description of what always and unavoidably happens, then there would be no point in prescribing that it should; whereas if the descriptive law does not in fact hold, then the basis of the supposed justification does not exist. Furthermore, even if an argument of this first sort could show that suicide is always immoral, it could scarcely provide a reason for insisting that it ought also to be illegal.

Second, it is urged that the suicide by his act deprives other people of the services which he might have rendered them had he lived longer. This can be a strong argument, especially where the suicide has a clear, positive family or public obligation. It is also an argument which, even in a liberal perspective, can provide a basis for legislation. But it is irrelevant to the circumstances which advocates of the legalization of voluntary euthanasia have in mind. In such circumstances as these, there is no longer any chance of being any use to anyone, and if there is any family or social obligation it must be all the other way—to end your life when it has become a hopeless burden both to yourself and to others.

Third, it is still sometimes maintained that suicide is in effect murder—"self-murder." To this, offered in a purely secular context, the appropriate and apparently decisive reply would seem to be that by parity of reasoning marriage is really adultery—"own-wife-adultery." For, surely, the gravamen of both distinctions lies in the differences which such paradoxical assimilations override. It is precisely because suicide is the destruction of oneself (by one's own choice), while murder is the destruction of somebody else (against his wishes), that the former can be, and is, distinguished from the latter.

Yet there is a counter to this own-wife-adultery-move. It begins by insisting, rightly, that sexual relations—which are what is common to both marriage and adultery—are not in themselves wrong: the crucial question is, "Who with?" It then proceeds to claim that what is common to both murder and suicide is the killing of a human being; and here the questions of "Which one?" or "By whom?" are not, morally, similarly decisive. Finally appeal may be made, if the spokesman is a little old-fashioned, to the Sixth Commandment, or if he is in the contemporary swim, to the Principle of the Absolute Sanctity of Human Life.

The fundamental difficulty which confronts anyone making this counter move is that of finding a formulation for his chosen principle about the wrongness of all killing, which is both sufficiently general not to appear merely question-begging in its application to the cases in dispute, and which yet carries no consequences that the spokesman himself is not prepared to accept. Thus, suppose he tries to read the Sixth Commandment as constituting a veto on any killing of human beings. Let us waive here the immediate scholarly objections: that such a reading involves accepting the mistranslation "Thou shalt not kill" rather than the more faithful "Thou shalt do no murder"; and that neither the children of Israel nor even their religious leaders construed this as a law forbidding all war and all capital punishment.[3] The question remains whether cur spokesman himself is really prepared to say that all killing, without any exception, is morally wrong.

It is a question which has to be pressed, and which can only be answered by each man for himself. Since I cannot give your answer, I can only say that I know few if any people who would sincerely say "Yes." But as soon as any exceptions or qualifications are admitted, it becomes excessively difficult to find any presentable principle upon which these can be admitted while still excluding suicide and assitance to suicide in a case of euthanasia. This is not just because, generally, once any exceptions or qualifications have been admitted to any rule it becomes hard or impossible not to allow others. It is because, particularly, the case for excluding suicide and assisting suicide from the scope of any embargo on killing people is so strong that only some absolutely universal rule admitting no exceptions of any sort whatever could have the force convincingly to override it.

Much the same applies to the appeal to the Principle of the Absolute Sanctity of Human Life. Such appeals were continually made by conservatives—many of them politically not Conservative but Socialist—in opposition to the recent efforts to liberalize the British abortion laws. Such conservatives should be, and repeatedly were, asked whether they are also opponents of all capital punishment and whether they think that it is always wrong to kill in a "just war." (In fact none of those in Parliament could honestly have answered "Yes" to both questions.) In the case of abortion their position could still be saved by inserting the qualification "innocent," a qualification traditionally made by cautious moralists who intend to rest on this sort of principle. But any such qualification, however necessary, must make it almost impossible to employ the principle thus duly qualified to proscribe all suicide. It would be extraordinarily awkward and far-fetched to condemn suicide or assisting suicide as "taking an innocent life."

Earlier in the present subsection I described the three arguments. I have been examining as secular. This was perhaps mislead-

---

[3] See, f.i., Joseph Fletcher, *Morals and Medicine* (1954; Gollancz, 1955), pp. 195–6. I recommend this excellent treatment by a liberal Protestant of a range of questions in moral theology too often left too far from liberal Roman Catholics.

ing. For all three are regularly used by religious people: indeed versions of all three are to be found in St. Thomas Aquinas's *Summa Theologica,* the third being there explicitly linked with St. Augustine's laboured interpretation of the Sixth Commandment to cover suicide.[4] And perhaps the incongruity of trying to make the amended Principle of the Absolute Sanctity of Innocent Human Life yield a ban on suicide is partly to be understood as a result of attempting to derive from secularized premises conclusions which really depend upon a religious foundation. But the next two arguments are frankly and distinctively religious.

The first insists that human beings are God's property: "It is our duty to take care of God's property entrusted to our charge— our souls and bodies. They belong not to us but to God";[5] Whoever takes his own life sins against God, even as he who kills another's slave sins against that slave's master";[6] and "Suicide is the destruction of the temple of God and a violation of the property rights of Jesus Christ."[7]

About this I restrict myself to three comments here. First, as it stands, unsupplemented by appeal to some other principle or principles, it must apply, if it applies at all, equally to *all* artificial and intentional shortening *or* lengthening of any human life, one's own *or* that of anyone else. Alone and unsupplemented it would commit one to complete quietism in all matters of life and death; for all interference would be interference with someone else's property. Otherwise one must find further particular moral revelations by which to justify capital punishment, war, medicine, and many other such at first flush impious practices. Second, it seems to presuppose that a correct model of the relation between man and God is that of slave and slave-master, and that respect for God's property ought to be the fundamental principle of morals. It is perhaps significant that it is to this image that St. Thomas and the pagan Plato, in attacking suicide, both appeal. This attempt to derive not only theological but all obligations from the putative theological fact of Creation is a

[4] Part II: Q. 64, A5. The Augustine reference is to *The City of God,* 1, 20. It is worth comparing, for ancient Judaic attitudes, E. Westermarck's *Origin and Development of the Moral Ideas.* Vol. 1, pp. 246–7.
[5] See the Rev. G. J. MacGillivray, "Suicide and Euthanasia," p. 10; a widely distributed Catholic Truth Society pamphlet.
[6] Aquinas, loc. cit.
[7] Koch-Preuss, *Handbook of Moral Theology,* vol. II, p. 76. This quotation has been taken from Fletcher, op. cit., p. 192.

common-place of at least one tradition of moral theology. In this derivation the implicit moral premise is usually that unconditional obedience to a Creator, often considered as a very special sort of owner, is the primary elemental obligation. Once this is made explicit it does not appear to be self-evidently true; nor is it easy to see how a creature in absolute ontological dependence could be the genuinely responsible subject of obligations to his infinite Creator. Third, this objection calls to mind one of the sounder sayings of the sinister Tiberius: "If the gods are insulted let them see to it themselves." This remark is obviously relevant only to the question of legalization, not to that of the morality or the prudence of the action itself.

The second distinctively religious argument springs from the conviction that God does indeed see to it Himself, with a penalty of infinite severity. If you help someone to secure euthanasia, "You are sending him from the temporary and comparatively light suffering of this world to the eternal suffering of hell." Now if this appalling suggestion could be shown to be true it would provide the most powerful moral reason against helping euthanasia in any way, and for using any legislative means which might save people from suffering a penalty so inconceivably cruel. It would also be the strongest possible prudential reason against "suiciding oneself."[8] (Though surely anyone who knowingly incurred such a penalty would by that very action prove himself to be genuinely of unsound mind; and hence not *justly* punishable at all. Not that a Being contemplating such unspeakable horrors could be expected to be concerned with justice!)

About this second, peculiarly religious, argument there is, it would seem, little to be done except: either simply to concede that for anyone holding this belief it indeed is reasonable to oppose euthanasia, and to leave it at that; or, still surely conceding this, to attempt to mount a general offensive against the whole system of which it forms a part.

(5) The final objection is one raised, with appropriate modifications, by the opponents of every reform everywhere. It is that even

---

[8] This rather affected-sounding gallicism is adopted deliberately: if you believe, as I do, that suicide is not always and as such wrong, it is inappropriate to speak of "committing suicide"; just as correspondingly if you believe, as I do not, that (private) profit is wrong, it becomes apt to talk to those who "commit a profit."

granting that the principle of the reform is excellent it would, if adopted, lead inevitably to something worse; and so we had much better not make any change at all. Thus G. K. Chesterton pronounced that the proponents of euthanasia now seek only the death of those who are a nuisance to themslves, but soon it will be broadened to include those who are a nuisance to others. Such cosy arguments depend on two assumptions: that the supposedly inevitable consequences are indeed evil and substantially worse than the evils the reform would remove; and that the supposedly inevitable consequences really are inevitable consequences.

In the present case we certainly can grant the first assumption, if the consequence supposed is taken to be large-scaled legalized homicide in the Nazi manner. But whatever reason is there for saying that this would, much less inevitably must, follow? For there are the best of reasons for insisting that there is a world of difference between legalized voluntary euthanasia and such legalized mass-murder. Only if public opinion comes to appreciate their force will there be any chance of getting the reform we want. Then we should have no difficulty, in alliance doubtless with all our present opponents, in blocking any move to legalize murder which might conceivably arise from a misunderstanding of the case for voluntary euthanasia. Furthermore, it is to the point to remind such objectors that the Nazi atrocities they probably have in mind were in fact not the result of any such reform, but were the work of people who consciously repudiated the whole approach to ethics represented in the argument of the present essay. For this approach is at once human and humanitarian. It is concerned above all with the reduction of suffering; but concerned at the same time with other values too, such as human dignity and respect for the wishes of the individual person. And always it is insistent that morality should not be "left in the dominion of vague feeling or inexplicable internal conviction, but should be . . . made a matter of reason and calculation."[9]

[9] J. S. Mill's essay on Bentham quoted in F. R. Leavis, *Mill on Bentham and Coleridge* (Chatto & Windus, 1950), p. 92.

ACTIVE AND PASSIVE EUTHANASIA

James Rachels

A distinction commonly cited in the discussion of euthanasia is that between the overt act of terminating a life and allowing a death to occur by refusing to act. Professor Rachels argues in this essay that the distinction is not only false; it may also lead to increased suffering.

James Rachels is a professor of philosophy at the University of Miami, Florida.

This article appeared in the New England Journal of Medicine, *volume 292, pages 78ff., January 9, 1975.*

The distinction between active and passive euthanasia is thought to be crucial for medical ethics. The idea is that it is permissible, at least in some cases, to withhold treatment and allow a patient to die, but it is never permissible to take any direct action designed to kill the patient. This doctrine seems to be accepted by most doctors, and it is endorsed in a statement adopted by the House of Delegates of the American Medical Association on December 4, 1973:

> The intentional termination of the life of one human being by another—mercy killing—is contrary to that for which the medical profession stands and is contrary to the policy of the American Medical Association.
>
> The cessation of the employment of extraordinary means to prolong the life of the body when there is irrefutable evidence that biological death is imminent is the decision of the patient and/or his immediate family. The advice and judgment of the physician should be freely available to the patient and/or his immediate family.

However, a strong case can be made against this doctrine. In what follows I will set out some of the relevant arguments, and urge doctors to reconsider their views on this matter.

To begin with a familiar type of situation, a patient who is dying of incurable cancer of the throat is in terrible pain, which can no longer be satisfactorily alleviated. He is certain to die within a few days, even if present treatment is continued, but he does not want to go on living for those days since the pain is unbearable. So he asks the doctor for an end to it, and his family joins in the request.

Suppose the doctor agrees to withhold treatment, as the conventional doctrine says he may. The justification for his doing so is that the patient is in terrible agony, and since he is going to die anyway, it would be wrong to prolong his suffering needlessly. But now notice this. If one simply withholds treatment, it may take the patient longer to die, and so he may suffer more than he would if more direct action were taken and a lethal injection given. This fact provides strong reason for thinking that, once the initial decision not to prolong his agony has been made, active euthanasia is actually preferable to passive euthanasia, rather than the reverse. To say otherwise is to endorse the option that leads to more suffering rather than less, and is contrary to the humanitarian impulse that prompts the decision not to prolong his life in the first place.

Part of my point is that the process of being "allowed to die" can be relatively slow and painful, whereas being given a lethal injection is relatively quick and painless. Let me give a different sort of example. In the United States about one in 600 babies is born with Down's syndrome. Most of these babies are otherwise healthy— that is, with only the usual pediatric care, they will proceed to an otherwise normal infancy. Some, however, are born with congenital defects such as intestinal obstructions that require operations if they are to live. Sometimes, the parents and the doctor will decide not to operate, and let the infant die. Anthony Shaw describes what happens then:

> When surgery is denied [the doctor] must try to keep the infant from suffering while natural forces sap the baby's life away. As a surgeon whose natural inclination is to use the scalpel to fight off death, standing by and watching a salvageable baby die is the most emotionally exhausting experience I know. It is easy at a conference, in

a theoretical discussion to decide that such infants should be allowed to die. It is altogether different to stand by in the nursery and watch as dehydration and infection wither a tiny being over hours and days. This is a terrible ordeal for me and the hospital staff—much more so than for the parents who never set foot in the nursery.*

I can understand why some people are opposed to all euthanasia, and insist that such infants must be allowed to live. I think I can also understand why other people favor destroying these babies quickly and painlessly. But why should anyone favor letting "dehydration and infection wither a tiny being over hours and days"? The doctrine that says that a baby may be allowed to dehydrate and wither, but may not be given an injection that would end its life without suffering, seems so patently cruel as to require no further refutation. The strong language is not intended to offend, but only to put the point in the clearest possible way.

My second argument is that the conventional doctrine leads to decisions concerning life and death made on irrelevant grounds.

Consider again the case of the infants with Down's syndrome who need operations for congenital defects unrelated to the syndrome to live. Sometimes, there is no operation, and the baby dies, but when there is no such defect, the baby lives on. Now, an operation such as that to remove an intestinal obstruction is not prohibitively difficult. The reason why such operations are not performed in these cases is, clearly, that the child has Down's syndrome and the parents and the doctor judge that because of that fact it is better for the child to die.

But notice that this situation is absurd, no matter what view one takes of the lives and potentials of such babies. If the life of such an infant is worth preserving what does it matter if it needs a simple operation? Or, if one thinks it better that such a baby should not live on, what difference does it make that it happens to have an unobstructed intestinal tract? In either case, the matter of life and death is being decided on irrelevant grounds. It is the Down's syndrome, and not the intestines, that is the issue. The matter should be decided, if at all, on that basis, and not be allowed to depend on the essentially irrelevant question of whether the intestinal tract is blocked.

* Shaw, Anthony, "Doctor, Do We Have a Choice?" *The New York Times Magazine,* January 30, 1972, p. 54.

What makes this situation possible, of course, is the idea that when there is an intestinal blockage, one can "let the baby die," but when there is no such defect there is nothing that can be done, for one must not "kill" it. The fact that this idea leads to such results as deciding life or death on irrelevant grounds is another good reason why the doctrine would be rejected.

One reason why so many people think that there is an important moral difference between active and passive euthanasia is that they think killing someone is morally worse than letting someone die. But is it? Is killing, in itself, worse than letting die? To investigate this issue, two cases may be considered that are exactly alike except that one involves killing whereas the other involves letting someone die. Then, it can be asked whether this difference makes any difference to the moral assessments. It is important that the cases be exactly alike, except for this one difference, since otherwise one cannot be confident that it is this difference and not some other that accounts for any variation in the assessments of the two cases. So, let us consider this pair of cases:

In the first, Smith stands to gain a large inheritance if anything should happen to his six-year old cousin. One evening while the child is taking his bath, Smith sneaks into the bathroom and drowns the child, and then arranges things so that it will look like an accident.

In the second, Jones also stands to gain if anything should happen to his six-year-old cousin. Like Smith, Jones sneaks in planning to drown the child in his bath. However, just as he enters the bathroom Jones sees the child slip and hit his head, and fall face down in the water. Jones is delighted; he stands by, ready to push the child's head back under if it is necessary, but it is not necessary. With only a little thrashing about, the child drowns all by himself, "accidentally," as Jones watches and does nothing.

Now Smith killed the child, whereas Jones "merely" let the child die. That is the only difference between them. Did either man behave better, from a moral point of view? If the difference between killing and letting die were in itself a morally important matter, one should say that Jones's behavior was less reprehensible than Smith's. But does one really want to say that? I think not. In the first place, both men acted from the same motive, personal gain, and both had exactly the same end in view when they acted. It may be inferred from Smith's conduct that he is a bad man, although that judgment may be withdrawn or modified if certain further facts are learned about him—for example, that he is mentally deranged. But would not the very same thing be inferred about Jones from his conduct? And would not the same further considerations also be relevant to any modification of this judgment? Moreover, suppose Jones pleaded, in his own defense, "After all, I didn't do anything except just stand there and watch the child drown. I didn't kill him; I only let him die." Again, if letting die were in itself less bad than killing, this defense should have at least some weight. But it does not. Such a "defense" can only be regarded as a grotesque perversion of moral reasoning. Morally speaking, it is no defense at all.

Now, it may be pointed out, quite properly, that the cases of euthanasia with which doctors are concerned are not like this at all. They do not involve personal gain or the destruction of normal healthy children. Doctors are concerned only with cases in which the patient's life is of no further use to him, or in which the patient's life has become or will soon become a terrible burden. However, the point is the same in these cases: the bare difference between killing and letting die does not, in itself, make a moral difference. If a doctor lets a patient die, for humane reasons, he is in the same moral position as if he had given the patient a lethal injection for humane reasons. If his decision was wrong—if, for example, the patient's illness was in fact curable—the decision would be equally regrettable no matter which method was used to carry it out. And if the doctor's decision was the right one, the method used is not in itself important.

The AMA policy statement isolates the crucial issue very well; the crucial issue is "the intentional termination of the life of one human being by another." But after identifying this issue, and forbidding "mercy killing," the statement goes on to deny that the cessation of treatment is the intentional termination of a life. This is where the mistake comes in, for what is the cessation of treatment, in these circumstances, if it is not "the intentional termination of the life of one human being by another?" Of course it is exactly that, and if it were not, there would be no point to it.

Many people will find this judgment hard to accept. One reason, I think, is that it is very easy to conflate the question of whether killing is, in itself, worse than letting die, with the very different question of whether most actual cases of killing are more reprehensible than most actual cases of letting die. Most actual cases of killing are clearly terrible (think, for example, of all the murders reported in the newspapers), and one hears of such cases every day. On the other hand, one hardly ever hears of a case of letting die, except for the actions of doctors who are motivated by humanitarian reasons. So one learns to think of killing in a much worse light than of letting die. But this does not mean that there is something about killing that makes it in itself worse than letting die, for it is not the bare difference between killing and letting die that makes the difference in these cases. Rather, the other factors—the murderer's motive of personal gain, for example, contrasted with the doctor's humanitarian motivation—account for different reactions to the different cases.

I have argued that killing is not in itself any worse than letting die; if my contention is right, it follows that active euthanasia is not any worse than passive euthanasia. What arguments can be given on the other side? The most common, I believe, is the following:

"The important difference between active and passive euthanasia is that, in passive euthanasia, the doctor does not do anything to bring about the patient's death. The doctor does nothing, and the patient dies of whatever ills already afflict him. In active euthanasia, however, the doctor does something to bring about the patient's death: he kills him. The doctor who gives the patient with cancer a lethal injection has himself caused his patient's death; whereas if he merely ceases treatment, the cancer is the cause of the death."

A number of points need to be made here. The first is that it is not exactly correct to say that in passive euthanasia the doctor does nothing, for he does do one thing that is very important: he lets the patient die. "Letting someone die" is certainly different, in some respects, from other types of action—mainly in that it is a kind of action that one may perform by way of not performing certain other actions. For example, one may let a patient die by way of not giving medication, just as one may insult someone by way of not shaking his hand. But for any purpose of moral assessment, it is a type of action nonetheless. The decision to let a patient die is subject to moral appraisal in the same way that a decision to kill him would be subject to moral appraisal: it may be assessed as wise or unwise, compassionate or sadistic, right or wrong. If a doctor deliberately let a patient die who was suffering from a routinely curable illness, the doctor would certainly be to blame for what he had done, just as he would be to blame if he had needlessly killed the patient. Charges against him would then be appropriate. If so, it would be no defense at all for him to insist that he didn't "do anything." He would have done something very serious indeed, for he let his patient die.

Fixing the cause of death may be very important from a legal point of view, for it may determine whether criminal charges are brought against the doctor. But I do not think that this notion can be used to show a moral difference between active and passive euthanasia. The reason why it is considered bad to be the cause of someone's death is that death is regarded as a great evil—and so it is. However, if it has been decided that euthanasia—even passive euthanasia—is desirable in a given case, it has also been decided that in this instance death is no greater an evil than the patient's continued existence. And if this is true, the usual reason for not wanting to be the cause of someone's death simply does not apply.

Finally, doctors may think that all of this is only of academic interest—the sort of thing that philosophers may worry about but that has no practical bearing on their own work. After all, doctors must be concerned about the legal consequences of what they do, and active euthanasia is clearly forbidden by the law. But even so, doctors should also be concerned with the fact that the law is forcing upon them a moral doctrine that may well be indefensible, and has a considerable effect on their practices. Of course, most doctors are not now in the position of being coerced in this matter, for they do not regard themselves as merely going along with what the law requires. Rather, in statements such as the AMA policy statement that I have quoted, they are endorsing this doctrine as a central point of medical ethics. In that statement, active euthanasia is condemned not merely as illegal but as "contrary to that for which the medical profession stands," whereas passive euthanasia is approved. However, the preceding considerations suggest that there is really no moral differences between the two, considered in themselves (there may be important moral differences in some cases in their *consequences,* but, as I pointed out, these differences may make active euthanasia, and not passive euthanasia, the morally preferable option). So, whereas doctors may have to discriminate between active and passive euthanasia to satisfy the law, they should not do any more than that. In particular, they should not give the distinction any added authority and weight by writing it into official statements of medical ethics.

THE INDIGNITY OF
"DEATH WITH DIGNITY"

Paul Ramsey

The term "death with dignity" has come to stand for a large area of theory and practice concerning the terminally ill. In a vividly written and argued essay, Professor Ramsey raises the question as to whether this term has not come to conceal the true loss and suffering death works on human existence.

Paul Ramsey is the Harrington Spear Paine Professor of Religion at Princeton University.

This article is taken from the Hastings Center Studies, *volume 2, number 2, May, 1974.*

Never one am I to use an ordinary title when an extraordinary one will do as well! Besides, I mean to suggest that there is an additional insult besides death itself heaped upon the dying by our ordinary talk about "death with dignity." Sometimes that is said even to be a human "right"; and what should a decent citizen do but insist on enjoying his rights? That might be his duty (if there is any such right), to the commonwealth, to the human race or some other collective entity; or at least, embracing that "right" and dying rationally would exhibit a proper respect for the going concept of a rational man. So "The Indignity of Death" would not suffice for my purposes, even though all I shall say depends on understanding the contradiction death poses to the unique worth of an individual human life.

The genesis of the following reflections may be worth noting. A few years ago,[1] I embraced what I characterized as the oldest

---

[1] Paul Ramsey, "On (Only) Caring for the Dying," *The Patient as Person* (New Haven: Yale University Press, 1971).

morality there is (no "new morality") concerning responsibility toward the dying: the acceptance of death, stopping our medical interventions for all sorts of good, human reasons, *only* companying with the dying in their final passage. Then suddenly it appeared that altogether too many people were agreeing with me. That caused qualms. As a Southerner born addicted to lost causes, it seemed I now was caught up in a triumphal social trend. As a controversialist in ethics, I found agreement from too many sides. As a generally happy prophet of the doom facing the modern age, unless there is a sea-change in norms of action, it was clear from these premises that anything divers people agree to must necessarily be superficial if not wrong.

Today, when divers people draw the same warm blanket of "allowing to die" or "death with dignity" close up around their shoulders against the dread of that cold night, their various feet are showing. Exposed beneath our growing agreement to that "philosophy of death and dying" may be significantly different "philosophies of life"; and in the present age that agreement may reveal that these interpretations of human life are increasingly mundane, naturalistic, antihumanistic when measured by *any* genuinely "humanistic" esteem for the individual human being.

These "philosophical" ingredients of any view of death and dying I want to make prominent by speaking of "The Indignity of 'Death with Dignity'." Whatever practical agreement there may be, or "guidelines" proposed to govern contemporary choice or practice, these are bound to be dehumanizing unless at the same time we bring to bear great summit points and sources of insight in mankind's understanding of mankind (be it Christian or other religious humanism, or religiously-dependent but not explicitly religious humanism, or, if it is possible, a true humanism that is neither systematically nor historically dependent on any religious outlook).

DEATH WITH DIGNITY IDEOLOGIES

There is nobility and dignity in caring for the dying, but not in dying itself. "To be a therapist to a dying patient makes us aware of the uniqueness of each individual in this vast sea of humanity."[2]

---

[2] Elisabeth Kübler-Ross, *On Death and Dying* (New York: Macmillan, 1969), p. 247.

It is more correct to say that a therapist brings to the event, from some other source, an awareness of the uniqueness, the once-for-allness of an individual life-span as part of an "outlook" and "onlook" upon the vast sea of humanity. In any case, that is the reflected glory and dignity of caring for the dying, that we are or become aware of the unique life here ending. The humanity of such human caring is apt to be more sensitive and mature if we do not lightly suppose that it is an easy thing to convey dignity to the dying. That certainly cannot be done simply by withdrawing tubes and stopping respirators or not thumping hearts. At most, those omissions can only be prelude to companying with the dying in their final passage, if we are fortunate enough to share with them—they in moderate comfort—those interchanges that are in accord with the dignity and nobility of mankind. Still, however noble the manifestations of caring called for, however unique the individual life, we finally must come to the reality of death, and must ask, what can possibly be the meaning of "death with dignity"?

At most we convey only the liberty to die with human dignity; we can provide some of the necessary but not sufficient conditions. If the dying die with a degree of nobility it will be mostly their doing in doing their own dying. I fancy their task was easier when death as a human event meant that special note was taken of the last words of the dying—even humorous ones, as in the case of the Roman Emperor who said as he expired, "I Deify." A human countenance may be discerned in death accepted with serenity. So also there is a human countenance behind death with defiance. "Do not go gentle into that good night," wrote Dylan Thomas. "Old age should rage and burn against the close of day; Rage Rage against the dying of the light." But the human countenance has been removed from most modern understandings of death.

We do not begin to keep human community with the dying if we interpose between them and us most of the current notions of "death with dignity." Rather do we draw closer to them if and only if our conception of "dying with dignity" encompasses—nakedly and without dilution—the final indignity of death itself, whether accepted or raged against. So I think it may be profitable to explore "the indignity of 'death with dignity'." "Good death" (euthanasia) like "Good grief!" are ultimately contradictions in terms, even if superficially, and before we reach the heart of the matter, there are distinctions to be made; even if, that is to say, the predicate "good" still is applicable in both cases in contrast to worse ways to die and worse ways to grieve or not to grieve.

"Death is simply a part of life," we are told, as a first move to persuade us to accept the ideology of the entire dignity of dying with dignity. A singularly unpersuasive proposition, since we are not told what sort of part of life death is. Disease, injury, congenital defects are also a part of life, and as well murder, rapine, and pillage. Yet there is no campaign for accepting or doing those things with dignity. Nor, for that matter, for the contemporary mentality which would enshrine "death with dignity" is there an equal emphasis on "suffering with dignity," suffering as a "natural" part of life, etc. All those things, it seems, are enemies and violations of human nobility while death is not, or (with a few changes) need not be. Doctors did not invent the fact that death is an enemy, although they may sometimes use disproportionate means to avoid final surrender. Neither did they invent the fact that pain and suffering are enemies and often indignities, although suffering accepted may also be ennobling or may manifest the nobility of the human spirit of any ordinary person.

But, then, it is said, death is an evolutionary necessity and in that further sense a part of life not to be denied. Socially and biologically, one generation follows another. So there must be death, else social history would have no room for creative novelty and planet earth would be glutted with humankind. True enough, no doubt, from the point of view of evolution (which—so far—never dies). But the man who is dying happens not to be evolution. He is a part of evolution, no doubt: but not to the whole extent of his being or his dying. A crucial testimony to the individual's transcendence over the species is man's problem and his dis-ease in dying. Death is a natural fact of life, yet no man dies "naturally," nor do we have occasions in which to practice doing so in order to learn how. Not unless the pursuit of philosophy is a practice of dying (as Plato's *Phaedo* teaches); and that I take to be an understanding of the human being we moderns do not mean to embrace when we embrace "death with dignity."

It is small consolation to tell mortal men that as long as you are, the death you contribute to evolution is not yet; and when death is, you are not—so why fear death? That is the modern equivalent to the recipe offered by the ancient Epicureans (and some Stoics) to undercut fear of death and devotion to the gods: as long as you are, death is not; when death is, you are not; there's never a direct encounter between you and death; so why dread death? Indeed, contrary to modern parlance, those ancient philosophers declared that death is *not a part of life;* so why worry?

So "death is not a part of life" is another declaration designed to quiet fear of death. This can be better understood in terms of a terse comment by Wittgenstein: "Our life has no limit in just the way in which our visual field has no limit."[3] We cannot see beyond the boundary of our visual field; it is more correct to say that beyond the boundary of our visual field *we do not see.* Not only so. Also, we do not see the boundary, the limit itself. There is no seeable bound to the visual field. *Death is not a part of life* in the same way that the boundary is not a part of our visual field. Commenting on this remark by Wittgenstein, James Van Evra writes: "Pressing the analogy, then, if my life has no end in *just the way* that my visual field has no limit, then it must be in the sense that I can have no experience of death, conceived as the complete cessation of experience and thought. That is, if life is considered to be a series of experiences and thoughts, then it is impossible for me to experience death, for to experience something is to be alive, and hence is to be inside the bound formed by death."[4] This is why death itself steadfastly resists conceptualization.

Still, I think the disanalogy ought also to be pressed, against both ancient and contemporary analytical philosophers. That notion of death as a limit makes use of a visual or spatial metaphor. Good basketball players are often men naturally endowed with an unusually wide visual field; this is true, for example, of Bill Bradley. Perhaps basketball players, among other things, strive to enlarge their visual fields, or their habitual use of what powers of sight they have, if that is possible. But ordinarily, everyone of us is perfectly happy within the unseeable limits of sight's reach.

Transfer this notion of death as a limit from space to time as the form of human perception, from sight to an individual's inward desire, effort and hope, and I suggest that one gets a different result. Then death as the temporal limit of a life-span is something we live toward. That limit still can never be experienced or conceptualized; indeed death is *never* a part of life. Moreover, neither is the bound-

---

[3] Wittgenstein, *Tractatus,* 6.4311.
[4] James Van Evra, "On Death as a Limit," *Analysis* 31 [5] (April, 1971), 170–76.

ary. Still it is a limit we conative human beings know we live *up against* during our life-spans. We do not live toward or up against the side-limits of our visual-span. Instead, within that acceptable visual limit (and other limits as well) as channels we live toward yet another limit which is death.

Nor is the following analogy for death as a limit of much help in deepening understanding. ". . . The importance of the limit and virtually *all* of its significance," writes Van Evra, "derives from the fact that the limit serves as an ordering device"—just as absolute zero serves for ordering a series; it is not *just* a limit, although nothing can exist at such a temperature. The analogy is valid so far as it suggests that we conceive of death not in itself but as it bears on us while still alive. As I shall suggest below, death teaches us to "number our days."

But that may not be its only ordering function for conative creatures. Having placed death "out of our league" by showing that it is not a "something," or never a part of life, and while understanding awareness of death as awareness of a limit bearing upon us only while still alive, one ought not forthwith to conclude that this understanding of it "exonerates death as the purported snake in our garden." Death as a limit can disorder no less than order the series. Only a disembodied reason can say, as Van Evra does, that "the bound, not being a member of the series, cannot defile it. The series is what it is, happy or unhappy, good or bad, quite independently of any bound as such." An Erik Erikson knows better than that when writing of the "despair and often unconscious fear of death" which results when "the one and only life cycle is not accepted as the ultimate life." Despair, he observes, "expresses the feeling that the time is short, too short for the attempt to start another life and to try out alternate roads to integrity."[5]

It is the temporal flight of the series that is grievous (not death as an evil "something" within life's span to be balanced, optimistically or pessimistically, against other things that are good). The reminder that death is *not a part of life,* or that it is only a boundary never encountered, is an ancient recipe that can only increase the threat of death on any profound understanding of human life. The dread of death is the dread of oblivion, of there being only empty room in one's stead. Kubler-Ross writes that for the dying,

[5] Erik Erikson, "Identity and the Life Cycle," *Psychological Issues,* I, [1] (New York: International University Press, 1959).

death means the loss of every loved one, total loss of everything that constituted the self in its world, separation from every experience, even from future possible, replacing experiences—nothingness beyond. Therefore, life is a time-intensive activity and not only a goods-intensive or quality-intensive activity. No matter how many "goods" we store up in barns, like the man in Jesus' parable we know that this night our soul may be required of us (Luke 12:13–21). No matter what "quality of life" our lives have, we must take into account the opportunity-costs of used time. Death means the conquest of the time of our lives—even though we never experience the experience of the nothingness which is natural death.

"Awareness of dying" means awareness of *that;* and awareness of that constitutes an experience of ultimate indignity in and to the awareness of the self who is dying.

We are often reminded of Koheleth's litany: "For everything there is a season, and a time for every matter under heaven: a time to be born and a time to die; a time to plant, and a time to pluck up what is planted," etc. (Eccles. 3:1,2). Across those words of the narrator of Ecclesiastes the view gains entrance that only an "untimely" death should be regretted or mourned. Yet we know better how to specify an untimely death than to define or describe a "timely" one. The author of Genesis tells us that, at 180 years of age, the patriarch Isaac "breathed his last; and he died and was gathered to his people, old and full of years . . ." (Gen. 35:29). Even in face of sacred Scripture, we are permitted to wonder what Isaac thought about it; whether he too knew how to apply the category "fullness of years" *to himself* and agreed his death was nothing but timely.

We do Koheleth one better and say that death cannot only be timely; it may also be "beautiful." Whether such an opinion is to be ascribed to David Hendin or not (a "fact of life" man he surely is, who also unambiguously subtitled his chapter on euthanasia "Let There Be Death"),[6] that opinion seems to be the outlook of the legislator and physician, Walter Sackett, Jr., who proposed the Florida "Death with Dignity" Statute. All his mature life his philosophy has been, "Death, like birth, is glorious—let it come easy." Such was by no means Koheleth's opinion when he wrote (and *wrote* beautifully) about a time to be born and a time to die. Dr. Sackett

---

[6] David Hendin, *Death as a Fact of Life* (New York: W. W. Norton, 1973).

also suggests that up to 90 percent of the 1,800 patients in state hospitals for the mentally retarded should be allowed to die. Five billion dollars could be saved in the next half century if the state's mongoloids were permitted to succumb to pneumonia, a disease to which they are highly susceptible. I suggest that the physician in Dr. Sackett has atrophied. He has become a public functionary, treating taxpayers' pocketbooks under the general anesthesia of a continuous daytime soap opera entitled "Death Can Be Beautiful!"

"Death for an older person should be a beautiful event. There is beauty in birth, growth, fullness of life and then, equally so, in the tapering off and final end. There are analogies all about us. What is more beautiful than the spring budding of small leaves; then the fully-leaved tree in summer; and then in the beautiful brightly colored autumn leaves gliding gracefully to the ground? So it is with humans." Those are words from a study document on Euthanasia drafted by the Council for Christian Social Action of the United Church of Christ in 1972. An astonishing footnote at this point states that "the naturalness of dying" is suggested in funeral services when the minister says "God has called" the deceased, or says he has "gone to his reward," recites the "dust to dust" passage, or note that the deceased led a full life or ran a full course!

Before that statement was adopted by that Council on Feb. 17, 1973, more orthodox wording was inserted: "Transformation from life on earth to life in the hereafter of the Lord is a fulfillment. The acceptance of death is our witness to faith in the resurrection of Jesus Christ (Rom. 8). We can rejoice." The subdued words "we can rejoice" indicate a conviction that *something* has been subdued. The words "acceptance of death" take the whole matter out of the context of romantic naturalism and set it in a proper religious context—based on the particular Christian tenet that death is a conquered enemy, to be accepted in the name of its Conqueror. More than a relic of the nature mysticism that was so luxurient in the original paragraph, however, remains in the words, "Death for an older person should be a beautiful event. There is beauty in birth, growth, fullness of life and then, *equally so,* in the tapering off and final end." (Italics added.) I know no Christian teaching that assures us that our "final end" is "equally" beautiful as birth, growth, and fullness of life. Moreover, if revelation disclosed any such thing it would be contrary to reason and to the human reality and experience of death. The views of our "pre-death morticians" are simply discordant with the experienced reality they attempt to beautify. So, in her recent book, Marya Mannes writes "the name of the oratorio is euthanasia." And her statement "dying is merely suspension within a mystery," seems calculated to induce vertigo in face of a fascinating abyss in prospect.[7]

No exception can be taken to one line in the letter people are being encouraged to write and sign by the Euthanasia Societies of Great Britain and America. That line states: "I do not fear death as much as I fear the indignity of deterioration, dependence and hopeless pain." Such an exercise in analyzing *comparative indignities* should be given approval. But in the preceding sentence the letter states: "Death is as much a reality as birth, growth, maturity, and old age—it is the one certainty." That logically leaves open the question what sort of "reality," what sort of "certainty," death is. But by placing death on a parity with birth, growth, maturity—and old age in many of its aspects—the letter beautifies death by association. To be written long before death when one is thinking "generally" (i.e. "rationally"?) about the topic, the letter tempts us to suppose that men can think generally about their own deaths. Hendin observes in another connection that "there is barely any relation between what people think that they think about death and the way they actually feel about it when it must be faced."[8] Then it may be that "the heart has its reasons that reason cannot know" (Pascal)—beforehand—and among those "reasons," I suggest, will be an apprehension of the ultimate (noncomparative) indignity of death. Talk about death as a fact or a reality seasonally recurring in life with birth or planting, maturity and growth, may after all not be very rational. It smacks more of whistling before the darkness descends, and an attempt to brainwash one's contemporaries to accept a very feeble philosophy of life and death.

Birth and death (our *terminus ad quo* and our *terminus ad quem*) are not to be equated with any of the qualities or experiences, the grandeur and the misery, in between, which constitutes "parts" of our lives. While we live toward death and can encompass our own dying in awareness, no one in the same way is aware of his own birth. We know that we were born in the same way we know

[7] Marya Mannes, *Last Rights* (New York: William Morrow, 1973), p. 6, (cf. 80, 133).
[8] Hendin, *Death as a Fact of Life,* p. 103.

that we die. Explanations of whence we came do not establish conscious contact with our individual origin; and among explanations, that God called us from the womb out of nothing is as good as any other; and better than most. But awareness of dying is quite another matter. That we may have, but not awareness of our births. And while awareness of birth might conceivably be the great original individuating experience (if we had it), among the race of men it is awareness of dying that is uniquely individuating. To encompass one's own death in the living and dying of one's life is more of a task than it is a part of life. And there is something of indignity to be faced when engaging in that final act of life. Members of the caring human community (doctors, nurses, family) are apt to keep closer company with the dying if we acknowledge the loss of all worth by the loss of him in whom inhered all worth in his world. Yet ordinary men may sometimes nobly suffer the ignobility of death.

By way of contrast with the "A Living Will" framed by the Euthanasia Society, the Judicial Council of the AMA in its recent action on the physician and the dying patient had before it two similar letters. One was composed by the Connecticut Delegation:

> *To my Family, my Physician*
> *my Clergyman, my Lawyer—*
>
> If the time comes when I can no longer actively take part in decisions for by own future, I wish this statement to stand as the testament of my wishes. If there is no reasonable expectation of my recovery from physical or mental and spiritual disability, I, ...
> ...., request that I be allowed to die and not be kept alive by artificial means or heroic measures. I ask also that drugs be mercifully administered to me for terminal suffering even if in relieving pain they may hasten the moment of death. I value life and the dignity of life, so that I am not asking that my life be directly taken, but that my dying not be unreasonably prolonged nor the dignity of life be destroyed. This request is made, after careful reflection, while I am in good health and spirits. Although this document is not legally binding, you who care for me will, I hope, feel morally bound to take it into account. I recognize that it places a heavy burden of responsibility upon you, and it is with the intention of sharing this responsibility that this statement is made.

A second letter had been composed by a physician to express his own wishes, in quite simple language:

To my Family, To my Physician—

Should the occasion arise in my lifetime when death is imminent and a decision is to be made about the nature and the extent of the care to be given to me and I am not able at that time to express my desires, let this statement serve to express my deep, sincere, and considered wish and hope that my physician will administer to me simple, ordinary medical treatment. I ask that he not administer heroic, extraordinary, expensive, or useless medical care or treatment which in the final analysis will merely delay, not change, the ultimate outcome of my terminal condition.

A comparison of these declarations with "A Living Will" circulated by the Euthanasia Society reveals the following signal differences: neither of the AMA submissions engages in any superfluous calculus of "comparative indignities"; neither associates the reality of death with such things as birth or maturation; both allow death to be simply what it is in human experience; both are in a general sense "pro-life" statements, in that death is neither reified as one fact among others nor beautified even comparatively.[9]

Everyone concerned takes the wrong turn in trying either to "thing-ify" death or to beautify it. The dying have at least this advantage, that in these projects for dehumanizing death by naturalizing it the dying finally cannot succeed, and death makes its threatening visage known to them before ever there are any societal or evolutionary replacement values or the everlasting arms or Abraham's bosom to rest on. Death means *finis,* not in itself *telos.* Certainly not a telos to be engineered, or to be accomplished by reducing both human life and death to the level of natural events.

"Thing-ifying" death reaches its highest pitch in the stated

---

[9] I may add that while the House of Delegates did not endorse any particular form to express an individual's wishes relating prospectively to his final illness, it recognized that individuals have a right to express them. While it encouraged physicians to discuss such matters with patients and attend to their wishes, the House nevertheless maintained a place for the conscience and judgment of a physician in determining indicated treatment. It did not subsume every consideration under the rubric of the patient's right to refuse treatment (or to have refused treatment). That sole action-guide can find no medical or logical reason for distinguishing, in physician actions, between the dying and those who simply have a terminal illness (or have this "dying life," Augustine's description of all of us). It would also entail a belief that wishing or autonomous choice makes the moral difference between life and death decisions which then are to be imposed on the physician-technician; and that, to say the least, is an ethics that can find no place for either reason or sensibility.

preference of many people in the present age for *sudden* death for death from unanticipated internal collapse, from the abrupt intrusion of violent outside forces, from some chance occurrence due to the natural law governing the operation of automobiles. While for a comparative calculus of indignities sudden *unknowing* death may be preferred to suffering knowingly or unknowingly the indignity of deterioration, abject dependence, and hopeless pain, how ought we to assess in human term the present-day absolute (noncomparative) preference for sudden death? Nothing reveals more the meaning we assign to human "dignity" than the view that sudden death, death as an eruptive natural event, could be a prismatic case of death with dignity or at least one without indignity. Human society seems about to rise to the moral level of the "humane" societies in their treatment of animals. What is the principled difference between their view and ours about the meaning of dying "humanely"? By way of contrast, consider the prayer in the Anglican prayer book: "From perils by night and perils by day, perils by land and perils by sea, and *from sudden death,* Lord, deliver us." Such a petition bespeaks an age in which dying with dignity was a gift and a task (*Gaube und Aufgaube*), a liberty to encompass dying as a final act among the actions of life, to enfold awareness of dying as an ingredient into awareness of one's self dying as the finale of the self's relationships in this life to God or to fellowman—in any case to everything that was worthy.

MAN KNOWS THAT HE DIES

Before letting Koheleth's "a time to be born and a time to die" creep as a gloss into *our* texts perhaps we ought to pay more attention to the outlook on life and death expressed in the enchantment and frail beauty of those words,[10] and ask whether that philosophy

---

[10] In the whole literature on death and dying, there is no more misquoted sentence, or statement taken out of context, than Koheleth's "time to be born and a time to die"—unless it be "Nor strive officiously to keep alive." The latter line is from an ironic poem by the nineteenth century poet Arthur Hugh Clough, entitled "The Latest Decalogue":

> "Thou shalt not kill; but need'st not strive
> Officiously to keep alive.
> Do not adultery commit;
> Advantage rarely comes of it:

can possibly be a proper foundation for the practice of medicine or for the exercise of the most sensitive care for the dying.

That litany on the times for every matter under heaven concludes with the words, "What gain has the worker from his toil?" (Eccles. 3:9). In general, the author of Ecclesiastes voices an unrelieved pessimism. He has "seen everything that is done under the sun," in season and out of season. It is altogether "an unhappy business that God has given to the sons of men to be busy with"—this birthing and dying, planting and uprooting; "all is vanity and seeking after wind" (Eccles. 1:3b, 14). So, he writes with words of strongest revulsion, "I hated life, because what is done under the sun was grievous to me"; "I hated all my toil and gave myself up to despair . . ." (Eccles. 2:17, 18a, 20).

After that comes the litany "for everything there is a season"—proving, as Kierkegaard said, that a poet is a man whose heart is full of pain but whose lips are so formed that when he gives utterance to that pain he makes beautiful sounds. Koheleth knew, as later did Nietzsche, that the eternal recurrence of birth and death and all things else was simply "the spirit of melancholy" unrelieved, even though there is nothing else to believe since God died. (The Pope knows: he was at the bedside.)

"Death with dignity" because death is a "part" of life, one only of its seasonal realities? If so, then the acceptable death of all flesh means death with the same signal indignity that brackets the whole of life and its striving. Dying is worth as much as the rest; it is no more fruitless.

"For the fate of the sons of men and the fate of the beasts is the same; as one dies so dies the other. They all have the same breath, and man has no advantage over the beasts; for all is vanity" (Eccles. 3:19). "Death with dignity" or death a part of life based on an equilibration of the death of a man with the death of a dog? I think that is not a concept to be chosen as the foundation of

---

> Thou shalt not steal; an empty feat,
> When it's so lucrative to cheat:
> Bear not false witness; let the lie
> Have time on its own wings to fly:
> Thou shall not covet; but tradition
> Approves all forms of competition.
> The sum of all is, thou shalt love
> If anybody, God above:
> At any rate, shalt never labor
> More than thyself to love thy neighbor."

modern medicine, even though both dogs and men are enabled to die "humanely."

Or to go deeper still: "death with dignity" because the dead are better off than the living? "I thought the dead who are already dead," Koheleth writes in unrelieved sorrow over existence, "more fortunate than the living who are still alive; and better than both is he who has not yet been, and has not seen the evil deeds that are done under the sun" (Eccles. 4:2,3). Thus the book of Ecclesiastes is the source of the famous interchange between two pessimistic philosophers, each trying to exceed the other in gloom: First philosopher: More blessed are the dead than the living. Second philosopher: Yes, what you say is true; but more blessed still are those who have never been born. First philosopher: Yes, wretched life; but few there be who attain to that condition!

But Koheleth thinks he knows some who have attained to the blessed goal of disentrapment from the cycles in which there is a time for every matter under heaven. ". . . An untimely birth [a miscarriage] is better off [than a living man], for it [a miscarriage] comes into vanity and goes into darkness, and in darkness its name is covered, moreover it has not seen the sun or known anything; yet it finds rest rather than he [the living]" (Eccles. 6:3b, 4,5). So we might say that death can have its cosmic dignity if untormented by officious physicians, because the dying go to the darkness, to Limbo where nameless miscarriages dwell, having never seen the sun or known anything. Thus, if dying with dignity as a part of life's natural, undulating seasons seems not to be a thought with much consolation in it (being roughly equivalent to the indignity besetting everything men do and every other natural time), still the dying may find rest as part of cosmic order, from which, once upon a time, the race of men arose to do the unhappy business God has given them to be busy with, and to which peaceful darkness the dying return.

Hardly a conception that explains the rise of Western medicine, the energy of its care of the dying, or its war against the indignity of suffering and death—or a conception on which to base its reformation! Dylan Thomas' words were directed against such notions: "The wise men at their end know dark is right,/Because their words had forked no lightning."

There is finally in Ecclesiastes, however, a deeper strand than those which locate men living and dying as simply parts of some malignly or benignly neglectful natural or cosmic order. From these more surface outlooks, the unambiguous injunction follows: Be a part; let there be death—in its time and place, of course (whatever that means). Expressing a deeper strand, however, Koheleth seems to say: Let the natural or cosmic order be whatever it is; men are different. His practical advice is: Be what you are, in human awareness apart and not a part. Within this deeper understanding of the transcendent, threatened nobility of a human life, the uniqueness of the individual human subject, there is ground for awareness of death as an indignity yet freedom to encompass it with dignity.

Now it is that Koheleth reverses the previous judgments he decreed over all he had seen under the sun. Before, the vale of the sunless not-knowing of a micarriage having its name covered by darkness seemed preferable to living; and all man's works a seeking after wind. So, of course, there was "a time for dying." But now Koheleth writes, ". . . there is no work or thought or knowledge or wisdom in Sheol, to which you are going" (Eccles. 9:10b). While the fate of the sons of men and the fate of the beasts are the same, still "a living dog is better than a dead lion"; and to be a living man is better than either, because of what Koheleth means by "living." "He who is joined with all the living has hope" (Eccles. 9:4), and that is hardly a way to describe dogs or lions. Koheleth, however, identifies the grandeur of man not so much with hope as with awareness, even awareness of dying, and the misery of man with the indignity of dying of which he, in his nobility, is aware. "For the living know that they will die," he writes, "but the dead know nothing . . ." (Eccles. 9:5). Before, the dead or those who never lived had superiority; now, it is the living who are superior precisely by virtue of their awareness of dying and of its indignity to the knowing human spirit.

Therefore, I suggest that Koheleth probed the human condition to a depth to which more than twenty centuries later Blaise Pascal came. "Man is but a reed, the feeblest in nature, but he is a thinking reed. . . . A vapour, a drop of water, is sufficient to slay him. But were the universe to crush him, man would still be nobler than that which kills him, for *he knows that he dies,* while the universe knows nothing of the advantage it has over him. Thus our whole dignity consists in thought."[11] (Italics added.)

[11] Pascal, *Pensées,* p. 347.

So the grandeur and misery of man are fused together in the human reality and experience of death. To deny the indignity of death requires that the dignity of man be refused also. The more acceptable in itself death is, the less the worth or uniqueness ascribed to the dying life.

TRUE HUMANISM AND THE DREAD OF DEATH

I always write as the ethicist I am, namely, a Christian ethicist, and not as some hypothetical common denominator. On common concrete problems I, of course, try to elaborate analysis at the point or on a terrain where there may be convergence of vectors that began in other ethical outlooks and onlooks. Still one should not pant for agreement as the heart pants for the waterbrooks, lest the substance of one's ethics dissolve into vapidity. So in this section I want, among other things, to exhibit some of the meaning of "Christian humanism" in regard to death and dying, in the confidence that this will prove tolerable to my colleagues for a time, if not finally instructive to them.

In this connection, there are two counterpoised verses in the First Epistle of St. John that are worth pondering. The first reads: "Perfect love casts out fear" (which being interpreted means: Perfect care of the dying casts out fear of one's own death or rejection of their dying because of fear of ours). The second verse reads: "Where fear is, love is not perfected" (which being interpreted means: Where fear of death and dying remains, medical and human care of the dying is not perfected). That states nothing so much as the enduring dubiety and ambiguity of any mortal man's care of another through his dying. At the same time there is here applied without modification a standard for unflinching care of a dying fellowman, or short of that of any fellow mortal any time. That standard is cut to the measure of the perfection in benevolence believed to be that of our Father in Heaven in his dealings with mankind. So there is "faith-ing" in an ultimate righteousness beyond the perceptible human condition presupposed by those verses that immediately have to do simply with loving and caring.

Whatever non-Christians may think about the *theology* here entailed, or about similar foundations in any religious ethics, I ask that the notation upon or penetration of the human condition be attended to. Where and insofar as fear is, love and care for the dying cannot be perfected in moral agents or the helping professions. The religious traditions have one way of addressing that problematic. In the modern age the problematic itself is avoided by various forms and degrees of denial of the tragedy of death which proceeds first to reduce the unique worth and once-for-all-ness of the individual life-span that dies.

Perhaps one can apprehend the threat posed to the dignity of man (i.e. in an easy and ready dignifying of death) by many modern viewpoints, especially those dominating the scientific community, and their superficial equivalents in our culture generally, by bringing into view three states of consciousness in the Western past.

The burden of the Hebrew Scriptures was man's obedience or disobedience to covenant, to Torah. Thus sin was the problem, and death came in only as a subordinate theme; and, as one focus for the problematic of the human condition, this was a late development. In contrast, righteousness and disobedience (sin) was a subordinate theme in Greek religion. The central theme of Greek religious thought and practice was the problem of death—a problem whose solution was found either by initiation into religious cults that promised to extricate the soul from its corruptible shroud or by belief in the native power of the soul to outlast any number of bodies. Alongside these, death was at the heart of the pathos of life depicted in Greek tragical drama, against which, and against the flaws of finitude in general, the major character manifested his heroic transcendence. So sin was determinative for the Hebrew consciousness; death for the Greek consciousness.

Consciousness III was Christianity, and by this, sin and death were tied together in Western man's awareness of personal existence. These two foci of man's misery and of his need for redemption— sin and death—were inseparably fused. This new dimension of man's awareness of himself was originally probed most profoundly by St. Paul's Letter to the Romans (5–7). Those opaque reflections, I opine, were once understood not so much by the intellect as along the pulses of ordinary people in great numbers, in taverns and market places; and it represents a cultural breakdown without parallel that these reflections are scarcely understandable to the greatest intelligences today. A simple night school lesson in them may be gained by simply pondering a while the two verses quoted above from St. John's Epistle.

The point is that according to the Christian saga the Messiah did not come to bring boors into culture. Nor did he bear epilepsy or psychosomatic disorders to gain victory over them in the flesh before the interventions of psychoneurosurgery. Rather is he said to have been born *mortal* flesh to gain for us a foretaste of victory over sin and death where those twin enemies had taken up apparently secure citadel.

Again, the point for our purposes is not to be drawn into agreement or disagreement with those theological affirmations, and it is certainly not to be tempted into endless speculation about an afterlife. Crucial instead is to attend to the notation on the human condition implied in all that. Death is an enemy even if it is the last enemy to be fully conquered in the Fulfillment, the eschaton; meanwhile, the sting of death is sin. Such was the new consciousness-raising that Christianity brought into the Western world. And the question is whether in doing so it has not grasped some important experiential human realities better than most philosophies, whether it was not attuned to essential ingredients of the human condition vis-a-vis death—whatever the truth or falsity of its theological address to that condition.

The foregoing, I grant, may be an oversimplification; and I am aware of needed corrections more in the case of Hebrew humanism than in the case of Greek humanism. The New Testament word, "He will wipe away every tear from their eyes, and death shall be no more, neither shall there be mourning nor crying nor pain any more, for the former things have passed away," (Rev. 21:3,4) has its parallel in the Hebrew Bible: "He will swallow up death forever, and the Lord God will wipe away tears from all faces . . ." (Isa. 25:8). Again, since contemplating the Lord God may be too much for us, I ask only that we attend to the doctrine of death implied in these passages: it is an enemy, surely, and not simply an acceptable part of the natural order of things. And the connection between dread of death and sin, made most prominent in Christian consciousness, was nowhere better stated than in Ecclesiastes: "This is the root of the evil in all that happens under the sun, that one fate comes to all. Therefore, men's minds are filled with evil and there is madness in their hearts while they live, for they know that afterward—they are off to the dead!"

One can, indeed, ponder that verse about the source of all evil in the apprehended evil of death together with another verse in Ecclesiastes which reads: "Teach us so to number our days that we may apply our hearts unto wisdom." The first says that death is an evil evil: it is experienced as a threatening limit that begets evil. The second says that death is a good evil: that experience also begets good. Without death, and death perceived as a threat, we would also have no reason to "number our days" so as to ransom the time allotted us, to receive life as a precious gift, to drink the wine of gladness in toast to every successive present moment. Instead, life would be an endless boredom and boring because endless; there would be no reason to probe its depths while there is still time. Some there are who number their days so as to apply their hearts unto eating, drinking and being merry—for tomorrow we die. Some there are who number their days so as to apply their hearts unto wisdom—for tomorrow we die. Both are life-spans enhanced in importance and in individuation under the stimulus of the perceived evil of death. Knowledge of human good or of human evil that is in the slightest degree above the level of the beasts of the field are both enhanced because of death, the horizon of human existence. So, debarment from access to the tree of life was on the horizon and a sequence of the events in the Garden of Paradise; the temptation in eating the fruit of the tree of knowledge of good and evil was because that seemed a way for mortal creatures to become like gods. The punishment of that is said to have been death; and no governor uses as a penalty something that anyone can simply choose to believe to be a good or simply receive as a neutral or dignified, even ennobling, part of life. So I say death may be a good evil or an evil evil, but it is perceived as an evil or experienced indignity in either case. Existential anxiety or general anxiety (distinguishable from particular fears or removable anxieties) means anxiety over death toward which we live. That paradoxically, as Reinhold Niebuhr said, is the source of all human creativity and of all human sinfulness.

Of course, the sages of old could and did engage in a calculus of comparative indignities. "O death, your sentence is welcome," wrote Ben Sira, "to a man worn out with age, worried about everything, disaffected and beyond endurance" (Ecclus. 41:2,3). Still death was a "sentence," not a natural event acceptable in itself.

Moreover, not every man grows old gracefully in the Psalms; instead, one complains:

> Take pity on me, Yahweh,
> I am in trouble now.
> Grief wastes away my eye,
> My throat, my inmost parts.
> For my life is worn out with sorrow,
> My years with sighs;
> My strength yields under misery,
> My bones are wasting away.
> To every one of my oppressors
> I am comtemptible,
> Loathsome to my neighbors,
> To my friends a thing of fear.
> Those who see me in the street
> Hurry past me.
> I am forgotten, as good as dead, in their hearts,
> Something discarded.   (Ps. 31:9–12)

What else is to be expected if it be true that the madness in men's hearts while they live, and the root of all evil in all that happens under the sun, lies in the simple fact that every man consciously lives toward his own death, knowing that afterward he too is off to the dead? Where fear is—fear of the properly dreadful—love and care for the dying cannot be perfected.

Unless one has some grounds for respecting the shadow of death upon every human countenance—grounds more ultimate than perceptible realities—then it makes good sense as a policy of life simply to try to outlast one's neighbors. One can, for example, *generalize,* and so attenuate our neighbors' irreplaceability. "If I must grieve whenever the bell tolls," writes Carey McWilliams, "I am never bereft: some of my kinsmen will remain. Indeed, I need not grieve much—even, lest I suggest some preference among my brethren, should not grieve much—for each loss is small compared to what remains."[12] But that solace, we know, is denied the dead who have lost everything making for worth in this their world. Realistic love for another irreplaceable, noninterchangeable individual human being means, as Unamuno wrote, care for another "doomed soul."

In this setting, let us now bring into consideration some em-

---

[12] Wilson Carey McWilliams, *The Idea of Fraternity in America* (Berkeley: University of California Press, 1973), p. 48.

pirical findings that in this day are commonly supposed to be more confirmatory than wisdom meditated from the heart.

In the second year anatomy course, medical students clothe with "gallows humor" their encounter with the cadaver which once was a human being alive. That defense is not to be despised; nor does it necessarily indicate socialization in shallowness on the students' part. Even when dealing with the remains of the long since dead, there is special tension involved—if I mistook not a recent address by Renée Fox—when performing investigatory medical actions involving the face, the hands, and the genitalia. This thing-in-the-world that was once a man alive we still encounter as once a communicating being, not quite as an object of research or instruction. Face and hands, yes; but why the genitalia? Those reactions must seem incongruous to a resolutely biologizing age. For a beginning of an explanation, one might take up the expression "carnal knowledge"—which was the best thing about the movie bearing that title—and behind that go to the expression "carnal *conversation*," an old, legal term for adultery, and back of both to the Biblical word "knew" in "And Adam *knew* his wife and begat. . . ." Here we have an entire anthropology impacted in a word, not a squeamish euphemism. In short, in those reactions of medical students can be discerned a sensed relic of the human being bodily experiencing and communicating, and the body itself uniquely speaking.

Notably, however, there's no "gallows humor" used when doing or observing one's first autopsy, or in the emergency room when a D.O.A. (Dead on Arrival) is brought in with his skull cleaved open. With regard to the "newly dead" we come as close as we possibly can to experiencing the incommensurable contrast between life and death. Yet those sequential realities—life and death—here juxtaposed never *meet* in direct encounter. So we never have an impression or experience of the measure and meaning of the two different worlds before which we stand in the autopsy and the emergency room. A cadaver has over time become almost a thing-in-the-world from which to gain knowledge of the human body. While *there* a little humor helps, to go about acquiring medical knowledge from autopsies requires a different sort of inward effort to face down or live with our near-experience of the boundary of life and death. The cleavage in the brain may be quite enough and more than enough to *explain* rationally why this man was D.O.A. But, I suggest, there can be no gash deep enough, no physical event destructive enough to account for the felt difference between life and death that we face here. The physician or medical student may be a confirmed materialist. For him the material explanation of this death may be quite sufficient rationally. Still the heart has its reasons that the reasons knows not of; and, I suggest, the awakening of these feelings of awe and dread should not be repressed in anyone whose calling is to the human dignity of caring for the dying.

In any case, from these empirical observations, if they be true, let us return to a great example of theological anthropology in order to try to comprehend why death was thought to be the assault of an enemy. According to some readings, Christians in all ages should be going about bestowing the gift of immortality on one another posthaste. A distinguished Catholic physician, beset by what he regarded as the incorrigible problems of medical ethics today, once shook his head in my presence and wondered out loud why the people who most believe in an after-life should have established so many hospitals! That seems to require explanation, at least as against silly interpretations of "otherworldliness." The answer is that none of the facts or outlooks cited ever denied the reality of death, or affirmed that death ever presents a friendly face (except comparatively). The explanation lies in the vicinity of Christian anthropology and the Biblical view that death is an enemy. That foundation of Western medicine ought not lightly to be discarded, even if we need to enliven again the sense that there are limits to man's struggle against that alien power.

Far from the otherworldliness or body—soul dualism with which he is often charged, St. Augustine went so far as to say that "the body is not an extraneous ornament or aid, but a part of man's very nature.[13] Upon that understanding of the human being, Augustine could then express a quite realistic account of "the dying process":

> Wherefore, as regards bodily death, that is, the separation of the soul from the body, it is good to none while it is being endured by those whom we say are in the article of death [dying]. For the very violence with which the body and soul are wrenched asunder, which in the living are conjoined and closely intertwined, brings with it a harsh experience, jarring horribly on nature as long as it continues, till there comes a total loss of sensation, which arose from the very interpenetration of flesh and spirit.[14]

[13] Augustine, *City of God,* Book I, Chapter XIII.
[14] *Ibid.,* Book XIII, Chapter VI.

From this Augustine correctly concludes: "Wherefore death is indeed . . . good to none while it is actually suffered, and while it is subduing the dying to its power . . . " His ultimate justifications attenuate not at all the harshness of that alien power's triumph. Death, he only says, is "meritoriously endured for the sake of winning what *is* good. And regarding what happens after death, it is no absurdity to say that death is good to the good, and evil to the evil."[15] But that is not to say that death as endured in this life, or as life's terminus, is itself in any way good. He even goes so far as to say:

> For though there can be no manner of doubt that the souls of the just and holy lead lives in peaceful rest, yet so much better would it be for them to be alive in healty, well-conditioned bodies, that even those who hold the tenet that it is most blessed to be quit of every kind of body, condemn this opinion in spite of themselves.[16]

Thus, for Biblical or later Christian anthropology, the only possible form which human life in any true and proper sense can take here or hereafter is "somatic." That is the Pauline word; we today say "psychosomatic." Therefore, for Christian theology death may be a "conquered enemy"; still it was in the natural order—and as long as the generations of mankind endure will remain—an enemy still. To pretend otherwise adds insult to injury—or, at least, carelessness.

There are two way, so far as I can see, to reduce the dreadful visage of death to a level of inherently acceptable indifference. One way is to subscribe to an interpretation of "bodily life" that reduces it to an acceptable level of indifference to the person long before his dying. That—if anyone can believe it today, or if it is not a false account of human nature—was the way taken by Plato in his idealized account of the death of Socrates. (It should be remembered that we know not whether Socrates' hands trembled as he yet bravely drank the hemlock, no more than we know how Isaac experienced dying when "fullness of years" came upon him. Secondary accounts of these matters are fairly untrustworthy.)

Plato's dialogue *The Phaedo* may not "work" as a proof of the immortality of the soul. Still it decisively raises the question of immortality by its thorough representation of the incommensurability

---

[15] *Ibid.,* Book XIII, Chapter VIII.
[16] *Ibid.,* Book XIII, Chapter XIX.

between mental processes and bodily processes. Few philosophers today accept the demonstration of the mind's power to outlast bodies because the mind itself is not material, or because the mind "plays" the body like a musician the lyre. But most of them are still wrestling with the mind-body problem, and many speak of two separate languages, a language for mental events isomorphic with our language for brain events. That's rather like saying the same thing as Socrates (Plato) while claiming to have gone beyond him (Soren Kierkegaard).

I cite *The Phaedo* for another purpose: to manifest one way to render death incomparably welcomed. Those who most have mature manhood in exercise—the lovers of wisdom—have desired death and dying all their life long, in the sense that they seek "in every sort of way to dissever the soul from the communion of the body"; "thought is best when the mind is gathered into herself and none of these things trouble her—neither sounds nor sights nor pain nor any pleasure—when she takes leave of the body. . . ." That life is best and has nothing to fear that has "the habit of the soul gathering and collecting herself into herself from all sides out of the body." (Feminists, note the pronouns.)

Granted, Socrates' insight is valid concerning the self's transcendence, when he says: "I am inclined to think that these muscles and bones of mine would have gone off long ago to Megara and Boeotia—by the dog, they would, if they had been moved only by their own idea of what was best. . . ." Still Crito had a point, when he feared that the impending dread event had more to do with "the same Socrates who has been talking and conducting the argument" than Socrates is represented to have believed. To fear the loss of Socrates, Crito had not to fancy, as Socrates charged, "that I am the other Socrates whom he will soon see, a dead body." Crito had only to apprehend, however faintly, that there is not an entire otherness between those two Socrates *now,* in this living being; that there was unity between, let us say, Socrates the conductor of arguments and Socrates the gesticulator or the man who stretched *himself* because his muscles and bones grew weary from confinement.

The other way to reduce the dreadful visage of death is to subscribe to a philosophy of "human life" that reduces the stature, the worth, and the irreplaceable uniqueness of the individual person (long before his dying) to a level of acceptable transiency or interchangeability. True, modern culture is going this way. But there have been other and better ways of stipulating that the image of death across the human countenance is no shadow. One was that of Aristotelian philosophy. According to its form-matter distinction, reason, the formal principle, is definitive of essential humanity. That is universal, eternal as logic. Matter, however, is the individuating factor. So when a man who bears a particular name dies, only the individuation disintegrates—to provide matter for other forms. Humanity goes on in other instances. Anything unique or precious about mankind is not individual. There are parallels to this outlook in Eastern religions and philosophies, in which the individual has only transiency, and should seek only that, disappearing in the Fulfillment into the Divine pool.

These then are two ways of denying the dread of death. Whenever these two escapes are *simultaneously* rejected—i.e., if the "bodily life" is neither an ornament nor a drag but a part of man's very nature; and if the "personal life" of an individual in his unique life-span is accorded unrepeatable, noninterchangeable value—then it is that Death the Enemy again comes into view. Conquered or Unconquerable. A true humanism and the dread of death seem to be dependent variables. I suggest that it is better to have the indignity of death on our hands and in our outlooks than to "dignify" it in either of these two possible ways. Then we ought to be much more circumspect in speaking of death with dignity, and hesitant to—I almost said—thrust that upon the dying! Surely, a proper care for them needs not only to know the pain of dying which human agency may hold at bay, but also care needs to acknowledge that there is grief over death which no human agency can alleviate.

EUTHANASIA: NONE DARE
CALL IT MURDER

Joseph Sanders

Euthanasia is plainly a form of homicide, but is it also murder? Is it, in other words, legal or illegal homicide. Sander's essay brings considerable clarity to the discussion of the legal status of euthanasia.

Joseph Sanders was a member of the Board of Editors of the Journal at the time this article was published.

This article is taken from the Journal of Criminal Law, Criminology, and Police Science, *volume 60, number 3.*

On August 9, 1967, Robert Waskin, a twenty-three year old college student, killed his mother by shooting her in the head three times. Warned by the police that he did not have to make a statement, Waskin allegedly said, "It's obvious, I killed her." He was arrested and charged with murder. Waskin's act, however, was a special type —a type that has troubled and perplexed both laymen and legal theorists. The homicide was a "mercy killing."

Waskin's mother was suffering from terminal leukemia. The doctors in the Chicago hospital where she was killed said that she had, at the most, a very few days to live. She wanted to die and had begged her son to kill her. Only three days before, she had tried to commit suicide by taking an overdose of sleeping pills. According to her husband and the doctors, she was suffering deep pain at the time she was shot.

In all American jurisdictions motive is no defense to a murder charge. If it is shown that the act was done with intent and premeditation, the motive for the crime is irrelevant. Motive can be taken into account by the judge in setting the sentence, but, for

Waskin, even the utmost leniency on a murder conviction would have resulted in a sentence of fourteen years in prison with no possibility of probation.

On January 24, 1969, however, after a seventeen month delay, a jury deliberated for only 40 minutes and found Waskin not guilty by reason of insanity. They further found that he was no longer insane, and he was released. Although it seems doubtful that Waskin was ever legally insane, the verdict, as we shall see, was entirely predictable.

The word *euthanasia* is generally used to describe a killing that is prompted by some humanitarian motive. Euthanasia, however, may vary with the nature of the act, the status of the actor and the victim, and the presence or absence of consent. The act itself may be one of commission or one of omission. The former, which is the concern of this paper, is at the present time some degree of criminal homicide.[1]

There are three reasonably identifiable groups against, or for

---

[1] There has never been a prosecution of a person for an act of omission with or without consent causing the death of any person falling within one of the groups subject to euthanasia. This fact, however, should not be interpreted as evidence of the infrequency of such acts. There is some evidence that these omissions make up the great majority of euthanasia cases in the United States. In a survey of 250 Chicago internists and surgeons by Levisohn, 156 responded to a questionnaire asking: " 'In your opinion do physicians actually practice euthanasia in instances of incurable adult sufferers?' Sixty-one percent agreed that physicians actually practiced it, if not in the affirmative at least in the negative or in terms of the omission to use every known medical measure to sustain life." Levisohn, *Voluntary Mercy Deaths,* 8 J. For. Med. 57, 68 (1961). Of the same 156 physicians, however, 72% said the practice should not be legalized.

Although this was not a random sample, still 38% or 95 of the Chicago physicians polled admitted knowing of acts of euthanasia, at least by omission. This survey refers only to acts against persons with incurable diseases. Similar results, however, might be expected in cases of old people dying of general deterioration. In both these cases the patient is usually near death and the physician inquires of the family if they wish him to use all possible means or permit the individual to "die in peace."

Williams has proposed a statute confirming the legality of acts of omission in relation to dying patients that would be useful in clarifying the law in this area. "For the avoidance of doubt, it is hereby declared that it shall be lawful for a physician whose patient is seriously ill— . . . to refrain from taking steps to prolong the patient's life by medical means;—unless . . . the omission was not made, in good faith for the purpose of saving the patient from severe pain in an illness believed to be of a incurable and fatal character." G. Williams, The Sanctity of Life and the Criminal Law 345 (1957). (Hereinafter referred to as Williams.)

whom euthanasia may be committed. The first group consists of persons with painful and terminal diseases such as cancer who, by definition, have at best a month or two, perhaps only a few days, to live. A second group consists of defective or degenerate persons, including the mentally ill, the retarded, those with gross physical defects, and old people suffering from senility. Some of these may be persons who have been rendered permanently unconscious by disease or accident and are being kept alive through artificial medical means. The third group is composed of infants and young children who suffer from gross mental or physical defects. The life expectancy of children in this group may be short, or perhaps even the same as normal infants.

Euthanasia may be performed upon the request of, or without the request of the victim. All those in group three and the insane in group two are incapable of consent. The consent issue, then, usually concerns persons in group one who suffer from painful terminal illnesses.

For purposes of legal analysis, persons committing euthanasia may be divided into two groups: physicians and all others. It has been suggested that under certain circumstances physicians should be allowed to perform euthanasia legally.

VOLUNTARY EUTHANASIA PERFORMED BY PHYSICIANS

It appears that neither consent of the victim, not the extremity of his suffering, or the imminence of his death are presently defenses to homicide. Demands have arisen from time to time to enact a statute permitting a physician to terminate the life of a consenting patient who is suffering from some incurable, painful and terminal illness. There are voluntary euthanasia societies in both England and the United States which have proposed legislation legalizing this type of euthanasia in order "to permit an adult person of sound mind, whose life is ending with much suffering, to choose between an easy death and a hard one; and to obtain medical aid in implementing that choice."[2]

Two types of statutes have been proposed by those who favor

---

[2] *Euthanasia Society, A Plan for Voluntary Euthanasia* (2d rev. ed. 1962) hereinafter cited as [*Euthanasia Society*].

legalizing voluntary euthanasia. The English Euthanasia Society proposal, typical of one type, requires a judicial investigation to assure the existence of the patient's consent and to prevent abuses. It has several requirements. The patient must be over twenty-one, of sound mind, in a hopeless condition and earnestly desirous of a painless death. He must make an application requesting euthanasia. His physician must combine this request with a written recommendation reporting on the patient's condition, and submit them to the court. The court then assigns a euthanasia referee who visits the patient and the physician in order to make himself personally aware of the circumstances of the case. If he agrees with the physician and believes the patient has given rational consent, he may then authorize the death. The authorization would be valid only for a limited period, and the patient may withdraw his consent at any time.

The eminent English legal authority, Glanville Williams, on the other hand, has proposed a statute that would give wide discretion to the physician. The proposed statute provides:

> It shall be lawful for a physician, after consultation with another physician, to accelerate by any merciful means the death of a patient who is seriously ill, unless it is proved that the act was not done in good faith with the consent of the patient and for the purpose of saving him from severe pain in an illness believed to be of an incurable and fatal character.[3]

If a physician is prosecuted, he can plead the statute and place the burden of proof on the state to show that his conduct did not fall under the act. Williams does suggest that the burden of proving consent could be placed on the doctor if this safeguard were deemed necessary. To protect himself if prosecuted, the physician could obtain a written request from a patient before performing euthanasia.

The main issue created by such proposals is whether a person dying in pain should have the privilege of choosing an easy death. There are several nonreligious objections to permitting such a choice.[4] The first is that it may be very difficult to establish satisfactorily the con-

---

[3] Williams 345.
[4] The religious issues involved in euthanasia are not discussed in this comment. Most such objections are based on the Fifth Commandment and the belief that our bodies and life are given by God and, therefore, He only has the right to take them away. *See* N. St. John-Stevas, *The Right to Life* (1964); J. Sullivan, *The Morality of Mercy Killing* (1949).

sent of the victim. If consent is not given until the final stages of a painful illness, the patient may be so wracked with pain or so doped with pain killers that he would be incapable of rational consent. If, on the other hand, consent is given earlier there is the possibility that a person will change his mind after he has become so ill that it is difficult to be sure what his true wishes are. Even an earlier signed document requesting euthanasia might then be contrary to his present intent. A dying person may change his mind several times even in one day, depending upon how he feels. Assuming this to be true, it seems difficult to devise any possible test of consent that would be more effective than the Euthanasia Society plan, which requires repeated rational requests to the physician and the referee.

A criticism that even the Euthanasia Society's proposal cannot meet, however, is that the patient's consent and the physician's decision may be based on factors other than the patient's own best interests and desires. The patient may request euthanasia in order to relieve his relatives' anguish, rather than his own pain. The physician will thus be forced to make life and death decisions while in the unenviable position of arbitrating between the patient and the family who oppose their dying relative's wishes. Perhaps many physicians would be unwilling to assume such a role. The present law does avoid such conflicts between the patient, the physician and the family by simply prohibiting euthanasia under any circumstances.

The advocates of voluntary euthanasia do not deny the difficulty in determining the reasons for the patient's request. They submit, however, that in resolving conflicts between the relatives and the patient, the patient's wishes should govern. If one of the patient's reasons for requesting euthanasia is to relieve anxiety in his family, this should not disqualify him. If, on the other hand, it were apparent that the relatives were pushing the sick person towards euthanasia, the doctor should refuse to perform the act. The referee proposed in the Euthanasia Society statute would provide extra protection against the possibility that the physician and the family might conspire to murder the patient.

A second objection to voluntary euthanasia is that the physician may make an incorrect diagnosis, or that a new cure might be discovered after the execution of the patient. This assumes that euthanasia may be performed long before the last stages of a fatal illness. The possibility of an incorrect diagnosis seems very remote in cases such as Mrs. Waskin's where death was clearly inevitable. But in the early stages of any illness mistaken diagnoses are possible and, like mistakes in the use of the death penalty, are incorrectible.

Although no one knows the precise number of mistakes that might be made, advocates of legalized euthanasia do not believe that the possibility of error is so great that euthanasia must be completely prohibited. Williams argues—and his critics partly concede— that the chance of incorrect diagnosis of cancer, the illness most likely to cause requests for euthanasia, is not very great. It might be, moreover, that the possibility of euthanasia as an alternative would cause the physician to take extra care in making his diagnosis, realizing that a mistake could not be corrected. The Euthanasia Society proposal does require the referee to make his own independent investigation and Williams' plan requires the independent judgment of two physicians.

Similar to the fear of incorrect diagnosis is the fear that a cure might be discovered the "morning after." Usually, however, there is a considerable period of time between the announcement of a new treatment and its general availability. If a cure is first announced shortly after the execution of a patient, it is unlikely that it would be distributed in time to save the individual. Of course, if legalized euthanasia were extended to persons with chronic as well as terminal illnesses, then this problem would be much greater. Under the present proposals, however, this remote possibility should not be an excuse for permitting the suffering of patients who desire euthanasia.

A third objection is that in view of modern medical techniques of controlling pain, including tranquilizers, analgesics, narcotics, anesthetics and glandular operations, the humanitarian goal of relieving suffering may be accomplished without resort to euthanasia. On the other hand, no adequate relief seems possible for several maladies. The Euthanasia Society of England gives as an example cancer of the throat, which makes any swallowing, and even breathing, extremely difficult and painful long before the patient is about to die. Also, emphysema and some lung cancers may cause shortness of breath and a constant feeling of suffocation. Severe strokes may cause a person to become little more than a vegetable, unable to move, speak or see.

Even if total pain relief were possible with the use of advanced medical techniques, many people would not be able to take advantage of them. Narcotics, still the most widely used analgesics, may reduce pain, but the side effects, including vomiting, nausea and long periods of consciousness of impending doom, may be just as undesirable. Moreover, if narcotics are used their effectiveness tends to wear off after continued use and may bring no relief unless the physician gives such a massive dose that it may cause death.

A final objection, the "wedge" argument, questions the presumed effects legalized euthanasia would have on society. Opponents submit that the creation of the right to choose an easy death under certain circumstances will weaken the psychological and moral fabric of society by reducing the absolute value placed on human life, and that it will eventually lead to the acceptance of the idea that others may have the right to choose death for an individual under certain circumstances.

Although anyone may commit suicide, what seems to bother many opponents of legalized euthanasia is not the right of the individual to choose an easy death, but the creation of a right of execution in another. They would perhaps be willing to grant the patient's right to die; what they do not wish to grant is the physician's right to kill.

But Williams and other advocates are not demanding that all should be forced to choose euthanasia, or that old people and the insane should be eliminated. Rather, proponents urge that society should not forbid this option to the group presently under consideration. They observe that the "wedge" argument may be raised against any new proposal; each new proposal should be weighed on its own merits. Simply because terrible consequences may be imagined is no reason, according to Williams, to reject a reasonable proposal. Replying to the observation of critics that the present demand for euthanasia is not sufficient to justify the risk of later expansion, Williams argues that if such a choice were possible and someone were permitted to perform the act, the number of persons requesting euthanasia would increase. He submits that their wishes overcome any inherent need of society to prohibit this practice because of some fear of future consequences.

Opponents of voluntary euthanasia believe, nevertheless, that there is no way to draft a statute to meet all four of their objections. Williams' proposal fails to provide what they consider to be the necessary safeguards against irrational or non-existing consent and mistaken diagnosis. Williams argues that if his type of statute is unacceptable for failure to protect against possible abuse, those opposing it should not argue that the safeguards incorporated at their demand, such as exist in the Euthanasia Society proposals, are so oppressive that they too are unacceptable. If we concede that some type of safeguard is required, the Euthanasia Society proposal indicates that the State should undertake to establish administrative bodies and have them make the final disposition in each case. This method would surely cause delays. More importantly, it conjures up visions, implyed in the "wedge" argument, of a society where the State would choose life and death. The Nazi experience is too fresh in many minds to permit this possibility.

Even if it is true that neither proposal fully meets all objections, the decision must be made whether the privilege of easy death is so valuable or the present system so unfair to both the physician and patient that some plan should be instituted. Assuming that the need for such a plan does outweigh the objections,[5] Williams' proposal, with a major qualification, seems superior. The Euthanasia Society type proposal suffers from delays at the crucial time after the patient and physician have reached a decision, and from its creation of a bureaucracy, which might establish for itself a vested interest in the maintenance and possible extension of the practice of euthanasia.

Although Williams' proposal lacks the safeguards of the Euthanasia Society proposal, hopefully the quality of physicians insures that abuses would be very infrequent, and with consultation and perhaps the development of euthanasia specialists trained in diagnostic work, mistakes would not be common enough to justify refusing euthanasia to those truly desiring it. Nonetheless, the physician should be required to show that he did have the patient's consent. This could consist of a written request. If it were proved that the deceased did not give his consent, the physician would be guilty of some degree of criminal homicide. In order to deal with the problem of an incorrect diagnosis, every voluntary mercy killing should be followed by an autopsy by another physician or the state coroner. A mistake could be the basis of a cause of action on behalf of the

[5] From a social science viewpoint, moral grounds seem to preclude empirical research as to any of the possible effects of a euthanasia statute, including mistakes in diagnosis and abuses of consent. The only way we may ever be able to know the actual demands for and effects of a statute and the willingness of physicians to use it, is to pass one and see how it operates.

relatives for malpractice. Perhaps an erring physician should not be permitted to perform any other mercy killings.

One of the effects of the foregoing restrictions would be to limit the number of mercy killings. Such requirements may discourage the doctor from performing euthanasia, or at least force him to wait until he was sure of his diagnosis even though the counter-risk would exist that by then his patient will no longer be capable of consent.

OTHER TYPES OF EUTHANASIA

Another classification would be involuntary euthanasia committed by physicians as well as voluntary and involuntary euthanasia performed by others. While these acts may have the same humanitarian under pinnings as those previously discussed, they lack either the request and consent of the victim or are performed by persons other than a physician, who presumably cannot be certain of the inevitable fatality of the victim's illness. Because of these factors, no one has suggested that these acts be legalized. Rather, the discussion has been whether the penalties for such crimes should be reduced.

Although most of the present debate about euthanasia concerns acts of commission by physicians, causing the death of consenting victims suffering from some incurable and painful illness, no known cases in the United States have involved this special type of mercy killing. A tabulation of American cases indicates the types of acts which have led to prosecution are one involuntary, one by a physician, and by others three were of a voluntary nature and seven involuntary.[6]

[6] a. Louis Greenfield chloroformed his imbecile teenage son to death. The boy reportedly had the mentality of a two year old. Greenfield said at the trial, "I did it because I loved him, it was the will of God." N.Y. Times, May 11, 1939, at 10, col. 2. He was acquitted of first degree manslaughter, N.Y. Times, May 12, 1939, at 1, col. 5.

b. Louis Repouille read about the Greenfield case. He said, "It made me think about doing the same thing to my boy." N.Y. Times, Oct. 14, 1939, at 21 col. 2. Repouille chloroformed his thirteen year old son, who had been blind for five years, bedridden since infancy and was also an imbecile, who never learned to talk. N.Y. Times, Oct. 13, 1939, at 25, col. 7. Repouille was indicted for first degree manslaughter but convicted of second degree manslaughter and freed on a suspended sentence of five to ten years. N.Y. Times, Dec. 25, 1941, at 44, col. 1.

In any given trial for euthanasia, in contrast to a decision involving the disposition of an ordinary murderer, the jury and judge need not consider aspects of rehabilitation, retribution or protection of society from dangerous behavior. The jury may still feel, however, that at least involuntary euthanasia is not a practice that should go completely unpunished, and by inference condoned, lest it become more common. In order, therefore, to show general opposition to this behavior and to dissuade others from a similar practice, the jury might prefer to stigmatize the actor and perhaps give him some minimal punishment. If forced to an election between conviction for murder and an acquittal or finding of insanity, however, the

---

c. John Noxon, a well-to-do lawyer, was charged with first degree murder for killing his six month old mongoloid son by wrapping him in a lamp cord and electrocuting him. Noxon claimed that the boy's death was an accident. N.Y. Times, Sept. 28, 1943, at 27, col. 2; N.Y. Times, Sept. 29, 1943, at 23, col. 7; N.Y. Times, Oct. 29, 1943, at 21, col. 7. Noxon was convicted of first degree murder. N.Y. Times, July 7, 1944, at 30, col. 2. His death sentence was commuted to life. N.Y. Times, Dec. 30, 1948, at 13, col. 5. Later his sentence was further reduced to six years to life to make parole possible. N.Y. Times, Dec. 30, 1948, at 5, col. 6. He was paroled shortly thereafter. N.Y. Times, Jan. 4, 1949, at 16, col. 3. The Massachusetts Supreme Court affirmed the trial court's decision and denied Noxon's request for a new trial, based on technical grounds, in Commonwealth v. Noxon, 319 Mass. 495, 66 N.E.2d 814 (1946).

d. Harry Johnson asphyxiated his cancer stricken wife. N.Y. Times, Oct. 2, 1938, at 1 col. 3. After a psychiatrist said he believed Johnson to have been "temporarily insane" the grand jury refused to indict him. N.Y. Times, Oct. 12, 1938, at 30, col. 4; N.Y. Times, Oct. 19, 1938, at 46, col. 1.

e. Eugene Braunsdorf took his 29 year old daughter, a "spastic incapable of speech," out of a sanitorium, and shot and killed her because he feared for her future should he die. He then attempted suicide by shooting himself in the chest twice. He was found not guilty by reason of insanity. N.Y. Times, May 23, 1950, at 25, col. 4.

f. Dr. Herman Sander was acquitted of the murder of his cancer stricken patient. N.Y. Times, Mar. 10, 1950, at 1, col. 4. Dr. Sander, for some unknown reason, had written on his patient's chart that he had given her ten c.c. of air intravenously four times and she died within ten minutes. N.Y. Times, Feb. 24, 1950, at 1, col. 1. At the trial, however, his defense was that the patient was already dead at the time of the injections. N.Y. Times, Mar. 7, 1950, at 1, col. 1. The patient apparently did not request death. The case turned on the causation question and did not live up to its billing as a case to decide the legality of euthanasia.

g. Miss Carol Ann Paget, a college girl, was indicted for second degree murder (carrying a mandatory life sentence) for killing her father while he was still under anesthetic following an exploratory operation which showed him to have cancer of the stomach. The girl apparently had a cancer phobia and was acquitted on grounds of "temporary insanity." N.Y. Times, Feb. 8, 1950, at 1, col. 2.

jury will usually acquit, not wishing, perhaps with good cause, to rely upon an executive pardon to mitigate the sentence.

The only middle ground available in American jurisdictions at the present time is to convict the defendant of a lesser offense, which by its definition rarely fits the facts of the case.[7] This can be

---

h. Harold Mohr killed his blind, cancer stricken brother and on a conviction of voluntary manslaughter with recommendation for mercy he was sentenced to three to six years and a $500 fine. N.Y. Times, Apr. 11, 1950, at 20, col. 5. He pleaded insanity and there was testimony tending to show that his brother had repeatedly requested to die. Some of the testimony, however, tended to show that Mohr was drinking at the time and two other brothers testified against him. N.Y. Times, Apr. 4, 1950, at 60, col. 4; N.Y. Times, Apr. 8, 1950, at 26, col. 1.

i. People v. Werner. The transcript of this case is presented in Williams, *Euthanasia and Abortion,* 38 U. Colo. L. Rev. 178, 184–87 (1966). The defendant, 69, pleaded guilty to manslaughter for the suffocation of his hopelessly crippled, bedridden wife. The court found him guilty, but then after hearing testimony of the defendant's children and others showing what great devotion the defendant had shown towards his wife and that the murder had been at her request, the court allowed the guilty plea to be withdrawn and a plea of not guilty entered. Held: not guilty. For a criticism of this obviously unorthodox procedure see 34 N. D. Law. 460 (1959). It is interesting to compare the events in the Werner case with article 37 of the Uruguayan Penal Code: "The judges are authorized to forego punishment of a person whose previous life has been honorable where he commits a homicide motivated by compassion, induced by repeated requests of the victim." Silving, *Euthanasia: A Study in Comparative Criminal Law,* 103 U. Pa. L. Rev. 350, 369 (1954).

j. Mrs. Wilhelmia Langevin, 56, shot her 35 year old son, an epileptic, with a deer rifle. She was indicted for first degree murder. N.Y. Times, Nov. 2, 1965, at 26, col. 6.

k. Robert Waskin. (The facts of this case are presented on page one of this article.)

The table below shows the various punishments inflicted on the persons above.

PUNISHMENT

First Degree Murder (1)	Lesser Degree Homicide (2)	Acquittal by Reason of Insanity (3)	Acquittal (3)	Refusal to Indict (1)
Noxon —4 years	Mohr Repouille	Paget Braunsdorf Waskin	Sander Greenfield Werner	Johnson

[7] Repouille's murder of his son was not involuntary, *supra* note 6b. Mohr's act was not an act of passion in the legal sense, *supra* note 6h. In relation to this point, Judge Learned Hand said in a later case to determine whether,

accomplished by indictment for a lesser offense or for several levels of homicide at once. It may be possible to indict for murder alone and then instruct and empower the jury to bring back a conviction for a lesser offense if it so desires, but this may not be permissible when the facts of a case cannot conceivably support the concept of a crime of passion or an involuntary act.[8]

There are at least three objectionable features to the present system. First, the consequence of applying what amounts to inapplicable and inadequate rules of law to these cases is that the results range from refusal to indict to findings of first degree murder, generally in the absence of any facts that might justify such wide variations. Secondly, since there is no conceptual legal niche for the handling of mercy killings, we are presently required to use legal fictions in dealing with the problem. Such fictions generally are undesirable since they tend to make the law appear hypocritical in the eyes of the public. Finally, the present system invites the possibility that in some future case an overly severe punishment may be inflicted. Several alternatives to the existing state of affairs are available.

One alternative is to use motive as a substantive criterion in deciding what offense has been committed. In American jurisdictions, motive is at best an evidentiary factor in prosecuting a case and an administrative tool in setting the punishment after it is determined by other means what offense was committed.

In some criminal codes of civil law countries, motive is a sub-

---

considering the murder, Repouille had possessed "good moral character" for five years preceding his petition necessary to qualify for citizenship: "Although it was inescapably murder in the first degree, not only did they [the jury] bring in a verdict that was flatly in the face of the facts and utterly absurd—for manslaughter in the second degree presupposes that the killing has not been deliberate—but they coupled even that with a recommendation which showed that in substance they wished to exculpate the offender." Repouille's petition for citizenship was denied, but Judge Hand virtually invited him to file a new one as soon as five years had elapsed from the date of his conviction. *Repouille* v. *United States,* 165 F.2d 152, 153 (2d Cir. 1947).

[8] *See* 41 C.J.S. *Homicide* §389-b (1944). Some prosecutors may say it is their duty to prosecute solely for the offense committed. Such a stance in effect forces the jury to do all the dirty work. The prosecutor has a duty to see that justice is done as well as to see that the law is upheld. In such a morally confused area as mercy killing, to stand back and shake one's head at the present state of the American Law is at best a cowardly point of view.

stantive element of the offense of homicide. Both the German and Swiss criminal codes provide for a finding of manslaughter, rather than murder, for homicides where the offender does not show either a reprehensible attitude or dangerous and inhumane behavior. This, of course, applies to almost all mercy killers.[9] The jury uses motive in deciding to convict for a lesser offense. In those countries, however, the use of motive avoids the conceptual and factual problems that are caused in the United States where this element theoretically should play no part in determining the actual offense committed. While the use of motive as a substantive element is conceptually appealing, it does not seem that euthanasia cases are so frequent or their disposition so unjust that they would justify what amounts to a massive overhaul in our conceptualization of the elements of homicide.

In Norway motive is not used to determine the actual offense committed, but it may be used to reduce the sentence imposed by statute when the victim is hopelessly ill. American jurisdictions have always used motive in determining the sentence, but this is not a statutory requirement, and the practice is handicapped in the case of capital offenses by the existence of high minimum sentences and the impossibility of probation. Uruguay is the only nation that actually offers the possibility of immunity to the mercy killer.

Norway and several other European countries have special provisions for homicide by request. In all of these states the penalties attached are less if a request can be shown. The purpose of the request is irrelevant so long as the actor responds to it out of altruistic motives. Since both of these defenses—homicide by request and reduction in sentence for motive—are applicable in Norway, a case such as Waskins' might lead to a dramatic reduction in sentence.

Another possibility is presented by the enactment of a diminished responsibility statute such as is now employed in England. The statute lessens the offense and punishment for persons who suffer from from some mental abnormality which is not sufficient to permit them to use the insanity defense. This, in fact may have been the situation with some of the defendants in the American cases.[10] The statute

[9] These statutes and all other information about Civil Law techniques in dealing with euthanasia, are taken from an excellent article by Helen Silving, *Euthanasia: A Study in Comparative Criminal Law,* 103 U. Pa. L. Rev. 350, 378, 380 (1950) [Hereinafter cited as Silving].

[10] Paget, *supra* note 6g.

has, however, been used for euthanasia cases in general, regardless of mental abnormality.[11] When applied to mercy killings, it reaches the same result as the law in Germany and Switzerland. However, while it is conceptually more in tune with the general elements of homicide already so well entrenched in the common law, its use does require one to indulge to some extent in the same type of legal fiction that is presently condemned.

One further alternative would be to do away with minimum punishments in all degrees of homicide. A person could be convicted of first degree murder and still be given a minimum sentence or be put on probation. This proposal seems superior to a specific statute for mercy killers, since this is a very hard crime to define, and any codification would probably lead to constant disputes over whether a certain case fits within the statute.

Although this is the easiest change and conceptually the least drastic, it also would have the effect of permitting anyone to receive a very short sentence, a result that might greatly confound those who believe murderers should be imprisoned for many years.[12] Another objection to this proposal might be that it would increase the possibilities for corruption, or that "soft judges" would return many truly dangerous criminals to the streets. The general movement towards more liberal sentencing power in other areas, however, has not proven especially corrosive.

It might be said that this proposal would weaken the legal supports indicating the high level of social condemnation with which the public views homicide. It is doubtful, however, whether this is the purpose of a minimum sentence; that function, if it exists, would seem to be performed adequately by the maximum sentence. Nor is it likely that the absence of a minimum sentence would lessen the deterrent effect of the law, if indeed any punishment so uncertain and delayed as imprisonment acts as a deterrent in the individual case.

If this plan is too drastic, perhaps a much lower minimum—one or two years—could be established. The one homicide where abuse

[11] Arthur Gray, 44, killed his son who had cancer of the spine, by giving him sleeping tablets. He pleaded guilty to manslaughter on grounds of diminished responsibility as the statute permits. The sentence was two year's probation. N.Y. Times, Oct. 7, 1965, at 1, col. 4.

[12] Other than protecting society, already discussed, the reason for a minimum sentence seems to be retribution, a purpose that is widely discredited as an objective of the criminal law.

through corruption might be most likely, and the defendant the most dangerous to society—murder for profit—could be made a special offense with a higher minimum sentence.

An examination of all of these alternatives, however, makes it questionable whether there should be any change at this time. Using motive as a substantive element is clearly too drastic a conceptual step and the use of diminished responsibility is only a fiction of a lesser degree. Finally, while a reduced minimum sentence for all homicides may be desirable, the proposition should be decided on its own merits, and the more rational handling of mercy killers would be only one rather small consideration.

The present system, as fictitious as it sometimes is, has not yet worked a great injustice on anyone committing euthanasia. Our system of trial by jury permits justice to be done without causing any tear in the conceptual fabric of the law; and although there is no available method of providing a minimum punishment for mercy killers, perhaps the anxiety and discomfort of going through a criminal trial is both a sufficient deterrent to others and an adequate display of public censure.

CONCLUSION

While the problems of euthanasia are legally intriguing and morally perplexing, legislative solutions seem to be far in the future. There is strong, organized opposition to voluntary euthanasia statutes from religious leaders and others, and from the law itself with respect to changes in the status of the involuntary mercy killer. The medical profession generally seems willing to permit the status quo to remain, partly perhaps because it permits a great deal of discretion with little fear of prosecution and partly perhaps because physicians do not wish to accept the extra burdens a statute might impose on them. On the other hand, there is little organized support for change in any of the areas. The people who would be most directly affected by change—dying persons—are in no position to argue for their preference.

As this comment has noted, there are valid reasons for opposing the legalization of voluntary euthanasia by physicians and perhaps little need for change in the other areas. As individuals live longer, however, and thus are more likely to contract painful and malignant diseases, and as medical discoveries make it possible to keep persons alive longer, the problems may magnify, and a more extended discussion will then be necessary. What individuals on both sides of the argument should keep in mind is that it is not they, at least at the present, who have to bear the consequences of their decisions. To quote Glanville Williams:

> The toad beneath the harrow knows
> Exactly where each toothpoint goes.
> The butterfly upon the road
> Preaches contentment to that toad.

ETHICS AND EUTHANASIA

Joseph Fletcher

In strong support of the practice of euthanasia, Professor Fletcher argues that there are circumstances when the active and intended ending of a life is justified. If the goal desired is the cessation of intolerable suffering, euthanasia is a morally acceptable means to that end.

Joseph Fletcher is the Robert Treat Paine Professor of Philosophy at the Episcopal Theological School.

This article is taken from To Live and To Die, *edited by Robert Williams, published by Springer-Verlag, New York, 1973.*

It is harder morally to justify letting somebody die a slow and ugly death, dehumanized, than it is to justify helping him to escape from such misery. This is the case at least in any code of ethics which is humanistic or personalistic, i.e., in any code of ethics which has a value system that puts humanness and personal integrity above biological life and function. It makes no difference whether such an ethics system is grounded in a theistic or a naturalistic philosophy. We may believe that God wills human happiness or that man's happiness is, as Protagoras thought, a self-validating standard of the good and the right. But what counts *ethically* is whether human needs come first—not whether the ultimate sanction is transcendental or secular.

What follows is a moral defense of euthanasia. Primarily I mean active or positive euthanasia, which helps the patient to die; not merely the passive or negative form of euthanasia which "lets the patient go" by simply withholding life-preserving treatments. The plain fact is that negative euthanasia is already a fait accompli in modern medicine. Every day in a hundred hospitals across the land decisions are made clinically that the line has been crossed from prolonging genuinely human life to only prolonging subhuman dying, and when that judgment is made respirators are turned off, life-perpetuating intravenous infusions stopped, proposed surgery canceled, and drugs countermanded. So-called "Code 90" stickers are put on many record-jackets, indicating "Give no intensive care or resuscitation." Arguing pro and con about negative euthanasia is therefore merely flogging a dead horse. Ethically, the issue whether we may "let the patient go" is as dead as Queen Anne.

Straight across the board of religious traditions there is substantial agreement that we are not morally obliged to preserve life in *all* terminal cases. (The religious-ethical defense of negative euthanasia is far more generally accepted by ministers and priests than medical people recognize or as yet even accept.) Humanist morality shows the same nonabsolutistic attitude about preserving life. Indeed, not only Protestant, Catholic, and Jewish teaching take this stance; but it is also true of Buddhist, Hindu, and Moslem ethics. In short, the claim that we ought always to do everything we can to preserve any patient's life as long as possible is now discredited. The last serious advocate of this unconditional pro-vitalist doctrine was David Karnofsky—the great tumor research scientist of the Sloan-Kettering Institute in New York. The issue about *negative* euthanasia is settled ethically.

Given modern medicine's capabilities always to do what is technically possible to prolong life would be morally indefensible on any ground other than a vitalistic outlook; that is, the opinion that biological survival is the first-order value and that all other considerations, such as personality, dignity, well-being, and self-possession, necessarily take second place. Vestigial last-ditch pro-vitalists still mumble threateningly about "what the Nazis did," but in fact the Nazis never engaged in euthanasia or mercy killing; what they did was merciless killing, either genocidal or for ruthless experimental purposes.

THE ETHICAL AND THE PRE-ETHICAL

One way of putting this is to say that the traditional ethics based on the sanctity of life—which was the classical doctrine of medical idealism in its prescientific phases—must give way to a code of ethics of the *quality* of life. This comes about for humane reasons. It is a result of modern medicine's successes, not failures. New occasions teach new duties, time makes ancient good uncouth, as Whittier said.

There are many pre-ethical or "metaethical" issues that are often overlooked in ethical discussions. People of equally good reasoning powers and a high respect for the rules of inference will still puzzle and even infuriate each other. This is because they fail to see that their moral judgments proceed from significantly different values, ideals, and starting points. If God's will (perhaps "specially revealed" in the Bible or "generally revealed" in his Creation) is against any responsible human initiative in the dying process, or if sheer life is believed to be, as such, more desirable than anything else, then those who hold these axioms will not find much merit in any case we might make for either kind of euthanasia—positive or negative. If, on the other hand, the highest good is personal integrity and human well-being, then euthanasia in either form could or might be the right thing to do, depending on the situation. This latter kind of ethics is the key to what will be said in this chapter.

Let's say it again, clearly, for the sake of truly serious ethical discourse. Many of us look upon living and dying as we do upon health and medical care, as person-centered. This is not a solely or basically biological understanding of what it means to be "alive" and to be "dead." It asserts that a so-called "vegetable," the brain-damaged victim of an auto accident or a microcephalic newborn or a case of massive neurologic deficit and lost cerebral capacity, who nevertheless goes on breathing and whose mid-brain or brain stem continues to support spontaneous organ functions, is in such a situation no longer a human being, no longer a person, no longer really alive. It is *personal* function that counts, not biological function. Humanness is understood as primarily rational, not physiological. This "doctrine of man" puts the *homo* and *ratio* before the *vita*. It holds that being human is more "valuable" than being alive.

All of this is said just to make it clear from the outset that biomedical progress is forcing us, whether we welcome it or not, to make fundamental *conceptual* changes as well as scientific and medical changes. Not only are the conditions of life and death changing, because of our greater control and in consequence our greater decision-making responsibility; our *definitions* of life and death also have to change to keep pace with the new realities.

These changes are signaled in a famous surgeon's remark recently: "When the brain is gone there is no point in keeping anything else going." What he meant was that with an end of cerebration, i.e., the function of the cerebral cortex, the *person* is gone (dead) no matter how many other spontaneous or artificially supported functions persist in the heart, lungs, and vascular system.[1] Such noncerebral processes might as well be turned off, whether they are natural or artificial.

This conclusion is of great philosophical and religious interest because it reaffirms the ancient Christian-European belief that the core of humanness, of the *humanum,* lies in the *ratio*—man's rational faculty. It is not the loss of brain functions in general but of cerebral function (the synthesizing "mind") in particular that establishes that death has ensued.

Using the old conventional conceptual apparatus, we naturally thought about both life and death as events, not as processes, which, of course, they are. We supposed that these events or episodes depended on the accidents of "nature" or on some kind of special providence. It is therefore no surprise to hear people grumbling that a lot of the decision making that has to be carried out in modern medical care is "playing God." And given that way of thinking the only possible answer to the charge is to accept it: "Yes, we *are* playing God." But the real question is: Which or whose God are we playing?

The old God who was believed to have a monopoly control of birth and death, allowing for no human responsibility in either initiating or terminating a life, was a primitive "God of the gaps"—a mysterious and awesome deity who filled in the gaps of our knowledge and of the control which our knowledge gives us. "He" was, so to speak, an hypothecation of human ignorance and helplessness.

In their growing up spiritually, men are now turning to a God who is the creative principle behind things, who is behind the test tube as much as the earthquake and volcano. This God can be believed in, but the old God's sacralistic inhibitions on human freedom and research can no longer be submitted to.

[1] The "brain death" definition of the Harvard Medical School's *ad hoc* committee is far too imprecise, effecting no real difference from the traditional clinical definition. The recent Kansas statute (Ann. Supp., 77–262, 1971) which is based upon it changes nothing since it requires absence of *brain* function, whereas what is definitive is cerebration, not just any or all brain functions regardless of whether they are contributory to personal quality.

We must rid ourselves of that obsolete theodicy according to which God is not only the cause but also the builder of nature and its works, and not only the builder but even the manager. On this archaic basis it would be God himself who is the efficient as well as the final cause of earthquake and fire, of life and death, and by logical inference any "interference with nature" (which is exactly what medicine is) is "playing God." That God, seriously speaking, is dead.

ELECTIVE DEATH

Most of our major moral problems are posed by scientific discoveries and by the subsequent technical know-how we gain, in the control of life and health and death. Ethical questions jump out at us from every laboratory and clinic. May we exercise these controls at all, we wonder—and if so, then when, where, how? Every advance in medical capabilities is an increase in our moral responsibility, a widening of the range of our decision-making obligations.

Genetics, molecular biology, fetology, and obstetrics have developed to a point where we now have effective control over the start of human life's continuum. And therefore from now on it would be irresponsible to leave baby-making to mere chance and impulse, as we once *had* to do. Modern men are trying to face up in a mature way to our emerging needs of quality control—medically, ecologically, legally, socially.

What has taken place in birth control is equally imperative in death control. The whole armory of resuscitation and prolongation of life forces us to be responsible decision makers about death as much as about birth; there must be quality control in the terminating of life as in its initiating. It is ridiculous to give ethical approval to the positive ending of subhuman life in utero, as we do in therapeutic abortions for reasons of mercy and compassion, but refuse to approve of positively ending a subhuman life in extremis. If we are morally obliged to put an end to a pregnancy when an amniocentesis reveals a terribly defective fetus, we are equally obliged to put an end to a patient's hopeless misery when a brain scan reveals that a patient with cancer has advanced brain metastases.

Furthermore, as I shall shortly expalin, it is morally evasive

and disingenuous to suppose that we can condemn or disapprove
positive acts of care and compassion but in spite of that approve
negative strategies to achieve exactly the same purpose. This contradiction has equal force whether the euthanasia comes at the fetal
point on life's spectrum or at some terminal point post-natally.

Only man is aware of death. Animals know pain, and fear it,
but not death. Furthermore, in humans the ability to meet death
and even to regard it sometimes as a friend is a sign of manliness.
But in the new patterns of medicine and health care patients tend
to die in a moribund or comatose state, so that death comes without the patient's knowledge. The Elizabethan litany's petition,
". . . from sudden death, good Lord, deliver us," has become irrelevant much if not most of the time.

It is because of this "incompetent" condition of so many of the
dying that we cannot discuss the ethical issues of elective death only
in the narrow terms of voluntary, patient-chosen euthanasia. A
careful typology of elective death will distinguish at least *four* forms
—ways of dying which are not merely willy-nilly matters of blind
chance but of choice, purpose, and responsible freedom (historical
ethics and moral theology are obviously major sources of suggestion
for these distinctions) :

(1) Euthanasia, or a "good death," can be *voluntary and direct,*
i.e., chosen and carried out by the patient. The most familiar way
is the overdose left near at hand for the patient. It is a matter of
simple request and of personal liberty. If it can be held in the abortion debate that compulsory pregnancy is unjust and that women
should be free to control their own bodies when other's lives (fetuses)
are at stake, do not the same moral claims apply to control of the
lives and bodies of people too? In any particular case we might
properly raise the question of the patient's competence, but to hold
that euthanasia in this category is justifiable entails a rejection of
the simplistic canard that all suicide victims are mentally disordered.

Voluntary euthanasia is, of course, a form of suicide. Presumably a related issue arises around the conventional notion of
consent in medical ethics. The codes (American Medical Association, Helsinki, World Medical Association, Nuremberg) all contend
that valid consent to any surgery or treatment requires a reasonable
prospect of benefit to the patient. What, then, is benefit? Could
death in some situations be a benefit? My own answer is in the
affirmative.

(2) Euthanasia can be *voluntary but indirect*. The choice might be made either in situ or long in advance of a terminal illness, e.g., by exacting a promise that if and when the "bare bodkin" or potion cannot be self-administered somebody will do it for the patient. In this case the patient gives to others—physicians, lawyers, family, friends—the discretion to end it all as and when the situation requires, if the patient becomes comatose or too dysfunctioned to make the decision pro forma. There is already a form called the Living Will, sent upon request to thousands by the Euthanasia Educational Fund (although its language appears to limit it to merely negative methods). This perfectly reasonable "insurance" device is being explored by more and more people, as medical prolongation of life tends to make them more afraid of senescence than of death.

Since both the common law tradition and statute law are caught practically unequipped to deal with this medical-legal lag, the problem is being examined worriedly and behind the scenes by lawyers and legislators. They have little or no case law to work with. As things stand now the medieval outlook of the law treats self-administered euthanasia as suicide and when effected by a helping hand as murder.

(3) Euthanasia may be *direct but involuntary*. This is the form in which a simple "mercy killing" is done on a patient's behalf without his present or past request. Instances would be when an idiot is given a fatal dose or the death of a child in the worst stages of Tay-Sachs disease is speeded up, or when a man trapped inextricably in a blazing fire is shot to end his suffering, or a shutdown is ordered on a patient deep in a mindless condition, irreversibly, perhaps due to an injury or an infection or some biological breakdown. It is in this form, as directly involuntary, that the problem has reached the courts in legal charges and indictments.

To my knowledge Uruguay is the only country that allows it. Article 37 of the *Codiga Penal* specifically states that although it is a "crime" the courts are authorized to forego any penalty. In time the world will follow suit. Laws in Colombia and in the Soviet Union (Article 50 of the Code of Criminal Procedure) are similar to Uruguay's, but in their codes freedom from punishment is exceptional rather than normative. In Italy, Germany, and Switzerland the law provides for a reduction of penalties when it is done upon the patient's request.

The conflict and tension between the stubborn prohibitionism on the one hand and a humane compassion on the other may be seen in the legal history of the issue in the United States. Eleven cases of "mercy killing" have actually reached the courts: one was on a charge of voluntary manslaughter, with a conviction and penalty of three to six years in prison and a $500 fine; one was for first-degree murder, resulting in a conviction, which was promptly reduced to a penalty of six years in jail with immediate parole. All of the other nine cases were twisted into "temporary insanity" or no-proof judgments—in short, no convictions.

(4) Finally, euthanasia might be *both indirect and involuntary*. This is the "letting the patient go" tactic which is taking place every day in our hospitals. Nothing is done for the patient positively to release him from his tragic condition (other than "trying to make him comfortable"), and what is done negatively is decided *for* him rather than in response to his request.

As we all know, even this passive policy of compassion is a grudging one, done perforce. Even so, it remains at least theoretically vulnerable to malpractice suits under the lagging law—brought, possibly, by angry or venal members of the family or suit-happy lawyers. A sign of the times was the bill to give negative euthanasia a legal basis in Florida, introduced by a physician member of the legislature.

But *ethically* regarded, this indirect-involuntary form of euthanasia is manifestly superficial, morally timid, and evasive of the real issue. I repeat: it is harder morally to justify letting somebody die a slow and ugly death, dehumanized, than it is to justify *helping* him to avoid it.

MEANS AND ENDS

What, then, is the real issue? In a few words, it is whether we can morally justify taking it into our own hands to hasten death for ourselves (suicide) or for others (mercy killing) out of reasons of compassion. The answer to this in my view is clearly Yes, on both sides of it. Indeed, *to justify either one, suicide or mercy killing, is to justify the other*.

The heart of the matter analytically is the question of whether the end justifies the means. If the end sought is the patient's death as a release from pointless misery and dehumanization, then the requisite or appropriate means is justified. Immanuel Kant said that if we will the end we will the means. The old maxim of some moral theologians was *finis sanctificat media*. The point is that no act is anything but random and *meaningless* unless it is purposefully related to some end or object. To be moral an act must be seeking an end.

However, to hold that the end justifies the means does not entail the absurd notion that *any* means can be justified by *any* end. The priority of the end is paired with the principle of "proportionate good"; any disvalue in the means must be outweighed by the value gained in the end. In systems analysis, with its pragmatic approach, the language would be: the benefit must repay the cost or the trade-off is not justified. It comes down to this, that in some situations a morally good end can justify a relatively "bad" means, on the principle of proportionate good.

The really searching question of conscience is, therefore, whether we are right in believing that *the well-being of persons* is the highest good. If so, then it follows that either suicide or mercy killing could be the right thing to do in some exigent and tragic circumstances. This could be the case, for instance, when an incorrigible "human vegetable," whether spontaneously functioning or artificially supported, is progressively degraded while constantly eating up private or public financial resources in violation of the distributive justice owed to others. In such cases the patient is actually already departed and only his body is left, and the needs of others have a stronger claim upon us morally. The fair allocation of scarce resources is as profound an ethical obligation as any we can imagine in a civilized society, and it arises very practically at the clinical level when triage officers make their decisions at the expense of some patients' needs in favor of others.

Another way of putting this is to say that the crucial question is not whether the end justifies the means (what else could?) but *what justifies the end?* And this chapter's answer is, plainly and confidently, that human happiness and well-being is the highest good or *summum bonum,* and that therefore any ends or purposes which that standard or ideal validates are just, right, good. This is what humanistic medicine is all about; it is what the concepts of loving concern and social justice are built upon.

This position comes down to the belief that our moral acts, including suicide and mercy killing, are right or wrong depending on the consequences aimed at (we sometimes fail, of course, through ignorance or poor reasoning), and that the consequences are good or evil according to whether and how much they serve humane values. In the language of ethics this is called a "consequential" method of moral judgment.

I believe that this code of ethics is both implicit and explicit in the morality of medical care and biomedical research. Its reasoning is inductive, not deductive, and it proceeds empirically from the data of each actual case or problem, choosing the course that offers an optimum or maximum of desirable consequences. Medicine is not a-prioristic or *prejudiced* in its ethos and modalities, and therefore to proscribe either suicide or mercy killing is so blatantly nonconsequential that it calls for critical scrutiny. It fails to make sense. It is unclinical and doctrinaire.

The problem exists because there is another kind of ethics, radically different from consequential ethics. This other kind of ethics holds that our actions are right or wrong according to whether they follow universal rules of conduct and absolute norms: that we ought or ought not to do certain things no matter how good or bad the consequences might be foreseeably. Such rules are usually prohibitions or taboos, expressed as thou-shalt-nots. Whereas this chapter's ethics is teleological or end-oriented, the opposite approach is "deontological" (from the Greek *deonteis,* meaning duty); i.e., it is duty-ethics, not goal-ethics. Its advocates sometimes sneer at any determination of obligation in terms of consequences, calling it "a mere morality of goals."

In duty-ethics what is right is whatever act obeys or adheres to the rules, even though the foreseeable result will be inhumane. That is, its highest good is not human happiness and well-being but obedience to a rule—or what we might call a prejudiced or predetermined decision based not on the clinical variables but on some transcending generality.

For example, the fifth of the Ten Commandments, which prohibits killing, is a no-no rule for nonconsequentialists when it comes to killing in the service of humane values like mercy and compassion, and yet at the same time they ignore their "moral law" when it comes to self-defense. The egocentricity and solipsism in this moral posture, which is a very common one, never ceases to bemuse consequentialists. You may end your neighbor's life for your own sake but you may not do it for his sake! And you may end your own life for your neighbor's sake, as in an act of sacrificial heroism, but you may not end your life for your own sake. This is a veritable mare's nest of nonsense!

The plain hard logic of it is that the end or purpose of both negative and positive euthanasia is exactly the same: to contrive or bring about the patient's death. Acts of deliberate omission are morally not different from acts of commission. But in the Anglo-American *law,* it is a crime to push a blind man off the cliff. It is not, however, a crime to deliberately not lift a finger to prevent his walking over the edge. This is an unpleasant feature of legal reasoning which is alien to ethics and to a sensitive conscience. Ashamed of it, even the courts fall back on such legal fictions as "insanity" in euthanasia cases, and this has the predictable effect of undermining our respect for the law.

There is something obviously evasive when we rule motive out in charging people with the crime of mercy killing, but then bring it back in again for purposes of determining punishment! It is also a menacing delimitation of the concepts of culpability, responsibility, and negligence. No *ethically* disciplined decision maker could so blandly separate right and wrong from motives, foresight, and consequences. (Be it noted, however, that motive is taken into account in German and Swiss law, and that several European countries provide for recognition of "homicide when requested" as a special category.)

It is naïve and superficial to suppose that because we don't "do anything positively" to hasten a patient's death we have thereby avoided complicity in his death. Not doing anything is doing something; it is a decision to act every bit as much as deciding for any other deed. If I decide not to eat or drink any more, knowing what the consequence will be, I have committed suicide as surely as if I had used a gas oven. If physicians decide not to open an imperforate anus in a severely 21-trisomy newborn, they have committed mercy killing as surely as if they had used a poison pellet!

Let the reader at this point now ask himself if he is a consequentialist or an a priori decision maker; and again, let him ask himself if he is a humanist, religious or secular, or alternatively has something he holds to be better or more obliging than the well-being of the patient. (Thoughtless religious people will sometimes point out that we are required to love God as well as our neighbors, but can the two loves ever come into conflict? Actually, is there any way to love God other than through the neighbor? Only mystics imagine that they can love God directly and discretely.)

Occasionally I hear a physician say that he could not resort to positive euthanasia. That may be so. What anybody would do in such tragic situations is a problem in psychology, however, not in ethics. We are not asking what we would do but what we should do. Any of us who has an intimate knowledge of what happens in terminal illnesses can tell stories of rational people—both physicians and family—who were quite clear ethically about the rightness of an overdose or of "turning off the machine," and yet found themselves too inhibited to give the word or do the deed. That is a phenomenon of primary interest to psychology, but of only incidental interest to ethics.

Careful study of the best texts of the Hippocratic Oath shows that it says nothing at all about preserving life, as such. It says that "so far as power and discernment shall be mine, I will carry out regimen for the benefit of the sick and will keep them from harm and wrong." The case for euthanasia depends upon how we understand "benefit of the sick" and "harm" and "wrong." If we regard dehumanized and merely biological life as sometimes real harm and the opposite of benefit, to refuse to welcome or even introduce death would be quite wrong morally.

In most states in this country people can and do carry cards, legally established (by Anatomical Gift Acts), which explain the carrier's wish that when he dies his organs and tissue should be used for transplant when needed by the living. The day will come when people will also be able to carry a card, notarized and legally executed, which explains that they do not want to be kept alive beyond the *humanum* point, and authorizing the ending of their biological processes by any of the methods of euthanasia which seems appropriate. Suicide may or may not be the ultimate problem of philosophy, as Albert Camus thought it is, but in any case it is the ultimate problem of medical ethics.

DILEMMAS OF "INFORMED CONSENT" IN CHILDREN

Anthony Shaw, M.D.

An obscure and difficult aspect of the law and the medical profession has to do with the medical care of infants who can have no part in the decisions affecting their life and death. Dr. Shaw presents a series of cases, mostly from his own practice, in which the dilemmas of euthanasia in child care are especially complicated.

Anthony Shaw is a member of the Pediatric Surgery Division of the Department of Surgery, University of Virginia Medical Center.

This article is taken from the New England Journal of Medicine, *volume 289, October 25, 1973.*

Numerous articles have been written about "rights" of patients. We read about "right to life" of the unborn, "right to die," of the elderly, "Bill of Rights" for the hospitalized, "Declaration of Rights" for the retarded, "right of Privacy" for the pregnant and, of course, "right to medical care" for us all.

Whatever the legitimacy of these sometimes conflicting "rights" there is at present general agreement that patients have at least one legal right: that of "informed consent"—i.e., when a decision about medical treatment is made, they are entitled to a full explanation by their physicians of the nature of the proposed treatment, its risks and its limitations. Once the physician has discharged his obligation fully to inform an adult, mentally competent patient, that patient may then accept or reject the proposed treatment, or, indeed, may refuse any and all treatment, as he sees fit. But if the patient is a minor, a parental decision rejecting recommended treatment is subject to review when physicians or society disagree with that decision.

The purpose of this paper is to consider some of the moral and ethical dilemmas that may arise in the area of "informed consent" when the patient is a minor. The following case reports, all but two from my practice of pediatric surgery, raise questions about the rights and obligations of physicians, parents and society in situations in which parents decide to withhold consent for treatment of their children.

Instead of presenting a full discussion of these cases at the end of the paper, I have followed each case presentation with a comment discussing the points I wish to make, the issues raised by that case to those raised in some of the other cases, and posing the very hard questions that I had to ask myself in dealing with the patients and parents. At present the questions are coming along much faster than the answers.

CASE REPORTS

A. Baby A was referred to me at 22 hours of age with a diagnosis of esophageal atresia and tracheoesophageal fistula. The infant, the firstborn of a professional couple in their early thirties, had obvious signs of mongolism, about which they were fully informed by the referring physician. After explaining the nature of the surgery to the distraught father, I offered him the operative consent. His pen hesitated briefly above the form and then as he signed, he muttered, "I have no choice, do I?" He didn't seem to expect an answer, and I gave him none. The esophageal anomaly was corrected in routine fashion, and the infant was discharged to a state institution for the retarded without ever being seen again by either parent.

Comment

In my opinion, this case was mishandled from the point of view of Baby A's family, in that consent was not truly informed. The answer to Mr. A's question should have been, "You *do* have a choice. You might want to consider not signing the operative consent at all." Although some of my surgical colleagues believe that there is no alternative to attempting to save the life of every infant, no matter what his potential, in my opinion, the doctrine of informed consent should, under some circumstances, include the right to withhold consent. If the parents do have the right to withhold consent for surgery in a case such as Baby A, who should take the responsibility for pointing that fact out to them—the obstetrician, the pediatrician or the surgeon?

Another question raised by this case lies in the parents' responsibility toward their baby, who has been saved by their own decision to allow surgery. Should they be obligated to provide a home for the infant? If their intention is to place the baby after operation in a state-funded institution, should the initial decision regarding medical or surgical treatment for their infant be theirs alone?

B. Baby B was referred at the age of 36 hours with duodenal obstruction and signs of Down's syndrome. His young parents had a 10-year-old daughter, and he was the son they had been trying to have for 10 years; yet, when they were approached with the operative consent, they hesitated. They wanted to know beyond any doubt whether the baby had Down's syndrome. If so, they wanted time to consider whether or not to permit the surgery to be done. Within 8 hours a geneticist was able to identify cells containing 47 chromosomes in a bone-marrow sample. Over the next 3 days the infant's gastrointestinal tract was decompressed with a nasogastric tube, and he was supported with intravenous fluids while the parents consulted with their ministers, with family physicians in their home community and with our geneticists. At the end of that time the B's decided not to permit surgery. The infant died 3 days later after withdrawal of supportive therapy.

Comment

Unlike the parents of Baby A, Mr. and Mrs. B realized that they did have a choice—to consent or not to consent to the intestinal surgery. They were afforded access to a wide range of resources to help them make an informed decision. The infant's deterioration was temporarily prevented by adequate intestinal decompression and intravenous fluids.

Again, some of the same questions are raised here as with Baby A. Do the parents have the right to make the decision to allow their baby to die without surgery?

Can the parents make a reasonable decision within hours or days after the birth of a retarded or brain-damaged infant? During that time they are overwhelmed by feelings of shock, fear, guilt, horror and shame. What is the proper role of the medical staff and the hospital administration? Can parents make an intelligent decision under these circumstances, or are they simply reacting to a combination of their own instincts and fears as well as to the opinions and biases of medical staff? Rickham[1] has described the interaction of physician and parents:

> Every conscientious doctor will, of course, give as correct a prognosis and as impartial an opinion about the possible future of the child as he can, but he will not be able to be wholly impartial, and, whether he wants it or not, his opinion will influence the parents. At the end it is usually the doctor who has to decide the issue. It is not only cruel to ask the parents whether they want their child to live or die, it is dishonest, because in the vast majority of cases, the parents are consciously or unconsciously influenced by the doctor's opinion.

I believe that parents often *can* make an informed decision if, like the B's, they are afforded access to a range of resources beyond the expertise and bias of a single doctor and afforded sufficient time for contemplation of the alternatives. Once the parents have made a decision, should members of the medical staff support them in their decision regardless of their own feelings? (This support may be important to assuage recurrent feelings of guilt for months or even years after the parents' decision.)

When nutritional and fluid support was withdrawn, intestinal intubation and pain medication were provided to prevent suffering. To what extent should palliative treatment be given in a case in which definitive treatment is withheld? The lingering death of a newborn infant whose parents have denied consent for surgery can have a disastrous effect on hospital personnel, as illustrated last year by the well publicized Johns Hopkins Hospital case, which raised a national storm of controversy. In this case, involving an infant with mongoloidism and duodenal atresia, several of the infant's physicians violently disagreed with the parents' decision not to allow surgey. The baby's lingering death (15 days) severely demoralized the nursing and house staffs. In addition, it prolonged the agony for the parents, who called daily to find out if the baby was still alive. Colleagues of mine who have continued to keep such infants on gastrointestinal decompression and intravenous fluids for weeks after the parents have decided against surgery have told me

[1] P. P. Rickham, *The Ethics of Surgery on Newborn Infants, Clin. Pediats.,* 8: 251–53, 1969.

of several cases in which the parents have finally changed their minds and given the surgeon a green light! Does such a change of heart represent a more deliberative decision on the part of the parents or merely their capitulation on the basis of emotional fatigue?

After the sensationalized case in Baltimore, Johns Hopkins Hospital established a committee to work with physicians and parents who are confronted by similar problems. Do such medical-ethics committees serve as a useful resource for physicians and families, or do they, in fact, further complicate the decision-making process by multiplying the number of opinions?

Finally, should a decision to withhold surgery on an infant with Down's syndrome or other genetically determined mental-retardation states be allowed on clinical grounds only, without clear-cut chromosomal evidence?

> C. I was called to the Newborn Nursery to see Baby C, whose father was a busy surgeon with 3 teen-age children. The diagnoses of imperforate anus and microcephalus were obvious. Doctor C called me after being informed of the situation by the pediatrician. "I'm not going to sign that op permit," he said. When I didn't reply, he said, "What would you do, doctor, if he were your baby?" "I wouldn't let him be operated on either," I replied. Palliative support only was provided, and the infant died 48 hours later.

Comment

Doctor C asked me bluntly what I would do were it my baby, and I gave him my answer. Was my response appropriate? In this case I simply reinforced his own decision. Suppose he had asked me for my opinion before expressing his own inclination? Should my answer in any case have simply been, "It's not my baby"—with a refusal to discuss the subject further? Should I have insisted that he take more time to think about it and discuss it further with his family and clergy, like the parents of Baby B? Is there a moral difference between withholding surgery on a baby with microcephalus and withholding surgery on a baby with Down's syndrome?

Some who think that all children with mongolism should be salvaged since many of them are trainable, would not dispute a decision to allow a baby with less potential such as microcephalic Baby C to die. Should, then, decisions about life and death be made on the basis of IQ? In a recent article,[2] Professor Joseph Fletcher outlined criteria for what he calls "humanhood"—minimal standards by which we could judge whether a living organism is or is not a human being. These criteria (further defined in Dr. Fletcher's article) include minimal intelligence, self-awareness, self-control, a sense of time, a sense of futurity, a sense of the past, the capability to relate to others, concern for others, communication, control of existence, curiosity, change and changeability, balance of rationality and feeling, idiosyncrasy and neocortical function. Dr. Fletcher also offers a shorter list of what a human being is not. By trying to arrive at a definition of what we call "human," Doctor Fletcher has, of course, stirred up a hornet's nest. But in so doing, he is not laying down a set of rigid standards but is issuing a challenge that should be a particularly attractive one to the medical profession. Is it possible that physicians and philosophers can agree on a "profile of man" that might afford more rational grounds for approaching problems in biomedical ethics?

D. In 1972 I wrote in a piece published by the New York Times, "Parents of mongoloids have the legal (and, I believe, the moral) responsibility of determining if their child with a potentially deadly but surgically correctable defect should live or die." After reading this article, Mr. D called me for advice concerning his 2-week-old grandson. This infant had been born in a New York hospital with Down's syndrome and with bilateral hydroureteronephrosis secondary to urethral valves, for the correction of which the family had refused surgery. Since the infant was becoming increasingly uremic, the family was being strongly pressured by the medical staff to consent to surgery. After an absolute refusal to sign, the family was ordered to take the infant home immediately despite the wish for the baby to die in the hospital. At my last conversation with the infant's grandfather, the family and the hospital had reached an impasse about discharge and the infant was dying slowly of uremis.

Comment

In threatening to discharge the dying infant, the medical staff was trying to coerce the family into signing consent for surgery.

[2] J. F. Fletcher. *Indications of Humanhood: a tentative profile of man.* The Hastings Center Report, vol. 2, no. 5, Hastings-on-Hudson, New York, Institute of Society, Ethics, and Life Sciences, November 1972, pp. 1–4.

Aside from the issue of coercion here, is providing facilities for dying patients a proper role for a hospital? The parents refused to take the infant home because of the devastating emotional impact that the dying baby would have on the entire family. The hospital wanted to discharge the infant partly because of the devastating emotional impact that the dying infant was having on the hospital staff. Can we prepare hospital, medical and paramedical personnel to accept the death of infants under these circumstances without the destruction of morale? Can we realistically expect hospital staff to be able to make such an emotional accommodation no matter how they view the situation from an intellectual standpoint? Finally, if the decision is not to operate, where does one draw the line between palliation of the infant's suffering and active shortening of the infant's life? This, of course, is one of the areas where the question of euthanasia has been raised. To my knowledge, the question of whether Baby D died at home or in the hospital finally became a legal matter to be resolved between the hospital's legal counsel and the family's attorney.

If the medical staff felt strongly that allowing Baby D to die for lack of simple surgery was immoral, why did they not obtain a court order permitting them to operate?

E. A court order *was* obtained for Baby E who was "reported" in Life Magazine 2 years ago. This infant, with Down's syndrome, intestinal obstruction and congenital heart disease, was born in her mother's car on the way to the hospital. The mother thought that the retarded infant would be impossible for her to care for and would have a destructive effect on her already shaky marriage. She therefore refused to sign permission for intestinal surgery, but a local child-welfare agency, invoking the state child-abuse statute, was able to obtain a court order directing surgery to be performed. After a complicated course and thousands of dollars worth of care, the infant was returned to the mother. The baby's continued growth and development remained markedly retarded because of her severe cardiac disease. A year and a half after the baby's birth, the mother felt more than ever that she had been done a severe injustice.

Comment

Is the crux of this case parental rights versus the child's right to life? Can the issue in this case be viewed as an extension of the basic dilemma in the abortion question? Does this case represent proper application of child-abuse legislation—i.e., does the parents' refusal to consent to surgery constitute neglect as defined in child-abuse statutes? If so, under these statutes does a physician's concurrence in a parental decision to withhold treatment constitute failure to report neglect, thereby subjecting him to possible prosecution?

Baby E's mother voluntarily took the baby home, but had she not done so, could the state have forced her to take the baby? Could the state have required her husband to contribute to the cost of medical care and to the subsequent maintenance of the infant in a foster home or institution?

If society decides that the attempt must be made to salvage every human life, then, as I have written, ". . . society *must* provide the necessary funds and facilities to meet the continuing medical and psychological needs of these unfortunate children."[3]

> F. Baby F was conceived as the result of an extramarital relation. Mrs. F had sought an abortion, which she had been denied. F was born prematurely, weighing 1600 g and in all respects normal except for the presence of esophageal atresia and tracheoesophageal fistula. Mrs. F signed the operative consent, and the surgery was performed uneventfully. Mrs. F fears that her husband will eventually realize that the baby is not his and that her marriage may collapse as a result of this discovery.

Comment

Like those of Mrs. E, Mrs. F's reasons for not wanting her baby were primarily psychosocial. However, Mrs. F never raised the question of withholding consent for surgery even though the survival of her infant might mean destruction of her marriage. Does the presence of mental retardation or severe physical malformation justify withholding of consent for psychosocial reasons (Babies B, C, D and E), whereas the absence of such conditions does not (Baby F)? If she had decided to withhold consent there is no doubt in my mind that I would have obtained a court order to operate on this baby, who appeared to be normal beyond her esophageal anomaly. Although I personally would not have objected to an abortion in this situation for the sociopsychologic reasons, I would not allow an otherwise normal baby with a correctable anomaly to

[3] A. Shaw, "Doctor, Do we have a choice?" *New York Times Magazine,* January 30, 1972, pp. 44–54.

perish for lack of treatment for the same reasons. Although those who believe that all life is sacred, no matter what its level of development, will severely criticize me for the apparent inconsistency of this position, I believe it to be a realistic and humane approach to a situation in which no solution is ideal.

Although my case histories thus far have dealt with the forms of mental retardation most common in my practice, similar dilemmas are encountered by other physicians in different specialties, the most obvious being in the spectrum of hydrocephalus and meningomyelocele. Neurosurgeons are still grappling unsuccessfully and inconsistently with indications for surgery in this group, trying to fit together what is practical, what is moral, and what is humane. If neurosurgeons disagree violently over criteria for operability on infants with meningomyelocele, how can the parents of such a child decide whether to sign for consent? Who would say that they *must* sign if they don't want a child whose days will be measured by operations, clinic visits and infections? I have intentionally omitted from discussion in this paper the infant with crippling deformities and multiple anomalies who does not have rapidly lethal lesions. Infants with such lesions may survive for long periods and may require palliative procedures such as release of limb contractures, ventriculoperitoneal shunts, or colostomies to make their lives more tolerable or to simplify their management. The extent to which these measures are desirable or justifiable moves us into an even more controversial area.

I must also point out that the infants discussed in the preceding case reports represent but a small percentage of the total number of infants with mental-retardation syndromes on whom I have operated. Once the usual decision to operate has been made, I, of course, apply the same efforts as I would to any other child.

G. Six-year-old boy G was referred to me because of increasing shortness of breath due to a large mediastinal mass. The parents had refused diagnostic procedures and recommended treatment until the child had become cachectic and severely dyspneic. His liver was enlarged. A thorough in-hospital work-up, including liver biopsy, bone-marrow aspiration, thoracentesis and mediastinal tomography failed to establish a diagnosis. The child was obviously dying of progressive compromise of his respiratory tract and vena-cava obstruction. His family belonged to a fundamentalist religious sect and firmly believed that the child would be healed by God. They refused to sign permission for exploratory thoracotomy. We spent 2 weeks trying to convince them that, although the boy's chances were slim in any case, his only hope lay in the possibility of our encountering a resectable tumor. When the parents refused to sign permission for surgery, a court order was obtained from the Juvenile Court Judge permitting surgery. The next day exploratory thoracotomy was carried out, and a non-resectable neuroblastoma was found. The child died a respiratory death 3 days later. Members of the family subsequently threatened the lives of the physicians and of the judge. A letter of inquiry was subsequently sent to me by their lawyer, implying an intention to sue. However, it was not followed up.

Comment

Some of the same questions are raised here as in the Jehovah's Witness cases. Does the parents' right to practice their religion include the right to deny their child medical or surgical treatment? The fact that I allowed a two-week delay before obtaining the court order indicates my strong feeling that a court order should be the last resort used to obtain parents' co-operation on behalf of their child. We persisted as long as we thought we might obtain such co-operation.

Should a court order be obtained by physicians only when they think their treatment will certainly save the child, or should they obtain an order so long as there is any possibility of helping the child? Were we justified in obtaining the court order and putting the parents and ourselves through such an ordeal when the odds against us of finding a curable lesion were so long? I believe the answer is yes. In making a decision to obtain a court order directing surgery, the physician must balance the risk for the child if surgery is withheld against the risk of surgery itself coupled with the demoralizing consequences for the family if the surgery fails. In G's case, in which his life expectancy without treatment appeared to be measurable in days, I believe that the decision to obtain a court order was appropriate.

Statutes on child abuse and neglect have on occasion been invoked to give a hospital or a physician temporary custody of a child whose parents' religion prevents lifesaving medical care. At the same time some states have worded their child-abuse statutes to avoid appearance of interfering with constitutional guarantees of freedom of religion. For example, in Virginia's child-abuse law, the following statement appears ". . . that a child who is being furnished Christian Science treatment by a duly accredited Christian Science practitioner shall not be considered for that reason alone a physically neglected child for the purposes of this section." However, the law may be invoked when, as a result of the practice of his parents' religion, a child's health can be demonstrated to be in jeopardy. For this reason, such religious exclusion clauses as the one just cited would not, in my opinion, be held applicable in G's case.

Several new questions arise when a child is an adolescent who himself refuses surgery on the basis of his sincere religious conviction. Then, one has to ask whether minors should be allowed to make life-and-death decisions about their own treatment. Should it depend on the degree of maturity of the child, or can one try to write into law an age at which a child's wishes should be seriously taken into consideration in medical decision making? In a sensitively written article Schowalter et al.[5] recently discussed the "agonizing dilemma" created for a hospital staff by a 16-year-old girl with uremia who, with her parents' consent, chose death over continued therapeutic efforts. The authors concluded that ". . . there are instances when a physician should honor an adolescent patient's wish to die." The case in point, although not terminal, had a poor prognosis. Suppose the patient had been a 16-year-old Jehovah's Witness with a ruptured spleen, who appeared to be mature and in full possession of his faculties and who, although he understood he would die without blood, refused to accept it?

H. Ten-year-old H was brought to the surgical clinic by her mother for removal of some cysts from the scalp. The family is well known to our hospital since most of its members have Gardner's syndrome and most of the senior family members either have enterostomies or have died of cancer of the gastrointestinal tract. H's mother has had rectal bleeding for the past year but has not permitted herself to be examined by a physician. She also would not permit H to have a barium-enema examination or sigmoidoscopy when this question was first raised. However, when excision of the scalp cysts was made contingent upon the mother's permitting evaluation of the child's colon, she consented. The barium-enema study and a proctosigmoidoscopy were negative. The cysts were excised. Since more cysts tend to form, we expect to be able to arrive at a regular quid pro quo that

[5] J. E. Schowalter, J. B. Ferholt, N. M. Mann, The Adolescent Patient's Decision to Die, *Pediatrics,* 51: 97–103, 1973.

will enable us to continue evaluating the child's colon until such time as the premalignant polyps are detected. We do not know what we will do if polyps begin to proliferate, making colectomy advisable before H achieves legal maturity. In all likelihood, the mother will not willingly permit us to perform major surgery on her child.

Comment

Here we found a substitute for judicial intervention. We called it "making a deal." If the mother had not consented to this bargain, would we have been justified in obtaining a court order for a diagnostic procedure? Would it not then be necessary to put the mother under long-term court supervision so that she would be forced to bring the child for regular diagnostic examinations and for resection when deemed necessary? It seems to me that such judicial intervention is proper when one is dealing with a potentially lethal condition in a young child and would be, I believe, fully sanctioned by the child-neglect laws of most states. Note that there is no question of religious freedom involved here. Should court orders also be sought in situations in which parents refuse treatment for children with diseases or deformities that, if untreated, will result in permanent physical or emotional damage but not death?

DISCUSSION

If an underlying philosophy can be gleaned from the vignettes presented above, I hope it is one that tries to find a solution, humane and loving, based on the circumstances of each case rather than by means of a dogmatic formula approach. (Fletcher has best expressed this philosophy in his book, Situation Ethics,[6] and in subsequent articles.[7]) This outlook contrasts sharply with the rigid "right-to-life" philosophy, which categorically opposes abortion, for example. My ethic holds that all rights are not absolute all the time. As Fletcher point out, ". . . all rights are imperfect and may be set aside if human *need* requires it." My ethic further considers quality of life as a value that must be balanced against a belief in the sanctity of life.

[6] J. F. Fletcher, *Situation Ethics: The New Morality,* Philadelphia, Westminster Press, 1966.
[7] *Idem: Ethical Aspects of Genetic Controls: Designed Genetic Changes in Man,* N. Engl. J. Med., 285: 776–783, 1971.

Those who believe that the sanctity of life is the overriding consideration in all cases have a relatively easy time making decisions. They say that all babies must be saved; no life may be aborted from the womb, and all attempts to salvage newborn life, whatever its quality and whatever its human and financial costs to family and society, must be made. Although many philosophies express the view that "heroic" efforts need not be made to save or prolong life, yesterday's heroic efforts are today's routine procedures. Thus, each year it becomes possible to remove yet another type of malformation from the "unsalvageable" category. All pediatric surgeons, including myself, have "triumphs"—infants who, if they had been born 25 or even five years ago, would not have been salvageable. Now with our team approaches, staged surgical technics, monitoring capabilities, ventilatory support systems and intravenous hyperalimentation and elemental diets, we can wind up with "viable" children three and four years old well below the third percentile in height and weight, propped up on a pillow, marginally tolerating an oral diet of sugar and amino acids and looking forward to another operation.

Or how about the infant whose gastrointestinal tract has been removed after volvulus and infarction? Although none of us regard the insertion of a central venous catheter as a "heroic" procedure, is it right to insert a "lifeline" to feed this baby in the light of our present technology, which can support him, tethered to an infusion pump, for a maximum of a year and some months?

Who should make these decisions? The doctors? The parents? Clergymen? A committee? As I have pointed out, I think that the parents must participate in any decision about treatment and that they must be fully informed of the consequences of consenting and of withholding consent. This is a type of informed consent that goes far beyond the traditional presentation of possible complications of surgery, length of hospitalization, cost of the operation, time lost from work, and so on.

It may be impossible for any general agreement or guidelines for making decisions on cases such as the ones presented here to emerge, but I believe we should bring these problems out into public forum because whatever the answers may be, they should not be the result of decisions made solely by the attending physicians. Or should they?

SUICIDE

In one respect suicide is the quintessentially private act. In almost every case it seems a decision made in the hidden counsel of a deeply troubled mind, and rarely is it the result of publicly reasoned reflection. In many instances we have no clue as to what that private deliberation might have been.

One might, in fact, want to argue that the true reasons for the act are unknown even to the person who makes a serious attempt to end his or her life. They are unknown either because they are unconscious reasons, or because they have to do with impersonal factors—such as economic hardship, dismal weather, or cultural meaninglessness—that have an undetected influence on the way one thinks about one's life.

This argument would suggest that the true reasons for suicide will not be learned from anything that passes through the conscious mind of a suicidal, self-destructive person, but only from the research of the psychoanalyst and the sociologist. There are, of course, grim limitations on the amount of data available to the psychoanalyst since the successful suicide is beyond interrogation. This is not to say that the psychiatric data available from unsuccessful suicides, or from the analyst's work with persons prior to their suicide, cannot be used to compose a portrait of a suicidal personality. A book like James Hillman's *Suicide and the Soul* is a good example of this.

The unreliability of personal data and the inaccessibility of psychoanalytic data offer a strong motive for discovering any correlation between the occurrence of suicide and societal factors. Emile Durkheim's epochal book, *Suicide,* published in 1897, was the first major attempt at such a study. While Durkheim's selection and use of the data have often been challenged, the manner of his approach to the study of suicide remains a prominent model for sociological research.

The sociological approach is not altogether uncontroversial, however. There are several serious difficulties that stand in the way of such studies. To begin with, anyone who approaches suicide from the public record must develop a reliable method of determining which deaths may be correctly cited as suicide. A second difficulty lies in ascertaining which data are to be coordinated with the patterns of known suicides. Suicide statistics, for example, indicate that the suicide rate among psychiatrists is markedly higher than the rate for the general population. How are we to decide which characteristics of the psychiatric profession (if any) are related to this accelerating rate?

A third and related difficulty in making use of publicly available data in the study of suicide has to do with the importance of *predicting* suicides. There is little point, beyond mere curiosity, in studying suicide if we cannot learn who are the persons most likely to commit suicide, and when they are most likely to do so. The recent emergence of suicide prevention as a major psychiatric and social strategy attests to the importance of knowing the patterns of predictable suicidal behavior. But it is admittedly unclear how one is to move from a generalization to a specific prediction. Knowing that the rate of suicide is higher among psychiatrists, or is higher in Hungary than almost all other Western nations, does not go very far in telling us which psychiatrists, or which citizens of Hungary, will kill themselves. However, since the stakes are high, thoughtful attention is being given to such studies in the hopes of increasing the usefulness of prediction.

As to the first difficulty—knowing from the public record which cases are properly to be regarded as suicides—there are strong arguments against the reliability of the most basic data. In a recent article entitled "Producing Suicides" James L. Wilkins draws into question the usefulness of suicide statistics on a number of grounds. Among these are the following: No death will be declared a suicide unless it has been so determined by a coroner. The coroner, however, is often dependent on what the police or the attending physician report to him. Moreover, coroners are not usually trained in the methods of criminal investigation and may neglect details that are medically irrelevant but critical in determining whether death occurred by suicide. The ability of the police to note such evidence is also not always reliable. Further, there often are influences on the police and the attending physician to suppress data indicating suicide. One study shows that the coroner conducted approximately 80% of his inquiries by phone.

To these difficulties, Wilkins continues, should be added the question of intent. Can a person afflicted with serious mental illness be said to have committed suicide if he or she takes an overdose of pills? Can a known alcoholic be said to have committed suicide if his or her body was found in an automobile left running in a garage? This overlooks the more puzzling question of suicidal behavior in general. How about deaths that occur as the consequence of long-term drug abuse, alcholic consumption, or unhealthful eating habits?

Wilkins also suggests that even when the facts are not in question, there might be conflicting explanations of them. He cites the following case, described from two points of view, one assuming death by suicide, the other death by accident.

(A) A young woman was found dead in Lake Michigan. The immediate cause of death was thought to be drowning or supposed drowning. A police officer testified that the area was not one used for swimming, that it was "windy" and the water was "choppy" on the day of death, and that no one saw her enter the water. The pathological examination revealed lacerations of both wrists, made prior to death. It also reported "hesitation marks," which are superficial cuts commonly found in suicides as a result of the individual tentatively trying out the instrument. The police officer also testified that her boyfriend and her best girlfriend said she "had been very despondent for about a month," because she felt that her chances for success in her art career were restricted due to her sex.

(B) A young woman was found dead in Lake Michigan, and the immediate cause of death was thought to be drowning or supposed drowning. It was not known precisely where she entered the water.

She was single and a college student. Her father testified that, when he had gone with her to the opera about a week before her death, she said she "felt very good," and that he also thought her mental condition was good. The police officer testified that no suicide notes were found, and that she was reported to have said that "suicide was a very poor way to solve problems." She had not been under psychiatric care and was, in the officer's view, of "sound mind." She had been "in the habit of taking walks" in the area where her body was found, and had been reported by her boyfriend to be "missing" for about a week prior to her death. Her clothing was not found. The officer testified that often there were scavengers in the area who might have taken it. Her mother added that the victim was an "excellent swimmer" and thought that her daughter removed her clothing after she was in the water as a safety measure.*

Wilkins indicates that the information for both (A) and (B) were taken from the same official document. The official judgment in the case was that the victim died of "undetermined cause," thereby eliminating suicide as the cause. Wilkins comments that while both accounts make good sense the stronger argument is that she died by suicide.

The opposite view concerning suicide rates is taken by Peter Cresswell in his article, "Suicide: the Stable Rates Argument."† Cresswell assumes that the basic stability in most suicide rates largely cancels out the difficulties cited above in gathering statistics. Existing variations do not suggest any factors as unpredictable as those listed by Wilkins.

The "stability" of suicide rates does not mean that they remain the same over a period of time, but that their fluctuation demonstrates trends in one direction or another. If Cresswell is right, and we can depend on the reliability of published statistics, then we might well look in any stable rate for a "link between individual action and social and other factors supposed to influence the incidence of suicide."‡ The first selection in this section indicates briefly what some of these trends are in an international comparison of suicide rates.

The second difficulty in using publicly available data, referred to above, lies in determining which factors may be supposed to have an influence on the incidence of suicide. The second and third

---

* Wilkins, "Producing Suicides," *American Behavioral Scientist,* pp. 195f.
† *Journal of Biosocial Science* (1974) 6, 151–61.
‡ Ibid., p. 158.

articles in this section address this question in two troublesome areas: suicide among physicians and suicide among American Indians. The data collected by the authors of these studies have gone far in isolating the relevant suicidogenetic factors, however serious problems of interpretation remain. In his study of suicides among physicians, for example, Mathew Ross reports that female physicians kill themselves at a rate four times greater than that for the general female population. Where do we find the "reason" for suicide in this statistic? Is there a cultural reason, or is it simply that female physicians have a much better knowledge of and greater access to drugs? In his suggested methods of suicide prevention among physicians Ross indicates that even with our limited knowledge we are greatly assisted in designing assistance programs for the suicidally prone physician.

In their study of suicide among American Indians, Resnik and Dizmang correlate suicide rates with such factors as the enforced residence on reservations, geographical isolation, widespread unemployment, and a frequency of alcoholism. The authors indicate that when such factors are involved the methods of prevention must be ineffective unless they include an improvement of the social conditions of the American Indian in general.

If we reconsider the fact, mentioned briefly above, that suicide is the quintessentially private act, we might suppose that there is at least one extremely useful source of information into the deliberations that preceded that act: suicide notes. The use of suicide notes as a research method has been attempted by a number of suicidologists. There are, however, serious difficulties in this method Compare, for example, the following notes cited in Edwin S. Shneidman's essay, "Suicide Notes Reconsidered."

> To my wife Mary: As you know, like we've talked over before our situation, I'll always love you will all my heart and soul. It could have been so simple if you had have given me the help that you alone knew I needed.
>
> This is not an easy thing I'm about to do, but when a person makes a few mistakes and later tried to say in his own small way with a small vocabulary that he is sorry for what has happened and promises to remember what has happened and will try to make the old Bill come home again, and do his best to start all over again, and make things at home much better for all concerned, you still refuse to have me when you as well as I know that I can't do it by myself, then there's only one thing to do.

I'm sorry honey, but please believe me this is the only way out for me as long as you feel as you do—This will put you in good shape. Please always take care of Betty and tell her that her Daddy wasn't too bad a guy after all. With all the love that's in me.

Yes, Mommie, now you have your car and a lot more too, even more than you had hoped for. At least you are better off financially than you were 6 years ago. The only pitiful thing about the whole situation is the baby and the nice car that I bought with blood money. I only hope I do a good job of it. Then your troubles will be over with. I know this is what you have been hoping for a long time. I'm not crazy, I just love you too much!!!

I love you—Daddy—Goodbye forever.

Dearest darling i want you to know that you are the only one in my life i love you so much i could not do without you please forgive me i drove myself sick honey please beleave me i love you again an the baby honey don't be mean with me please I have lived fifty years since i met you, I love you—I love you. Dearest darling i love you i love you. Please don't discraminat me darling i know that i will die dont be mean with me please i love you more than you will ever know darling please an honey Tom i know don't tell Tom why his dady said good by honey. Can't stand it any more. Darling i love you. Darling i love you.

Dear Mary. I am writing you, as our Divorce is not final, and will not be till next month, so the way things stand now you are still my wife, which makes you entitled to the things which belong to me, and I want you to have them. Don't let anyone take them from you as they are yours. Please see a lawyer and get them as soon as you can. I am listing some of the things, they are: A Blue Davenport and chair, a Magic Chef Stove, a large mattress, an Electrolux cleaner, a 9 x 12 Rug redish flower design and pad. All the things listed above are all most new. Then there is my 30-30 rifle, books, typewriter, tools and a hand contract for a house in Chicago, a Savings account in Boston, Mass. Your husband, William H. Smith.

Good by Kid. You couldn't help it. Tell that brother of yours, When he gets where I'm going. I hope I'm a foreman down there. I might be able to do something for him.§

Those interested in pursuing this line of research will find a useful bibliography of studies of suicide notes in Shneidman's essay. These notes are poignant, occasionally bizarre, and often suggestive, but they offer no easily generalizable characteristics. Shneidman attempts to categorize them under different types, but the effort is uncon-

§ These are taken from Edwin S. Shneidman, "Suicide Notes Reconsidered."

vincing. We want to know much more about the circumstances, much more about the rest of the suicide's own life. It is obvious that there are many details in the notes that would look different to us if we could interview the writers of those notes at length.

The final two essays in this section were selected with these difficulties in mind. Jerome A. Motto's "The Right to Suicide" takes seriously the possibility that the suicidally prone person may not be hopelessly confused or driven by forces beyond the edge of his or her own rational control. He introduces the reader to the subtleties involved in discussing suicide with someone seriously contemplating the act and able to make clear all the reasons for committing it. If we know precisely *who* might commit suicide, and *why,* what is the appropriate response?

This line of reflection is carried further, and possibly to an extreme many persons would find unacceptable, in James Hillman's daring book, *Suicide and the Soul,* from which the last essay in this section was excerpted. Hillman, a Jungian analyst, insists strongly that suicide must be seen as a *choice*—a choice which a person makes from within. We cannot therefore come to anything like an adequate understanding of suicide, Hillman argues, by studying it from the outside. Suicide statistics tell us nothing, he suggests, nor does categorizing suicides under such terms as anomic, altruistic, political, religious, submeditated, or any number of others. This is not to say that the act of suicide is so private and subjective that we cannot understand it at all; it is rather to insist that inasmuch as suicide is an act of the soul we shall understand what it means to a person only by the sort of communication we might regard as soul to soul.

This brings Hillman to a startling conclusion. Inasmuch as medicine, the law, theology, and even society see in suicide a threat to values by which these sciences proceed, they are all opposed to suicide. Suicide ends life; therefore, medicine, which is committed to prolonging life, finds itself contradicted; both theology and the law see suicide as a variety of murder; and society views the act as directly threatening to the social fabric. But each of these approaches, Hillman argues, are from the outside, and therefore none of them has a true understanding of what the soul has chosen when one chooses to kill oneself. Therefore, the task of the analyst is simply to understand what suicide means to the psyche—and in no way must the analyst oppose the act. Indeed, the path to life is marked by the freedom of the soul to choose its own death.

SUICIDE—INTERNATIONAL COMPARISONS

The statistical table shown below, and the following analysis of the figures, are taken from the Statistical Bulletin of the Metropolitan Life Insurance Company. The table is offered here as a sample of the kind of study that can be made of mortality statistics available from the organizations cited at the bottom of the table. Other issues of the Bulletin may also be consulted for studies of mortality figures in categories other than suicide.

This article is taken from the Metropolitan Life Insurance Company Statistical Bulletin, *volume 53, August, 1972.*

A marked change has occurred during the past fifteen years in the pattern of suicide mortality in a number of countries.

Broadly speaking, suicide rates among males in the United States and Canada have risen sharply at ages under 45 but have declined at ages 45 and older. In Western Europe the increases in suicide rates reported for males at the younger ages have been much smaller, as have been the decreases at the older ages. Despite these differences, suicide rates among males in the United States continue to run below those in Western Europe, except for Norway, the Netherlands, the United Kingdom, and Ireland. Suicide rates among females in the United States have risen even more sharply than for males at ages under 65, whereas in the more industrialized countries of Western Europe (United Kingdom, Belgium, France, Germany, and Switzerland) the corresponding suicide rates have generally either declined or exhibited little change. Despite their recent uptrend, suicide rates among females in the United States remain quite low as compared with those in Western Europe, with only Norway and Scotland reporting lower rates.

Between 1956–57 and 1966–67, the latest years for which detailed figures are available, suicide rates among young men rose

MORTALITY FROM SUICIDE, AGES 15 AND OVER
United States, Canada, and Selected Countries, 1956–57 and 1966–67

Average Annual Death Rate* per 100,000

Country	Male								Female							
	1956–57				1966–67				1956–57				1966–67			
	15–24	25–44	45–64	65 and Over	15–24	25–44	45–64	65 and Over	15–24	25–44	45–64	65 and Over	15–24	25–44	45–64	65 and Over
United States																
White	6.4	16.0	34.2	50.0	10.4	20.0	32.9	40.3	1.9	5.8	9.6	8.4	3.3	9.5	12.5	9.0
Nonwhite	5.5	11.5	11.3	15.6	8.4	15.6	13.3	13.5	1.3	2.6	2.7	2.7	3.5	5.0	3.5	3.3
Total	6.3	15.5	32.1	47.5	10.1	19.6	31.0	38.1	1.9	5.5	9.0	8.0	3.3	9.0	11.7	8.5
Canada	6.1	13.7	27.2	29.1	11.0	17.6	26.8	24.6	1.2	4.5	8.7	5.8	2.4	7.3	10.5	5.5
Denmark	14.9	32.8	58.5	59.2	9.4	26.4	46.2	43.7	6.0	17.5	26.1	28.3	5.6	12.7	23.3	18.4
Norway	5.0	12.9	23.3	29.0	6.4	11.5	20.0	17.4	†	1.6	7.0	5.6	(1.1)	3.7	7.3	5.8
Sweden	11.0	30.3	60.2	59.7	15.3	35.5	53.1	47.0	5.4	9.8	16.1	12.1	7.5	13.2	19.3	12.7
Netherlands	2.8	5.8	14.2	29.9	4.0	8.2	16.0	27.1	(0.7)	3.6	11.5	19.2	1.1	4.5	10.4	13.5
Wgt. Avg.	7.2	18.4	37.7	43.4	8.1	19.0	33.3	34.8	2.9	7.5	14.9	16.5	3.5	8.1	14.9	13.0
United Kingdom	4.3	10.9	26.0	41.0	6.3	12.4	19.5	26.0	1.9	5.8	16.6	18.8	3.1	7.1	14.1	15.9
England & Wales	4.4	11.1	27.1	43.3	6.5	12.5	19.6	27.1	2.0	6.0	17.4	20.0	3.2	7.3	14.5	17.0
Northern Ireland	†	6.8	7.9	(12.6)	†	10.7	15.6	(12.6)	†	†	7.2	†	†	6.0	8.0	(8.0)
Scotland	4.5	10.1	20.5	26.7	5.2	11.9	19.1	18.3	(1.5)	5.4	11.5	10.1	2.6	5.9	12.1	7.3
Ireland	†	6.1	8.2	10.8	†	3.6	7.3	11.1	†	†	(0.9)	†	†	†	(2.5)	†
Belgium	5.7	12.7	36.6	68.4	7.1	15.2	34.7	65.9	3.8	5.9	14.6	19.9	3.0	7.0	14.3	23.1
Germany, Fed. Rep.	17.2	25.2	45.5	49.3	18.4	30.8	51.5	52.7	7.5	11.3	21.5	20.6	5.1	12.9	24.1	25.7
Switzerland	27.1	30.2	57.1	68.3	19.8	30.3	47.3	51.1	5.8	11.6	19.6	20.5	6.0	11.3	15.2	18.1
Austria	18.5	32.2	61.1	63.8	20.3	37.3	54.8	66.3	7.5	14.8	22.9	25.6	5.4	11.0	23.1	29.7
France	6.0	20.6	51.5	71.9	7.4	21.4	45.8	61.9	3.6	6.0	15.4	21.2	3.6	7.1	13.8	17.1
Wgt. Avg.	10.5	18.8	41.0	54.1	11.0	22.4	38.2	48.2	4.7	8.1	17.9	20.1	4.0	9.3	17.7	20.1
Italy	4.3	7.8	21.1	27.6	3.4	6.1	14.1	24.6	3.0	3.5	7.1	7.6	2.5	2.9	5.2	6.4
Portugal	7.9	11.4	36.6	60.9	5.8	15.1	31.9	52.6	4.4	3.4	7.0	8.2	3.7	4.8	6.1	11.3
Japan	53.1	31.8	39.9	87.6	14.5	18.5	26.0	59.8	35.4	18.8	22.5	57.7	12.5	12.0	16.0	46.4

* Adjusted in basis of age distribution of the United States population, 1940—except for rates at ages 15–24. † Less than 10 deaths—rate not computed. ( ) denotes rate based on 10–20 deaths.

Note: Ireland—data for 1957 not available; figures used are for 1956.

Source of basic data: Reports of the Division of Vital Statistics, National Center for Health Statistics, and World Health Organizations, World Health Statistics Annuals.

markedly in the United States and Canada, but increased to only a minor extent in Western Europe. More particularly, the suicide rate for white males aged 15–24 in the United States rose from 6.4 to 10.4 per 100,000, or by more than three fifths; among nonwhite males at these ages the suicide rate climbed by over one half, from 5.5 to 8.4 per 100,000. In Canada the suicide rate among males at these ages increased by 80 percent, from 6.1 to 11.0. On the other hand, in the industrialized countries of Western Europe the suicide rate among males aged 15–24 increased only slightly; in Scandinavia and the Netherlands as a group, the corresponding suicide rate rose by about 10 percent. In contrast, the suicide rate among Japanese males declined at these ages from the extremely high rate of 53.1 reported in 1956–57 to 14.5 per 100,000 in 1966-67 or by over 70 percent—indicative, perhaps, of the extent to which the Japanese are adopting Western European attitudes.

In the United States and Canada the suicide rate among men in the age group 25–44 increased appreciably, but not as sharply as at ages under 25. The suicide rate in the United States for white males aged 25–44 increased from 16.0 per 100,000 in 1956–57 to 20.0 in 1966–67; among nonwhite males the rate rose from 11.5 to 15.6 per 100,000. Canadian males in this age group recorded an increase in suicides of about 30 percent. In the industrialized countries of Western Europe as a group, the suicide rate among males at ages 25–44 increased from 18.8 to 22.4, but in the Scandinavian countries and the Netherlands suicides showed only a small increase at these ages. As at the younger ages, Japanese males aged 25–44 recorded a marked decline from 31.8 to 18.5 per 100,000.

In the age range 45–64 white males in the United States registered a small decline in suicide, from 34.2 to 32.9 per 100,000, but nonwhite males at these ages recorded an increase, from 11.3 to 13.3 in the more industrialized countries of Western Europe, as well as in the Scandinavian countries and the Netherlands, men in this age range experienced a small decrease in the suicide rate. Japanese men at these ages reported a distinctly lower suicide rate in 1966–67 than in 1956–57, with a drop from 39.9 to 26.0 per 100,000.

Among United States white males aged 65 and older the suicide rate declined by about a fifth, from 50.0 to 40.3 per 100,000; among nonwhite males at these ages the rate fell from 15.6 to 13.5 per 100,000. Canadian males at these ages experienced a decline of about 15 percent in the suicide rate. Males aged 65 and older in the industrialized countries of Western Europe and in Scandinavia and the Netherlands as a group reported decreases in suicide rates of about 10 and 20 percent, respectively.

Between 1956–57 and 1966–67 suicide rates among young women increased appreciably in the United States and Canada, but declined in Western Europe and Japan. Specifically, the suicide rate among white women in the United States aged 15–24 rose from 1.9 to 3.3 per 100,000 population, or by more than 70 percent; the suicide rate among nonwhite women at these ages increased from 1.3 to 3.5, or more than one and one half times. In Canada the suicide rate among women at ages 15–24 just about doubled. In the Scandinavian countries and the Netherlands as a group, suicides among women aged 15–24 rose from 2.9 per 100,000 in 1956–57 to 3.5 in 1966–67, but in the industrialized countries of Western Europe the rate among women at these ages decreased about 15 percent. Among Japanese women in this age range the suicide rate declined to a much greater extent—from 35.4 to 12.5, or by nearly two thirds.

Among white females in the United States at ages 25–44 the suicide rate increased by nearly two thirds, from 5.8 per 1,00,000 in 1956–57 to 9.5 in 1966–67; the rate among nonwhite females virtually doubled, from 2.6 to 5.0 per 100,000. Among Canadian women in this age range the suicide rate rose from 4.5 to 7.3 per 100,000, or by over three fifths. In the industrialized countries of Western Europe the suicide rate among women aged 25–44 increased moderately—from 8.1 to 9.3 per 100,000. Women at these ages in the Scandinavian countries and the Netherlands as a group experienced a very small increase in the suicide rate. As at the younger ages the suicide rate among Japanese women aged 25–44 fell more sharply—by more than a third.

In the United States both white and nonwhite females in the age range 45–64 have recently experienced distinctly higher suicide rates than those of a decade ago. Among white women the rate rose from 9.6 per 100,000 in 1956–57 to 12.5 per 100,000 in 1966–67; among nonwhite women the rate increased from 2.7 per 100,000 in the earlier years to 3.5 per 100,000 in the later years. In Canada the corresponding suicide rate rose by about a fifth from 8.7 to 10.5 per 100,000. The suicide rate among women at these ages in the industrialized countries of Western Europe declined by about 10 percent, but dropped by nearly a third in Japan.

The suicide rate among white females at ages 65 and over increased slightly in the United States, from 8.4 to 9.0 per 100,000, but rose by about a fifth among nonwhite women. In the more industrialized countries of Western Europe the suicide rate among women at these ages remained virtually unchanged. However, women in Canada and Japan, as well as those in the Scandinavian countries and the Netherlands, reported lower suicide rates.

In 1966–67 suicide rates in all age groups were significantly higher among males than among females in each of the countries here considered. The greatest differential between the sexes was manifest in the United States for both whites and nonwhites; the least differential was exhibited in Japan at the younger ages. The race differential in suicide rates in the United States declined somewhat between 1956–57 and 1966–67.

Statistics on reported suicides, although based on official figures, are not completely reliable because of the reluctance to admit this cause of death publicly and because of the difficulty in many instances of determining whether or not death was due to an accident or to suicide. However, many of the trends in suicide to which this article calls attention have been very pronounced and appear to be significant despite the questionable accuracy of some of the rates reported.

The reasons for the changes in the pattern of suicide rates are not clear. Increased social pressures among younger people and among women may have played an important role in the rise in the suicide rates in these groups in the United States, Canada, and certain other countries. Throughout the world individuals are finding it increasingly difficult to deal with personal problems in the face of a decline in traditional value systems and the growing complexities of a rapidly changing world.

SUICIDE AMONG PHYSICIANS

Mathew Ross, M.D.

It is frequently noted by students of suicidal behavior that the suicide rates among physicians is unusually high. This is a study that investigates some of the circumstances surrounding this phenomenon.

Mathew Ross, M.D., is a psychiatrist practicing in Chestnut Hill, Mass.

This article is taken from Diseases of the Nervous System, *volume 34, pages 145–50, March, 1973.*

Physician suicide rates vary from country to country. In the United States, suicide causes more physician deaths than do automobile accidents, plane crashes, drownings, and homicide combined. Everywhere suicide among physicians is high. In fact, data indicate that physicians take their own lives with greater frequency than do other members of the general population.

Incidence

The current annual suicide rate among American physicians removes from society a number equal to that of an average medical school graduating class. Historically, the United States physician suicide death rate per 100,000 reported in the 1890's averaged 41, or about 1 in 50 of all M.D. deaths; during 1912–1921 on the average, it fell to 39.8, rose to 45.4 in 1925, and in 1938–1942 leveled off at 38.7. The variations in the next decade were modest. For the 3-year period 1949–1951, the ratio of actual to expected physician suicides was 102.8%. The physician suicide death rate reported in the 1965–1967 period was 33/100,000, double that for white American males.

Not only do physicians take their own lives with greater frequency than other members of the general population but in most instances at an earlier age.

Recently, in the U.S.A. suicides accounted for 28% of physician deaths in the under 40 age group compared with 9% for white males of the same age.

Among medical students, suicide is the second most common cause of death. In the period 1947–67 among a population of 85,299 medical students, attending 50 US medical schools, the reported rate of death from suicide was significantly higher than among a reference population matched as closely as possible for age, sex, race and residence. It seems to be increasing more rapidly as well.

One may well wonder what lies behind these startling statistics.

This paper attempts to make physicians aware of some aspects of the problems and what they can do about it. There is considerable evidence that the recognition of the suicide-prone physician leaves much to be desired for, although useful diagnostic procedures are at hand, physicians are not always alert to their appropriate application.

The factors leading to suicide are exceedingly complex; indeed, it is an outcome of many forces in the life of an individual. Surely it is not an isolated event unrelated to the rest of an individual's life, nor is it solely a reaction to external pressures.

Nevertheless, because suicidal risk is often recognizable, predictable, and preventable, efforts must be made to improve the diagnostic efforts and therapeutic and preventive management of those physicians who make suicidal gestures and attempts—and all too often succeed! Suicidal attempts and acts are cries for help and should be responded to directly and immediately.

Diagnosis

How may we recognize the danger? From a review of the pertinent literature of the past 75 years of suicide among physicians there emerges this composite picture of the type of physician, especially in the U.S.A., considered to be a high suicide risk: This 48 year old doctor graduated at or near the top of his high prestige medical school class, and now he practices a peripheral specialty associated with chronic problems, where satisfactions are difficult and laggard. Because he is active, aggressive, ambitious, competitive, compulsive, enthusiastic and individualistic, he is apt to be easily frustrated in his need for achievement and recognition, and in meeting his goals. Unable to tolerate delay in gratification, he may use large amounts of anesthetics or psychoactive drugs in his practice. Add a nonlethal annoying physical illness, mood swings, a problem with drugs and alcohol—itself perhaps a reflection of suicide proneness—in one who may feel a lack of restraints by society, and one has a likely enough combination to induce sufficient anxiety and depression to seek psychiatric help, but these are also the very traits which so often make a worthwhile relationship with a psychiatrist most difficult. Self-seeking and self-indulgent, versatile and resourceful, his lack of control may often lead him to hasty, impulsive or immature behavior—possibly suicide.

Several significant early signs of emotional disturbance among doctors stand out and are reflected particularly in the conduct of his profession:

1. Hurried existence
2. Self-doubts about the ordinary medical procedures.
3. Extensive tension when confronted with difficult diagnostic problems.
4. Gradual neglect of his practice.

Among physicians who committed suicide, colleagues have noticed a change in behavior, and increasing indecisiveness, disorganization, and depression for two to four months preceding suicide.

Role Strain

For the person highly committed to his role in the practice of medicine, the gradual development of role strain, which sociologists define as "the state in which there is no doubt about the role in which one performs, but the social institutions and norms to support role performance are missing or inadequate," appears almost inevitable. Present day facilities for the delivery of medical care do not match the desire to provide it.

Many psychiatrically ill physicians comment on being overloaded with work and responsibility and are dissatisfied with their working conditions as a whole. About half of them feel that their professional work is wholly or partly to blame for their illness. They point out that because of the demands on the physician's time and knowledge, he constantly feels threatened, not only by his patients, but also by his colleagues, to maintain his professional competence. In addition, he is expected to fulfill his obligations as a husband, father, and civic leader. The demand that he be all things to all people potentially facilitates emotional decompensation. Duffy and Litin[1] remind us that medical practice is hard work for anyone, but it is harder work for those who use the profession vicariously to give solace to others rather than themselves. In their study, this group was the most prone to drug abuse. Psychiatrists who have cared for drug-using physicians are impressed by the doctor's need to be needed. In a word, the virtue of altruism is more taxing if it is an adaptation to earlier deprivation.

Health Status

Virtually all persons who commit suicide are psychiatrically ill. A careful U.S. study indicated that none of the physicians who committed suicide was considered to be in good mental health at the time of suicide, less than one-half enjoyed good physical health, the remainder suffered from health problems of varying severity. Among physicians who suicide, there is a high coincidence of psychiatric morbidity, alcoholism and drug addiction.

Depression

The most frequent precursor to suicide is depression. Indications are that as many as 75% of physicians who commit suicide are either depressed or otherwise emotionally disturbed. Depressed physicians fearing further loss of self-esteem are especially loath to seek psychiatric help. Before seeking such help, physicians may compound the problem by self-medication.

Alcoholism and Drug Addiction

Studies indicate a high incidence of alcohol and drug use among physicians who are psychiatric patients.

The physician who has established a dependency on alcohol represents a high risk of becoming a drug addict.

[1] J. C. Duffy and E. M. Litin, Journal of the American Medical Association 189:989–92, 1964.

Estimates of the incidence of narcotics addiction in physicians vary from 30 to 100 times that in the general population.

Among physician suicides, alcoholism was associated with 40% and drug abuse with 20%. About 10% of U.S. physician addicts commit suicide.

THE SUICIDAL ACT

Method

The method of suicides is somewhat predictable on the basis of the means that are most available, or with which the person is most familiar.

U.S. physicians, both male and female, use drugs far more frequently in suicide than do their counterparts in the general population. The high frequency of death by suicide among female physicians may reflect, in part, a high proportion of successful attempts through knowledge of lethality of various readily available poisons.

Correlates

Admittedly, the factors leading to suicide are exceedingly complex. The suicidal act is not an isolated event unrelated to the rest of an individual's life, nor is it solely a reaction to external pressures, but it is an outcome of many forces in the life of an individual.

Correlates considered significant in studies of suicide among physicians include:

Age

Not only do physicians take their own lives with greater frequency than other members of the general population but in most instances at an earlier age.

Recently, in the U.S.A., suicides accounted for 28% of physician deaths in the under 40 age group compared with 9% for white males of the same age.

Gender

Female physicians' suicides—40.5 per 100,000—represent the highest reported rate for any group of females, nearly four times that of the female general population of U.S. females over age 25.

In the U.S., the suicide rate among women is less than one-third that for men, but the suicide rate among female physicians is higher than among male physicians: females account for 6.5% of physician suicides as opposed to only 3.6% of total physician deaths.

There are those who maintain that professional women who select male-oriented careers are likely to be ambitious, competitive, compulsive, individualistic, intelligent, scholarly, and unmarried and that female physicians may select a medical career to compete with men or to avoid competing with women, and this personality constellation is highly significant. Others indicate that the high frequency of death by suicide among female physicians and chemists may reflect, in part, a high proportion of successful attempts through knowledge of lethality of various readily available poisons for the rates are not elevated among women in nursing and teaching.

Specialty

There is a considerable variation in the rate of suicide among the various medical and surgical specialties: In the U.S.A. psychiatry, opthalmology and anesthesiology lead all the rest. The specialties with low rates, pediatrics, dermatology, surgery and pathology have, in common, more frequently a generally short term and less intense emotional relationship to the patient. Psychiatry, medical school faculty, and public health men are involved in long-term planning, while being somewhat alien in the mainstream of medicine. The marked difference in rate by specialty raises the question as to whether or not the job influences the susceptibility.

PREVENTION

What can be done to prevent suicide among physicians and medical students?

Early recognition and prompt appropriate treatment are still mainstays of preventive psychiatry. If prevention is to become significantly more than a pious hope, students and faculty must be more keenly alerted and become more effective intervenors.

When one considers that medical students live near and work in what are proclaimed to be the country's best medical facilities and its best physicians, one wonders about the overall continuing sensitivity of medical school faculty to medical student health and more particularly attitudes towards psychiatric illness.

One-quarter to one-third of medical students get some psychiatric treatment. Nevertheless, earlier, more astute and continuous surveyance appear indicated, in view of the data which indicate that in the period 1947–67 among a population of 85,299 medical students, attending 50 US medical schools, the reported rate of death from suicide was significantly higher than among a reference population matched as closely as possible for age, sex, race and residence. It seems to be increasing more rapidly as well.

Although psychosocial studies of applicants to medical school and medical school students are legion, the exact incidence of psychiatric difficulties among medical students are unknown. For at least the past 35 years, it has been a rather general assumption that it is relatively high.

As a teaching device, a reasonably thorough health screening has distinctly good educational value to young people coming into medicine and so does the provision of adequate psychiatric services to students.

Greater emphasis on the psychiatric screening coupled with an efficient student health service might improve the efficiency of the preadmission screening of medical students in regard to their mental health.

Third and fourth year students tend to get extensive corridor care from faculty, a practice which is to be deplored not only for its potential hazards, but also because of the questionable educational effects. There is reason to believe that, in most instances, the medical student does not take the opportunity to turn to the psychiatrist in the medical school for help when his emotional burden becomes severe. In part, this may be due to a subtle but demeaning attitude toward emotional illness and psychiatric help inculcated in the medical school years, and perhaps the student, his professors, and the school—all must accept some responsibility for this attitude toward psychiatry and psychiatric treatment.

Improved standards in teaching psychiatry at both under-graduate and postgraduate levels and improved liaison between psychiatrists and members of other branches of medicine would be welcome, as would be a review of educational programs concerning suicide, alcohol and drugs, especially as these relate to the health of students themselves.

Medical schools must assume greater responsibility for teaching their students that they represent a high risk population for alcohol and drug abuse, and that unchecked, the virtues of the good physician can increase the risk. No physician, whatever his rationalization, should write a prescription for himself for a drug that will make his brain feel better, sleep better or work better. This will not be easy for the student to hear.

Interns and Residents

In the period 1965–66, 16 suicides among interns and residents were recorded in the obituary columns of The Journal of the American Medical Association.

Internship and residency training are periods of great stress for the young physician who, when fresh from medical school, is expected to assume the responsibilities of his chosen profession and specialty. Great thought and care as to the quality of educational training, and their medical performance is always under constant scrutiny in terms of their knowledge and ability; yet little organized attention is given to the state of their emotional health.

Likewise, it is imperative that the physician in training attempt to understand and accept his emotional needs in his training. His particular set of emotional vulnerabilities, coupled with the vagaries of his life work will, in great measure, determine the success or failure of his emotional adjustment.

We must devote as much attention to the emotions of the physician in training as to his medical skill. It must be the responsibility of those physicians who were charged with working closely with young doctors to be alert to the serious emotional stresses which may be present, as well as the proficiency of their medical performance.

The Physician as a Patient

The extreme defensiveness of doctors about admitting psychological problems is a barrier to therapy, and yet in some instances the doctor's own resistance, hesitation, and delay in getting into active therapy is frequently compounded as a result of unwitting neglect by the family and colleagues who rationalized that he, as a physician, ought to know what and how to take care of himself. He doesn't. Indeed, one is well advised to observe as the cardinal principle in management to the physician-patient purposely omitting the fact of his special medical education. It is improper to assume that a physician's past medical information adds up to special personality controls or particular immunity from emotional conflicts.

Knowledgeable, experienced psychiatrists have remarked that the physician-patient is treated with special restraint, often to his detriment so that techniques, such as court commitment, firm probation and control, and convulsive treatments were rarely used even though hospitalization often has the preventive effect expected of it.

It is imperative that the staff clearly state and define their relationship with the patient, and emphasize his responsibility in cooperating with them as a patient. One must avoid special considerations or privileges for the physician, as well as the many other more subtle pitfalls in dealing with a "special patient."

The behavior of a physician-patient, once admitted to a psychiatric service, has consistently shown certain common characteristics that probably relate to his professional identity and his difficulty in accepting his illness and his status as a patient. He tends to be quite manipulating of his environment, generally remaining aloof from other patients, and seemingly unable to assume the role of a patient in the social structure of the ward. This situation is not without strain for the hospital staff who must cope with their own feelings of insecurity in dealing with the physician as a patient, but the physician-patient tends to manipulate the staff. He prefers to be aloof from other patients, is frequently hostile to his therapist, and often demands premature, immediate discharge from the hospital.

Overt hostility by the patient toward the therapist is common. Once the acute phase of the illness has passed, there may often be a demand for immediate release. Denial is a common defense mechanism in therapy, and suggestions for follow-up psychotherapy after discharge are often met with ambivalence. Few physicians return following discharge, either for psychiatric or nonpsychiatric reasons.

For the psychiatrist looking after a fellow physician there is definitely an added burden of responsibility. The stirred up positive and negative counter-transference feelings, especially the identification, are well known. There is little comfort and much truth in the aphorism "doctors make the worst patients."

Indeed, the fact that many of the decedents were getting some form of psychiatric treatment at the time of death raises important issues in regard to the treatment.

Role of Professional Organization

Long ago, Durkheim felt that the most effective way to prevent suicides was to strengthen the role of the professional organization intrinsic to each occupation. Thus, the attitudes of medical societies, hospital committees, and licensing authorities should be supportive and encouraging rather than restrictive or punitive. Most would agree that those social groups which presumably represent the physician, the various medical associations, have the most apathetic kind of membership—they represent neither the collective conscience of their members, nor places of psychic protection and refuge.

The American Psychiatric Association established in 1972 a Task Force on Suicide Prevention with a focus at the outset on the incidence of suicide among psychiatrists. Possibly one outcome of the study may be the development of a network of interested and capable colleagues to forestall the distressing incidence of suicide among physicians.

SUMMARY

A review of the available literature of suicide among physicians indicates that (1) physician suicide varies from country to country, (2) suicide among physicians is high, (3) suicide among female physicians is very much higher than among male physicians, (4) there is a high incidence of psychiatric morbidity, alcoholism and drug addiction among physician suicides, (5) as in suicides among other age groups, there are significant variable correlates of age, gender, type of medical practice and specialty, the state of physical and emotional health, the use of alcohol and drugs, professional and psychosocial factors, (6) preventive action is both possible and desirable.

SUICIDAL BEHAVIOR AMONG AMERICAN INDIANS

H. L. P. Resnik, M.D.
Larry H. Dizmang, M.D.

Among the anomalies that show up on a closer examination of suicide statistics are exceptionally high rates among selected areas of the population. A poignant example of a disproportionate increase in suicide frequency is studied here by Dr. Resnik and Dr. Dizmang. Such studies as these not only highlight particular human tragedies; they also urge the thoughtful student to search for social remedies.

At the time this article was written H. L. P. Resnik was Chief of the Center for Studies of Suicide Prevention at the National Institute of Mental Health and Larry H. Dizmang was Coordinator of Intramural Research at the Center.

This article is taken from the American Journal of Psychiatry, *volume 127, page 7, January, 1971.*

The framework within which we propose to discuss suicidal behavior among American Indians is a sociocultural one. By so doing we do not mean to minimize the role of intrapsychic dynamic mechanisms or of neurophysiologic or biochemical concomitants of depression and suicide. However, the sociocultural determinants apply so clearly that we believe it is an unwarranted luxury to talk about individual dynamics or neurobiochemistry outside the context of the broad sociocultural picture.

American Indian culture is at least as diverse as the broad spectrum of cultures that currently exist in the United States; that is, the Indians of the Northeast, the Penobscot in Maine, and the Iroquois in New York State differ immeasurably from the Seminole in Florida. Different from all of these are the warlike nomadic

Sioux and Apache and the more agrarian and community-settled Hopi and Navaho. When we say that the tribes differ from each other, we mean in their most important respects—language, culture, and tradition. They also differ in their attitudes toward suicidal behavior—the most warlike usually condoned acts of self-destruction in battle or when captured; for others, suicide was related to un-requited love or guilt over homicides or was considered acceptable behavior for the aged.

Although significant steps have been taken in recent years to advance the health of these people, infant mortality rates are ap-proximately 50 percent higher, tuberculosis is found eight times more frequently, and cirrhosis of the liver is 4.5 times more frequent than among the general population. The average age at death of an Indian is 44 years, while that of the white is 65 years. With a birth rate twice that of the general population, and inadequate housing to begin with, there is also gross overcrowding. In addition, the un-employment rate among Indians is 40 percent—more than ten times the national average.

Today the majority of Indians live on lands held in trust for them by the U.S. government. Mrs. Leah Manning, a social worker of Indian descent, summarized the effects of such conditions in a paper written for a study group at the Southwest Conference on Suicide Prevention, held in Denver in 1969:

> These lands have been set aside either by executive order or by special purchases and are known as reservations. They were estab-lished initially in an attempt to ease the hostilities created by west-ward expansion. Upon these tracts of land, tribal groups once inde-pendent were forced to settle; years of conflict over land ownership, use, and income derived therefrom have continued. Each reservation and its residents have had their unique historical experiences with the United States Government, and attitudes both toward the tribe and by the tribe reflect these experiences in many ways. For exam-ple, one tribal group was given the opportunity to choose between two possible sites, while another tribal group was ordered to settle on a specified reservation. In many cases, groups of Indians with differing languages, separate traditions, and even traditional hostili-ties were assigned to live together on the same reservation. In other cases, a single tribal group might inhabit a reservation alone, or, re-lated groups might be assigned to live on different reservations. Ad-justment to reservation life at best was quite alien to a number of

tribes who were nomadic and migrant, whereas other tribes, more agrarian and settled, found the adjustment an easy one to make, especially if they remained on their hereditary land.

At times, pressures on one reservation became great and individuals or whole families moved back and forth from reservation to reservation to join other family members for prolonged visits. The reservations were usually on tracts of arid, often uninhabitable land, at considerable distances from urban communities. The Department of the Interior, through its Bureau of Indian Affairs, was responsible for the health, education, welfare, and economic problems of the Indians, who were wards of the government. Recently, responsibility for health care has been assigned to the Public Health Service and this augurs well. Continued pressures in a variety of ways from the dominant culture have vacillated from attempting to bring about total assimilation to fostering Indian pride in being "more Indian." Indians have seen these efforts as directed *at* them and feel they were allowed little chance to make their own adjustments to the new set of circumstances they were forced to face. It is encouraging to note that recent action by both the President and the Congress seems aimed at correcting such inequities.

These introductory remarks should make it clear that when one speaks of suicidal behavior among American Indians one must first recognize the wide range of Indians included—their traditions, their degrees of social disintegration, and their geography.

THE SUICIDE RATE

Overall, the suicide rate for American Indians is only slightly higher than the national average of 11 per 100,000. For some reservations, however, it grossly exceeds that figure, ranging from five to ten times the national average. In fact, within certain Indian nations, such as the Apache, where the average rate is significantly higher, the frequency varies from reservation to reservation. This is also true among the Pueblo Indians, where the average rate is low but certain reservations have exceedingly high rates. Some of the distinguishing characteristics of reservations where the rate tends to be high include dissolution of the traditional family structure, high levels of unemployment coupled with inadequate job training programs, significant alcoholism, and a high index of more insidious self-destructive behavior, such as automobile fatalities and other accidents.

In addition to the high suicide rate on some reservations, one of the most distinguishing and disturbing characteristics of Indian suicidal behavior is its occurrence almost uniquely in those aged 35 or younger. This is in sharp contrast to the figures on completed suicides among the non-Indian population in the United States, where the trend is to a steady increase in suicide as age advances. However the figures on attempted suicides in the Indian and non-Indian populations appear less disparate, since both are higher in middle age.

By the time the Indian reaches adolescence, the sum of the variables that we have outlined briefly has fostered a high degree of alienation during a normally tumultuous period of psychological identity striving. Because the matrix of the Indian's early years is that of a culture in relative dissolution, the Indian youth not only experiences the very personal identity crisis of adolescence, but he also has the additional burden of the identity crisis of his culture. He is neither an Indian with a sense of pride and self-respect for his people and his culture nor able to identify with the culture and tradition of the dominant group. The Indian adolescent, then, begins to experience early a sense of identity diffusion and the resulting psychological chaos of not knowing who he really is or whether he even has a right to exist. Although it is obvious, we will simply state here that such crises are not unique to the American Indian; they are shared in varying degrees by blacks, Puerto Ricans, and Mexican-Americans.

The psychological helplessness and increasing feelings of hopelessness engendered by such circumstances may often make a self-sought death an idealized solution. Suicide becomes, paradoxically, the only way an Indian adolescent, caught up in a cultural and personal identity crisis, can have any sense of gaining control over his constant anxiety and of exercising mastery over his destiny.

Suicide rates among Indians seem to arise from the same social influences that have been reported to underlie suicidal behaviors generally.[1] It is our clinical impression that if one could apply a

---

[1] J. Douglas, *The Social Meanings of Suicide* (Princeton: Princeton University Press, 1967).

valid measurement of social and family disorganization to a given reservation and then rank all the Indian reservations on this basis, the suicide rate would approximate closely the increases in family and social disorganization. We agree with Barter[2] that social disorganization (with, we would add, its resultant anomie), geographic isolation, parental loss, and the high incidence of alcoholism, all of which have been reported by various investigators to be related to suicidal behavior, characterize the Indian reservations that show the highest rates of suicide.

GEOGRAPHIC ISOLATION

Locating Indian reservations many miles from areas of urban growth and economic development has effectively isolated the Indian. This is only one more factor that prevents the Indian from developing any meaningful interaction with the non-Indian population. Visits to the few small towns that border the reservations are usually for "looking and drinking" or to obtain the menial and undesirable jobs in the community. The reservations themselves often cover such large areas in terms of square miles that many families live in virtual isolation from one another. On the reservation, there are often few mechanisms for meaningful social interaction among the Indians themselves. Recent attempts by the federal government to relocate (and integrate) large numbers of Indians closer to urban areas, where there are opportunities for further acculturation and jobs and job training are available, fail to take into consideration their lack of some of the basic social skills necessary to function in a white urban community. A large percentage of the Indians who are relocated or who migrate independently fail to last more than a year in the new area. This inevitably results in a "trek back to the reservation" with an increased sense of personal failure, frustration, and hopelessness. Those who do remain away for more than a year exist socially and economically at a very marginal level; there is serious question whether an urban life has more to offer than the reservation.

When we attempt to isolate the influences that have led to the

[2] J. Barter, "Suicide in Western Indian Population," read at the Southwest Regional Conference on Suicide Prevention (Denver, Colo., September 11, 1969).

current disruption of the Indian family structure, as well as its larger cultural base, a number of factors appear relevant. Let us consider the Cheyenne tribe in Montana as an example.[3] When they were finally vanquished by the white man the Cheyenne were placed on a reservation in Montana. The buffalo, their primary source of food, were gone by then. Since these nomadic plains dwellers had lost their earlier agricultural skills, the alternative to starvation was for the government to ship in food to sustain them. A long and painful history of demeaning welfare dependency followed. The Cheyenne quickly lost their self-respect and pride as the white man proceeded to "civilize these primitive people." The Indians were forbidden to hold their traditional sun dance or to carry out any other "primitive and barbaric rituals." In a government-sponsored program to improve health conditions, the men were forced to cut their long hair, a prized symbol of strength. Without further elaboration of the details, the Northern Cheyenne were systematically stripped of their identity as a proud and strong people, and their culturally evolved ways of providing for themselves and maintaining their self-esteem were lost.

A second example of events that led to family and cultural dissolution in many Indian tribes is clearly outlined by the history of the Shoshone-Bannock in Idaho.[4] This tribe, not as well organized as the Cheyenne, had been easily defeated by the white man. When they were assigned to their reservation, the government disrupted their long-standing extended family patterns by assigning land plots to nuclear families. It was traditional then (and still is) that a band made up of several extended families had much greater loyalty to one another than to members of other groups. Even today extended family ties on the Shoshone-Bannock reservation are much stronger than the relationship between neighbors. However, the extended family became fragmented because of the great distances between the nuclear families' plots of land: this pattern of land settlement resulted in a great disruption of child-rearing patterns as well as a loss of self-esteem and, as with the Cheyenne, loss of the ability to sustain themselves in their usual nomadic food-gathering patterns.

---

[3] L. H. Dizmang, "Suicide Among The Cheyenne Indians," *Bulletin of Suicidology* 8–11 (July 1967).
[4] L. H. Dizmang, "Observations on Suicidal Behavior Among the Shoshone-Bannock Indians," read at the first annual National Conference on Suicidology (Chicago, Ill., March 20, 1968).

These examples illustrate some of the stresses that disrupt the social structure of the Indian family. Indian men were early faced with overwhelming frustration and loss of self-esteem. Traditionally, their values were centered on strong family leadership, acts of bravery and physical strength, and respect for parents, grandparents, and tradition. Such behaviors were no longer possible. The increasing frustration and the ready availability of alcohol (which was abundantly supplied by those who would facilitate the denigration of these people) caused an increase in alcoholism to such proportions that it is currently almost epidemic on Indian reservations. Many suicides and most of the suicide attempts occur during periods of intoxication.

RESULTS OF FAMILY DISORGANIZATION

Disorganization of the family has resulted in a diminution of the father's authority, his alcoholism, and ultimately his inability to continue in a family unit where he sees himself as weak, useless, and a failure; it has transformed him from a physically actively outdoor male to a dependent position as a welfare recipient. He frequently abandons his wife and children. In the absence of meaningful male models within the family, the boys and young men of the tribe try, generally unsuccessfully, to locate an appropriate substitute within the community. When a leader is chosen, it is often a boy somewhat older than themselves who has had no more positive direction than they. Mrs. Manning has pointed out that these sex-role conflicts have been less a problem for Indian girls, since they still find the traditionally valued role of mother and wife reasonably attractive. Whereas the grandfather-teacher has little or nothing to offer, the grandmother-teacher still functions in a more active and dominating way within the Indian household, thus reinforcing the relative role reversal. It is amazing that all of this has occurred within *less* than one century.

The loss of prestige and respect on the part of the father and his increased tendency toward alcoholism have fostered a lessening of parental responsibilities and familial ties. The incidence of disrupted marriages is extremely high, with the father often deserting his wife and large family. We know that parental loss and early separation may contribute to depression in later years. Dizmang,

Watson, and May[5] have found that 70 percent of adolescent Indian youths who completed suicide, compared with only 15 percent of a control group, had had more than one significant caretaker before the age of 15.

Separation from parents occurs even when the family structure has been relatively successful in withstanding the numerous insults that we have indicated. The ultimate culprit is the school system. Education poses a great problem for Indian children and youths simply because they are most often educated by non-Indians in schools where the skills and values of the majority society are taught. Although this may be construed as an attempt to prepare the Indian to function away from the reservation, there are many reasons why this educational system is dysfunctional both to the Indian and to the non-Indian society, whose efforts to help him end by frustrating his children.

The crux of the problem lies with language. Most Indians are raised in homes where the language spoken is that of their tribe rather than English. The Indian youngster is best able to conceptualize, and thus to learn, in his native language. Since the schools generally use English as the medium of instruction, this language difference presents a serious handicap for the Indian child. (This is also true for other underprivileged children, who do better when teachers and instructional materials use terms and language familiar to them.) The American Indian languages are not only extremely different from English and all other Indo-European languages in their grammatical structures, but they are also rooted in a very different perception of the universe. The languages are so different that during World War II the U.S. Army successfully used uncoded Navaho to send messages; it was a "code" the Japanese did not crack. It should also be noted that the various Indian languages are as different from one another as are the various European languages.

The Indian education system is further complicated by the fact that Indian children as young as seven years old are sent to boarding schools, usually off the reservation and often thousands of miles away from their parents, whom they visit infrequently. This

[5] L. H. Dizmang, J. Watson, P. A. May et al., "Adolescent Suicide at Fort Hall Indian Reservation," read at the 123rd annual meeting of the American Psychiatric Association (San Francisco, Calif, May 11–15, 1970).

isolation further fractionates the family. Since these boarding schools are attended by children from different tribes, some of the children may even be linguistically isolated from their classmates.

When there are educational facilities nearby they may be restricted, e.g., an Indian school with inferior teaching standards and facilities; or the Indian student may enter the existing school system to find that his fellow students have received better preparatory educations and understand English far better than he does. Saslow and Harrover have summarized studies that suggest that the Indian, as a member of a minority group, is often open to ridicule about his Indian identity.

In summary, when an Indian enters the educational system, he is handicapped because: 1) his primary language is not English. 2) he has perceptions of life different from those on which the English language is based, and 3) he has values—both cultural and socioeconomic that are different from those of his white teachers and classmates.

The "crossover effect" is a recognized phenomenon among Indian students: when compared to other students, Indian children achieve satisfactorily in the early grades, fall behind in the middle grades, and grossly underachieve through the high school years. This phenomenon demonstrates the overt manifestations of the alienation process occurring in a great number of Indian youth. Approximately half of all Indian children drop out before completing high school.

CONCLUSIONS

The Indian adolescent, having experienced a constant struggle to derive an individual identity from a highly disrupted family setting, must also face the problem of delineating a social identity from a badly disorganized culture. He is caught between two cultures—he is unprepared for the one and feels the other, toward which he is ambivalent, has failed him. Saslow and Harrover[6] postulated that "the culture shock of having to renounce, with the beginning of school, much of what has been learned before school, undoes the pattern of trust and personal worth developed up to that

[6] H. L. Saslow, "Research on Psycho-social Adjustment of Indian Youth," *American Journal of Psychiatry* 125: 224, 231 (1968).

time. With traditions crumbling, it is even possible to suggest that this pattern might not be well developed." McNickle,[7] a Flathead Indian, was more optimistic and held out the possibility that the young Indian can use skills acquired from the majority culture to support his traditional society.

The Indian adolescent has a double identity crisis—the expected adolescent turmoil, plus a cultural crisis. How does he cope with it? Frequently, with suicide; with alcoholism; with violence, even homicide; with reckless driving; with victim-precipitated homicides. We do not believe this is necessarily specifically Indian; we believe it can also apply to other minority group children.

Programs for suicide prevention on Indian reservations must recognize these social problems and must be prepared to work actively toward their solution. Any program that aims at primary prevention does best to involve itself with issues we have briefly outlined. That is not to say that building treatment facilities, training indigenous crisis intervenors (including shamans), and making more mental health professionals available can be put off any longer. The Center for Studies of Suicide Prevention does not anticipate that its preventive efforts can succeed unless Indians are involved in planning and operating relevant programs of prevention. At this time, suicide is not seen as a unique symptom, but rather as a glaring symptom, of their collective helplessness and hopelessness.

[7] D. McNickle, "The Sociocultural Setting of Indian Life," *American Journal of Psychiatry* 125: 219, 223 (1968).

THE RIGHT TO SUICIDE:
A PSYCHIATRIST'S VIEW

Jerome A. Motto, M.D.

It is reasonable to assume that there are persons who might de-cide on taking their lives after a rational and realistic assessment of their circumstances. Dr. Motto, a psychiatrist, proposes this view of suicide and discusses what implications this has for those close to anyone who is contemplating suicide.

Jerome A. Motto is professor of Psychiatry at the University of California Medical School at San Francisco.

This article is taken from Life Threatening Behavior, *volume 2, number 3, Fall, 1972.*

To speak as a psychiatrist may suggest to some that psychiatrists have a certain way of looking at things. This would be a misconception, though a common one. I know of no professional group with more diverse approaches to those matters concerning it than the American psychiatric community. All physicians, however, including psychiatrists, share a tradition of commitment to both the preservation and the quality of human life. With this one reservation, I speak as a psychiatrist strictly in the singular sense.

The emergence of thoughts or impulses to bring an end to life is a phenomenon observed in persons experiencing severe pain, whether that pain stems from physical or emotional sources. Thus physicians, to whom persons are inclined to turn for relief from suffering, frequently encounter suicidal ideas and impulses in their patients. Those who look and listen do, at least.

From a psychiatric point of view, the question as to whether a person has the right to cope with the pain in his world by killing himself can be answered without hesitation. He does have that right. With a few geographical exceptions the same can be said from the legal and social point of view as well. It is only when philosophical or theological questions are raised that one can find room for argument about the right to suicide, as only in these areas can restrictions on behavior be institutionalized without requiring social or legal support.

The problem we struggle with is not whether the individual *has* the right to suicide; rather, we face a twofold dilemma stemming from the fact that he does have it. Firstly, what is the extent to which the exercise of that right should be subject to limitations? Secondly, when the right is exercised, how can we eliminate the social stigma now attached to it?

Putting limitations on rights is certainly not a new idea, since essentially every right we exercise has its specified restrictions. It is generally taken for granted that certain limitations must be observed. In spite of this, it is inevitable that some will take the position that unless the right is unconditional it is not "really" granted.

I use two psychological criteria as grounds for limiting a person's exercise of his right to suicide: (*a*) the act must be based on a realistic assessment of his life situation, and (*b*) the degree of ambivalence regarding the act must be minimal. Both of these criteria clearly raise a host of new questions.

REALISTIC ASSESSMENT OF LIFE SITUATION

What is reality? Who determines whether a realistic assessment has been made? Every person's perception is reality to *him,* and the degree of pain experienced by one can never be fully appreciated by another, no matter how empathic he is. Differences in capacity to *tolerate* pain add still another crucial yet unmeasurable element.

As formidable as this sounds, the psychiatrist is obliged to accept this task as his primary day-to-day professional responsibility, whether or not the issue of suicide is involved. With an acute awareness of how emotions can—like lenses—distort perceptions which in turn shape one's thoughts and actions, and with experience in understanding and dealing with this underlying substrate of emotion, he is constantly working with his patients on the process of differentiating between what is realistic and what is distorted. The former must be dealt with on a rational level; the latter must be explored and modified till the distortion is reduced at least to the point where it is not of handicapping severity. He is aware of the nature and extent of his own tendency to distort ("Physician, heal thyself"), and realizes that the entire issue is one of degree. Yet he must use his own perception of reality as a standard, shortcomings notwithstanding, realizing full well how much information must be carefully considered in view of the frailty of the human perceptual and reality-testing apparatus.

Some persons have a view of reality so different from mine that I do not hesitate to interfere with their right to suicide. Others' perceptions are so like mine that I cannot intercede. The big problem is that large group in between.

In the final analysis, then, when a decision has to be made, what a psychiatrist calls "realistic" is whatever looks realistic to *him*. At the moment of truth, that is all any person can offer. This inherent human limitation in itself is a reality that accounts for a great deal of inevitable chaos in the world; it is an article of faith that not to make such an effort would create even greater chaos. On a day-to-day operational level, one contemporary behavioral scientist (Diggory, 1968, p. 18) expressed it this way: "No doubt the daily business of helping troubled individuals, including suicides, gives little time for the massive contemplative and investigative efforts which alone can lead to surer knowledge. And the helpers are not thereby to be disparaged. They cannot wait for the best answers conceivable. They must do only the best they can *now*."

Thus if I am working with a person in psychotherapy, one limitation I would put on his right to suicide would be that his assessment of his life situation be realistic as *I* see it.

A related concept is that of "rational suicide," which has enjoyed a certain vogue since at least the seventeenth century, when the "Rationalist Era" saw sharp inroads being made into the domination of the church in determining ethical and social values (Sprott, 1961). According to one contemporary philosopher (Pepper, 1967, p. 121), "the degree of rationality of the [suicidal] act would depend on the degree of rationality of the philosophy which was guiding the person's deliberations." Rationality is defined as a means of problem solving, using "methods such as logical, mathematical, or experimental procedures which have gained men's confidence as reliable tools for guiding instrumental actions." The rationality of one's philosophy is determined by the degree to which it is free of mysticism. Further, "A person who is considering how to act in an intensely conflicting situation cannot be regarded as making the most rational decision, unless he has been as critical as possible of the philosophy that is guiding his decision. If the philosophy is institutionalized as a political ideology or a religious creed, he must think critically about the institution in order to acquire maximum rationality of judgment. This principle is clear enough, even if in practice it is enormously difficult to fulfill" (Pepper, 1967, p. 123).

The idea of "rational suicide" is a related yet distinctly different issue from the "realistic assessment of one's life situation" referred to above. Making this assessment involves assembling and understanding all the facts clearly, while the idea of a "rational suicide" can only be entertained after this assessment is done and the question is "what to do" in the light of those facts.

The role of the psychiatrist and the thinking of the rationalist tend to merge, at one point, however. In the process of marshaling all the facts and exploring their meaning to the person, the psychiatrist must ensure that the patient does indeed critically examine not only his perception of reality but his own philosophy. This often entails making that philosophy explicit for the first time (without ever using the term "philosophy"), and clarifying how it has influenced his living experience. The implication is clear that modification of the person's view of his world, with corresponding changes in behavior, may lead to a more satisfying life.

The rationalist concedes that where one's philosophy is simply an "intellectual channeling of emotional forces," rational guidelines have severe limitations, since intense emotional conflicts cut off rational guidance. These circumstances would characterize "irrational" grounds for suicide and would identify those persons whose suicide should be prevented.

The argument for "rational suicide" tends to apply principally to two sets of circumstances: altruistic self-sacrifice for what is perceived as a noble cause; and the severe, advanced physical illness with no new therapeutic agents anticipated in the foreseeable future. This does not help us very much because these circumstances generate relatively little real controversy among behavioral scientists. The former situations are not usually recognized till after the act, and the latter at present are receiving a great deal of well-deserved attention from the point of view of anticipating (and sometimes hastening) the foreseeable demise in comfort and dignity.

Our most difficult problem is more with the person whose pain is emotional in origin and whose physical health is good, or at most constitutes a minor impairment. For these persons, the discussion above regarding "rational" and "irrational" distinctions seems rather alien to the clinical situation. This is primarily due to the rationalist's emphasis on intellectual processes, when it is so clear (at least to the psychiatrist) that it is feelings of worthiness of love, of relatedness, of belonging, that have the strongest stabilizing influence on the suicidal person.

I rarely hear a patient say, "I've never looked at it that way," yet no response is more frequently encountered than, "Yes, I understand, but I don't feel any differently." It is after a continuing therapeutic effort during which feelings of acceptance and worthiness are generated that emotional pain is reduced and suicidal manifestations become less intense. Either exploring the philosophy by which one lives or carefully assessing the realities of one's life can provide an excellent means of accomplishing this, but it is rarely the influence of the philosophy or the perception of the realities per se that brings it about. Rather, it is through the influence of the therapeutic relationship that the modified philosophy or perception develops, and can then be applied to the person's life situation.

MANIFESTATIONS OF AMBIVALENCE

The second criterion to be used as the basis for limiting a person's exercise of his right to suicide is minimal ambivalence about ending his life. I make the assumption that if a person has no ambivalence about suicide he will not be in my office, nor write to me about it, nor call me on the telephone. I interpret, rightly or wrongly, a person's calling my attention to his suicidal impulses as a request to intercede that I cannot ignore.

At times this call will inevitably be misread, and my assumption will lead me astray. However, such an error on my part can be corrected at a later time; meanwhile, I must be prepared to take responsibility for having prolonged what may be a truly unendurable existence. If the error is made in the other direction, no opportunity for correction may be possible.

This same principle regarding ambivalence applies to a suicide prevention center, minister, social agency, or a hospital emergency room. The response of the helping agency may be far from fulfilling the needs of the person involved, but in my view, the ambivalence expressed is a clear indication for it to limit the exercises of his right to suicide.

REDUCING THE STIGMA OF SUICIDE

The second horn of our dilemma about the right to suicide is the fact that the suicidal act is not considered respectable in our society. It can be maintained that granting a right but stigmatizing the exercise of that right is tantamount to not having granted it in the first place. In order to develop a realistic approach to this problem it is necessary to reduce the negative social implications attached to it.

The first step is to talk about it freely—with each other, with doctors, ministers, patients, and families. Just as with past taboos— TB, cancer, sex (especially homosexuality), drug addiction, abortion—it will gradually lose the emotional charge of the forbidden. The second step is the continued institutionalization of supportive and treatment services for suicidal persons, through local, state, and federal support.

News media should be responsible for reporting suicidal deaths with dignity and simplicity, without attempting either to cover up or sensationalize pertinent information. In an economically competitive field this would not be a reasonable expectation unless it were made part of an accepted ethical code.

Instruction regarding this problem should be provided as a matter of course in the education and training for all health care personnel, emergency services (police, firemen), behavioral sciences (psychology, sociology, anthropology), and those to whom troubled people most often turn, such as ministers, teachers, and counselors. In short, every person who completes the equivalent of a high school education would be provided with an orientation toward the problem of suicide, and those responsible for responding to others in stressful circumstances should be prepared to assist in providing—or at least locating—help when needed.

A question has been raised whether incorporating concern for suicide into our social institutions might depersonalize man to some extent. I would anticipate the contrary. The more our social institutions reflect awareness of and concern for man's inner life and provide means for improving it, the greater is the implied respect for that life—even if this takes the form of providing a dignified means of relinquishing it.

It seems inevitable to me that we must eventually establish procedures for the voluntary cessation of life, with the time, place, and manner largely controlled by the person concerned. It will necessarily involve a series of deliberate steps providing assurance that appropriate criteria are met, such as those proposed above, as we now observe specific criteria when a life is terminated by abortion or by capital punishment.

The critical word is "control." I would anticipate a decrease in the actual number of suicides when this procedure is established, due to the psychological power of this issue. If I know something is available to me and will remain available till I am moved to seize it, the chances of my seizing it now are thereby much reduced. It is only by holding off that I maintain the option of changing my mind. During this period of delay the opportunity for therapeutic effort—and the therapy of time itself—may be used to advantage.

Finally, we have to make sure we are not speaking only to the strong. It is too easy to formulate a way of dealing with a troublesome problem in such a manner, that if the person in question could approach it as we suggest, he would not be a person who would have the problem in the first place.

When we discuss—in the abstract—the right to suicide, we tend to gloss over the intricacies of words like "freedom," "quality of life," "choice," or even "help," to say nothing of "rational" and "realistic." Each of these concepts deserves a full inquiry in itself, though in practice we use them on the tacit assumption that general agreement exists as to their meaning.

Therefore it is we who, in trying to be of service to someone else, have the task of determining what is rational for us, and what our perception of reality is. And we must recognize that in the final analysis it will be not only the suicidal person but we who have exercised a choice, by doing what we do to resolve our feelings about this difficult human problem.

SUICIDE AS THE
SOUL'S CHOICE

James Hillman

*"Until we can say no to life, we have not really said yes to it,"
Hillman writes in this essay, offering a daring interpretation of
suicide as an authentic choice of the soul, or person. Suicide is
therefore regarded not as the dilemma of a troubled person, but
as a legitimate possibility, given the inner freedom of the soul—
a freedom without which there can be no health.*

*James Hillman is a psychoanalyst, practicing in Zurich, and an
author of several volumes on analytic psychology.*

This essay is taken from Suicide and the Soul, *Harper and Row,
1964.*

Said first by Plato (*Phaedo* 64), repeated in other places at other
times, exaggerated, contested, torn from context, the philosophers'
maxim holds true: philosophy is the pursuit of death and dying.
The old natural philosopher, who was usually both physician and
philosopher, pondered with the skull upon his table. Not only did
he see death from the viewpoint of life. He viewed life through
the sockets of the skull.

Life and death come into the world together; the eyes and the
sockets which hold them are born at the same moment. *The moment
I am born I am old enough to die.* As I go on living I am dying.
Death is entered continuously, not just at the moment of death as
legally and medically defined. Each event in my life makes its contribution to my death, and I build my death as I go along day by
day. The counter position must logically also follow: any action
aimed against death, any action which resists death, hurts life.
Philosophy can conceive life and death together. For philosophy
they need not be exclusive opposites, polarised into Freud's Eros

and Thanatos, or Menninger's Love against Hate, one played against the other. One long tradition in philosophy puts the matter in quite another way. Death is the only absolute in life, the only surety and truth. Because it is the only condition which all life must take into account, it is the only human *a priori*. Life matures, develops, and aims at death. Death is its very purpose. We live in order to die. Life and death are contained within each other, complete each other, are understandable only in terms of each other. Life takes on its value through death, and the pursuit of death is the kind of life philosophers have often recommended. If only the living can die, only the dying are really alive.

Modern philosophy has come again to death, a main current of its tradition. Through the problem of death, philosophy and psychology are rejoining. Freud and Jung, Sartre and Heidegger, have placed death in the middle of their works. Most of Freud's followers rejected his metapsychology of death. Yet today, psychotherapy is fascinated with Heidegger, whose central theme is a metaphysics of death. Heidegger's Germanic language borne on a Black Forest wind is not what interests analysts. Nor is his logic of use, because it does not correspond with psychological facts. When he says that death is the fundamental possibility yet cannot be experienced as such, he is but repeating the rationalist arguments that existence and death (being and not-being) are logical contraries: where I am death is not, where death is I am not. Bridgman (who committed suicide in his old age) reasons in the same way: "There is no operation by which I can decide whether I am dead; 'I am always alive'." This line of thinking is taken by those who have trouble separating the realm of psychological experience from the realm of mentation or rational consciousness. This line argues that dying can be experienced, but not death. If we follow along we are led into foolishness, for we will have to say sleep and the unconscious can also not be experienced. Such quibbles no more affect psychological experience than do logical oppositions obtain in the soul.

Death and existence may exclude each other in rational philosophy, but they *are not psychological contraries*. Death can be experienced as a state of being, an existential condition. The very old sometimes inform us of experiences of finding themselves in another world which is not only more real but from which they view this. In dreams and in psychosis one can go through the anguish of dying, or one is dead; one knows it and feels it. In visions, the dead return and report on themselves. Every analysis shows death experiences in all variety, and we shall turn to examples shortly. The experience of death cannot be forced into a logical definition of death. What gives Heidegger—that unpsychological man—his influence in psychotherapy is one crucial insight. He confirms Freud by placing death at the centre of existence. *And analysts cannot get on without a philosophy of death.*

But philosophers provide answers to questions no more than analysts, or rather they provide many sorts of answers by splitting questions open to reveal many seeds of meaning. An analyst turning towards philosophy will not get the same defined viewpoint towards death and suicide as he will from systems of religion, law, and science. The one answer he will get from philosophy is philosophy itself; for when we ask about death we have begun to practise philosophy, the study of dying. This kind of answer is also psychotherapy.

To philosophise is partly to enter death; philosophy is death's rehearsal, as Plato said. It is one of the forms of the death experience. It has been called "dying to the world." The first movement in working through any problem is taking the problem upon oneself as an experience. One enters an issue by joining it. One approaches death by dying. Approaching death requires a dying in soul, daily, as the body dies in tissue. And as the body's tissue is renewed, so is the soul regenerated through death experiences. Therefore, working at the death problem is both a dying from the world with its illusory sustaining hope that there is no death, not really, and a dying into life, as a fresh and vital concern with essentials.

Because living and dying in this sense imply each other, any act which holds off death prevents life. "How" to die means nothing less than "how" to live. Spinoza turned the Platonic maxim around, saying, *Ethics* IV, 67) the philosopher thinks of nothing less than death, but this meditation is not of death but of life. Living in terms of life's only certain end means to live aimed towards death. This end is present here and now as the purpose of life, which means the moment of death—at any moment—is every moment. *Death cannot be put off to the future and reserved for old age.* By the time we are old we may no longer be able to experience death; then it may be merely to go through its outer motions. Or, it may have already been experienced, so that organic death has lost all sting. For organic death cannot undo the fundamental accomplishments of the soul. *Organic death has absolute power over life when death has not been allowed in life's midst.* When we refuse the experience of death we also refuse the essential question of life, and leave life unaccomplished. Then organic death prevents our facing the ultimate questions and cuts off our chance for redemption. To avoid this state of soul, traditionally called damnation, we are obliged to go to death before it comes to us.

Philosophy would tell us that we build towards death from day to day. We build each our own "ship of death" within ourselves. From this standpoint, by making our own deaths we are killing ourselves daily, so that each death is a suicide. Whether "from a lion, a precipice, or a fever," each death is of our own making. Then we need not beg with Rilke, "O Lord, give each man his own death", since just that God does give us, though we do not see it because we do not like it. When a man builds the structure of his life upwards like a building, climbing step by step, storey by storey, only to go out the high window or to be brought low by heart attack or stroke, has he not fulfilled his own architectural plan and been given his own death? In this view, suicide is no longer one of the ways of entering death, but *all death is suicide,* and the choice of method is only more or less evident, whether car-crash, heart-attack, or those acts usually called suicide.

By consciously going towards death, philosophy says we build the better vessel. Ideally, as we age, this building becomes more incorruptible, so that the passage to it from the failing flesh may be without fear, felicitous and easy. This death we build within us is that permanent structure, the "subtle body," in which the soul is housed amidst the decay of impermanence. But death is no easy matter; and dying is a rending business, ugly, cruel, and full of suffering. Going towards death consciously as philosophy proposes must therefore be a major human achievement, which is held up to us by the images of our religious and cultural heroes.

An analyst may do well to consider philosophy as a first step in his struggle with the suicide problem. Suicide can be for some an act of unconscious philosophy, an attempt to understand death by joining it. The impulse to death need not be conceived as an anti-life movement; it may be a demand for an encounter with absolute reality, *a demand for a fuller life through the death experience.*

Without dread, without the prejudices of prepared positions, without a pathological bias, suicide becomes "natural." It is natural because it is a possibility of our nature, a choice open to each human psyche. The analyst's concern is less with the suicidal choice as such, than it is with helping the other person to understand the meaning of this choice, *the only one which asks directly for the death experience.*

A main meaning of the choice is the importance of death for individuality. As individuality grows so does the possibility of suicide. Sociology and theology recognise this, as we have seen. Where man is law unto himself, responsible to himself for his own actions (as in the culture of cities, in the unloved child, in protestant areas, in creative people), the choice of death becomes a more frequent alternative. In this choice of death, of course, the opposite lies concealed. Until we can choose death, we cannot choose life. *Until we can say no to life, we have not really said yes to it,* but have only been carried along by its collective stream. The individual standing against this current experiences death as the first of all alternatives, for he who goes against the stream of life is its opponent and has become identified with death. Again, the death experience is needed to separate from the collective flow of life and to discover individuality.

Individuality requires courage. And courage has since classic times been linked with suicide arguments: it takes courage to choose the ordeal of life, and it takes courage to enter the unknown by one's own decision. Some choose life because they are afraid of death and others choose death because they are afraid of life. We cannot justly assess courage or cowardice from the outside. But we can understand why the problem of suicide raises these questions of courage, since the suicide issue forces one to find his individual stand on the basic question—to be or not to be. The courage to be— as it is modishly called—means not just choosing life out there. The real choice is choosing oneself, one's individual truth, including the ugliest man, as Nietzsche called the evil within. To continue life, knowing what a horror one is, takes indeed courage. And not a few suicides may arise from an overwhelming experience of one's own evil, an insight coming more readily to the creatively gifted, the psychologically sensitive, and the schizoid. Then who is the coward and who casts the first stone? The rest of us brutish men who go about dulled to our own shadows.

Each analysis comes upon death in one form or another. The dreamer dies in his dreams and there are deaths of other inner figures; relatives die; positions are lost never to be regained; deaths of attitudes; the death of love; experiences of loss and emptiness which are described as death; the sense of the presence of death and the terrible fear of dying. Some are "half in love with easeful death" for themselves or wish it for others, wanting to be killed or to kill. There is death in soaring sunwards like young Ikaros, in climbing for power, in the arrogant ambitions of omnipotence fantasies, where in one stroke of hatred and rage all enemies vanish. Some seem driven to death; others are hounded by it; still others are drawn to it by a call from what can only be empirically described as "the other side," a longing for a dead lover, or parent, or child. Others may have had an acute mystical vision as an encounter with death which has haunted their lives, forming an un-understood experience towards which they yearn. For some, each separation is death, and parting is dying. There are those who feel cursed, certain their life is an ineluctable progress into doom, a chain of destiny, the last link called suicide. Some may have escaped death in a holocaust or war and not yet have inwardly escaped, and the anxiety is enacted again and again. Phobias, compulsions, and insomnia may reveal a core of death. Masturbation, solitary and against the call of love and, like suicide, called the "English disease," evokes fantasies of death. Death can impinge upon the moral "how" of the individual's life: the review of life, one's faith, sins, destiny; how one got to where one is and how to continue. Or, whether to continue.

To understand all these death patterns, analysis cannot turn anywhere but to the soul to see what it says about death. Analysis develops its ideas on death empirically from the soul itself. Again Jung has been the pioneer. He simply listened to the soul tell its experiences and watched the images of the goal of life which the living psyche produces out of itself. Here, he was neither philosopher, nor physician, nor theologian, but psychologist, student of the soul.

He discovered that death has many guises and that it does not usually appear in the psyche as death *per se,* as extinction, negation, and finality. Images of dying and ideas of death have quite other meanings in dreams and fantasies. The soul goes through many death experiences, yet physical life goes on; and as physical life comes to a close, the soul often produces images and experiences that show continuity. The process of consciousness seems to be endless. *For the psyche, neither is immortality a fact, nor is death an end.* We can neither prove nor disprove survival. The psyche leaves the question open.

Searching for proof and demonstration of immortality is muddled thinking, because proof and demonstration are categories of science and logic. The mind uses these categories and the mind is convinced by proof. That is why the mind can be replaced by machines and the soul not. Soul is not mind and has other categories for dealing with its problem of immortality. For the soul, the equivalents of proof and demonstration are belief and meaning. They are as difficult to develop and make clear, as hard to wrestle with, as is proof. The soul struggles with the after-life question in terms of its experiences. Out of these experiences, not out of dogma or logic or empirical evidence, the positions of faith are built. And the fact alone that the psyche has this faculty of belief, unaffected by proof or demonstration, presses us towards the possibility of psychic immortality. Psychic immortality means neither resurrection of the flesh nor personal after-life. The former refers to immortality of the body, the latter to immortality of the mind. Our concern is with immortality of the soul.

What might be the function of these categories of belief and meaning in the soul? Are they not part of the soul's equipment— as proof and demonstration are used by the mind—for dealing with reality? If so, then the objects of belief may indeed be "real." This *psychological argument for immortality* has as its premise the old correspondence idea that the world and the soul of man are intimately linked. The psyche functions in correspondence with objective reality. If the soul has a function of belief it implies a corresponding objective reality for which belief has its function. This psychological position has been stated in the theological arguments that only believers get to Heaven. Without the function of belief, there is no corresponding reality of Heaven.

This psychological approach to immortality can be put another way: following Jung, the concept of energy and its indestructibility was an ancient and widespread notion associated in countless ways with the idea of the soul, long before Robert Mayer formulated the conservation of energy into a scientific law. We cannot get away from this primordial image even in modern scientific psychology, which still speaks of the psyche in dynamic terms. What is immortality and reincarnation of the soul in psychology is conservation and transformation of energy in physics. The mind's certainty that energy is "eternal" is given by law in physics. This corresponds with the soul's conviction that it is immortal, and the sense of immortality is the inner feeling of the eternity of psychic energy. *For if the psyche is an energetic phenomenon, then it is indestructible.* Its existence in "another life" cannot be proved any more than the existence of the soul in this life can be proved. Its existence is given only psychologically in the form of inner certainty, i.e., belief.

When we ask why each analysis comes upon the death experience so often and in such variety, we find, primarily, *death appears in order to make way for transformation.* The flower withers around its swelling pod, the snake sheds its skin, and the adult puts off his childish ways. The creative force kills as it produces the new. Every turmoil and disorder called neurosis can be seen as a life and death struggle in which the players are masked. What is called death by the neurotic mainly because it is dark and unknown is a new life trying to break through into consciousness; what he calls life because it is familiar is but a dying pattern he tries to keep alive. The death experience breaks down the old order, and in so far as analysis is a prolonged "nervous breakdown" (synthesising too as it goes along), *analysis means dying.* The dread to begin an analysis touches these deep terrors, and the fundamental problem of resistance cannot be taken superficially. Without a dying to the world of the old order, there is no place for renewal, because, as we shall consider later, it is illusory to hope that growth is but an additive process requiring neither sacrifice nor death. The soul favours the death experience to usher in change. Viewed this way, a suicide impulse is a transformation drive. It says: "Life as it presents itself must change. Something must give way. Tomorrow and tomorrow and tomorrow is a tale told by an idiot. The pattern must come to a complete stop. But, since I can do nothing about life out there, having tried every twist and turn, I shall put an end to it here, in my own body, that part of the objective world over which I still have power. I put an end to myself."

When we examine this reasoning we find it leads from psychology to ontology. The movement towards a complete stop, towards that fulfillment in stasis where all processes cease, is an attempt to enter another level of reality, to move from becoming to being. To put an end to oneself means to come to one's end, to find the end or limit of what one is, in order to arrive at what one is not—yet. "This" is exchanged for "that"; one level is wiped out for another. *Suicide is the attempt to move from one realm to another by force through death.*

This movement to another aspect of reality can be formulated by those basic opposites called body and soul, outer and inner, activity and passivity, matter and spirit, here and beyond, which become symbolised by life and death. The agony over suicide represents the struggle of the soul with the paradox of all these opposites. The suicide decision is a choice between these contradictions which seem impossible to reconcile. Once the choice is made, ambivalence overcome (as the studies of Ringel and of Morgenthaler on suicide notes show), the person is usually deliberate and calm, giving no sign of his intention to kill himself. He has crossed over.

This calm corresponds with the death experience of the physically dying, of whom Sir William Osler said, "A few, very few, suffer severely in the body and fewer still in the mind." The death agony usually takes place before the moment of organic death. Death comes first as an experience of the soul, after which the body expires. "Fear," says Osis, "is not a dominant emotion in the dying," whereas elation and exaltation occur frequently. Other investigations of dying report similar findings. The fear of dying concerns *the experience of death,* which is separable from physical death and not dependent upon it.

If suicide is a transformation impulse we can regard today's concern with mass suicide through the Bomb as an attempt of the collective psyche at renewal by ridding itself of the binds of history and the weight of its material accumulations. In a world where things and the physical life overwhelmingly predominate, where goods have become the "good," that which would destroy them and us with them because of our attachments will, of course, become "evil." Yet, could this evil not somewhere be a good in disguise, by showing how shaky and relative our current values are? Through the Bomb we live in the shadow of death. Where it may bring the death experience nearer, it must not mean that mass suicide is also closer. Where life is clung to, suicide takes on the compulsive attraction of "over-kill." But where collective death is lived with—as in the Nazi concentration camps or during war—suicide is seldom. The point is: *the more immanent the death experience, the more possibility for transformation.* The world is closer to a collective suicide, yes; that this suicide must actually occur, no. What must occur if the actual suicide does not come is a transformation in the collective psyche. The Bomb may thus be God's dark hand which He has shown before to Noah and the peoples of the Cities of the Plain, urging not death, but a radical transformation in our souls.

In individuals where the suicide impulse is not directly associated with the ego, but seems a voice or figure or content of the unconscious that pushes or leads or orders the person to self-murder, again it can be saying: "We cannot meet one another again until a change takes place, a change which ends your identification with your concrete life." *Suicide fantasies provide freedom from the actual and usual view of things,* enabling one to meet the realities of the soul. These realities appear as images and voices, as well as impulses, with which one can communicate. But for these conversations with death one must take the realm of the soul—with its night spirits, its uncanny emotions and shapeless voices, where life is disembodied and highly autonomous—as a reality. Then what appear as regressive impulses can reveal their positive values.

For instance, a young man who would hang himself after an examination failure is drawn to choke off his spirit, or blow out his brains, after having tried too hard to fly too high. Death is dark and easeful; passivity and the inertia of matter draw him down again. Melancholy, that black affliction in which so many suicides occur, shows the pull of gravity downwards into the dark, cold bones of reality. Depression narrows and concentrates upon essences, and suicide is the final denial of existence for the sake of essence. Or, a dead father figure (as Hamlet's ghost) continues to fascinate a woman through suicide thoughts. When she turns to face him she finds him saying: "You are lost in the mundane because you have forgotten your father and buried your aspirations. Die and ascend." Even in those suicide notes where a husband kills himself ostensibly to remove the obstacle to his wife's freedom and happiness, there is an attempt to achieve another state of being through suicide. There is an attempt at transformation.

Transformation, to be genuine and thorough, always affects the body. Suicide is always somewhere a body problem. The transformations from infancy to childhood are accompanied by physical changes both in body structure and libidinal zones; so, too, the major transforming moments of life at puberty, menopause, and old age. Crises are emotional, transfusing the body with joy and anguish and altering looks and habit. Initiation rites are ordeals of the flesh. The death experience emphasises transformation in the body and *suicide is an attack on bodily life.* The Platonic idea that the soul was trapped in the body and released by death has relevance here. Some feel themselves alien in their own bodies all their lives. To encounter the realm of the soul as a reality equal to the usual view of reality, a dying to the world is indeed required. This may produce the impulse to destroy the bodily trap. And, because we can never know whether the old idea of immortal soul in mortal body is true or not, the analyst will at least consider suicide in the light of a body–soul opposition.

The attack on bodily life is for some an attempt *to destroy the affective basis of ego-consciousness.* Suicidal mutilations are extreme distortions of this form of the death experience. Such mutilations can be understood in the light of Eastern meditation techniques or in the universal imagery of sacrificing the animal carrier, bodily life. Because images and fantasies impel action, methods are used for killing off the affective impulse from psychological contents. Memory is washed of desire. For action to be purged of impulse and for image to be free for imaginative play and meditative concentration, bodily desire must die. It must not die directly through suicide, which in this case would be a concrete misinterpretation of a psychological necessity. The necessity is simply that, for an awareness beyond egocentric limitations, affect and image must be separated. This separation proceeds through the introversion of the libido, archetypally represented by the incest complex. Then bodily desire unites with the soul, rather than with the world. The affective impulse becomes then wholly psychic through this conjunction and is transformed.

When the psyche persists in presenting its demands for transformation it may use, besides death, other symbols showing birth and growth, transitions of place and time, and the like. Death, however, is the most effective because it brings with it that intense emotion without which no transformation takes place. The death experience challenges most, requiring a vitally whole response. It means all process is stopped. It is the confrontation with tragedy, for there is no way out, except onward, into it. Tragedy is born *in extremis,* where one is cornered into making a *salto mortale* towards another plane of being. Tragedy is the leap out of history into myth; personal life is pierced by the impersonal arrows of fate. *The death experience offers each life the opening into tragedy,* for, as the Romantics saw it, death extinguishes the merely personal and transposes life on to the heroic key where sounds not only adventure, experiment, and absurdity, but more—the tragic sense of life. Tragedy and death are necessarily interwoven, so that the death experience has the bite of tragedy, and the tragic sense is the awareness of death.

The other symbols of transformation (as birth, growth, transitions of place and time) all openly indicate a next stage. They present this next stage before the present one is over. They unfold new possibilities, affording hope; whereas the death experience never feels like a transition. It is the major transition which, paradoxically, says there is no future. The end has come. It is all over, too late.

Under the pressure of "too late," knowing that life went wrong and there is no longer a way out, suicide offers itself. *Then suicide is the urge for hasty transformation.* This is not premature death, as medicine might say, but the late reaction of a delayed life which did not transform as it went along. It would die all at once, and now, because it missed its death crises before. This impatience and intolerance reflects a soul that did not keep pace with its life; or, in older people, a life that no longer nourishes with experiences a still-hungering soul. For the old there is guilt and sin to be expiated, and so I am my own executioner. The spouse is dead. There may be no certainty about an after-life reunion, yet there may at least be a possibility of joining on the "other side," whereas here is but barren grief. Or there is the sense of having already died; an apathetic indifference that says, "I don't care if I live or die." The soul has already left a world through which the body moves like painted cardboard. In each case time is out of joint and suicide would set it right.

When analysis presents the death experience it is often associated with those primary images of the soul, the anima and animus. The struggles with the seductions of the anima and the plots of the animus are contests with death. These struggles are more lethal in adult life than are the parental threats of the negative mother and father images. The challenges of the anima and animus threaten even the life of the organism, because the core of these archetypal dominants is psychoid, that is, bound up with the physical life of the body through emotion. Disease, crime, psychosis, and addiction are only some of the crasser manifestations of the death aspects of the anima and animus archetypes. Again and again, the animus appears as the killer and the anima as the temptress who seemingly leads a man into life but only to destroy him. The psychology of Jung offers deep insights into these specific carriers of death in the soul.

In analysis a person finds death all about him, especially in dreams. There he cuts up the old order with knives, burns it, and buries it. Buildings crumble; there is rot, worms, or fire in the walls. He follows funeral processions and enters graveyards. There sounds uncanny music. He sees unknown corpses, watches women at their prayers, and hears the bell toll. His name is inscribed in a family album, a register, or a stone. Parts of his body disintegrate; the surgeon, the gardener, and the executioner come for dismemberment. A judge condemns, a priest performs last rites. A bird lies fallen on its back. It is twelve o'clock, or happenings come in dark threes. Claws, coffins, shrouds, grimacing masks with teeth appear. Scythes, serpents, dogs, bones, white and black horses, ravens portend destruction. A thred is cut, a tree felled. Things go up in smoke. There are signs of gates and thresholds. He is led downward by an ambiguous female; or, if a woman, disembodied eyes, fingers, wings, and voices indicate to her a dark way. Or there can be a marriage, intercourse with an angel, a weird dance, rioting at a wake, an ancestral banquet of symbolic foods, or a journey to a happy paradisical land. A sense of dampness is felt, as of the tomb, and a sudden gust of chill wind. There is death by air, by fire, by water, and by burial in the earth. Coma, ecstasy, and the trance of effortless passivity float the dreamer away. Or he is caught in a net or a web. He witnesses the death of all the carriers of no longer viable ways of adaptation, as favourites of childhood, world heroes, even as beloved pets and plants and trees. As old relationships fade in daily life there are departures and he loses habitual ways of behaving, he finds himself a hermit in a cave, by a stagnant pool, in the desert thirsting, at the abyss edge, or on a far island. Again, he is threatened by forces of nature (the sea or lightning) chased by packs of animals, of murderers (robbers and ravishers), or sinister machines. Or, he may turn upon himself.

The varieties of imagery for experiencing death would seem

unlimited. Each tells the way the conscious view of death is reflected by the unconscious, ranging from sweet escape to brutal murder. Each time that one experiences these images and a new turn of suffering begins, a piece of life is being given over and we go through loss, mourning, and grief. With it comes loneliness and a vacuum. Each time something has come to a stop.

Where the death experience insists on a suicidal image, then it is the patient's "I" and everything he holds to be his "I" which is coming to its end. The entire network and structure is to be broken, every tie slipped, every bond loosed. The "I" will be totally and unconditionally released. The life that has been built up is now a cage of commitments to be sprung; for a man it is often with the violence of masculine force and for a woman a dissolution into the soft reception of nature through drowning, asphyxiation, or sleep. What comes next no longer matters in the sense of "will it be better or worse"; what comes next will for sure be something else, completely, the Wholly Other. What comes next is irrelevant, because it leads away from the death experience and saps it of its effect.

This effect is all that counts. How it comes and when it comes are questions secondary to why it comes. *From the evidence which the psyche produces out of itself, the effect of the death experience is to bring home at a critical moment a radical transformation.* To step in at this moment with prevention in the name of life's preservation would frustrate the radical transformation. A thorough crisis is a death experience; we cannot have the one without the other. From this we are led to conclude that the experience of death is requisite for psychic life. This implies that the suicidal crisis, because it is one of the ways of experiencing death, must also be considered necessary to the life of the soul.

DEATH AND THE LAW

One of the assumptions running through all the essays collected in this book is that death is an issue in the way persons live with each other. On the one hand, the occurrence of death leaves a deep mark on the social fabric, requiring us to reorder and sometimes even reconstitute the collective structures of our lives; on the other, the occurrence of death is itself often the direct or indirect result of the way we have arranged our societies. This is not to say, of course, that death cannot also provoke a personal crisis, that the prospect of our own death cannot cause a radical shift in our individual self-understanding. We are concerned here with death as a social issue, and not as a personal crisis, but this is not to conceal the fact that the two are rarely so neatly separable.

To refer to death as a social issue is to indicate that there is a serious disagreement over the appropriate action concerning death. Death does not in itself, however, constitute the issue; the issue lies in a conflict of social policy, in a conflict of the public will. There are instances of directly administered death that excite little public debate. War, for example, particularly a popular war, may be opposed by only an insignificant number of politically impotent protesters. And there are instances in which public policy has a widespread *indirect* effect on mortality, but often goes unchallenged.

Treatment of the aged, the use of chemicals in food production and processing, and governmentally monitored safety regulations are but a few of the areas in which public policy has some effect on how and when people die. While none of these is without controversy, the public's interest seems more focused on such issues as euthanasia, abortion, organ transplantation, and capital punishment.

We might sharpen the nature of these issues by observing that each of the latter can ultimately be understood as the issue of homicide. In euthanasia and abortion the question is whether killing can be legally sanctioned. In organ transplantation the question often arises whether the donor, particularly in heart transplants, is being unnecessarily killed. It is worth repeating that the dispute in these areas does not arise from the fact of death itself, but from the meaning of that death in the social context. The law, in other words, does not prohibit killing in all cases, but only in some.

Since the issues of euthanasia and abortion have been dealt with earlier, with extended discussion of the appropriate legal sanctions or prohibitions, this section will address three other areas of controversial legislation: capital punishment, the statutory defintion of death, and the anatomical gift act.

The fact that death itself is not the issue, but rather the social meaning of that death, is immediately evident when we compare the character of the debate surrounding capital punishment with the abortion discussion. It is, in fact, possible to argue *against* abortion and *for* capital punishment. A notable instance of this is the article by Brendan F. Brown, "Individual Liberty and the Common Good," in the present section. In what way is the homicide involved in capital punishment to be distinguished from the kind of killing involved in abortion? The heart of Brown's argument lies in the free choice of the criminal. If the murderer has willfully degraded the human nature of another person, or even his own nature, he "has forfeited his right to be treated in every instance as if he had human dignity." Therefore, when society decides to kill its murderers it is killing those persons who are without human dignity, and this is killing in a very different sense.

Brown's reasoning touches on the point that lies at the center of the deterence argument: that is, that the prospect of one's own death would deter one from taking the death of another. If one, knowing that one's own life is at stake, murders another anyway, one has, in fact, chosen one's own death. When this reasoning is pushed a bit more it can even be said that capital punishment is not the state's act of taking life as much as it is the criminal's act of taking his or her own.

There are, of course, other arguments favoring the death penalty that have nothing to do with deterence. There is a strong desire among many to exact death as the penalty for murder if only because it is a fitting penalty for such a weighty crime. This retributive impulse lies behind the article by Carol S. Vance, a district attorney and, at the time the article was written, the President of the National District Attorney's Association. There is no apology in Vance's reasoning for asking the state to commit homicide.

The Supreme Court's highly controversial decision on capital punishment, *Furman* v. *Georgia*, summarized in the first selection of this section, shows the recalcitrance on the part of the judiciary in asking directly for the state to commit murder. The majority view is largely developed around the difficulty of finding any ground for saying that capital punishment is not itself the very crime which the punishment is designed to eliminate. By saying that it is "cruel and unusual" and therefore in violation of the Eighth and Fourteenth Amendments, the justices seem to be ruling against the retributive function of the death penalty. However, only two of the justices actually declared the penalty unconstitutional. The others indicated the inconsistent application of the penalty, suggesting that it is the incomplete and perhaps prejudiced views of the jurors and judges in capital cases that leads to the death penalty, and not the criminal's willful choice to put aside his own dignity as a human being.

The controversy surrounding capital punishment is a reflection of a deep division in the attitudes of the public toward death. The controversy surrounding the statutory definition of death and the donation of organs is much more a reflection of the technical sophistication of medical science. In these areas legislation is designed only to advance life and to prevent any unnecessary taking of life. The discussion of these issues is often technical and loaded with hair-splitting distinctions, but the stakes are high. Because organ transplantation can save or improve the lives of many thousands of persons, it is obviously desirable to find a way of increasing the supply of available healthy organs. At the same time the very technology that has made transplantation possible has also made possible a previously unimagined continuation of life. The question now turns around whether what is being kept alive by machines is in fact a person or only an organism forever incapable of retrieving those characteristics essential to personhood.

The Uniform Anatomical Gift Act, included here along with a commentary from the *Journal of the American Medical Association,* represents the combined labor of many experts to unravel the complexities of law and medicine and produce a legally valid and medically useful piece of legislation. The article by Capron and Kass, "Standards for Determining Human Death," is also the concluding statement of a long and careful discussion by experts. Whereas the Uniform Anatomical Gift Act has the status of law, the legislation proposed by Capron and Kass has not yet been enacted into law.

CAPITAL PUNISHMENT
AND THE LAW

*This article summarizes the current legal status of capital punish-
ment as it makes its way through the courts under various cases and
proposed legislation. The author shows the unresolved subtleties
in this issue as they now come before the courts and legislatures.*

This article appeared, unsigned, in the Annual Survey of American Law, *1973/74.*

[*Editor's note: The reader who wishes to do further research on
the subject of this article is advised to consult the extensive footnotes included in its original publication.*]

In *Furman* v. *Georgia,* the Supreme Court, in a per curiam opinion,
held that the imposition of capital punishment in the cases before
it would be unconstitutional as "cruel and unusual punishment in
violation of the Eighth and Fourteenth Amendments." The five
Justices concurring in the result delivered separate opinions expressing
a variety of reasons to support the ruling: capital punishment is imposed discriminatorily against the poor and members of minority
groups, is inherently cruel because of its uniqueness and extreme
severity, serves no legitimate legislative purpose, is repugnant to the
values of modern society, and, because of the juries' broad discretion
in imposing it, has been inflicted in an arbitrary and "freakish" manner which belies and defeats any valid state interest.

Since, however, only two of the Justices (Brennan and Marshall)
expressed the belief that capital punishment is unconstitutional *per
se, Furman* has not mandated the end of the death penalty altogether, and the past year has witnessed efforts by legislatures and
courts to rewrite or interpret state capital punishment statutes so as
to ensure their validity. These efforts have been aimed primarily at

eliminating the element of the jury's discretion which Justices Stewart and White found objectionable in *Furman*.

The reinstitution of the death penalty by various state legislatures has included the following approaches, both individually and collectively: (1) mandatory death for first degree murder and other first degree capital offenses, (2) specifying which aggravating and mitigating circumstances determine when the death penalty, or a lesser penalty, is to be imposed, and (3) specifying those particular fact patterns (*e.g.*, the commission of a murder while under a sentence of life imprisonment, the assassination of a governor) which mandate imposition of the death penalty.

It is questionable, however, whether the first of these approaches, the mandatory death penalty for first degree capital offenses, is an effective solution to the problem of discretion. Although a jury under such a system has no choice in the mode of punishment to be meted out, it does have discretion in determining the crime of which a defendant is guilty. If found guilty of first degree murder, a defendant will suffer death; if found guilty of second degree murder, he will live. Thus, the jury still has a choice between life and death. The only way to eliminate this element of discretion is to allow no distinction between the punishment for first and second degree murder. However, such a broad scope of the death penalty would pose two new problems. First, it is doubtful whether the public would tolerate or endorse a policy of sentencing to death all persons found guilty of homicide, without regard to the mitigating factors usually associated with second degree murder. Second, such a broad application of the death penalty may encompass some individuals for whom the punishment of death would not be a rational state response; under such circumstances the death penalty would serve no valid legislative purpose and thus might be unconstitutional.

The establishment of specific aggravating and mitigating circumstances for determining when the death penalty is to be imposed could be one solution to this problem of "degrees." However, some of the states which have adopted statutes of this nature have not used them to supplant the traditional "degree" murder statutes, but rather to supplement them. Only Utah and Connecticut have instituted a statutory scheme which requires a determination to be made, first, as to whether or not a defendant is guilty of murder in a specific fact pattern, and then, as to what aggravating or mitigating factors exist. All other states which have adopted the approach of aggravating/mitigating circumstances still retain a preliminary investigation into the degree of murder; only if the individual is found guilty of first degree murder does the aggravating/mitigating statute come into play. Thus, the problem of "degrees" remains.

The amount of discretion may even be increased if the aggravating/mitigating statute enumerates vaguely worded circumstances which are open to varying interpretations or fails to provide guidelines as to how to weigh each circumstance or resolve combinations of conflicting circumstances. Nevertheless, in *State* v. *Dixon,* the Supreme Court of Florida upheld that state's capital punishment statute, despite assertions that it suffered from these flaws. Defendants criticized in particular the enumeration of two aggravating circumstances as failing to provide meaningful guidelines in sentencing: conduct creating a "great risk of death to many persons" and offenses which were termed "especially heinous, atrocious or cruel." The court, however, concluded that the meaning of these aggravating circumstances was easily comprehensible to a person of ordinary intelligence, and hence they were not excessively vague.

The most interesting and novel aspect of the *Dixon* opinion was the majority's approach to the issue of discretion in general. Florida's statutory scheme provides for a post-conviction hearing before the convicting jury in order to determine what sentence to impose. The jury "weighs" the aggravating and mitigating evidence presented, but its determination is not binding. Rather, its decision has the status of a mere recommendation which the judge, after similarly "weighing" the evidence, is free to disregard. Since the statute merely lists the aggravating and mitigating circumstances without giving any guidance as to how to weigh them, and since the judge can disregard the jury's recommendation and impose a greater or lesser penalty as he sees fit, the scheme appears on its face to involve a considerable degree of discretion.

The majority was convinced, however, that the existence of five steps between a defendant's conviction and his sentencing to death, when combined with the aggravating/mitigating statute, eliminated the danger of unbridled discretion and ensured that the sentencing process was "a matter of reasoned judgment." The court in *Dixon* concluded that *Furman* did not mandate the end of all discretion, as it believed that some discretion was inevitable at every stage of the judicial process and that the legislature could not provide "computer justice." Rather, *Furman* merely required that any discretion in the sentencing process be controlled and reasoned, rather than arbitrary. The *Dixon* majority concluded that Florida's statute met this requirement, emphasizing in particular that the provision for automatic review of a death sentence by the Supreme Court of Florida guaranteed uniformity of result in similar cases.

While Florida's scheme appears to minimize the possibility of "freakish" results, the result in *Dixon* may be inconsistent with *Furman.* As Judge Ervin noted in dissent, several of the statutes invalidated in the aftermath of *Furman* provided for similar sentencing and review procedures. Furthermore, many of these statutes also required the weighing of aggravating and mitigating circumstances, either statutorily or as part of the state's case law.

Judge Ervin's dissent in *Dixon* also raised an interesting argument which, if valid, may affect all legislative approaches to the reinstatement of the death penalty. This argument, based on the equal protection clause, was that since the taking of an individual's life constitutes an infringement of his "fundamental rights," it will not suffice for a state to show merely a reasonable or "valid" interest in the imposition of the death penalty; it must instead prove a "compelling" interest. Absent such a "compelling state interest," a determination by a state that those guilty of certain offenses should suffer a punishment as severe and irrevocable as death, while others do not, is not sustainable. Judge Ervin noted that the Florida legislature apparently had attempted merely to "fit" its statute into the *Furman* opinions and had not shown a compelling interest in reinstating the death penalty. Furthermore, he stated that it is difficult to maintain that any state has such a compelling state interest as long as states differ as to whether or not, and for what crimes, they will impose capital punishment. Judge Ervin thus believed that the only death statute which would reflect a compelling state interest would be a national, uniform standard.

This conclusion, though interesting, is flawed. Under such a view of the equal protection clause, no state could differ at all from its sisterstates in any law which distinguishes among different classes of citizens in an area of fundamental rights. The equal protection clause has never been given a scope so broad that it would dissolve distinctions between states as well as between citizens.

The third approach taken by state legislatures in reinstating the death penalty, that of enumerating specific fact patterns which mandate death (*e.g.,* the commission of a murder while under life imprisonment, the assassination of a governor) has been adopted by some states either as a preliminary determination before an inquiry into aggravating or mitigating circumstances, or as an absolute determinant of when the death penalty is to be imposed. Such a procedure may be a viable, totally non-discretionary approach to the reinstatement of capital punishment, so long as the fact patterns themselves are not vague or otherwise open to variant interpretations which could allow discretion. However, there has not yet been any case law since *Furman* ruling on the constitutionality of statutes reflecting this approach.

It must be borne in mind, however, that the previous discussion is based on the assumption made by most courts and legislatures since *Furman* that discretion in and of itself is a fatal flaw in any capital punishment statute. If, however, a statute permitting discretion is constitutional as long as it is not carried out in a discriminatory or freakish manner, the mandatory death penalty and aggravating/mitigating statutes may all be constitutional.

The death penalty has been reinstated, not only by the legislatures, but indirectly by courts as well. Two state courts have accomplished this by striking the discretionary provisions and converting the enactments into mandatory death statutes. In *State* v. *Dickerson,* the Supreme Court of Delaware invalidated the state's "mercy" statute, which gave the jury discretion to recommend the reduction of a death sentence to one of life imprisonment, but left in force the statute which mandated a death penalty for first degree murder. The court reached this result by applying Delaware's severance statute, which allowed a court to invalidate only those provisions or portions of a statutory scheme found to be unconstitutional. In *State* v. *Waddell* the Supreme Court of North Carolina reached a similar result, despite the fact that its code, unlike the one involved in *Dickerson,* did not contain a severence provision and that its mercy provision was not embodied in a separate statute. The North Carolina court found a basis for severance of the statute in the legislative history of the Act. Thus, both North Carolina and Delaware have been left with mandatory death penalties.

These decisions, in addition to presenting the problems inherent in all mandatory death provisions, are questionable in several respects. First, they constitute interference in the legislative realm and are quite possibly contrary to the legislative intent. The "mercy" provisions of both Delaware and North Carolina were relatively recent enactments by the state legislatures as compared to the older death statutes; it appears from this legislative history that North Carolina and Delaware were moving away from a mandatory death sentence and towards a decrease in capital punishment, rather than in the direction the courts have chosen. Furthermore, *Dickerson* and *Waddell* are contrary to the view taken by most courts after *Furman,* which believed that the Supreme Court's ruling prevented the states from sentencing anyone to death under their existing statutes. All of these courts reduced the death sentences to life imprisonment, and none suggested that they had any power to rewrite the statutes by striking only their discretionary provisions.

The *Dickerson* and *Waddell* courts found a legislative intent to have a mandatory death penalty from the fact that the legislature had repeatedly refused to pass bills which would have abolished capital punishment entirely; the legislature, therefore, probably would not accept a severance of the statute which would yield that result. At best, however, this legislative history is inconclusive since, when faced with the question of total abolition of capital punishment, the legislature was not faced with the possibility of the sole alternative being a mandatory death penalty. In fact, when considering attempts to legislate mandatory capital punishment, the North Carolina legislature rejected such proposals.

These decisions thus evidence a "boomerang" effect of *Furman.* Rather than abolishing or limiting the death penalty in this country, *Furman* in some instances seems to have become the source of stricter death penalties, through both judicial and legislative action. By virtue of these judicial reinstatements, the task of changing the law has fallen upon lobbyists against capital punishment, rather than upon those who favor it.

One must question, however, whether these judicial reinstatements of the death penalty will withstand scrutiny by the Supreme Court. Two Supreme Court Justices have indicated opposition to the death penalty in any form whatsoever. The four dissenting opinions in *Furman* were founded on disapproval of the Court's interference in matters properly within the legislature's competence. This forecasts a minimum of six judges who would probably overrule judicial reinstatements of capital punishment, on the basis of either the unconstitutionality of the death penalty itself or the impropriety of judicial interference in legislative matters.

INDIVIDUAL LIBERTY AND
THE COMMON GOOD

Brendan F. Brown

In previous essays in the present volume authors have opposed and supported abortion on such grounds as the personhood of the fetus and the fetus's right to life. Professor Brown opposes abortion in this essay on an altogether different ground: natural law. The same appeal to natural law, however, leads him to support capital punishment, clearly indicating that natural law is not opposed to homicide as such, but only certain forms of homicide. The first part of Brown's essay is summarized.

Brendan F. Brown is a professor emeritus, at Loyola University School of Law.

This article, originally entitled "Individual Liberty and the Common Good—the Balance: Prayer, Capital Punishment, Abortion," appeared in the Catholic Lawyer, *summer, 1974.*

[Brown reminds the reader that the American constitution was written by persons committed to the philosophy of natural law. The distinctive features of natural law are that it is discoverable in nature by the exercise of reason, and that it originates in a "higher authority," that is, it is divinely established. The fact that natural law is believed by many to originate in the divine will does not mean that one must be a believer in God either to know what the law is or to obey it. The law is rational and objective and can therefore be found and understood by any rational person regardless of his or her faith.

There are, of course, other philosophies of law. Common law, for example, is neither discoverable by reason nor divinely instituted. It is the cumulated wisdom of a people through a continuous history. The theory of law identified with the philosopher Immanuel

Kant is still different. For Kant the origin of law is the innate sense of good and evil, along with the felt constraint to do one's duty as it is understood within.

Brown strongly insists that it was the philosophy of natural law that informed the authors of the principal American juridical institutions, including the constitution, and that to interpret the constitution by any other philosophy is therefore a violation of the intent of the nation's founders.

An aspect of natural law important to Brown is the subtle balance between *individual dignity* and the *common good*. He understands the individual's dignity to consist chiefly in terms of liberty—but liberty with limits. A person is not free simply to do all he or she is able to do, but free to do whatever will not diminish the liberty—or dignity—of others. It is possible, of course, but rarely the case, that all of an individual's desires will be both rational and consistent with the common good. More frequently there are some areas of conflict in which individual liberty must be restricted—though never eliminated (except in properly applied capital punishment, as Brown will argue). The United States constitution is designed to create a juridical commonwealth in which such conflicts are sharply reduced.

The Supreme Court, by Brown's account, has on several significant occasions abandoned the original philosophy of natural law—sometimes to judge according to social convention, sometimes to add to the scope of individual liberty. It is in this latter category that Brown feels the court has most seriously erred. He cites five cases in which commitment to the common good was exchanged for an unduly high valuation of personal privacy. Two of these cases have to do with prayer in the public schools, one with capital punishment, and two with abortion.

Brown's view of the school prayer issue is, briefly, that the dignity of the dissenting children was not threatened by the practice of beginning the school day with a simple prayer. He appears to be arguing that the reason no one's dignity was being diminished by this practice is that the prayers did, after all, acknowledge the existence of the very source of the laws that guarantee human dignity. To have thrown out the prayers because some children were embarrassed is like throwing out the truth because it breaks in on someone's privacy. "There are still those who believe that the world is flat," Brown writes. "But the liberty to believe this does not prevent the teaching of the contrary."

He states his case against the court's decisions on the death penalty and abortion as follows.]

In *Furman* v. *Georgia,* the capital punishment case, one of the petitioners, Furman, had been convicted of murder, and the two other petitioners had been convicted of rape. In each instance, the jury, which had been given the discretion to impose the death penalty, exercised that discretion in favor of that penalty. The Supreme Court held, in a 5-4 per curiam opinion, "that the imposition and carrying out of the death penalty in these cases constitutes cruel and unusual punishment in violation of the Eighth and Fourteenth Amendments."

The holding in *Furman* by the five Justices "did not purport to prohibit, although it did not approve, a statute where the death penalty is mandatory for a particular crime." Regardless of the constitutionality of more narrowly drawn death penalty statutes, it has been observed that the *Furman* Court "has prohibited capital punishment in the overwhelming majority of cases where it has previously been imposed for rape and murder at the discretion of the jury." It may be that "in addition, *Furman* may contain the seeds, in the opinions of Justices Brennan and Marshall, of a complete proscription of the death penalty in the future."

The reasoning behind the decision was that it was cruel and unusual punishment to allow a jury, after it had found an accused guilty of murder or rape, to sentence him to either death or imprisonment. This was on the apparent premise that capital punishment itself, however carried out, was cruel and unusual. The illegality of one of the two choices left to the discretion of a jury constitutionally voided the statute which attempted to confer the discretion. It is submitted that the real reason was to enlarge the individual liberty of the convicted. For almost two hundred years the words "cruel and unusual punishment" in the Constitution had meant only such obviously unreasonable punishments as cutting off a man's hand for theft, or crucifixion for murder or rape. Prior cases had interpreted the eighth amendment as forbidding "torturous or barbaric penalties," or cruel methods of carrying out a sentence of capital punishment.

The argument that capital punishment is cruel and unusual is clearly specious. According to a natural law approach, a punishment is not cruel and unusual when it is necessary to carry into effect the death penalty as an essential protection of the common good, and when it is not used as an end in itself, such as inflicting pain as a matter of revenge or sadism. There must be a reasonable relation between the gravity of the crime and the penalty imposed. The penalty should fit the crime as well as the criminal. Obviously, death would be an excessive punishment for offenses other than murder, rape, or treason. It should also be understood that capital punishment is justified only when the criminal in question has, beyond a reasonable doubt, committed the crime with full knowledge that his act is evil and antisocial. Likewise, the crime must be a great injustice against the human dignity of the victim, as in murder or rape, or the life of a justly ruling state, as in treason.

What weight is to be given to the values which are to be balanced in the area of capital punishment? On one side of the scale is the freedom of the convict not to forfeit his life. On the other is the right of society to have the common good protected against the gross injustice which such crimes as murder inflict. The formula is that the greater weight should be given to the social claim as long as this does not deprive the individual of a liberty which is absolutely indispensable for the preservation of his human dignity. According to this formula, the scale should be tipped in favor of the social interest.

The claim of society to protect itself by recourse to capital punishment is not unreasonable. While it is not certain that capital punishment protects society by deterrence, the conclusion that it does is not unreasonable. Life imprisonment may not be adequate as a punishment by society because it is common knowledge that sentences of life imprisonment are seldom, if ever, fully served. Whether capital punishment protects society by way of deterrence is a conclusion of fact, which cannot be resolved with certainty. But the conclusion of the members of the forty legislatures in the respective states who enacted the death penalty is surely not less valid in this matter than that of the Justices of the Supreme Court. What superior wisdom do judges have to reach the factual conclusion that capital punishment is not necessary as a deterrent, and as a definitive means of permanently preventing a repetition of the crime?

Recourse to the death penalty by society does not deprive the convict of any essential of his human dignity. The criminal has surrendered his human dignity during the commission of his crime. The commission of a grave crime, such as murder or rape, involves the self-inflicted degradation of the criminal's human dignity, along with that of his innocent victim. How does freedom from the fear of the death penalty enhance the essential human dignity of a murderer or rapist, before, during, or after the commission of his crime? Indeed, it will aid him in his purposes for he will have the certain knowledge that his own life is not in danger.

The criminal is not morally or legally free to degrade human nature—either his own or that of another. He has forfeited his right to be treated in every instance as if he had human dignity if society decides that capital punishment is the only way in which it can protect itself. The common good is adversely affected when the individual inflicts a serious wound upon his own human dignity or that of another because each individual is related sociologically to every other individual within the unity of society. In one sense, each is like a cell in the body social. The tainted human dignity of an unjust aggressor has never been allowed to outweigh the right of personal self-defense to protect life or limb. Nor has the morally impaired human dignity of persons killed while waging an unjust war been held to outweigh the right of a state to wage a just war of self-defense, except by a small percentage of pacifists.

The criterion to be followed, according to natural law doctrine, in determining whether society should have recourse to the protection of capital punishment is objective, not subjective. The criterion is not the will of the people, or the frequency or the infrequency of capital punishment, or the subjective, philosophical preference of a particular justice. A law made by a majority of the people, for example, that all persons, upon reaching the age of one hundred, should be put to death by public authority because this was necessary for the common good would not be binding. The human dignity of these centenarians, never tainted by the commission of great crime, would outweigh any economic advantage of society by their execution. But it would be otherwise in the case of the great criminal, whose human dignity has been impaired by the permanent, irrevocable and irreversible results of his offense, with reference to himself and his victim. This is so despite the religious necessity of forgiveness and possible rehabilitation.

Finally, capital punishment serves such goals as giving the criminal his due and reinforcing public morality. According to natural law philosophy, crime is a great injustice, not only against society, but also against the victim and his family. In addition to protecting society, therefore, capital punishment vindicates the human dignity of the victim. It would be vengeance for a member of the dead victim's family to give the convict his due, but it becomes a matter of social justice when society inflicts the death penalty.

The two abortion cases, *Roe* v. *Wade* and *Doe* v. *Bolton,* were decided by the Supreme Court in 1973. In the former, a pregnant unmarried woman sued on behalf of herself and all other women so situated to void the Texas statute which forbade her an abortion. In the second case, a married woman sued to void a Georgia statute which obliged her to conform to certain medical practices before she had a right to an abortion. In each case, the Court declared the anti-abortion statute unconstitutional on the ground that it violated the fourteenth amendment by a denial of liberty and privacy without due process of law. In so doing, the Supreme Court stretched the doctrine of due process to unprecedented lengths and imposed such limits upon permissible abortion legislation "that no abortion law in the United States remained valid." The Court concluded that patient and physician were free to end any pregnancy during the first trimester without regulation by the state. The state may not interfere with the liberty of the woman even to protect her health during this stage of pregnancy. State regulation, if any, is constitutionally permitted only at the point of viability, *i.e.,* "when a fetus can survive with artificial aid outside the mother's body."

Here again, the Court balanced individual liberty, now extended under the notion of privacy, to the detriment of the common good. The Court made the same philosophical mistake it had made in the prayer and capital punishment cases, and much earlier in the freedom of contract and property cases. It started its judicial reasoning from the subultimate value of liberty, which can have no genuine judicial significance except as an instrumental value to protect human dignity as necessary for the common good. In fact, the error was compounded by starting with privacy, a sub-subultimate value.

In both *Wade* and *Bolton,* the liberty of a woman to destroy the fetus at will was on one scale. On the other, was the common good of society, requiring the protection of human life. Individual liberty was given such weight in the balancing process as to deny the right of society to protect what is now regarded by the best scientific evidence as human life. This life starts with the zygote or first fertilized cell.

The growth of the embryo "has been traced in a continuous line from a single unfertilized ovum through the unbroken processes of fertilization, cell division, segmentation, implantation of the blastocyst in the uterine wall, and gradual fetal development to the point of birth." It is manifest that "the advance of embryology and medicine over the past century and a half rendered untenable any notion that the fetus suddenly 'came to life' in a physiological sense at a definable point during pregnancy."

In any event, "the recent scientific evidence about the humanity of the zygote is enough to raise a reasonable doubt . . ." which must be placed on the scale. If present human life is not on the scale, with absolute certainty, it is at least possibly there, if not probably. The burden of proof is upon those who claim that there is no possible human life during the first twelve weeks of pregnancy.

It is obvious that abortion destroys something which otherwise could have matured into a human being. But only human life can so mature. May any Justice of the United States Supreme Court deny that at one time he was a zygote? Would he have given his mother the constitutional right to abort him during the first twelve weeks of her pregnancy?

How does the liberty to destroy what is now human life, or probably human life, and in the due course of nature, certain human life, contribute in any way to the safeguarding of the human dignity of the pregnant women? The arbitrary killing of the unborn any time from the moment of conception is an unnatural interference with an essential life function, and hence a vitiation of human dignity. Is it not akin to the mutilation of an important organ, or suicide? Liberty must not be allowed just for the sake of liberty.

Is it any wonder that one of the dissenting Justices, Mr. Justice Rehnquist, wrote that "the disaster would have been less complete" had the Court applied at least a traditional rationality standard. Professor Tribe has stated: "What makes *Roe* unusual, as Professor Ely rightly observes, is that, for reasons the Court never adequately explains, 'the liberty involved is accorded a . . . stringent protection, so stringent that a desire to preserve the fetus' existence is unable to overcome it.' "

In the abortion cases, the Court extracted the sub-subultimate right of privacy from the subultimate right of liberty, and gave it such unprecedented weight that it may be balanced against the common good, conceivably, so as to legalize homosexual marriages, eliminate all legal restrictions on what was formerly regarded as obscene conduct, and permit the free sale and use of narcotics. Sacrificed on the altar of privacy would be social consciousness.

The alternative is either to repudiate liberty as the ultimate value or accept the rule of physical force by some anti-democratic state form. The social interest will sooner or later assert itself. The fixed pattern of human nature ultimately demands and obtains a rational balance between the aspiration to be free and the necessity of living in society.

REINSTATEMENT OF THE DEATH PENALTY

Carol S. Vance

This essay is a strongly argued bid by a working district attorney for renewed effort to write legislation for capital punishment that would meet the Supreme Court's objections as they were stated in Furman v. Georgia *(see the first selection in this chapter). The first part of Vance's essay, in which the Supreme Court decision is summarized, has been deleted for publication here.*

Carol S. Vance is the District Attorney of Harris County, Texas, and at the time this article appeared was the president of the National District Attorney's Association.

This article is taken from the Notre Dame Lawyer, *volume 48, page 850.*

The question is not, should there be a death penalty. The vast majority of Americans have answered that question through their elected representatives in forty states and a United States Senate that unanimously enacted an air piracy statute just a few months ago. The people speaking through referendums such as the one in California where over two to one (67.5 to 32.5%) voted in favor of the death penalty, also want the death penalty.

The more subtle and realistic question is: Is the death penalty worth the trouble in light of the many obstacles not the least of which is the *Furman* v. *Georgia* opinion?

Before I go into my reasons, let me clear up one matter where I believe the majority of the Supreme Court is off base. Many opponents of capital punishment tender the same fallacious reasoning. They assume that since so few receive the death penalty, this is a form of discrimination. Nothing could be further from the truth. If we were to extend this line of reasoning, *the very same* argument could be made against a natural life sentence, life imprisonment, or any long term of years.

The average sentence for murder in my jurisdiction, Harris County (a country of approximately 2 million persons), is somewhere in the neighborhood of 12 years. Of the homicides the last full year of the death penalty, 1971, there were 277 cases tried for murder with malice (first-degree murder); 154 were convicted, and there were three death penalties and nine life sentences. Nearly every word written in *Furman* v. *Georgia* would be equally applicable for the nine who received life imprisonment.

Why do so few cases receive the most stringent penalties? In my jurisdiction, out of 100% of the homicides committed, 10% will not be arrested, 25% will not be indicted, and another 10% will be dismissed on insufficient evidence or acquitted after trial. Of the 45% who are tried for murder and convicted, the conviction will be for a lesser offense than first-degree murder about half the time. In this weeding-out process some guilty men will not receive the punishment due them. Yet no one would seriously contend that because many guilty parties get off, all should be acquitted in order to insure equal justice.

Actually there is a fairly universal concensus on which cases should receive the harshest penalties. Consider the following murder cases for example. Some 70% of the killings are between persons who knew each other. Nearly all of these occur in a state of passion over such things as a 50 cents pool bet, dancing with the wrong person, or even more likely a domestic quarrel. These crimes are extremely serious, but any jury would laugh at the prosecutor seeking the death penalty in a typical crime of passion situation. It is only in the bizarre murder, the killing for hire or during another serious crime, and a few other isolated instances that the people of this country want to see the death penalty applied. And these crimes are a small percentage of the overall murders. The prosecutors of Texas (as well as any judge or defense attorney) can listen to a set of facts and tell you whether it is a death penalty case. A recent survey of the Texas District and County Attorneys Association revealed that in the past five years there were only 87 cases where the district attorneys sought the death penalty. In 37 of these instances (over 40%) juries rendered a death penalty verdict.

The truth of the matter is that there *should* be very few death penalty sentences. Only a very few cases warrant this extreme measure. It takes two essential ingredients to obtain a death penalty: (1) overwhelming proof of the defendant's guilt and (2) an extremely aggravated fact situation. What is so surprising is Justice White's and Justice Stewart's conclusion that there is something highly improper in so few people receiving the death penalty.

If there is any injustice in those cases deserving the death penalty, it is that some defendants escape with life imprisonment or a term of years due to superior defense counsel or an unusually sympathetic jury. But by anyone's standards this is less of an injustice that the murderer who goes free because he is never arrested or his case is dismissed due to a missing witness, the *Miranda* decision, or a motion to suppress.

There is no question that an unusually talented defense counsel with relatively unlimited resources can sharply reduce the odds of a defendant's receiving the death penalty. Although this may be a valid argument against the death penalty, it should equally apply to any defendant who receives life, or for that matter is even convicted, if the defendant did not have the very best lawyer in the state representing him.

If then, the death penalty is to be meted out very sparingly, why is it worth the trouble? Although rehabilitation and punishment are generally considered reasonable purposes of imprisonment, some patterns of criminal conduct indicate that the criminal is hopeless. Why should we take a chance with a murderer, whose past history indicates is likely to kill again?

In a sense, the criminal is taking his own life when he commits a capital crime. Society is responsible for the safety and security of its members. Therefore, it has the right to remove a person who threatens this safety and security.

But perhaps the most important argument for capital punishment is that it is a deterrent. There are some people who fear nothing but death itself, and to place society's innocent in the hands of these uncontrollables without hope of fair recompense would be to play the fool. In law enforcement, idealism untempered with realism is sheer folly.

The death penalty deterred an escapee from a Texas prison. The inmate abducted a woman, stole her car and headed west. When asked why he didn't kill this person who told police his direction of travel that led to his capture, the inmate, already under a life sentence, said he didn't want to ride "Old Sparky." I have talked to robbers, who said the only reason they didn't kill the only eye witness was the threat of the electric chair.

Even England, upon allegedly abolishing the death penalty, kept it for second-offender murders, for killing a prison guard and for killing a policeman. Wasn't this hypocritical? Apparently they believed it a deterrent for the killer of the guard or the policeman, or at least the second time around.

And if Charles Manson and his companions were executed tomorrow, might not some future defendant think twice before shooting, beating and stabbing seven innocent victims a total of 1,691 times to satisfy a lustful and depraved desire? What about the next airline bomber? Future victims need all the protection society can give them.

There is no way to measure or predict how many murderers are deterred by the death penalty. Since the moratorium on the death penalty which lasted about ten years, crimes of violence have drastically increased. In my opinion, a death penalty, even sparingly used, would cut down on certain types of murders such as premeditated murder and killings during robberies.

One last thing worthy of mention is that in certain cases society expects justice or retribution. If we were to ignore the retribution aspect and concentrate solely on rehabilitation, murderers would receive the lowest sentences as a group because they are the least likely as a group to repeat. Once caught, Adolf Eichmann would probably be one of the better risks. There are some cases that call for the death penalty. Even Justice Stewart in his opinion said:

> On that score I would say only that I cannot agree that retribution is a constitutionally impermissible ingredient in the imposition of punishment. The instinct for retribution is part of the nature of man, and channeling that instinct in the administration of criminal justice serves an important purpose in promoting the stability of a society governed by law. When people begin to believe that organized society is unwilling or unable to impose upon criminal offenders the punishment they "deserve" then there are sown the seeds of anarchy —of self-help, vigilante injustice, and lynch law.[1]

We must recognize that retribution is an ingredient of justice— particularly where a human life is unlawfully taken. Otherwise, we would not impose any penalty for the typical fit of passion killer

[1] 408 U.S. at 308.

who does not need to be rehabilitated and who is the least likely to be deterred by any punishment.

I do think the death penalty is worth the effort. In the interest of justice as well as public safety, I hope most of the states enact appropriate statutes. In this regard, legislation similar to Florida's should be preferred. It allows participation by the jury, but the judge makes the final decision. The Florida statute sets up exacting guidelines where the death penalty is applicable—including statutory mitigating and aggravating factors. Lastly, it provides for sentencing review by the state's supreme court and thus a system for statewide uniformity.

A STATUTORY DEFINITION OF THE STANDARDS FOR DETERMINING HUMAN DEATH: AN APPRAISAL AND A PROPOSAL

Alexander Morgan Capron
Leon R. Kass

Carefully weighing the risks, but also the necessity, for legal guidance on the question of determining human death, the authors of this invaluable essay propose legislation intended to provide a humanly just and medically useful path through this persistent issue.

At the time this essay was published Alexander Morgan Capron was an assistant professor of law, University of Pennsylvania and Leon R. Kass was the executive secretary of the Committee on the Life Sciences and Social Policy, National Research Council— National Academy of Sciences.

This article is taken from the University of Pennsylvania Law Review, *volume 121, page 87.*

[Owing both to the increasing technical competence in sustaining at least the appearance of life, and to the growing demand for organs for transplantation, there is an acute need for legal clarification and guidance on a definition of death. So far the courts have defined death in its most unambiguous sense—as the permanent cessation of all vital signs. This means that in cases where a person is kept "alive" by mechanical devices, even when there is no hope of returning to consciousness or other behavioral characteristics essential to human personality, the removal of such devises is considered an act of murder.

The Ad Hoc Committee of the Harvard Medical School to

Examine the Definition of Brain Death has provided its famous definition of irreversible coma (see *A Definition of Irreversible Coma,* p. 355 in the present volume) which has received widespread agreement in the medical community, but it is still possible that a physician will judge someone dead by the Harvard criteria and be prosecuted for breaking the law.

Capron and Kass, following their participation in discussions held by the Research Group on Death and Dying of the Institute of Society, Ethics and the Life Sciences, wrote a long, carefully researched paper making the case for legal action in this matter. It is not sufficient to leave the issue to physicians, they argue, because there are philosophical questions involved in the definition of death which go beyond the competence of most physicians. It is obvious that the public ought to be involved in the development of policy in this area; however, involving the public will not bring to the discussion a sufficient knowledge of the technical issues involved. To allow the courts to resolve the question is not much better since the courts can only respond to litigants, and litigants will come only from those who have the money and the energy to press their cases. Moreover, it would be a slow process at best.

This leaves the legislatures. Capron and Kass acknowledge that there is always the risk that definition of death legislation may be poorly written, leaving the public unsure of its intent. Legislatures may also be moved by powerful lobbies. But they believe that with care these drawbacks can be eliminated, and that there are great advantages: it will provide a *uniform* guide to the physician and others involved, and will reduce the amount of individual interpretation in any one case, providing an unambiguous expression of the public will. The question then is what such legislation should include. The following excerpt from their article details the authors' proposal for legislation.

Students wishing to do further research in this issue are referred to the complete text of the article in the *University of Pennsylvania Law Review* [vol. 121:87]. The extensive footnotes included with the original publication of the article have been omitted here.]

Arguments both for and against the desirability of legislation "defining" death often fail to distinguish among the several different subjects that might be touched on by such legislation. As a result, a mistaken impression may exist that a single statutory model is, and must be, the object of debate. An appreciation of the multiple meanings of a "definition of death" may help to refine the deliberations.

Death, in the sense the term is of interest here, can be defined purely formally as the transition, however abrupt or gradual, between the state of being alive and the state of being dead. There are at least four levels of "definitions" that would give substance to this formal notion; in principle, each could be the subject of legislation: (1) the basic concept or idea; (2) general physiological standards; (3) operational criteria; and (4) specific tests or procedures.

The *basic concept* of death is fundamentally a philosophical matter. Examples of possible "definitions" of death at this level include "permanent cessation of the integrated functioning of the organism as a whole," "departure of the animating or vital principle," or "irreversible loss of personhood." These abstract definitions offer little concrete help in the practical task of determining whether a person has died but they may very well influence how one goes about devising standards and criteria.

In setting forth the *general physiological standard(s)* for recognizing death, the definition moves to a level which is more medicotechnical, but not wholly so. Philosophical issues persist in the choice to define death in terms of organ systems, physiological functions, or recognizable human activities, capacities, and conditions. Examples of possible general standards include "irreversible cessation of spontaneous respiratory and/or circulatory functions," "irreversible loss of spontaneous brain functions," "irreversible loss of the ability to respond or communicate," or some combination of these.

Operational criteria further define what is meant by the general physiological standards. The absence of cardiac contraction and lack of movement of the blood are examples of traditional criteria for "cessation of spontaneous circulatory functions," whereas deep coma, the absence of reflexes, and the lack of spontaneous muscular movements and spontaneous respiration are among criteria proposed for "cessation of spontaneous brain functions" by the Harvard Committee.

Fourth, there are the *specific tests and procedures* to see if the criteria are fulfilled. Pulse, heart beat, blood pressure, electrocardiogram, and examination of blood flow in the retinal vessels are among the specific tests of cardiac contraction and movement of the blood. Reaction to painful stimuli, appearance of the pupils and their responsiveness to light, and observation of movement and breathing over a specified time period are among specific tests of the "brain function" criteria enumerated above.

There appears to be general agreement that legislation should not seek to "define death" at either the most general or the most specific levels (the first and fourth). In the case of the former, differences of opinion would seem hard to resolve, and agreement, if it were possible, would provide little guidance for practice. In the case of the latter, the specific tests and procedures must be kept open to changes in medical knowledge and technology. Thus, arguments concerning the advisability and desirability of a statutory definition of death are usually confined to the two levels we have called "standards" and "criteria," yet often without any apparent awareness of the distinction between them. The need for flexibility in the face of medical advance would appear to be a persuasive argument for not legislating any specific operational criteria. Moreover, these are almost exclusively technical matters, best left to the judgment of physicians. Thus, the kind of "definition" suitable for legislation would be a definition of the general physiological standard or standards. Such a definition, while not immutable, could be expected to be useful for a long period of time and would therefore not require frequent amendment.

There are other matters that could be comprehended in legislation "defining" death. The statute could specify who (and how many) shall make the determination. In the absence of a compelling reason to change past practices, this may continue to be set at "a physician," usually the doctor attending a dying patient or the one who happens to be at the scene of an accident. Moreover, the law ought probably to specify the "time of death." The statute may seek to fix the precise time when death may be said to have occurred, or it may merely seek to define a time that is clearly after "the precise moment," that is, a time when it is possible to say "the patient is dead," rather than "the patient has just now died." If the medical procedures used in determining that death has occurred call for verification of the findings after a fixed period of time (for example, the Harvard Committee's recommendation that the tests be repeated after twenty-four hours), the statute could in principle assign the "moment of death" to either the time when the criteria were first met or the time of verification. The former has been the practice with the traditional criteria for determining death.

Finally, legislation could speak to what follows upon the determination. The statute could be permissive or prescriptive in determining various possible subsequent events, including especially the pronouncement and recording of the death, and the use of the body for burial or other purposes. It is our view that these matters are best handled outside of a statute which has as its purpose to "define death."

PRINCIPLES GOVERNING THE FORMULATION OF A STATUTE

In addition to carefully selecting the proper degree of specificity for legislation, there are a number of other principles we believe should guide the drafting of a statute "defining" death. First, the phenomenon of interest to physicians, legislators, and laymen alike is human death. Therefore, the statute should concern the death of a human being, not the death of his cells, tissues or organs, and not the "death" or cessation of his role as a fully functioning member of his family or community. This point merits considerable emphasis. There may be a proper place for a statutory standard for deciding when to turn off a respirator which is ventilating a patient still clearly alive, or, for that matter, to cease giving any other form of therapy. But it is crucial to distinguish this question of "when to allow to die?" from the question with which we are here concerned, namely, "when to declare dead?" Since very different issues and purposes are involved in these questions, confusing the one with the other clouds the analysis of both. The problem of determining when a person is dead is difficult enough without its being tied to the problem of whether physicians, or anyone else, may hasten the death of a terminally-ill patient, with or without his consent or that of his relatives, in order to minimize his suffering or to conserve scarce medical resources. Although the same set of social and medical conditions may give rise to both problems, they must be kept separate if they are to be clearly understood.

Distinguishing the question "is he dead?" from the question "should he be allowed to die?" also assists in preserving continuity with tradition, a second important principle. By restricting itself to the "is he dead?" issue, a revised "definition" permits practices to move incrementally, not by replacing traditional cardiopulmonary standards for the determination of death but rather by supplementing them. These standards are, after all, still adequate in the majority of cases, and are the ones that both physicians and the public are in the habit of employing and relying on. The supplementary standards are needed primarily for those cases in which artificial means of support of comatose patients render the traditional standards unreliable.

Third, this incremental approach is useful for the additional and perhaps most central reason that any new means for judging death should be seen as just that and nothing more—a change in method dictated by advances in medical practice, but not an alteration of the meaning of "life" and "death." By indicating that the various standards for measuring death relate to a single phenomenon legislation can serve to reduce a primary source of public uneasiness on this subject. Once it has been established that certain consequences—for example, burial, autopsy, transfer of property to the heirs, and so forth—follow from a determination of death, definite problems would arise if there were a number of "definitions" according to which some people could be said to be "more dead" than others.

There are, of course, many instances in which the law has established differing definitions of a term, each framed to serve a particular purpose. One wonders, however, whether it does not appear somewhat foolish for the law to offer a number of arbitrary definitions of a natural phenomenon such as death. Nevertheless, legislators might seek to identify a series of points during the process of dying, each of which might be labelled "death" for certain purposes. Yet so far as we know, no arguments have been presented for special purpose standards except in the area of organ transplantation. Such a separate "definition of death," aimed at increasing the supply of viable organs, would permit physicians to declare a patient dead before his condition met the generally applicable standards for determining death if his organs are of potential use in transplantation. The adoption of a special standard risks abuse and confusion, however. The status of prospective organ donor is an arbitrary one to which a person can be assigned by relatives or physicians and is unrelated to anything about the extent to which his body's functioning has deteriorated. A special "definition" of death for transplantation purposes would thus need to be surrounded by a set of procedural safeguards that would govern not only the method by which a person is to be declared dead but also those by which he is to be classified as an organ donor. Even more troublesome is the confusion over the meaning of death that would probably be engendered by multiple "definitions." Consequently, it would be highly desirable if a statute on death could avoid the problems with a special "definition." Should the statute happen to facilitate organ transplantation, either by making more organs available or by making prospective donors and transplant surgeons more secure in knowing what the law would permit, so much the better.

If, however, more organs are needed for transplantation than can be legally obtained, the question whether the benefits conferred by transplantation justify the risks associated with a broader "definition" of death should be addressed directly rather than by attempting to subsume it under the question "what is death?" Such a direct confrontation with the issue could lead to a discussion about the standards and procedures under which organs might be taken from persons near death, or even those still quite alive, at their own option or that of relatives, physicians, or representatives of the state. The major advantage of keeping the issues separate is not, of course, that this will facilitate transplantation, but that it will remove a present source of concern: it is unsettling to contemplate that as you lie slowly dying physicians are free to use a more "lenient" standard to declare you dead if they want to remove your organs for transplantation into other patients.

Fourth, the standards for determining death ought not only to relate to a single phenomenon but should also be applied uniformly to all persons. A person's wealth or his "social utility" as an organ donor should not affect the way in which the moment of his death is determined.

Finally, while there is a need for uniformity of application at any one time, the fact that changes in medical technology brought about the present need for "redefinition" argues that the new formulation should be flexible. As suggested in the previous section, such flexibility is most easily accomplished if the new "definition" confines itself to the general standards by which death is to be determined and leaves to the continuing exercise of judgment by physicians the establishment and application of appropriate criteria and specific tests for determining that the standards have been met.

THE KANSAS STATUTE

The first attempt at a legislative resolution of the problems discussed here was made in 1970 when the State of Kansas adopted

"An Act relating to and defining death." The Kansas statute has received a good deal of attention; similar legislation was enacted in the spring of 1972 in Maryland and is presently under consideration in a number of other jurisdictions. The Kansas legislation, which was drafted in response to developments in organ transplantation and medical support of dying patients, provides "alternative definitions of death," set forth in two paragraphs. Under the first, a person is considered "medically and legally dead" if a physician determines "there is the absence of spontaneous respiratory and cardiac function and . . . attempts at resuscitation are considered hopeless." In the second "definition," death turns on the absence of spontaneous brain function if during "reasonable attempts" either to "maintain or restore spontaneous circulatory or respiratory function," it appears that "further attempts at resuscitation or supportive maintenance will not succeed." The purpose of the latter "definition" is made clear by the final sentence of the second paragraph:

> Death is to be pronounced before artificial means of supporting respiratory and circulatory function are terminated and *before any vital organ is removed for the purpose of transplantation.*

The primary fault with this legislation is that it appears to be based on, or at least gives voice to, the misconception that there are two separate phenomena of death. This dichotomy is particularly unfortunate because it seems to have been inspired by a desire to establish a special definition for organ transplantation, a definition which physicians would not, however, have to apply, in the draftsman's words, "to prove the irrelevant deaths of most persons." Although there is nothing in the Act itself to indicate that physicians will be less concerned with safeguarding the health of potential organ donors, the purposes for which the Act was passed are not hard to decipher, and they do little to inspire the average patient with confidence that his welfare (including his not being prematurely declared dead) is of as great concern to medicine and the State of Kansas as is the facilitation of organ transplantation. As Professor Kennedy cogently observes, "public disquiet [over transplantation] is in no way allayed by the existence in legislative form of what appear to be alternative definitions of death." One hopes that the form the statute takes does not reflect a conclusion on the part of the Kansas legislature that death occurs at two distinct points during the process of dying. Yet this inference can be derived from the Act, leaving open the prospect "that X at a certain stage in the process of dying can be pronounced dead, whereas Y, having arrived at the same point, is not said to be dead."

The Kansas statute appears also to have attempted more than the "definition" of death, or rather, to have tried to resolve related questions by erroneously treating them as matters of "definition." One supporter of the statute praises it, we think mistakenly, for this reason: "Intentionally, the statute extends to these questions: When can a physician avoid attempting resuscitation? When can he terminate resuscitative efforts? When can he discontinue artificial maintenance?" To be sure, "when the patient is dead" is one obvious answer to these questions, but by no means the only one. As indicated above, we believe that the question "when is the patient dead?" needs to be distinguished and treated separately from the questions "when may the doctor turn off the respirator?" or "when may a patient—dying yet still alive—be allowed to die?"

A STATUTORY PROPOSAL

As an alternative to the Kansas statute we propose the following:

A person will be considered dead if in the announced opinion of a physician, based on ordinary standards of medical practice, he has experienced an irreversible cessation of spontaneous respiratory and circulatory functions. In the event that artificial means of support preclude a determination that these functions have ceased, a person will be considered dead if in the announced opinion of a physician, based on ordinary standards of medical practice, he has experienced an irreversible cessation of spontaneous brain functions. Death will have occurred at the time when the relevant functions ceased.

This proposed statute provides a "definition" of death confined to the level of *general physiological standards,* and it has been drafted in accord with the five principles set forth above in section V. First, the proposal speaks in terms of the *death* of a *person.* The determination that a person has died is to be based on an evaluation of certain vital bodily functions, the permanent absence of which indicates that he is no longer a living human being. By concentrating on the death of a human being as a whole, the statute rightly disregards the fact that some cells or organs may continue to "live" after this point, just as others may have ceased functioning long before the determination of death. This statute would leave for resolution by other means the question of when the absence or deterioration of certain capacities, such as the ability to communicate, or functions, such as the cerebral, indicates that a person may or should be allowed to die without further medical intervention.

Second, the proposed legislation is predicated upon the single phenomenon of death. Moreover, it applies uniformly to all persons, by specifying the circumstances under which each of the standards is to be used rather than leaving this to the unguided discretion of physicians. Unlike the Kansas law, the model statute does not leave to arbitrary decision a choice between two apparently equal yet different "alternative definitions of death." Rather, its second standard is applicable only when "artificial means of support preclude" use of the first. It does not establish a separate kind of death, called "brain death." In other words, the proposed law would provide two standards gauged by different functions, for measuring different manifestations of the same phenomenon. If cardiac and pulmonary functions have ceased, brain functions cannot continue; if there is no brain activity and respiration has to be maintained artificially, the same state (*i.e.,* death) exists. Some people might prefer a single standard, one based either on cardiopulmonary or brain functions. This would have the advantage of removing the last trace of the "two deaths" image, which any reference to alternative standards may still leave. Respiratory and circulatory indicators, once the only touchstone, are no longer adequate in some situations. It would be possible, however, to adopt the alternative, namely that death is *always* to be established by assessing spontaneous brain functions. Reliance only on brain activity, however, would represent a sharp and unnecessary break with tradition. Departing from continuity with tradition is not only theoretically unfortunate in that it violates another principle of good legislation suggested previously, but also practically very difficult, since most physicians customarily employ cardiopulmonary tests for death and would be slow to change, especially when the old tests are easier to perform, more accessible and acceptable to the lay public, and perfectly adequate for determining death in most instances.

Finally, by adopting standards for death in terms of the cessation of certain vital bodily functions but not in terms of the specific criteria or tests by which these functions are to be measured, the statute does not prevent physicians from adapting their procedures to changes in medical technology.

A basic substantive issue remains: what are the merits of the proposed standards? For ordinary situations, the appropriateness of the traditional standard, "an irreversible cessation of spontaneous respiratory and circulatory functions," does not require elaboration. Indeed, examination by a physician may be more a formal than a real requirement in determining that most people have died. In addition to any obvious injuries, elementary signs of death such as absence of heartbeat and breathing, cold skin, fixed pupils, and so forth, are usually sufficient to indicate even to a layman that the accident victim, the elderly person who passes away quietly in the night, or the patient stricken with a sudden infarct has died. The difficulties arise when modern medicine intervenes to sustain a patient's respiration and circulation. As we noted in discussing the Harvard Committee's conclusions, the indicators of brain damage appear reliable, in that studies have shown that patients who fit the Harvard criteria have suffered such extensive damage that they do not recover. Of course, the task of the neurosurgeon or physician is simplified in the common case where an accident victim has suffered such gross, apparent injuries to the head that it is not necessary to apply the Harvard criteria in order to establish cessation of brain functioning.

The statutory standard, "irreversible cessation of spontaneous brain functions," is intended to encompass both higher brain activities and those of the brainstem. There must, of course, also be no spontaneous respiration; the second standard is applied only when breathing is being artificially maintained. The major emphasis placed on brain functioning, although generally consistent with the common view of what makes man distinctive as a living creature, brings to the fore a basic issue: What aspects of brain function should be decisive? The question has been reframed by some clinicians in light of their experience with patients who have undergone what they term "neocortical death" (that is, complete destruction of higher brain capacity, demonstrated by a flat E.E.G.). "Once neocortical death has been unequivocally established and the possibility of any recovery of consciousness and intellectual activity [is] thereby excluded, . . . although [the] patient breathes spontaneously, is he or she alive?" While patients with irreversible brain damage from cardiac arrest seldom survive more than a few days, cases have recently been reported of survival for up to two and one-quarter years. Nevertheless, though existence in this state falls far short of a full human life, the very fact of spontaneous respiration, as well as coordinated movements and reflex activities at the brainstem and spinal cord levels, would exclude these patients from the scope of the statutory standards. The condition of "neocortical death" may well be a proper justification for interrupting all forms of treatment and allowing these patients to die, but this moral and legal problem cannot and should not be settled by "defining" these people "dead."

The legislation suggested here departs from the Kansas statute in its basic approach to the problem of "defining" death: the proposed statute does not set about to establish a special category of "brain death" to be used by transplanters. Further, there are a number of particular points of difference between them. For example, the proposed statute does not speak of persons being "medically and legally dead," thus avoiding redundancy and, more importantly, the mistaken implication that the "medical" and "legal" definitions could differ. Also, the proposed legislation does not include the provision that "death is to be pronounced before" the machine is turned off or any organs removed. Such a *modus operandi*, which was incorporated by Kansas from the Harvard Committee's report, may be advisable for physicians on public relations grounds, but it has no place in a statute "defining" death. The proposed statute already provides that "Death will have occurred at the time when the relevant functions ceased." If supportive aids, or organs, are withdrawn after this time, such acts cannot be implicated as having caused death. The manner in which, or exact time at which, the physician should articulate his finding is a matter best left to the exigencies of the situation, to local medical customs or hospital rules, or to statutes on the procedures for certifying death or on transplantation if the latter is the procedure which raises the greatest concern of medical impropriety. The real safeguard against doctors killing patients is not to be found in a statute "defining" death. Rather, it inheres in physicians' ethical and religious beliefs, which are also embodied in the fundamental professional ethic of *primum non nocere* and are reinforced by homicide and "wrongful death" laws and the rules governing medical negligence applicable in license revocation proceedings or in private actions for damages.

The proposed statute shares with the Kansas legislation two

features of which Professor Kennedy is critical. First, it does not require that two physicians participate in determining death, as recommended by most groups which set forth suggestions about transplantation. The reasons for the absence of such a provision should be obvious. Since the statute deals with death in general and not with death in relation to transplantation, there is no reason for it to establish a general rule which is required only in that unusual situation. If particular dangers lurk in the transplantation setting, they should be dealt with in legislation on that subject, such as the Uniform Anatomical Gift Act. If all current means of determining "irreversible cessation of spontaneous brain functions" are inherently so questionable that they should be double-checked by a second (or third, fourth, etc.) physician to be trustworthy, or if a certain means of measuring brain function requires as a technical matter the cooperation of two, or twenty, physicians, then the participation of the requisite number of experts would be part of the "ordinary standards of medical practice" that circumscribe the proper, nonnegligent use of such procedures. It would be unfortunate, however, to introduce such a requirement into legislation which sets forth the general standards for determining who is dead, especially when it is done in such a way as to differentiate between one standard and another.

Kennedy's second objection, that a death statute ought to provide "for the separation and insulation of the physician (or physicians) attending the patient donor and certifying death, from the recipient of any organ that may be salvaged from the cadaver," is likewise unnecessary. As was noted previously, language that relates only to transplantation has no place in a statute on the determination of death.

CONCLUSION

Changes in medical knowledge and procedures have created an apparent need for a clear and acceptable revision of the standards for determining that a person has died. Some commentators have argued that the formulation of such standards should be left to physicians. The reasons for rejecting this argument seem compelling: the "definition of death" is not merely a matter for technical expertise, the uncertainty of the present law is unhealthy for society and physicians alike, there is a great potential for mischief and harm through the possibility of conflict between the standards applied by some physicians and those assumed to be applicable by the community at large and its legal system, and patients and their relatives are made uneasy by physicians apparently being free to shift around the meaning of death without any social guidance. Accordingly, we conclude the public has a legitimate role to play in the formulation and adoption of such standards. This article has proposed a model statute which bases a determination of death primarily on the traditional standard of final respiratory and circulatory cessation; where the artificial maintenance of these functions precludes the use of such a standard, the statute authorizes that death be determined on the basis of irreversible cessation of spontaneous brain functions. We believe the legislation proposed would dispel public confusion and concern and protect physicians and patients, while avoiding the creation of "two types of death," for which the statute on this subject first adopted in Kansas has been justly criticized. The proposal is offered not as the ultimate solution to the problem, but as a catalyst for what we hope will be a robust and well-informed public debate over a new "definition." Finally, the proposed statute leaves for future resolution the even more difficult problems concerning the conditions and procedures under which a decision may be reached to cease treating a terminal patient who does not meet the standards set forth in the statutory "definition of death."

THE UNIFORM ANATOMICAL GIFT ACT: A MODEL FOR REFORM

Alfred M. Sadler, Jr., M.D.

Blair L. Sadler

E. Blythe Stason

The legal and medical tangle surrounding the problem of organ donation and transplantation has been significantly reduced by the proposal of the "Uniform Anatomical Gift Act," printed and analyzed in this essay.

Alfred M. Sadler and Blair L. Sadler are staff members of the National Institutes of Health and served as consultants to the National Conference of Commissioners on Uniform State Laws, which drafted the Uniform Anatomical Gift Act. E. Blythe Stason is a professor at the Vanderbilt University School of Law and the chairman of the special committee that drafted the Act.

This article is taken from the Journal of the American Medical Association, *volume 206, page 2501, December 9, 1968.*

Few events in recent legal history have as great a potential for beneficial impact on the medical community as the final approval of the Uniform Anatomical Gift Act on July 30, 1968, at the most recent National Conference of the Commissioners on Uniform State Laws. The Uniform Act, which is appended, received the endorsement of the American Bar Association on Aug. 7, 1968. The Act is designed to facilitate the donation and use of human tissues and organs for transplantation and other medical purposes and provides a favorable legal environment for such activities.

The National Conference of Commissioners on Uniform State

Laws is composed of law professors, lawyers, and judges, representing every state, whose function is to help make state laws more uniform and up to date. The Uniform Anatomical Gift Act is the product of three years of intensive study by a special committee of the conference and is particularly timely because of the many legal questions emphasized by recent heart transplant operations. Earlier drafts of this Act have been reviewed by medical and scientific groups, including the Committee on Tissue Transplantation of the Division of Medical Sciences of the National Research Council.

PERSPECTIVE

Because of the extraordinary legal complexities in this area, a few words of perspective are in order. The donation and procurement of human tissue can be effected from both living and dead persons. In the former case, such as the transplantation of a kidney, the primary legal concern is obtaining adequate informed consent authorizing the surgical removal. This may become complicated if the prospective donor is a minor or is incompetent. The crucial point is that, while the donation and procurement of tissue from a living donor (eg, a paired organ) may raise serious ethical and legal issues such as informed consent, there is no doubt as to the right of a competent, adult individual to make such a donation and thus there is no need for statutory donation authority.

If use of an organ or tissue after death of the donor is involved, many additional questions appear. These problems result from the existence of four very important but frequently competing interests which the law had endeavored to recognize. (1) The wishes of the deceased, (2) the wishes of the surviving spouse and other appropriate next of kin, (3) the need for organs, tissue, and cadavers for medical education, research, and therapy including transplantation, and (4) the need of society to determine the cause of death in certain circumstances.

The present laws relevant to these interests are a confusing mixture of old common law dating back to the 17th century and numerous state statutes. The state statutes are highly variable and many issues remain unsettled. Laws have been enacted in 40 states and the District of Columbia which provide for the donation before death of all or part of the human body for medical or scientific purposes.

Four other states provide for the donation of eyes only (Alaska, Georgia, Maine, and West Virginia). Six states have no donation statutes (Delaware, Idaho, New Hampshire, Utah, Vermont, and Wyoming). Although these laws were designed to eliminate the uncertainties of the common law and to fill the vacuum left by other statutes relating to autopsies, unclaimed bodies, and medical examiners, they are generally incomplete and inadequate.

To facilitate donation, adequately clarify existing uncertainties, and to protect physicians who wish to procure and use human tissue, a comprehensive donation statute which includes at least the following 13 provisions is needed. Prior to March 1968 when donation statutes were enacted in Kansas and Maryland, none of the existing state laws contained more than eight of these provisions and many contained only five or six.

THE UNIFORM ANATOMICAL GIFT ACT

The Uniform Anatomical Gift Act contains all of these important provisions and serves as an excellent model for state legislation. The Uniform Act is based on the belief that an individual should be able to control the disposition of his own body after death and that his wishes should not be frustrated by his next of kin. To encourage donations and to help meet the increasing need for organs and tissue, unnecessary and cumbersome formalities should be eliminated and only those safeguards required to protect the other varied interests involved should be included. The rights of the appropriate next of kin should be clearly provided, physicians working in this area should be protected, and the public interests in a dead body, as represented by the medical examiner, should be maintained. With this philosophy in mind, an analysis of the Uniform Act follows with emphasis on its 13 most important provisions:

1. *Individual Authority to Donate.*—The core of the Uniform Act grants authority to any individual of sound mind and 18 years of age or more to give all or part of his body for any purpose specified later in the Act, the gift to take effect upon death. This crucial provision provides the donation authority which does not exist under common law. Under common law, the next of kin have the right and the authority to control the disposition of a dead body.

2. *Next of Kin Authority to Donate.*—The Uniform Act speci-

fically provides that the next of kin may donate the body or parts of the deceased and enumerates an order of priority beginning with the surviving spouse. It is important to include this in the statute since donation authority of the next of kin based on common law is vague and unclear. Only 17 of the existing statutes contain a provision dealing with the authority of next of kin.

3. *Possible Conflict Between Donor and Next of Kin.*—A statement is needed concerning priorities between the donor and his next of kin and concerning conflicting wishes between next of kin to avoid the uncertainty that would confront physicians. Uncertainty could arise in the following situation: (1) The deceased expressed the desire not to have his body or parts donated. Under the Uniform Act the wishes of the deceased would prevail. Only five statutes contain such provisions. (2) The deceased made a valid donation under the statute and the next of kin object. To deal with this possible conflict, 20 state statutes specifically provide that the next of kin shall comply with the wishes of the deceased. The Uniform Act provides that the donation by the deceased is paramount to the wishes of the next of kin. (3) Conflicts between next of kin. The Uniform Act creates six classes of next of kin who may donate, in order of priority beginning with the surviving spouse. If it is known that a gift by a member of a class is opposed by a member of the same of a prior class, the gift shall not be accepted.

4. *Donees.*—Permissible Donees.—Existing statutes reveal considerable diversity concerning possible donees. It is desirable to limit donees to those persons or institutions licensed or authorized to practice medicine and to engage in tissue banking or related matters. The Uniform Act is comprehensive and includes tissue banks, specified persons, licensed hospitals, and accredited medical and dental schools.

Obligations of the Donee.—Although the donee should be under no obligation to accept a gift, most statutes are silent on this point. The Uniform Act provides that the donee may reject the gift and requires that, following the removal of the part named, custody of the remaining parts shall be transferred to the next of kin or other persons under obligation to dispose of the body.

The Open-Ended Donation and the Unavailable Donee.—The Uniform Act provides that if the gift is open ended and no donee is named, it may be accepted and used by the attending physician. If a donee is designated but is not readily available at the time and place of death, the attending physician may accept and use the gift. These important provisions are not found in most donation statutes.

5. *Purposes for Which Donations Can Be Made.*—Again, there is a considerable diversity among the statutes. Some are unduly restrictive or vague and do not provide for all relevant purposes. The provisions of the Uniform Act are comprehensive in this respect and include medical and dental education, research, advancement of medical or dental science, therapy, and transplantation.

6. *Mechanism of Gift—Wills.*—Some of the statutes, particularly those first enacted, are based on laws relating to wills. Consequently, many donations are not valid unless they have been made in accordance with highly restrictive notarization, recording, and filing requirements, which severely reduce the number of donations and limit their effectiveness. The Uniform Act eliminates these requirements and provides that the gift is effective immediately upon death without waiting for probate.

7. *Mechanism of Gift—Other Written Instruments.*—Many statutes also provide that any written instrument is valid if witnessed by two persons. This represents a considerable improvement because it provides much greater flexibility by eliminating many of the procedural technicalities of wills. It may not be helpful in the accident situation, however, where time is frequently very limited, the prospective donor unconscious, and existence of a written donation instrument unknown.

8. *Mechanism of Gift—Cards.*—In light of these problems, it would be highly desirable if an easily carried card could serve as a valid mechanism. Florida, Kansas, Maryland, Louisiana, California, and the Uniform Act specifically provide that a properly executed card carried on the donor's person or in his effects will suffice. Although the language "written instrument" would literally include a properly executed card, it is unlikely that many legislatures had a wallet-sized card in mind. It seems wise to include this device in the statute to give it greater visibility and official legislative approval. This will be especially important in light of its enormous potential for facilitating donations in the future.

In this regard it would be equally desirable to develop a uniform instrument of gift which would apply to all types of tissue and would be universally used. The commentary of the Uniform Act will contain model forms for use by an individual and by his next of kin.

Forms were not included in the Act itself because it was felt that the individual states should have the choice to develop their own. It is hoped that as states adopt the Uniform Act, they will follow the model forms included in the commentary.

9. *Mechanism of Gift by Next of Kin—Recorded Telephonic Consent.*—The Uniform Act simplifies the gift procedure dealing with donations by the next of kin in two important ways. First, the requirements for witnesses are eliminated. Second, consent may be given by telegraphic, recorded telephonic, or other recorded message. The advantage of obtaining consent from next of kin by telegraph or recorded telephone message is clear when the deceased and the next of kin are far apart and time is very limited.

10. *Revocation or Amendment of Gift.*—Only four states make adequate provision for amendment or revocation. In the interests of respecting the final wishes of the donor, every reasonable means for changing one's intent should be made available. The Uniform Act lists six ways in which a donation can be modified, including an oral statement witnessed by two persons.

11. *Protection From Liability for Physicians and Others Acting in Accordance With the Statute.*—Although many statutes contain provisions protecting the physician who removed an organ or tissue from civil liability, only eight extend the protection to include both civil and criminal proceedings. The Uniform Act protects all persons concerned, including physicians, next of kin, funeral directors, and medical examiners. The protection applies to both civil and criminal proceedings.

12. *The Problem of Conflict of Laws.*—Until the Uniform Act is universally adopted, conflicts between the diverse donation laws of various states are inevitable. For example, a resident of state A makes a valid gift under the donation statute in state A and then dies in state B which either has no donation statute or has one that differs significantly from that of state A. Which law should apply? There are no cases on this point. The Uniform Act protects the physician in this situation by insulating him from liability if he acts in good faith and in accordance with the terms of either of the relevant state laws.

13. *The Time of Death.*—The problem of defining death has received considerable attention in recent months and was the subject of lengthy discussion by the Commissioners on Uniform State Laws. There are presently no laws in the United States which attempt to

define death. The moment of death has traditionally been regarded as a question for medical determination and not the proper subject for codification by law. The commissioners have chosen to maintain this policy and unanimously concluded that it would be unwise to incorporate a definition of death into the Uniform Act. Medical authorities are currently seeking a consensus on relevant criteria for a definition of death and suitable medical guidelines are being proposed.

The commissioners believed that it was appropriate to deal with the possible conflict of interest which could arise if one physician were to care for both a potential donor and potential recipient of a transplantable organ. On the other hand, they recognized the importance of maintaining adequate channels of communication between those physicians representing the donor and those physicians administering to the recipient. Effective communication is essential to the successful transplantation of a vital organ. Consequently, the Uniform Act provides that "the time of death shall be determined by a physician who attends the donor at his death, or if none, the physician who certifies the death. This physician shall not participate in the procedures for removing or transplanting a part.

CONCLUSION

The Uniform Anatomical Gift Act has provided a sorely needed model for reform of the current legal structure relating to the donation and use of organs and tissue for transplantation and other medical purposes. The act represents a major step towards resolving many of the existing legal uncertainties and, at the same time, does not intrude into those questions which require unhampered medical judgment.

There is reason to be optimistic about the prospect for adoption of the Uniform Act by the individual states. Since March 1968, Kansas, Maryland, Louisiana, and California have passed new donation statutes based on the second tentative draft of the Uniform Act. This draft has also been introduced into the Pennsylvania legislature. Many other states are already planning to consider the Uniform Act at their next legislative sessions.

The legal profession has reached a consensus on this highly complex area so vital to law, medicine, and the general public. The medical community is progressing towards a similar consensus on difficult issues such as the definition of death. It now remains for all interested members of both professions to support the adoption of the Uniform Anatomical Gift Act in their respective states.

UNIFORM ANATOMICAL GIFT ACT

(*Copy of final draft as approved on July 30, 1968, by the National Conference of Commissioners on Uniform State Laws*)

An act authorizing the gift of all or part of a human body after death for specified purposes.

SECTION 1. (*Definitions*)

(a) "Bank or storage facility" means a facility licensed, accredited or approved under the laws of any state for storage of human bodies or parts thereof.

(b) "Decedent" means a deceased individual and includes a stillborn infant or fetus.

(c) "Donor" means an individual who makes a gift of all or part of his body.

(d) "Hospital" means a hospital licensed, accredited or approved under the laws of any state and includes a hospital operated by the United States government, a state or a subdivision thereof, although not required to be licensed under state laws.

(e) "Part" includes organs, tissues, eyes, bones, arteries, blood, other fluids and other portions of a human body, and "part" includes "parts."

(f) "Person" means an individual, corporation, government or governmental subdivision or agency, business trust, estate, trust, partnership or association or any other legal entity.

(g) "Physician" or "surgeon" means a physician or surgeon licensed or authorized to practice under the laws of any state.

(h) "State" includes any state, district, commonwealth, territory, insular possession, and any other area subject to the legislative authority of the United States of America.

SECTION 2. (*Persons Who May Execute an Anatomical Gift*)

(a) Any individual of sound mind and 18 years of age or more may give all or any part of his body for any purposes specified in section 3, the gift to take effect upon death.

(b) Any of the following persons, in order of priority stated, when persons in prior classes are not available at the time of death, and in the absence of actual notice of contrary indications by the decedent, or actual notice of opposition by a member of the same or a prior class, may give all or any part of the decedent's body for any purposes specified in section 3.

    (1) the spouse,

    (2) an adult son or daughter,

    (3) either parent,

    (4) an adult brother or sister,

    (5) a guardian of the person of the decendent at the time of his death,

    (6) any other person authorized or under obligation to dispose of the body.

    (c) If the donee has actual notice of contrary indications by the descedent, or that a gift by a member of a class is opposed by a member of the same or a prior class, the donee shall not accept the gift. The persons authorized by subsection (b) may make the gift after death or immediately before death.

    (d) A gift of all or part of a body authorizes any examination necessary to assure medical acceptability of the gift for the purposes intended.

    (e) The rights of the donee created by the gift are paramount to the rights of others except as provided by section 7(d).

SECTION 3. (*Persons Who May Become Donees, and Purposes for Which Anatomical Gifts May Be Made*) The following persons may become donees of gifts of bodies or parts thereof for the purposes stated:

    (1) any hospital, surgeon, or physician, for medical or dental education, research, advancement of medical or dental science, therapy or transplantation; or

    (2) any accredited medical or dental school, college or university for education, research, advancement of medical or dental science or therapy; or

    (3) any bank or storage facility for medical or dental education, research, advancement of medical or dental science, therapy or transplantation; or

    (4) any specified individual for therapy or transplantation needed by him.

SECTION 4. (*Manner of Executing Anatomical Gifts*)

    (a) A gift of all or part of the body under section 2(a) may be made by will. The gift becomes effective upon the death of the testator without waiting for probate. If the will is not probated, or if it is declared invalid for testamentary purposes, the gift, to the extent that it has been acted upon in good faith, is nevertheless valid and effective.

    (b) A gift of all or part of the body under section 2(a) may also be made by document other than a will. The gift becomes effective upon the death of the donor. The document, which may be a card designed to be carried on the person, must be signed by the donor, in the presence of 2 witnesses who must sign the document in his presence. If the donor cannot sign, the document may be signed for him at his direction and in his presence, and in the presence of 2 witnesses who must sign the document in his presence. Delivery of the document of gift during the donor's lifetime is not necessary to make the gift valid.

(c) The gift may be made to a specified donee or without specifying a donee. If the latter, the gift may be accepted by the attending physician as donee upon or following death. If the gift is made to a specified donee who is not available at the time and place of death, the attending physician upon or following death, in the absence of any expressed indication that the donor desired otherwise, may accept the gift as donee. The physician who becomes a donee under this subsection shall not participate in the procedures for removing or transplanting a part.

(d) Notwithstanding section 7(b), the donor may designate in his will, card or other document of gift the surgeon or physician to carry out the appropriate procedures. In the absence of a designation, or if the designee is not available, the donee or other person authorized to accept the gift may employ or authorize any surgeon or physician for the purpose.

(e) Any gift by a person designated in section 2(b) shall be made by a document signed by him, or made by his telegraphic, recorded telephonic or other recorded message.

SECTION 5. (*Delivery of Document of Gift*) If the gift is made by the donor to a specified donee, the will, card, or other document, or an executed copy thereof, may be delivered to the donee to expedite the appropriate procedures immediately after death, but delivery is not necessary to the validity of the gift. The will, card or other document, or an executed copy thereof, may be deposited in any hospital, bank or storage facility or registry office that accepts them for safekeeping or for facilitation of procedures after death. On request of any interested party upon or after the donor's death, the person in possession shall produce the document for examination.

SECTION 6. (*Amendment or Revocation of the Gift*)

(a) If the will, card or other document or executed copy thereof has been delivered to a specified donee, the donor may amend or revoke the gift by:

(1) the execution and delivery to the donee of a signed statement, or

(2) an oral statement made in the presence of 2 persons and communicated to the donee, or

(3) a statement during a terminal illness or injury addressed to an attending physician and communicated to the donee, or

(4) a signed card or document found on his person or in his effects.

(b) Any document of gift which has not been delivered to the donee may be revoked by the donor in the manner set out in subsection (a) or by destruction, cancellation, or mutilation of the document and all executed copies thereof.

(c) Any gift made by a will may also be amended or revoked in the manner provided for amendment or revocation of wills, or as provided in subsection (a).

SECTION 7. (*Rights and Duties at Death*)

(a) The donee may accept or reject the gift. If the donee accepts a gift of the entire body, he may, subject to the terms of the gift, authorize embalming and the use of the body in funeral services. If the gift is of a part of the body, the donee, upon the death of the donor and prior to embalming, shall cause the part to be removed without unnecessary mutilation. After removal of the part, custody of the remainder of the body vests in the surviving spouse, next of kin or other persons under obligation to dispose of the body.

(b) The time of death shall be determined by a physician who attends the donor at his death, or, if none, the physician who certifies the death. This physician shall not participate in the procedures for removing or transplanting a part.

(c) A person who acts in good faith in accord with the terms of this Act, or under the anatomical gift laws of another state (or a foreign country) is not liable for damages in any civil action or subject to prosecution in any criminal proceeding for his act.

(d) The provisions of this Act are subject to the laws of this state prescribing powers and duties with respect to autopsies.

SECTION 8. (*Uniformity of Interpretation*) This Act shall be so construed as to effectuate its general purpose to make uniform the law of those states which enact it.

SECTION 9. (*Short Title*) This Act may be cited as the Uniform Anatomical Gift Act.

DEATH AND THE AGING

Aging is an elusive category. In one respect it means passing through time, "growing older." But this is a characteristic of every existing thing. Nothing living or unliving is unaffected by the passage of time. In this sense aging is merely a characteristic of existing.

In another respect we often use the category of aging as a way of indicating the movement of a living organism toward death. When we speak of the "aged" we usually mean persons close to death, However, the death toward which the aging process is directed is of a certain sort usually referred to as a "natural" death. One does not "age" toward suicide or death by cancer. Indeed, any death but a natural death is an interruption of the aging process.

This still does not clarify the matter, however, for the term "natural death" is open to a great many interpretations. One might, in fact, go so far as to argue that death is not natural at all, that it is rather the failure of the natural processes of life. Or, at the other extreme, one might insist that any form of death is natural. Why should cancer or heart failure be less natural than death by old age?

To make the discussion still more complicated it should be noted that there is considerable doubt as to whether old age can even be considered a cause of death. Listing old age as a cause of death in the very old may simply be an expression of disinterest on the part of the attending physician in discovering the actual medical cause. Moreover, even the process of aging is itself exceedingly difficult to describe, for it is by no means obvious which physiological processes are to be included under the term.

What then *is* aging? It is certain that we can use the term without being confused by it. But, if so, we do not mean by it simply existing, nor do we mean by it simply advancing toward an inevitable death. It would appear that the term is usually used in a comparative sense. When we speak of the "aged" we are speaking of the characteristics shared by another, say, the "young." Aging is then a relational term. To be of great age is not to have some specific combination of physical qualities, but simply to have lived longer than most other persons.

This means that it is misleading to speak of aging as an exclusively medical or physiological category. It is also appropriate to speak of it in social, cultural, or even political terms. There are, of course, certain medical problems and certain physiological disabilities more widely shared among the old than among the young, but the issue concerning the aged and death has less to do with these than with the fact that the elderly are in a disadvantaged position in society.

The four articles in this section address chiefly the consequences of this disadvantaged position. The first, Richard A. Kalish's "The Aged and the Dying Process," deals with what could be considered the political nature of aging, that is, the question of the power to make decisions affecting one's own life—and death. A frequent consequence of aging is the increased dependence of the aged on others. This owes in part to the diminished capacities that come with the aging process, but also in part to the social isolation of the old, which forces them out of normal employment patterns and into specialized institutions. Kalish has studied some of the patterns of powerlessness among the elderly as they approach death. He finds that such decisions as those affecting *who* it is that dies, *where* they die, and *when* and *how* they die, are increasingly made *for* the aged, and not *by* the aged.

The second article, "Aspects of Old Age in Age-Specific Mortality Rates," by W. R. Bytheway, addresses the *social* character of aging. Although Bytheway's paper is coldly empirical in style and deals with mortality rates in Scotland it offers a brutal portrait of old age that has universal application. He shows by the use of mortality rates alone how the social context is profoundly altered with an increase in age, particularly among those who survive into very old age. It is a statistical confirmation of the isolating effect of aging.

The third essay in this section, "On Aging, Dying, and Denying," by Carpenter and Wylie, surveys some of the *institutional* abuse suffered by the aging, and particularly the aging who are also terminally ill. "A patient with no future at all attracts both hostility and denial," the authors state, then indicate some of the ways in which that hostility and denial are expressed in institutions designed for the care of the old.

The fourth and final piece is excerpted from Sharon R. Curtin's book, *Nobody Ever Died of Old Age*. Curtin's work has the distinction of combining the political with the social aspects of aging in a way that shows the reader its cultural and personal nature as well. Hers is a very personal account of experiences with a number of aging people. It does not pretend to be an empirical study that shows the larger picture, but is rather an intimate study that allows the lives of the aged to emerge through the printed page with a special force. It is therefore a report that makes no attempt to conceal the author's own impassioned responses: sometimes confused, sometimes angry, but also often touched and thrilled by the ability of some of the old to survive illness and social rejection. Curtin does what the statistics cannot do in themselves, but without doing which they are useless: she appeals to the heart.

THE AGED AND THE DYING PROCESS: THE INEVITABLE DECISIONS

Richard A. Kalish

Professor Kalish, a noted author in the field of death and dying, here addresses the often hidden issue of the decisions of life and death affecting the elderly—decisions in which they themselves have little or no part.

Richard A. Kalish is a professor of behavioral sciences at the Graduate Theological Union, Berkeley, and holds consultation and workshops on aging and death.

This article is taken from the Journal of Social Issues, *volume 21, page 85, 1965.*

The dying process, like any other stage in human development, is influenced by numerous decisions. Although we often perceive the events that surround dying as automatic, inevitable, or beyond our control, in actuality they are constantly affected by cultural traditions and human decision-makers.

The decisions "who," "where," "when," and "how" are part of the dying process of each individual. This paper will explore and speculate upon the decisions and decision-makers involved in the dying process of the aged individual, although we recognize that comparable problems are faced when dying occurs at any age. We will deal with such decisions as who lives and who dies, where death occurs, how and when death comes about, who is to be with the dying patient, and how he is to learn of his imminent dying. Omitted for now will be such vital and relevant matters as war, fallout, air and water pollution control, socialized medicine, crime and accident prevention, and food and drug inspection, although each demands decisions which bear an obvious relationship to the dying process.

An important thread running through numerous behavioral science discussions of dying is the degree to which death and the dying are avoided (e.g., Wahl, 1959). Although the professional behavioral scientist studying these topics is no longer venturing into quite the taboo area reported by Feifel (1963), he is still likely to be accused of investigating a "morbid" topic. Even the geriatrician or gerontologist, while acknowledged to be making a pertinent contribution, seem to elicit wistful smiles and "I don't think I could take work like that" statements from his professional confreres.

Those who work with geriatric patients also find their own feelings make their work more difficult. A competent physician spends a sleepless week trying to decide how to inform a cheerful, alert octogenarian that her illness is terminal. A geriatric hospital nurse quickly explains that she *never* upsets a patient by telling him of the death of a close friend and ward-mate (thus leaving him to contemplate the significance of the empty bed). A young internist abruptly and affectlessly informs an elderly woman that she will be dead of cancer within three months (it took her six months, but the doctor had achieved his real goal, which was to propel her death away from his consciousness). A nursing home aide tells her friend that "Right after work, I go home, take a stiff shot, and forget about that depressing place until I show up in the morning." A Veterans Administration social worker encourages the son of a dying World War I veteran to avoid letting his father learn of his condition, and thus both the son and the social worker can suppress the coming death encounter—at least for a while.

Probably one of the most interesting and most telling examples of how the dying are avoided was cited in Bowers, *et al.* (1964). One of the authors, Lawrence LeShan, computed the length of time it took hospital nurses to respond to call lights for terminal cases and compared it to the time for non-terminal cases; the nurses, although not the observer, were startled to learn how much they delayed answering the ring of the dying.

In essence, the number and proportion of the post-65-year-olds are increasing, as are the facilities and the professional, financial, and political interest. At the same time, the personal encounter with the aged and the dying still seems highly upsetting and is most commonly avoided. Within this framework, we can better understand that the increasing need to examine our decisions regarding the dying process has outdistanced our willingness to do so. As a result, many decisions involving the dying process are ignored, avoided, postponed, or not seen as occurrences which involve decisions in the first place.

THE DECISIONS AND THE DECISION-MAKERS

In a large West Coast city, it has been reported to the author, a carefully selected panel of physicians and non-physicians must decide which of numerous applicants will be entitled to the use of highly limited medical facilities necessary to extend their lives by several years. At present, those rejected can expect to live only a very brief time. Rarely do we see, except for juries and the military, a more obvious (and probably anguishing) demand for making decisions regarding who lives and who dies. Most decisions involving the dying process are less dramatic, and most decision-makers are less aware of their role in the decision-making process. Nonetheless, society is constantly involved in decisions regarding the "who," the "where," the "when," and the "how" of dying.

WHO LIVES AND WHO DIES?

Determining who dies is certainly one of the most vital decisions made concerning the dying process. Such factors as age, race, sex, finances, and—perhaps—personality seem to affect decisions and decision-makers.

Age. Research has indicated that the lives of younger people are considered to be worth much more time and expense than the lives of the elderly (Kastenbaum, 1964a), and have more social value (Glaser and Strauss, 1964). Research and treatment of children and adolescents elicit more sympathy and attract more workers than research and treatment of the aged, and psychotherapy for the aged holds little interest for many, perhaps most, therapists (Kastenbaum, 1964b). The reasons for this are many, varied, and consistent with the value systems most widely maintained in our society. Although geriatrics and gerontology have received a recent impetus in this country, this author feels they still lag behind study and care of other age-groupings. Thus, probably without being fully aware of what they are doing, physicians, nurses, psychologists, social workers, and those responsible for the policies of funding organizations have helped decide who shall live and who shall die.

Race. Differential treatment of Negroes by physicians, teachers, lawyers, policemen, realtors, and employers, to name just a few, has contributed to the higher rate of Negro mortality at all ages. In some instances—those that often make the headlines—the Negro has been the victim of a direct attempt upon his life, or of overt exclusion from adequate medical care or legal protection. But more frequently, and probably more destructive, the Negro is selected to die sooner because of subtler causes, such as having to spend a higher proportion of his income on housing, leaving less for food and medical care, or for being forced to live in less advantageous sections of the community, regardless of income. In addition, of course, are his lesser job opportunities and more limited access to the type of information and education that provides the sort of knowledge and understanding that extends life.

Sex. Women, as is well known, live longer than men. Whatever constitutional bases might determine this differential life expectancy, we may speculate that certain implicit cultural norms are also involved. To give but one example: our cultural traditions allow women to seek medical care, but encourage a moderate to high degree of spartanism for men. Thus, the male may die sooner, partly as the result of his decision to adhere to the standard male role.

Finances. The indigent can receive competent medical care, which they pay for largely with time; the wealthy can receive competent medical care, which they can pay for readily with money. For the great majority of the elderly, however, medical care takes a high proportion of their financial assets. With Medicare, the economic advantages of the wealthy are considerably reduced, but many differences still exist, such as the opportunity to make long-term use of good nursing home facilities.

Personality. Personality not only affects the ability of an individual to seek and profit from medical and related help, but affects the responses an individual elicits from others. In a geriatric facility, for example, we observe the pleasant and cooperative patient receiving better care and treatment on the ward than the irritable and belligerent patient. The patient who growls at the physician may get a more superficial examination than the one who cooperates; the good-natured aged woman is wheeled to the sunny spot on the porch and is taken to activities, while her grumpy, complaining ward-mate is left in bed longer, is spoken to less frequently, and is less likely to receive extra attention.

Thus, as the result of age, race, sex, finances, and personality, decisions are made which affect who lives and who dies. These decisions are made by medical personnel, hospital ward personnel, other patients, relatives—just about everyone, including the elderly patients themselves. Such decisions are based upon tacit assumptions and cultural values that need illumination and thorough dialogue.

DECIDING WHERE THE DEATH OCCURS

Traditionally, people died in their homes. Only a few decades ago, the hospital was considered the "place where people went to die," and was avoided by many, including the dying, for that very reason. Now, perhaps ironically, that the hospital is seen as being primarily for short-term care, people enter more readily—and die there more often. However, many terminal patients prefer to die at home. The administrator of one large hospital, which averages some 600 deaths annually, has suggested that the dying process could and should occur at home more frequently than it now does. At this hospital, the next-of-kin are often asked if they wish to take the patient home, where he can die in familiar surroundings, rather than in the impersonal hospital where the ebb and flow of events is controlled by routine and by strangers.

But how does the family feel? Both professional literature (e.g., Kalish, in press) and personal experience remind us constantly of the degree to which the dying person is avoided in our society. One highly emotional forty-ish housewife exclaimed that she would never be able to live in her house again, if her aged father were to die there. Another woman of similar age and duties agreed with her 79-year-old father's complaint that "no one is allowed to die at home any more—and what's worse, they won't even leave the poor body around long enough for a wake. No, they ship it off to a funeral home right away." In between is a variety of expressed attitudes. (These quotations were extracted from interviews the author recently conducted with adult children of geriatric hospital patients; analysis of these data is still in process.)

Sometimes the decision to hospitalize is made because adequate care is lacking at home, or because the fight for life can be made more effectively in a medical facility. Often, however, the decision is made by default since the participants, the patient, his family, and the physician, are never actively aware that the possible alternative decision to die at home is a reasonable one. Some may feel the sacrifice of a few days of life is a not unreasonable exchange for the opportunity to die at home. Although, for the most part, the next-of-kin interviewees felt that their parent did not care where he died, only two of the 37 felt the elderly person would prefer the hospital, while eight stated that home was preferable.* A large proportion of dying geriatric patients are not sufficiently lucid, of course, to know where they are when they die. Nonetheless, whatever is known about their wishes may be respected.

The elderly themselves, however, frequently wish to be removed from their home when they become unable to take care of themselves of cannot afford to hire others who can care for them. Unlike other places and other times, the elderly are so much concerned lest they become a "burden" on others that they often decide to place themselves in nursing homes or similar facilities. They thus divest themselves of the right to be cared for by their children, a right that the contemporary Japanese or traditional American or European would take as his due.

When asked how they themselves felt about growing old, our sample of adult children most frequently mentioned their fear of "being a burden." In a geriatric facility, the "burdensome" quality of daily (and often abrasive) contact with children is substantially eliminated. It absolves the guilt of the parent and multiplies the guilt of the children, according to clinicians in the geriatrics field.

The fear of becoming a burden is not the only pressure upon the elderly to decide to live, and thus die, in nursing homes. Some prefer to be where medical care is more readily available; others prefer the impersonal care; sometimes an aged parent believes that his effect upon the people with whom he lives is destructive. A number of elderly persons also prefer to avoid the role reversal in which the once-dominant parent must regress to the status of helpless infant, nurtured by the children he once nurtured himself; a geriatric facil-

---

* The author feels that respondents, who were responsible for the hopitalization in the first place, would tend to under-estimate their parents' desires to return home to die.

ity enables him to maintain the original parent-child relationship intact as long as possible.

Thus, the elderly person may prefer to die at home, with his possessions surrounding him, and with familiar faces near. Nonetheless, a barrage of medical, psychological, and financial pressures often produces the decision to die in a hospital or geriatric facility.

Numerous researchable problems emerge in considering where the dying process occurs. We could attempt to learn where the elderly patient prefers to die, and what relationship this bears to his feelings at previous developmental stages. We could also investigate how different types of geriatric patients are affected by various living (and dying) arrangements. The possibility that separation from family through placement in a nursing home leads to premature death is one contemplated study. We recognize the impact of separation upon infants and children; perhaps the aged person, often highly dependent also, would have similar reactions to this type of separation. It would also be valuable to learn who actually makes the decision, on what basis, and with what implications for the psychological functioning of all those concerned.

WHEN DOES THE PATIENT DIE?

How long is existence to be extended? Some physicians believe it is their responsibility to maintain existence as long as possible, while others interpret their role more flexibly. This decision becomes more difficult as the definition of "living" becomes more complex. Shneidman (1963) has discussed this problem at some length, but for present purposes we need to keep in mind that the cessation of the heart beat is technically the end of life only because we continue to accept this traditional definition. Could the future define the end of life as the end of self-awareness? If it seems axiomatic that life continues as long as the heart beats, what will define "life" when an artificial or transplanted heart becomes an actuality? We might keep a beating heart encased indefinitely within an otherwise lifeless body. When does life cease? Who is to decide?

A hospital administrator has suggested that a panel be established to decide when life has, for practical purposes, ended, and the heart may be allowed to stop beating. When one physician berated him for "playing God," his rejoinder was that the physician was "playing God" by sustaining existence beyond the time that God apparently had decided it should cease. Although it is clearly murder to remove an intravenus tube from a dying patient, the act of not inserting it in the first place is a totally different matter. The battle lines on this issue are just being drawn, and its resolution is far in the future.

If it is "playing God" to make a decision affecting the length of life, then physicians and next-of-kin are both forced into this controversial role. Whether or not to operate on an elderly person is a decision which often must be made. Any surgery, of course, entails risk, and an operation on the elderly entails more than the normal amount. The decision must be made as to whether the possible reduction of suffering or extension of life is worth the risk of death on the operating table. Someone must make the decision—usually the physician and the patient jointly or, if the patient is not sufficiently lucid, the next-of-kin. And the need for such a decision immediately creates other decisions. Who determines whether a patient is sufficiently lucid to make decisions involving his own life and death? The aged, even those who frequently seem disoriented, often have days or hours when they appear alert. Does the physician obtain permission for a dangerous operation during a lucid period? Does he by-pass the patient altogether?

The answer seems to depend upon the individual physician and his interaction with both patient and family. In actual practice, the physician may decide whom to ask and when to ask, often based, consciously or unconsciously, on his perceptions of how to receive the response he wishes. Obviously, he will consider professional ethics, legal restrictions, the possibility of incurring family wrath, or a malpractice lawsuit. When indigents without families are involved, the decision may be influenced by the sort of operation or treatment needed for instruction for the interne and resident staff. In the case of clearly senile patients, decisions regarding the dying process are made by the physician, often in conjunction with the family. Sometimes the family members appreciate having a part in the decision-making process; at other times, they resent the physician for forcing them into taking a share of responsibility, even though the medical man must be the final decision-maker. It is he who must decide which relative is the proper one to represent the patient, and when the interests of the patient conflict with the decisions suggested by the family. In more than one case, the physician has had to evaluate the financial investment the family has in the patient's death.

Provocative ethical and legal problems emerge from this discussion, although somewhat tangential to the immediate topic. At what point do "you" cease to be "yours?" That is, when do you cease to have responsibility for what happens to your body or your thinking? Lack of responsibility for "you" ceases before death, if evidence can be given that "you" are not capable of taking responsibility. Thus, "you" may be medicated, sedated, tranquillized, operated upon, fed, bathed, and dressed without the prerogative of being an agent in the decision-making process.

THE "HOW" DECISIONS

To an appreciable extent, we are unable to control how we die, any more than we can control when we die. However, the modern world certainly makes more effective decisions regarding the "how" and "when" of the dying process than ever before. Ignoring for this presentation such death-decisions as suicide or homicide, we need to consider the condition of the patient as he goes through the dying process.

Most people would probably accept the premise that the physician should reduce the suffering of a dying person as much as possible. But the reduction of discomfort often requires sedation, sometimes to the point that the patient leads an almost vegetative, albeit comfortable, existence. Is this preferable to having pain, but remaining alert and able to communicate? Who makes this decision? Sometimes the decision of when to die depends directly upon the decision how to die. A patient may need to decide whether to live a substantial number of years in pain, or a lesser number of comfortable years. Additional decisions include who will be with the patient as he dies and how the patient is informed of his terminal condition.

WHO IS WITH THE PATIENT AS HE DIES?

Do elderly patients want their families with them as they die? Generalizing from our sample of 37, their adult children believe so. Do the family members want to be there? The answer is again, generally, in the positive, although frequently with the qualification that "father can recognize me," or "if there is any point in it." The range of responses is great, however, from: "I don't want to be within twenty miles at that point," (from a very emotional housewife) to "I'd sit with him day and night in case he could talk to me for a few minutes before he dies," (from the daughter of a man whose stroke a year earlier left him almost completely paralyzed).

But decisions regarding who can stay with the dying are not always left to the patient or to the individual family members. An adult may make the decision that the patient's grandchildren should not see him dying, although the grandchildren might wish to do so; a physician might decide that the terminal illness is contagious and the patient should be isolated; a hysterical son might be kept from his mother's side "for his own good" or for hers.

INFORMING THE TERMINAL GERIATRIC PATIENT

The patient's "right to know" has generated more questions than answers and each question requires a decision. One school of thought insists that the patient be apprised, as objectively as possible, of his condition. Another school believes that the patient should be protected against such knowledge, which will rob him of hope and perhaps hasten his death. Intermediate positions call for discussing the possible seriousness, but purposely remaining unduly optimistic; answering only direct questions; being vaguely encouraging without giving specific information; telling the patient things will get worse before they get better, which often deflects further questioning; and so forth. The decision must be made, not only what to tell the patient, but who is to do the telling: The physician? The next-of-kin? A social worker or psychologist? Or a chance hint inadvertently supplied by a visitor or nurse?

Informing the terminally ill person of his condition is not a popular task. Ward personnel usually avoid it at all costs, sometimes being obviously and ridiculously optimistic in their patient contact to do so. Family members and physicians are likely to pass the buck back and forth to each other, until the patient senses the situation and grasps for himself what is happening without being told. In many instances the patient understands his condition long before the attending doctor or relative has even decided whether or not to present the information. On other occasions, the patient becomes

terminal and dies without ever attaining sufficient lucidity to understand the significance of what is happening to him.

Dr. Weisman, a consultant psychiatrist on a research project for
the aged, to whom the author is indebted to his writings of and his
personal contacts, believes that few dying patients need to be told
they are nearing death, but that many more would like to discuss
their prognosis than doctors and nurses generally realize.

"Most patients already sense the diagnosis long before they are
told," (Weisman and Hackett, 1962), and misleading or patronizing
answers to serious questions will only alienate the physician and the
patient. Although the doctor should convey only that information
which the patient is emotionally and intellectually able to absorb, he
should respond so that the patient finds his words understandable
and according to the meaning the patient intended. Questions such
as "Will I ever leave here?" or "Will I die soon?" may be circum-
vented or rephrased, but the meaning the patient is communicating
should never be distorted. In no instance should the patient be told a
falsehood or given an inappropriately optimistic outlook. Most dying
patients, Dr. Weisman feels, are afraid of losing their last enduring
relationships. "Focus upon the time that is left and concentrate upon
the patient's residue of autonomy, control, choice, and responsibility."
This author would agree and believes that emphasis should be upon
the participation of the patient and upon his ability to choose, rather
than upon a specific estimate of the remaining time, which is rarely
a crucial issue and which, perhaps fortunately, cannot be predicted
as accurately as other aspects of a fatal illness.

A CONCLUDING NOTE

In a sense we each make daily decisions affecting the dying
processes of ourselves and others. The food we decide to eat, the
speed at which we drive our car, the ballot we cast, the charity donation we make, all these influence dying, although we may be only
sporadically aware of it. We also tend to be unaware of some of the
basic assumptions we have regarding dying. For example, care
offered in the hospital is better for the dying person than care offered
elsewhere. Dying usually means pain and discomfort. The death of a
child is "worse" than the death of an elderly person. Existence
should be extended as long as possible. Living, except for isolated

cases, is better than dying. Women are constitutionally pre-disposed to live longer than men. These are but a few of the underlying premises we maintain, often without evaluation, that affect our decisions as we manipulate the process of dying.

ASPECTS OF OLD AGE IN AGE-SPECIFIC MORTALITY RATES

W. R. Bytheway

A strange and tragic arithmetic in the mortality statistics causes painful social reordering, Professor Bytheway shows in this precise but understated profile of the increasing isolation of the aged.

W. R. Bytheway is on the faculty of the Medical Sociology Unit, Center for Social Studies, University of Aberdeen, Scotland.

This article is taken from the Journal of Biosocial Science, *volume 2, page 337, October, 1970.*

INTRODUCTION

A review of the literature on social gerontology reveals a notable absence of any discussion of the definition of old age. This is perhaps to be expected since old age is both a readily acceptable conceptual category and increasingly used as an important indicator of social problems. Consequently it is defined either as being over a particular chronological age, or as possessing certain characteristics known to be associated with old age (e.g. membership of an old people's home, widowhood, grandparenthood). Generally there is little discussion of alternative definitions, or of the broader implications of the definition used.

Similarly, although there are studies, such as Rose's study (1965) of the "group consciousness" of the aged, specifically investigating the "ageing subculture" from a sociological perspective, there is little consideration of the effect of the constant drain of members through death upon that subculture. To draw a rather simplified analogy, if a football match is played and each player is allowed to stop playing and go home when he feels tired, then the character of the game will change with time not only as a result of the players becoming tired, but also due to the decreasing number of players. Social gerontologists have studied in some detail whether the players mind getting tired, how they adjust their play to their tiredness, and how to postpone as long as possible their decision to leave the field. They have not studied directly the effect of depletion upon the remaining players and the characteristics of their game.

This paper argues that, by relating old age and death in small human groups, an alternative approach both to defining old age and to studying the aetiology of certain old age problems is achieved. However, it must be emphasized that the paper is primarily an exercise, first, in drawing certain inferences about statistically rational attitudes and behaviour resulting from the effects of the peculiar association between the probability of death and chronological age, and, second, in estimating the statistical probabilities of certain characteristics. No claim is made that these are equivalent to actual attitudes and behaviour held generally by old people. Finally, the data used to describe this peculiar association is drawn from the 1966 annual report of the Registrar General for Scotland (1968). For simplicity of exposition the analysis has been based solely on male death rates.

AGE, DEATH, AND REFERENCE GROUPS

A person B is defined as being an acquaintance of another person A if A is able to associate either a name or a face with B, even if this requires a certain amount of prompting by a mutual acquaintance. Of the population of people known to A at any one time, a certain number of them he can identify as being of a similar age to himself. The actual difference in ages may be up to about 20%, but the essential criterion is that A sees these acquaintances as being of his own age. This set will be referred to as his peer acquaintances. The complementary terms "peer bereaved" and "peer deceased" will be used for A and B respectively, when B dies and when B was, at the time of death, an acquaintance of A (according to the above definition).

It is events occurring to A's peer acquaintances that are his crucial sources of information about age-appropriate behaviour. He ignores the fact that his parents married when his father was 35, when he is aware that all his old school friends are married and he is 25 years old next week. Similarly the man in his early 50s forgets that his parents are growing roses for next year's horticultural show, when the man with whom he was vying for promotion died from a stroke over the weekend. His peer acquaintances constitute a reference group which is a powerful influence upon his age-specific behaviour. To quote Loether (1967):

> "The possibility of one's own death is most likely to enter awareness when one's relatives or friends die. Particularly when acquaintances of one's own age die, one is likely to be thinking about death in more personal terms,"

and Vischer (1966):

> "A seventy-four year old man told me that when he read the death notices he always attached great importance to the age of the dead person. If the person was younger than he was, then he did not feel particularly concerned; he felt satisfied to have attained a greater age himself. And if the dead person was considerably older, then this gave him fresh courage. But if he read of the death of somebody of the same age as himself, it invariably left him with a sense of shock."

This paper argues that, with the perception that some of his peer acquaintances have died not as the result of tragic accidents but, as it were, of their own accord (as a result of reaching the "natural" end of their lives), A makes a number of crucial adjustments. He begins to see death as normative behaviour for his age group. The deceased are no longer parties to deviant acts. The deceased have behaved appropriately for their age. Deaths of his friends may have a certain poignancy. He attends their funerals, but these are anticipated (if random) events which become part of his regulated life, like visits from his adult children, and wins on the horses. Giese (1961) found that for some old people, "funerals of old friends no longer occasioned such grief."

AGE OF ONSET OF PEER BEREAVEMENT

The average age-specific incidence of peer bereavement can be calculated from standard mortality rates. The percentages of all peer acquaintances who die between certain ages, can be simply estimated from the same percentage in the general population.

Almost one in three of the 50-year-old man's peer acquaintances will die before they all retire at the age of 65 (Table 1). This is a proportion which seems unexpectedly high when reading some gerontological literature which emphasizes the normality of death

TABLE 1

Percentage of peer acquaintances dying between certain ages

Age group (years)	Percent Dying
50–59	16
50–64	31
50–69	47
50–74	63

in old age, and abnormality of "premature" death (Parsons, 1964). Clearly, people who reach the age of 65, who have had no experience of death are, in a similar (i.e. statistical) sense, markedly abnormal.

Without interviewing old people directly, it is possible, making certain assumptions, to investigate in more detail the statistical aspects of experience of death. The basic assumption is that a man in his later years who has thirty-two acquaintances of exactly his own age throughout his old age, is a reasonable approximation to the archetypical ageing man. It is also assumed that, upon the death of one of the thirty-two, a substitute acquaintance is immediately found. As a result of what is learnt about him, inferences can be made about the corresponding histories of old men with fewer or more acquaintances, or with younger or older acquaintances. The number thirty-two was chosen primarily for arithmetic convenience.

Table 2 is based upon the expected ages (based upon statistical averages) at which acquaintances die. A further necessary assumption is that one died on his 50th birthday (again arbitrarily chosen). The last death before the one at age 45 was well before his 40th birthday. It is clear from the last column that the rate of change in the expected lengths of intervals is greater in the early and mid-fifties than in the late fifties and sixties. Whereas there is only one

TABLE 2

Expected ages of deaths within thirty-two acquaintances

Order of death	Age		Interval length (months)	Percentage decrease in interval length
	Years	Months		
1	45	5		
			55	
2	50	0		
			38	32
3	53	2		
			26	29
4	55	4		
			23	15
5	57	3		
			19	16
6	58	10		
			17	15
7	60	3		
			14	11
8	61	5		
			12	11
9	62	5		
			11	13
10	63	4		
			10	8
11	64	2		
			10	8
12	65	0		

death every 5 years during the forties, there is one death in every 18 months in the late fifties.

However, it is possible that, despite the changes in the expected lengths of intervals between deaths, the actual lengths between deaths are sufficiently sporadic for most men to be left unaware of any change. Table 3 gives the expected incidence of one or two deaths per year in 10-year intervals within thirty-two acquaintances of the same ageing man. As was clear from Table 2, he can expect one death somewhere between the ages of 35 and 45. There is an approximately 1-in-3 chance that he will lose two acquaintances between two successive birthdays in the period between his 45th and 55th birthdays, and he can expect two such instances between the ages of 55 and 64.

TABLE 3

Expected number of times in periods of 10 years that an ageing person loses at least one, or at least two, peer acquaintances between successive birthdays (It is assumed that he has thirty-two peer acquaintances all the same age as himself, and that he finds a substitute immediately following each death of a peer acquaintance)

	Age group (years)			
	35–44	45–54	55–64	65–74
At least 1 death/year	1·0	2·6	5·6	8·5
At least 2 deaths/year*	0·05	0·35	1·9	5·6

* The expected interval between two deaths is approximately 6 months. It is not the occurrence of two deaths separated by less than a year, rather two deaths occurring between two birthdays.

Thus, if this ageing man suddenly perceives death to be possible for his age group in non-accidental circumstances, by inference from either a perceived increased frequency of peer bereavements, or on the occurrence of more than one death within a short period of time, then this can be expected to occur during his fifties, and almost certainly before he retires at the age of 65. If he then goes on to see this as an indicator of old age, and in so far as people "enter old age," then the final conclusion from these results is that it seems reasonably likely that a considerable proportion of people will be in the throes of entering old age well before they retire at the age of 65.

DEATH AND MARRIAGE

Whereas it might be relatively easy for the ageing man to adjust his relationships with his set of friends and acquaintances in order to accommodate the possible disruption caused by peer bereavement, membership of a marriage can only be adjusted at a considerable cost. Most people find old age subject to enough change without attempting divorce as well. Thus, the only future for the marriage is the inevitable death of one of the partners and the widowhood of the other. Despite differences between the age-specific death rates for the two sexes, and small differences in the ages of husband and wife, the respective chances of husband or wife being widowed are unlikely to be particularly dissimilar for most of the lives of most marriages. However, due to the high stakes involved, and despite acknowledgment of the chance element, it is possible that both partners will have firmly established expectations about who will bury whom, calculated from results in the reference group, and perhaps more particularly, from the common knowledge that women, on average, live longer than men.

Since the reference group, and indeed the sociologist's random sample, uses the year lived and not the life lived as its unit of enumeration, then the likelihood of the wife being widowed is generally over-estimated since the widowed wife can expect more years of widowhood than the widowed husband can. (This may be due only to differences in age-specific mortality rates and remarriage rates between widows and widowers, but the data of Shurtleff (1955) suggests that the mortality of men is increased proportionately more as a result of widowhood than that of women.) In order to estimate the chances of the husband or the wife being widowed, it is essential that this is based upon the ratio of men who eventually became widowers to women who eventually become widows, rather than the ratio of widowers to widows at any one point in time. In Scotland, in 1966, there were thirty-four widows for every ten widowers, but as a result of deaths of married people there were only twenty-two widows created for every ten widowers created. This suggests that for every twelve marriages where the wife is bound to be widowed, there are twenty where the husband and wife are equally likely to be widowed. Clearly it would take only a small imbalance in age or health in the appropriate direction for each partner in the typical marriage partnership to have equal chances of being the first to die.

However, not only is the outcome itself of interest, but also the time of outcome. Death can come sooner than expected. At 50, the Scottish male can expect 21 years and 9 months more of life, his female counterpart can expect 26 years and 5 months more. It may come as something of a surprise for him to learn that he can expect only 16 or 17 years more married life, assuming both partners are of the same age. This anomaly is simply due to the fact that the marriage as opposed to the individual's life can be ended by either of two deaths. In so far as one in eight married 50-year-old Scottish males can expect to be widowed before the age of 65, then the problems of young male widowhood referred to by Blau (1961) will be characteristic, primarily, of men in their fifties and early sixties.

However, slightly over 50% of marriages will remain intact

until after retirement at 65. Of these, only 30% will survive a further 10 years, again assuming both partners are of the same age. Given the marriage does survive, then a number of problems appear, resulting from the relative rarity of such successes. First, most of the couple's acquaintances will be involved in the new world of widowhood. It will be difficult for the old couple to partake jointly in social activities as before. Blau (1961) found this to be true, suggesting that particularly young widows and particularly old married couples have certain problems in common. However, the old married couple would seem to have certain additional problems. Long-surviving marriages are celebrated achievements for reasons similar to those for celebrating longevity itself. However, whereas those who failed to achieve longevity are dead, a proportion of those who failed to celebrate their golden wedding anniversary are alive but widowed. It is obviously difficult to live with success in the company of those who have failed.

Yet even at 75 one of the couple will still eventually be faced with joining the ranks of the widowed. Whereas the young widow is the pioneer of a difficult but new way of life, one of the old married couple will inevitably have to adjust to this change at a very late stage in his or her life. Further to this, since their marriage has confounded all expectations, on what basis can they now anticipate who will be the deceased and who the bereaved? Both have entered "bonus time." Not only do they themselves have less confidently held expectations about the future, but the statistician is also less confident in predicting the outcome. The ratio of male death rates to female death rates is shown in Table 4.

TABLE 4

Ratio of male death rates to female death rates

Age group (years)	Ratio
40–44	1·47
45–49	1·67
50–54	1·69
55–59	1·88
60–64	2·08
65–69	1·84
70–74	1·64
75–79	1·48
80 +	1·26

The ratio following the age of 75 is lower than in any age group since the age of 40. This is further reflected in the ratio of bereaved wives to bereaved husbands (for marriages where both partners at the time of first death are in the same age group) shown in Table 5.

As a final description of this difference, the man of 75 is subject, on average, to death rates similar to those of a woman 4 years his elder, the man of 60 is equivalent, in the same sense, to a woman 7 years his elder.

TABLE 5

Ratio of bereaved wives to bereaved husbands

Age groups (years)	Ratio
40–44	1·44
45–49	1·97
50–54	1·85
55–59	2·15
60–64	2·37
65–69	2·05
70–74	1·93
75 +	1·53

Although this reduced differentiation is unlikely to be perceived through reference groups, and is certainly not common knowledge, so that it is very unlikely that the old married couple could be aware of it, it is in itself a considerable structural change which could be an important consideration in the planning of certain social welfare services.

SOCIAL ISOLATION

The paradox of old age isolation is that, in certain perspectives, it is an inevitable threat and, in others, a rare condition. In the perspective of maximum life-spans it is inevitable, since a high proportion of people over 80 would be isolated if no adjustments were to be made, but, in the perspective of all people living at a particular time, the percentage who are isolated through old age will be small. Relatively few people will eventually be faced with the prospect of isolation in old age; most will die first. For example, if there is a group of six men of a similar age, each knows and interacts with each of the other five as long as they are both alive, but none of the six interact with any other persons, then only one of the six will ever be socially isolated (17% of the original population), although for that particular man, without adjustment, it was unavoidable.

Thus, it is increasingly important for the increasingly old person, if he wishes to avoid isolation, to attempt actively to extend the membership of his set of acquaintances. If he is seen to possess some positively valued attributes (e.g. health, wealth, power or wisdom), or if he finds other persons who are themselves in need of friendship, he may be successful. However, if for instance A offers friendship to B, B considers A, sees A as having little to offer, sees A as having the greater need for their mutual interaction, sees this greater need being translated into demands (in terms of time and decision making) that might disrupt B's present social world, perhaps sees A as being older (than B) and therefore making even greater demands (visits to hospitals, financial help, help to avoid being placed in an institution, help in bereavement, help during A's own death passage), and, as a consequence of all this, B refuses A's offer.

There is some evidence from two papers by Blau that those who are in danger of isolation may experience these difficulties in attempting to avoid isolation. Blau's study (1961), mentioned in the previous section, found that younger widowers suffered a drop in friendship participation as a result of their bereavement. In an earlier paper (Blau, 1956), she also found that, in comparing old people who saw themselves as members of a "bunch of friends" with others of a similar age who did not, the former were more likely to see themselves as middle-aged rather than old. There is likely to be little sympathy in a bunch of "middle-aged" old people with an appeal for friendship from a single "old-aged" old person. The data of Batten, Barton, Durstine & Osborn (1966) show that people over 65 become increasingly dependent upon younger people for friends.

Although some may be able to continue in isolation, there are certain institutionalized procedures whereby isolated old persons, either on their own initiative or on someone else's, can congregate together. Both the isolation and the need for some of the institutions would not exist without the fact of a permanent and increasing rate of depletion in old age peer groups. The following results describe the effect of this depletion upon the incidence of isolation.

A group of thirty-two men have a certain pattern and amount of interaction. With succeeding deaths, certain policies are adopted towards adjusting the pattern of interaction. Interaction with persons outside the thirty-two is ignored, and substitutes are not admitted into the group as result of deaths. This latter assumption contrasts with that of the earlier section since that was concerned primarily with the experience of death between the ages of 50 and 65. In this section the focus is primarily upon people in their 70s and 80s for whom depletion of acquaintances is particularly marked, and who will have found substitution increasingly difficult. There are two parameters of interest: first, the number who lose all their interactors before their own death and, second, for these isolates the

TABLE 6

Expected incidence and length of isolation in a group of thirty-two old men

Pattern of interaction	Amount of interaction	Policy of adjustment	Average no. of isolates	Isolate's average length of isolation (units of rank)
A	5	i	5·3	4·7
A	2	i	10·7	8·3
A	1	i	16·0	11·0
B	5	i	4·8	4·9
B	5	ii	14·5	10·4

average length of time in isolation, in units of rank, the thirty-two being ranked according to the order of death. The unit of one rank is approximately equivalent to a year. Apart from the first four (occurring at rather wider intervals), deaths between the fifth at the age of 60 years 8 months and twenty-fifth at 79 years 10 months are expected to occur at intervals of about a year according to the 1966 Scottish male mortality rates. The rather sparser data would suggest that deaths after the twenty-fifth can be expected to follow at roughly similar intervals.

Table 6 gives average values for these two parameters for a number of different situations, depending upon the initial pattern and amount of interaction and the policy of adjustment to death. There were two initial patterns of interaction considered:

A. Groups of a certain fixed size are formed at random. There is complete interaction within each group (each member interacts with each other) but none between groups. Each of the thirty-two belongs to a group, although there may be one group where some are in the thirty-two and some not.

B. Interaction within the thirty-two is distributed at random, such that each member has a fixed amount of interaction.

The values for pattern A were found by direct calculation based upon probabilities. The values for pattern B are based upon the results of ten replications using random numbers to generate the order of death. Each and every person interacts with only a fixed number of other persons. In Table 6, this number is 1, 2 or 5. Finally the policy of adjustment assumed is one of the following:

i. No action is taken following a death. Consequently, a member is isolated only when all of his initial interactors have died.

ii. As (i) but with the additional policy: If following any death, a pair of interactors differ by more than 1 in their respective numbers of interactors, then they permanently cease interacting. Example: If A interacts with B, A has three interactors in all (including B), and B has only one (i.e. A), then they cease interacting, and consequently A has only two interactors, and B is isolated. A does not readjust further until after a further death. We shall say "A has rejected B." Thus, following a death, a member may reject only one interactor, but may be rejected by any number of his interactors.

Comparing A5i (pattern A, 5 interactors and policy i) with B5i, it is clear that the initial pattern of interaction A or B, given similar amounts of adjustment, has little effect upon the two parameters. Comparing within the two patterns, the effect of enforcing policy (ii) is seen to be approximately equivalent to reducing the initial group size in pattern A from 6 to 2. It more than trebles the number of isolates and more than doubles their expected length of isolation.

This suggests that the probability of isolation may be significantly affected by reaction and adjustment to particular deaths by the group as a whole, at least in comparison to the effect of varying numbers of interactors per person.

Although this is only simulated data, resulting from a rather tenuous model, it does suggest that social isolation in old age is a phenomenon the occurrence of which will depend in large part upon the characteristics of both the small human group and of the relationships between pairs of friends or acquaintances. It would seem unlikely that the characteristics of the isolate himself are the dominant factors contributing to the creation of his current demise.

ON AGING, DYING, AND DENYING: DELIVERING CARE TO OLDER DYING PATIENTS

James O. Carpenter

Charles M. Wylie, M.D.

The difficulties of providing adequate care to the terminally ill have been widely chronicled, but when the terminally ill are also aged they have a combination of problems which, in the opinion of the authors, causes them to be treated by the medical staff with "both hostility and denial." The authors show that such treatment is both costly in human terms and unnecessary in medical terms.

James O. Carpenter is an assistant professor of public health administration and associate director of the Program in Health Gerontology at the University of Michigan School of Public Health. Charles M. Wylie is a professor and director of public health administration at the same school and director of the Program in Health Gerontology.

This article is taken from Public Health Reports, *volume 89, number 5, September/October, 1974.*

Dying in old age is a subject of distant postponable concern to most health professionals since they are interested primarily in the prevention and adequate treatment of disease. Even those who are close to the care of dying older patients are uncomfortable in confronting the specter of death in their clients. In the health professions, the overwhelming commitment of training, talent, and funds to curing and healing, although important, may weaken the thrust for better care of the dying and render it unlikely that an older person's last days will be spent in a supportive social environment in which his death is regarded as an individual and unique event. A patient with no future at all attracts both hostility and denial. When death becomes inevitable, many health professionals withdraw from its bruising assault and redirect their efforts elsewhere.

Yet, many readers of this journal are deeply interested and involved in comprehensive health care, which—if it is truly comprehensive—should help dying older patients as well as younger curable patients. There is a rising concern about the delivery of humane care, a push for open discussion of complex moral issues, and a growing recognition that we must openly communicate with both the terminally ill patient and his family. As a first step in overcoming our aversion to dealing with death at an advanced age, we need to examine the complex issues associated with the management of the older dying patient. That is the purpose of our paper.

SOCIOLOGICAL PERSPECTIVES

Technological and other advancements have rendered obsolete many attributes of the older person, such as his wisdom, that were highly valued in the more rural society of 19th century America. The power that the older person enjoyed in the extended family of the past has also been reduced in the emergent nuclear family of industrialized society. In modern society older parents may continue to help their children, and in turn, the children may assist their elders. The power of the older family member over family decisions, however, has faded in comparison with that of earlier decades.

Today some 25 percent of the persons aged 65 and over live alone or with nonrelatives. About three times as many older women as men live alone or with nonrelatives, a circumstance reflecting, among other things, the greater life expectancy among women. Older women also appear to be at greater risk of institutionalization. In the segment of the older population residing alone or with unrelated persons, social disengagement and isolation may occur. These observations suggest the need for health and social support services to compensate for the possible absence of family members of older patients facing death.

To understand the possibilities for improving the care given the older dying person, we must consider the social climate in which the older population lives. Many older people subsist on small, fixed incomes in an inflationary economy; in 1970 half of those who were not living with their families had incomes below the poverty level. Some older citizens have been forced to retire, while others have done so voluntarily. For both groups, retirement may have entailed a reduction of activities, loss of contact with their working colleagues, and a reduced income.

A century ago about two-thirds of U.S. men aged 65 and older were still in the labor force, compared with only 25 percent today. The shift from having one's hours dictated by the work organization to having free time and a reduced income has implications for the quality of life of the older person. Because an older person not in the work force is no longer seen by society as being "productive," he may find himself regarded as having a lower social status. Many older people cope successfully with this transition. Socially isolated retirees seem to have the most difficulty in adjusting to their new status. Indeed, one investigation disclosed a "low will to live" in 48 percent of socially isolated retired steelworkers in contrast with only 7 percent of the retirees who were socially integrated. As one retired worker pointed out, "I don't worry about the next life. I've got enough hell right here." Not surprisingly, those older persons who find themselves socially devalued and isolated may experience depression and hold negative views of themselves and of life in general.

Presumably the younger person looks to the future, whereas the older person is seen as engaging in a review of his past life. Although such a review may be helpful to many older persons, for the socially isolated who have experienced social estrangement, this period of life review may parallel a process of social disengagement, of dying socially. And social death, the extreme stage of social isolation, may contribute in complex ways to biological death.

To a considerable extent modern society defies age and denies death. Our health care providers come from such a society, and therefore few can conceive realistically of their own senescence and death, even though they recognize that death is a universal phenomenon. Their training in this area has been inadequate so that they are often only able to react as laymen to dying patients, rather than on the basis of sound academic knowledge. Thus, both at the beginning and in the midst of the professional's career, education must increasingly focus on the dynamics of senescence and dying and on management of the dying patient. When, through such education, we as health providers come to realize that our own deaths are likely to take place in a health care setting, a large step will have been taken toward improving the environment of the older dying patient.

STRESSES OF BEREAVEMENT AND RELOCATION

The great impact of bereavement on the health of older survivors is now well documented. In a study of 4,486 widowers aged 55 years and older, Parkes and associates found that 213 had died within 6 months after the loss of their wives.[1] This figure was 40 percent higher than the expected mortality for married men of the same age. After the 6-month period the death rate of the widowers dropped to that of married men. The authors point out that "if as seems most likely, the painful effects of bereavement on physical health are a response to psychological stress, then anything that mitigates this stress can be expected to reduce the risk of its physical effects." Other research, suggesting that grief is a syndrome leading to greater use of physicians for both psychiatric and nonpsychiatric symptoms, clearly shows the need for preparing physicians, nurses, and others to deal with the physical and psychological needs of the bereaved.

Unfortunately, few health agencies use death notifications or other approaches to single out older persons who may need supportive care. Yet, health professionals and community volunteers might help blunt some of the sharp and traumatic edges of grief in the bereaved elderly. In one pilot treatment program designed to assist the bereaved, a psychiatric social worker was accepted by 90 percent of the persons who were contacted. More communities might organize widow to widow programs in which widowed volunteers give support to newly bereaved women, with some mutual benefit accruing to both groups.

Through what practical steps can we help the bereaved? Gerber has suggested the following approach: (*a*) help the person express, verbally and emotionally, the pain, sorrow, and common feelings of guilt; (*b*) facilitate his gradual return to social activities with friends or relatives; (*c*) help him deal with such practicalities as legal prob-

[1] C. M. Parkes, B. Benjamin, and M. G. Fitzgerald, "Broken Heart: A Statistical study of Increased Mortality among Widowers," *British Medical Journal* 5646:740–43 (March 22, 1969).

lems; (*d*) mediate referral for health care if indicated; and (*e*) offer assistance in making future plans. Few health care providers may now be ready to give such help and many may doubt that it should be part of a comprehensive health and social support system, but such steps seem essential if we are to reduce the unnecessarily high incidence of disease and distress during bereavement.

Faced with increasing illness and reduced social support, some older persons head inescapably toward a new life within institutional walls. Thus, the issues of death and dying are for the older person often intertwined with those of living an institution. Gustafson provocatively conceives of the "career" of many nursing home patients as that of a dying trajectory.[2] Markson is among those who suggest that hospitals and comparable institutions have used other facilities, such as psychiatric hospitals, as dumping grounds for dying older persons.[3] As Glaser points out, hospital beds, in which care that is technically good is given, are thus "freed up" by referring older persons to marginal institutions.[4] Such institutions, in turn, have few resources to meet the complex medical, emotional, and social needs of the dying elderly.

Studies of enforced relocation suggest that moving the older patient against his or her will to another location may speed the downhill course to death. Even awaiting such a move has been shown to have negative effects. For example, Prock found that people awaiting relocation to an old age home had a worse psychological status than those who were already institutionalized.[5] Among their characteristics were "general anxiety and tension, high emotional reactivity, a sense of helplessness and powerlessness, a tone of depression accompanied by low self-esteem, interpersonal patterns suggesting an active withdrawal from those around them, and some signs of ego disorganization. A quality of 'my life is over' permeated the waiting list group."

Older people waiting to move to a new location can best be

[2] E. Gustafson, "Dying: The Career of the Nursing Home Patient," *Journal of Health and Social Behavior* 13: 226–35 (September 1972).

[3] E. Markson, "A Hiding Place to Die," *Transaction* 9: 48–54 (November–December 1971).

[4] B. A. Glaser, "The Social Loss of Aged and Dying Patients," *Gerontologist* 6: 77–80 (June 1966).

[5] V. Prock, "Effects of Institutionalization: A Comparison of Community, Waiting List, and Institutionalized Aged Persons," *Americal Journal of Public Health* 59: 1837–44 (October 1969).

described as dying socially. The anticipatory grief associated with the expected loss of familiar surroundings and of close friends, relatives, and even of staff members of an institution where they have been living may precipitate adverse biological changes. One resident of a medical care facility, when informed that she had to be moved because the facility was closing down, said that she would rather die than move to the new nursing home. Two days later she was dead; whether by coincidence or cause and effect is not known. Clearly, the increased morbidity and mortality that may occur in older people confronted with involuntary relocation should be prevented whenever possible. Since the older patients who are to be relocated are the persons most concerned in such moves, it helps to give them an active role in the advance planning and decision making about the move and to have them visit the new facility before they actually move. The resulting lessening of uncertainty and fear reduces the patients' anticipatory grief and its adverse effects.

SITE OF DEATH

Advances in technology, the concentration of modern, complex medical equipment in major hospitals, and the wide variety of specialists engaged in delivering care are among the factors that have increased the proportion of deaths occurring within institutional walls. The encouragement that insurance gives to hospitalization, the paucity of home health care services, the loss with the advance in age of many friends and relatives, and the limited financial resources of many of the elderly may further contribute to this pattern for the older population. Lerner reports that for the nation as a whole, 50 percent of all deaths in 1949 and 61 percent of all deaths in 1958 occurred within institutions.[6] Today the figure is probably 70 percent.

The way the environment of the older dying person is organized within an institution (including the beliefs, values, and behavior of the institution's staff), its organizational goals, and the available resources considerably affect the care and support he is given. In the general hospital, for example, the dying patient and family

[6] M. Lerner, "When, Why and Where People Die," *The Dying Patient*, O. Brim, Jr., H. Freeman, S. Levine, and N. Scotch, eds. (Russell Sage Foundation: New York, 1970) pp. 5–29.

members undergo an experience that to them is unique and moving, but that is more common and less personal to the staff. Routine patient care and routine administrative activities continue, accompanied perhaps by impersonality or even a withdrawal of interest from the dying patient. In long-term institutions, the older person may be assigned to the "vegetable garden"—an area where the soil is rarely tilled sufficiently to nurture dignity and social support in the face of death. Kastenbaum calls for professionals to recognize that many of the dying are conscious of their surroundings and miss those interpersonal relationships which have steadily been withdrawn.[7] On some wards older dying patients may be treated as if they were already dead, or at least as if they were deeply unconscious, childlike, and unaware of what people were saying around their beds.

Hinton and others have noted the covert reluctance of some staff members to care for the dying person.[8] Markson described hospitals in which a combination of great age and terminal illness apparently would cause a patient to be despised by medical and lay personnel alike. Unless death came on schedule, the hospitals would suggest transfer of the patient to a State mental hospital. Even in an intensive care unit of a hospital where younger patients predominate, the staff may use detachment, constant activity, and other measures to cope with the frequent deaths that occur. Coombs and Goldman describe how laughter helped the staff of one such hospital unit relieve some stresses, while other staff members were helped by intentionally losing themselves in their work.[9] They found that the delicate balance between detachment and concern was most often tipped by the patient's age; the weight of many years appeared to tip the scales decisively in the direction of detachment.

In a study of possible "dead on arrivals" in a hospital emergency room. Sudnow found that "the older the patient, the more likely is his tentative death taken to constitute pronouncible death. . . . Very old patients who are initially considered to be dead solely on the basis of the ambulance driver's assessment of that possibility

[7] R. Kastenbaum, "The Mental Life of Dying Geriatric Patients," *Proceedings of the Seventh International Congress of Gerontology* (H. Egermann: Vienna, Austria, 1966) pp. 153–59.

[8] J. Hinton, Dying, Second Edition (Penguin Books: Baltimore, Md., 1972).

[9] R. H. Coombs and L. J. Goldman, "Maintenance and Discontinuity of Coping Mechanisms in an Intensive Care Unit," *Social Problems* 20: 342–53 (winter 1973).

were seen to be put in an empty room to wait several moments before a physician arrived. . . . The older the person, the less thorough is the examination he is given. . . . "[10] Routinized practices like these emerge as an organization seeks to meet curative, youth-oriented goals, goals that, in turn, may reflect the views of the broader "gerontophobic" society.

No institution is immune to the social sterotypes of its surrounding culture. Comfort is of the opinion that a fear of aging and confrontation with one's own mortality are often reflected in a "gerontophobia" that adversely affects the care of the older patient.[11] Death in an old patient may sometimes be treated as a social gain for all concerned since resources will no longer seem to be drained away by a person considered to be of low social value. Yet an emphasis upon cure, however essential it may be for all health institutions, should not prevent them from giving the humane care needed by the older dying patient and his family.

A CHANCE TO LIVE

The elderly patient dying in a humane and caring environment is our major theme. We would not, however, like this major thrust to obscure another shortcoming in the health care given the older person—the failure to rediagnose when a new emergency arises. It is easier to accept an established diagnosis for an elderly patient than to repeat the diagnostic effort when a new emergency occurs. It is often simpler to label a condition as terminal illness rather than to rediagnose the condition, but upon rediagnosis, a new and controllable disease may be unexpectedly found. That the extra effort can prove worthwhile is exemplified by the following case.

Over a 3-week period, headache developed in a 74-year-old retired merchant; he had difficulty in speaking and experienced weakness in the right side of the body. When he became unconscious he was admitted to the hospital with spasticity of the right arm and leg. A cerebral thrombosis had been diagnosed 2 years before, and with little effort the man's condition could have been diagnosed as the terminal stage of a second stroke. However, a more extensive diag-

[10] D. Sudnow, "Dead on Arrival," *Transaction* 5: 36–45 (November 1967).
[11] A. Comfort, "On Gerontophobia," *Medical Opinion Review* 3: 31–37 (September 1967).

nostic effort was considered worthwhile to insure that no error had occurred. A large clot within the skull, apparently caused by a relatively minor and unmentioned accident, was thereupon discovered and surgically removed. Antibiotics for pneumonitis, good nursing care, and restoration of the fluid and electrolyte balance greatly improved the patient's condition. After several weeks he returned to the normal activities of a man in his seventies.

CONCLUSION

The major objective of health care is to improve the quality of life. We do this partly by preventing and controlling disease so that the person continues to function for as long as possible; we also alleviate the distress of disease and impairment so that life continues to be worthwhile even though accompanied by some undesirable conditions. Health providers may not always feel compelled to prolong in the aged the grave discomfort of terminal illness. Nevertheless, there is some purpose in endowing the last stages of life with those ingredients of health care that will help the dying patient feel that he is still part of a humane and caring society, which continues its concern for the individual even when health services cannot be justified by cost-benefit analyses.

SOCIAL DEATH AND AGING

Sharon R. Curtin

The aged are not only neglected by social policy and legislation, often with considerable suffering; they are avoided and over-looked in our ordinary social behavior. This peculiar invisibility that attaches to old age is movingly described in Curtin's book, Nobody Ever Died of Old Age, *from which this excerpt is taken.*

Sharon R. Curtin, a freelance writer, wrote her study of the aged after winning an Atlantic Grant.

This excerpt is taken from Nobody Ever Died of Old Age *by Sharon R. Curtin (*Little, Brown and Co., Boston, 1972*).*

The Gruner family had spent three days in the psychiatric emergency room of City Hospital. Father, mother, and daughter sat stoically, feet flat on the floor, untouched by the little mad bits of drama around them. Mr. Gruner was eighty-one, strong-featured and rather handsome, with iron-gray hair and a fine broad forehead. From the chin down he was withered and emaciated; I wondered where he got the energy to continue the rolling, jerking motions of Parkinson's disease. His hands were in constant motion, pill-rolling, drawing against his chest, back to his knees; he occasionally jostled the arm of his wife. She sat quietly most of the time, looking like she was still waiting on Ellis Island. Every half hour or so, she would jump up and begin shouting incomprehensible sentences, punctuated by throwing her hands in the air in an appeal to God. No one could understand her, she seemed to be speaking a combination of Yiddish and gibberish; yet everyone knew she was complaining. Her voice was the voice of all our aged grandparents: You never come to see me, you don't eat right, you're too thin, when are you going to get married and settled down?

Most of Mrs. Gruner's complaints seemed to be directed at the daughter, Anna, who sat a little apart from her parents and turned angrily away whenever anyone tried to speak to her. She had terrible acne, the kind that leaves your skin raw and red between pustules. The large nose, noble on her father, stuck out between her diseased cheeks like the beak of a sad parrot. Anna had been born late in her parents' life. She had been shy and alone, partly because of the acne, partly because she was raised by aging parents who understood little what a girl wanted or dreamed about. It was understood by her that she was brought into the world for one purpose: to take care of her parents. She had worked as a bookkeeper for a few years, but when her father began to have trouble getting around because of the Parkinson's disease, she quit to stay home and help her mother. The family had always been a tight, self-sufficient unit; her mother was suspicious of strangers and did not encourage friendships. Anna never had a friend. She had been raised to do her duty, and her duty was her parents. This new trouble, this being thrown out of their home, was more than she could manage. She felt she had failed her parents, had failed to protect them from danger. So she sat, guilty and despairing, not hearing her mother's shouts, but only that inner voice saying, you failed, you failed, it's all your fault, you did it, you failed.

The family had been brought to the psychiatric emergency room by the police. They had barricaded the door against a city marshal who had come to evict them from their home. The patrolmen were called and finally had to break down the door of the apartment. One policeman was treated for deep scratches on his face, inflicted by Anna when he tried to carry her from the apartment. The Gruners had occupied that apartment for thirty years.

The police report said that the condition of the apartment was enough to turn your stomach. Most of the windows were broken and repaired with pieces of cardboard; the walls bore evidence of furious family fights. Neighbors reported that for three years the family seldom left the building, having their groceries delivered and leaving their garbage in the halls for other tenants to remove. Mrs. Gruner's brother visited occasionally, but for the last few months, the family would not see him.

The family had little in the way of possessions; most of the furniture was broken, old, useless. The city marshal reported that it was barely worth the effort it took to carry things down four flights of stairs. Exactly what happened to it then was anybody's guess; since the Gruners had been taken away by the police, their few possessions had probably been taken by scavengers. The family was left with nothing but the clothes they wore.

The police did not want to arrest the family, even though they could be charged with assault. Since the combined weight of all three Gruners barely equaled that of one New York City patrolman, embarrassment motivated mercy, and the officers decided the whole family was crazy enough to be locked up in an institution. The patrol car brought the family to the emergency room and no one there knew what to do with them. The social worker on duty sent the family to a "Welfare Hotel" downtown; the family refused to stay there. One of the attendants on duty knew of an apartment available; the family refused to stay there, stating that they wanted only to go home. For three days the staff of the emergency room tried to find a home, a roof, a member of their family, someplace, anyplace. The Gruners refused to move. The old lady kept getting crazier and crazier; now she wasn't even speaking Yiddish, but just jumping up and screaming now and then. Anna was sullen and withdrawn, refusing to speak. Mr. Gruner just sat, that beautiful old head perched on top of the physical ruin, shaking and jerking more than ever.

So it went for four days. The police brought them in early Friday morning, and on Tuesday they still sat in the emergency room. Here was a family, thrown out of their home, all possessions lost, all nightmares realized; and they sat in a row like they were waiting for a train to come and take them away. They ate cookies and sodas from the vending machines; they shook and mumbled and stared; they smelled.

No one wanted to admit an entire family to the psychiatric ward upstairs. The old man needed medical care; his Parkinsonian symptoms could be controlled, possibly relieved completely. All three were badly undernourished, thin and rickety, pale and gray. Anna's skin was a mess. Of the three the old lady was the healthiest physically, and the craziest. However, before they had been thrown out of their apartment, they managed to escape the eyes of any social agency, and functioned quite well outside of an institution. Something obviously had to be done; the sight of the family sitting hour after hour, day after day, just sitting in that cold drab waiting room waiting for someone to tell them what to do; the sight of such complete abdication of self was beginning to upset the staff. The decision was made to admit them temporarily to the psychiatric ward; to keep the old couple together in one room, and give Anna a room close by; and to ensure proper medical treatment for all three Gruners. The psychiatrists accepted this compromise unwillingly; they weren't interested in trying to work with an old lady who couldn't speak English, an old man jerking, rolling the minutes away, a middle-aged spinster quite awesome in her ugliness. Psychiatrically, they just weren't very interesting.

Everything was so accidental. If the landlord had not wanted to renovate the building, he wouldn't have pushed for eviction. If the marshal had served warrants on the Gruners so they could have known about the coming eviction, they might have tried to do something about it before that day. If the family hadn't been so frightened, they might not have fought the police, and would have just ended up walking the streets. But every step, every little incident, led them down the path to the state mental hospital; not so much because they were mad, or dangerous, or even unable to function. They just had no place else to go, and no strength to find a place, and were just weird enough for society to accept the burden of their support. They were poor, they were old, they were dirty, and they wouldn't cooperate. So, after a few weeks in the relative opulence of a city hospital receiving ward, the whole family was moved to a nearby state mental hospital. This time they were separated. Anna was sent to a regular ward, and her parents were sent to the geriatric section.

By this time I had come to know the family fairly well. Since they had been ripped from a home of thirty years, pulled rudely and brutally out of an environment they felt safe in, and all trace of their furniture and possessions had disappeared, they were increasingly disoriented. The old lady remained totally suspicious; finally one day, she pointed at me and said, "You Jewish?"

"No," I replied. That was the end of our conversations.

"She's not Jewish," the old lady would hiss whenever I came into the room. "Don't trust her, she's not Jewish." She was a thoroughly disagreeable old lady, full of petty suspicions, a tiny, boxed-in little mind, shrinking ever tighter inside herself. Nothing I could do could touch or move her; somehow, I was responsible for all their troubles, I was one of them, one of the enemy, a holder of the large keys that kept them locked in the hospital. "Don't trust her," the whisper would come with me into the room, filling the air with silent suspicion. And the old lady was right in some way; I was an agent, a part of the machine that was pulling, pushing, moving them around. I had the keys, she was a prisoner. I had some of the power to keep her locked up for the rest of her natural life.

Because of her suspicious and uncooperative behavior, the old lady succeeded in getting herself labeled psychotic. "Senile dementia, with paranoid ideas." Her behavior was certainly strange, She would come out of the room she shared with her husband, clutching a filthy paper bag containing all her personal things—a comb, a toothbrush, old tissues, some bright-colored yarn, her reading glasses, a piece of mirror—and, standing tightly up against the doorjamb, she would dart her eyes up, down, across the hall before moving an inch. And that is how she moved: inch by inch, shoulder tight up against the wall, eyes constantly moving, ready for danger and betrayal at every step. You could hear her slithering down the hall, sounding for all the world like an upright snake. And a few steps behind, slightly stumbling, a little unsteady, moved the old man.

Mr. Gruner was a little apologetic about everything. He seemed to say excuse me to the very air he breathed; to hesitate before each bite of food, as if he wasn't sure it was his to chew; to sit and walk in a way that made you understand perfectly the word "self-effacing."

He and his wife had come to the United States sixty years ago, newly married and full of hope. They had paid their third-class passage with her wedding dowry. The village gathered silently to watch them leave; Mrs. Gruner cried all the way across, he told me.

"Now the village we were born in, the country of our birth, has disappeared. Yes, gone, the casualty of a revolution, a world war, geopolitics; now a whole people have lost their history. I find that sad in my old age. I remember my native dress, even my language. I close my eyes and try and imagine what has taken its place. Is there nothing? The emptiness causes a pain, a sadness of the spirit. A nation gone. This has something to do with why Sarah feels so confused now; so many things disappearing. She has no tears left. First her village gone, then her country. She never got accustomed to all the changes. Maybe if we hadn't left our village . . ."

And he would sit quietly for a few minutes, proud head bowed over his ruined body. In the hall I could hear Mrs. Gruner sliding down the wall, following her own path.

Mr. Gruner had been a printer, a typesetter, a skilled man before the Parkinson's disease became too debilitating. He had been a good union man, a fighter in the early days, and when he talked about those days when he had been trying to help organize the printer's union he seemed taller and more sure of himself. "Those were the days," he said, "the days when I was a man, when I took care of my family and fought the bosses at the same time. I was not a big man, but strong, strong in my heart. The union was the big thing, the important work of my life. Being a printer was a skill, a job for the hands; but the union was my heart. I was a workingman, yes, but a union man. That is important, those days. Even now it makes a difference. Typesetters make good money now, because me and mine went without food, without heat, to show the bosses we were stronger. We won so many fights, so many battles. But the war still goes on, you know, the war between big money and little workers. To work hard, always work hard, that is good and right for men and women; but you should have enough to live, to eat, to buy books. Only then you can call your soul and mind free. This old body of mine—look at it. Shaking away, getting better, maybe, but no good. The hands are no good anymore, and sometimes I can't even read. But when my check comes, my pension check that I get because I fought for a union, then I am a man again. It is not a gift, that money; neither is the other check, the social security check. I worked. My wife worked. Now we are old, and these are wages due us for a life of work, a good life."

"Don't trust her . . ." hissed Mrs. Gruner.

"We've had a hard time," continued the old man. His head, that beautiful strong head above the ruined body, was straight and proud as he talked about the past. "And my wife, she learned sometimes you can't trust anyone. One of her friends reported us to the police, and a goon squad broke up our home looking for union literature. And there were other times . . . in the old country . . . so excuse her. She gets a little confused, and doesn't understand you are trying to help, trying to find us a new home. Sometimes, even I can't remember why the police wrecked our home this time. I've been retired a long time; but maybe someone has a very long memory, and is trying to get us still. But they can't change things now. The union, the union is strong, now."

Mr. Gruner and I would have long conversations about the old days while Mrs. Gruner would act out her private fantasies around us. She would sometimes dart around the room, as if looking for a place to hide, and would stop suddenly, glance slyly in my direction, and move back to the wall. Most of the day she spent moving rest-lessly, endlessly, up and down the corridor. One day I noticed that her endless sliding, moving so close to the baseboard, was removing ten years' accumulation of dirt. You could see a little path, a place where some of the original pattern of the tile was showing through layers of old wax, old dirt, old soap. That was on "her" side of the corridor; the other side remained as dark and filthy as before. I pointed this out to one of the attendants one afternoon, saying that Mrs. Gruner was really cleaning the corners for them. As we stood in the hall laughing at the power of mad feet, Mrs. Gruner came sliding down the hall in our direction. The aide went over and took the old lady by the arm, laughingly urging her to clean the other side of the corridor. "Come on, honey, walk down *this* side for a bit. Come on, don't be so stubborn, move down this side." A desperate pulling match began; Mrs. Gruner was plainly terrified to leave "her" side of the corridor, for whatever crazy reasons, and the aide was bigger, stronger, and very insistent. Mrs. Gruner began to scream, to wail a high keening note, and spat in the attendant's face. The aide released the old lady, shoving her abruptly against the wall. Another aide came down the hall, and the two of them locked the old lady in a seclusion room for the rest of the day. "Patient became violent," read the report.

The ward staff began to talk about giving Mrs. Gruner shock treatments and separating her from her husband to prevent any deterioration in his condition. The doctor was moderate and very scientific; he said that shock treatments are particularly effective in cases of senile depression or when patients are violent. The social worker said it was important to maintain the family unit, but that the behavior of one must not be allowed to influence the other members, and that Mrs. Gruner was frequently upsetting to every-one. The attendants reported that Mrs. Gruner was uncooperative and suspicious, sometimes refusing to make her bed or bathe herself according to schedule. The recreation worker said that Mrs. Gruner did not participate in any ward activities. Everyone seemed to agree that the disagreeable old lady should have a hundred and thirty volts of electricity sent through her brain for three tenths of a second. Since all three members of the family were formally committed to a mental hospital, no approval from anyone else was necessary.

ECT. Electro-convulsive-therapy. I didn't even know they used it any more; I thought that since the so-called tranquilizing drugs were developed, shock treatment had largely been discontinued. In fact, at this particular hospital, no area was set aside for ECT and recovery rooms. But it seemed that patients could be sent down the street to the city hospital where facilities were available—and used.

The patient is sedated, wheeled into a room, the sticky jelly applied to both temples, and cold electrodes, running on wires from a little black box, are applied over the jelly. There is no noise, maybe just a little zzss! and the patient goes into a severe convulsion. Throws a fit. Muscles strain against the straps, jerking, pulling, twitching; a hollow gasping moan comes from the rubber tube placed in the mouth of the patient, and in a few seconds it is all over.

Except little bits and pieces of memory are wiped out. The patients are subdued, confused, disoriented for days after ECT. Yes, sometimes depressed people become less depressed, and violent people become less violent. You could say it is effective and, if judged by simple empirical standards, therapeutic. But I am prejudiced; it has always seemed to me that shock therapy is a violent, evil act in itself; when I was in nurse's training, I refused to hold the electrodes against the temple of the patients, refused finally to even watch, because it seemed to me the treatment was so much worse than the disease. The eyes of people who have had shock treatment always seem pained and a little vague. They spend a good deal of time trying to fill in the holes left by the hundred and thirty volts; the mind doesn't like to miss bits of history. Mrs. Gruner had suffered enough rude shocks lately—the loss of her home, the long confused days in the hospital waiting room, the move to the state hospital—and certainly had reason enough to act a little weird, even to act very weird. After all, she was eighty years old and had a right to some aberrant behavior. So I argued against ECT.

"Sentiment wins," said the doctor. "We'll let you try and straighten her out without shock. But her behavior must improve within a week or . . ." and he waved a languid arm in the general direction of something.

I left the meeting considerably shaken; Mrs. Gruner was not going to respond to any magic therapy of mine within a week. All I had done was buy a little time. And protect my own conscience by taking a principled stand I knew would be overruled any moment. I stood in the corridor and looked at Mrs. Gruner's little path. Now what, for God's sake? Her brother would not accept any responsibility; Anna was just beginning to pull herself together, and was looking for a part-time job and a place to live; and Mr. Gruner was still in no physical shape to be moved out of the hospital.

The state mental hospital. Not too many old people end up there. Those wards are really the end of the road. The geriatric section is always the most unattractive, poorly lighted, no brightness, no pictures, no laughter. Just long green corridors, lined by doors; white-gowned nurses moving silently, expressionless; large wards with beds filling the room, allowing no space for anything. Two things impress you: the silence and the smell of urine.

The door of the elevator would open quietly and the smell would tell you it was the geriatric section. When you stepped off, you found yourself trying to walk very quietly, as if not to wake a sleeping child. There were people there, you could feel them, but not a sound . . . then a door would open, you heard the heavy keys clanking at the belt of an attendant, and you knew there was life. I visited the Gruners infrequently; the old lady still did not trust me, but she always remembered me. I would try and bring the old man a copy of the Jewish newspaper, and he would smile sweetly, move his head in a courtly Old World manner, and ask me to sit down.

"Tell me," he said one day. "What is this shock treatment they want to do? Is it a good thing? Is my wife, then, being treated by old-fashioned methods? She is difficult, and old, and not easy to understand; but she does no harm."

They were so helpless. And so was I. I could no more stop the doctors from doing whatever they pleased to the old couple than they could. Once inside, once clamped in the public jaws of the mental hospital, the doctor knows best, knows all, makes all the decisions. Even if you are clever, and not too mad, you can't escape the force of decisions made by a man who may or may not have real interest in your case. Doctors who choose to practice in a state institution are not always imaginative and open-minded in their approach to problems. And Mrs. Gruner was a problem. I thought wildly of telling Mr. Gruner to gather his things together, take his wife by the hand and escape . . . where? He was looking at me, blue eyes a little watery with concentration, waiting for an answer.

"I think shock treatment is not a good thing. But your wife . . . if you could get her to be a little more polite to the attendants, participate more . . . she's such a cranky old lady . . . can you do anything with her?"

"My dear. No one has been able to change Sarah's ways for years;

she has just been getting worse. I think that is what growing old is all about: whatever you are, it just gets worse. Like me, my shaking; fifty years ago no shaking, forty years ago a little tremor, thirty years ago I shake like a mild chill, and today—a regular earthquake, my body. The medicine helps me, but pills won't make Sarah an easy woman. Maybe for her the shock treatment will give a little rest from her meanness." His eyes were so blue, so kind; he was reassuring me, trying to say accept, accept, we can't change it by ourselves. "It isn't so bad here. And Anna is beginning to free herself. She, too, will never be a happy woman, but she should not be here. Here is for the old, and others who care nothing for their surroundings, such drab colors, such tasteless food. This is for the old and the mad. Not for Anna. She is not much to look at, but she can still find some satisfaction. In books, or movies, or a little dog, maybe. She should not be here. You get her out. Let the old care for the old; and you stop worrying."

My eyes were on the little path left by Mrs. Gruner around the edge of the floor. If they gave her shock treatment, could she move to the other side of the corridor? Would she learn to play musical chairs, or bingo, or whatever childish games were offered? I didn't think so; I thought they might slow her down for a little bit, but unless they were willing to burn out her mind, burn out all the stubbornness, all the meanness, all the secret parts of her head, she would remain a very, very difficult old lady. That was what Mr. Gruner was trying to say. I had to trust her as he did.

"Mr. Gruner, I'm sorry. I really don't think you belong here, but I don't know how to get you out."

"I know, I know. There is a story about a room that only has a way in, no way out. You enter that room, and it is not a pleasant room, but you can't leave. The only way out, the characters find, is by death. That is what this place is to me. I know. I hope the wait is not too long; some of those people, vegetables lying in their own dirt, some of them have been here since this hospital opened. They are fed, cleaned, turned. They are not alive. And it it not easy for the staff to take care of them—look at their faces. The living pinched and hardened by caring for the dying. You must not get angry at them, they do a very hard job."

He was correct, of course. I did get very angry at the staff; at their coldness, their harshness, their sloppiness. They cared nothing for their patients. I don't know why they even did their job, except, maybe because someone like Mr. Gruner come along, someone to talk to, someone who tries to understand. His careful courtesy and manner made him the darling of the ward, just as her crabbiness made his wife the pest. His clothing was always clean, and picked carefully from the piles of donated things sent to the ward. Special little things had a way of appearing on his tray at dinner. They fussed about his hair, which was really beautiful, thick and gray, brushed into high waves above his forehead. But his wife continued to wear almost the same clothes; I'm sure they were changed sometimes, but on her they always looked the same. She still hissed suspiciously at everyone and looked madly around corners. Nothing suited her.

I stopped seeing the Gruners when Anna left the hospital. For one thing, she wasn't there to make me feel guilty with her pitted face. For another, the trips upstairs were getting too depressing. The feeling of death and decay and madness was in every corner of the hospital, but on the geriatric wards you could taste it. I could not keep going up that elevator to talk to a ruined old man who had totally accepted his fate. Nothing could touch him; he had made his peace a long time ago. But I had not, and did not think I could tolerate seeing so much of the dirty inner workings of the society, the last place they reserve for the old, the senile, the mad, the dying. There was no room for dignity in that place, no space for a good place to die.

DEATH AND THE CARING INSTITUTIONS

In the introduction to this volume we discussed the interdependency of persons on each other—not as a result of human socialization, but as the very basis of it. We are not first persons, then dependent on each other for the sustenance of our personhood. Personhood is the very expression of our dependence on each other. As we noted, death is that phenomenon which most vividly exposes this feature of personal existence. It does so in two ways: first, every death indicates the degree to which other persons are able, or willing, to prevent the cessation of life; second, every death represents a loss to the human community, causing it to undergo some degree of change both at the level of institutions and at the level of individuals.

One manifestation of the almost universal societal responsibility to sustain the living and to protect them against death is the development of institutions of caring. As one examines the cultural history of such institutions, it seems to be the case that they have come into being for largely technological reasons. That is, it is simpler and more efficient to care for the sick and dying in a setting where there is a concentration of the necessary human skills and technical devices. It is telling that in cultures where no technology for treating the sick has developed, there is rarely any attempt to gather the ailing into one place—even though they might be isolated from the rest of the society.

There is another, less obvious, reason for the institutionalization of health care. If the sick must be protected by society against death, society must be protected in turn against the diseases carried by the sick. Therefore, the caring institutions also serve the function of removing the ill from normal social intercourse. The benevolent face of this strategy is the desire to check the spread of disease. But another face of this same impulse is far less commendable: the desire to remove the ailing from sight, and therefore from mind. What lies at the bottom of this latter desire is perhaps impossible finally to say, but certainly it involves the unpleasantness, and perhaps even the horror, of being confronted with human frailty, for it is an undeniable reminder of one's own ultimate vulnerability.

There is a vast literature on the psychological, sociological, medical, scientific, and economic aspect of hospitals and other institutions of caring. There is recently a burgeoning interest in caring for the terminally ill in particular—an interest quite probably awakened by Elisabeth Kübler-Ross's now famous book *On Death and Dying* in which she showed, among other things, how the caring institution even hid from itself the fact that some of its patients were actually dying.

The essays included in this section address the two sides of the question concerning the character of such institutions: their technological function, and their isolating function.

As it has been observed above, the sophistication of technology has meant that the "ordinary" course of death can be interrupted, frequently putting medical staffs in the position of having to decide when the life-sustaining devices should be "turned off." When this issue is discussed under the heading of euthanasia, the question is whether the decision to allow the patient to follow the ordinary course toward death is in fact homicide; and, even if it is, whether it is justifiable under certain circumstances.

When we look at the question of technology as it serves the institutions of caring, there is another issue: since it is now possible to transplant some vital organs from one person to another, at what point may we say that it is ethically permissable to remove the organ in question from the still living donor? The question here is primarily ethical, and not medical. The medical possibility only raises the ethical question; it does not provide a solution.

It has long been recognised that there is an acute need for a workable definition of death. The most famous attempt to provide such a definition is the "Report of the Ad Hoc Committee of the Harvard Medical School to Examine the Definition of Brain Death." The publication of this report in 1968, however, seemed to arouse the controversy more than conclude it, although the report was widely accepted in the medical profession. The text of the report is the first selection in this section.

The second selection is an appraisal of the Harvard report by a task force of the Hastings Institute of Society, Ethics, and the Life Sciences. In this appraisal the Harvard report is certainly considered an important step toward dealing with the problem, but one that leaves too many questions unsolved. Some of them are philosophical and terminological: What, after all, *is* death? Which *kind* of death is the report concerned with? Are the central terms in the report too ambiguous to guard against dangerous misinterpretation? And some of the questions are medical: Can the EEG be used in such a decisive manner?

The Hastings Institute appraisal indicates the level, both philosophically and technically, of the continuing discussion of the problem of definition—a problem that would not exist if it were not for the capacity of the caring institution so effectively to concentrate life sustaining expertise and equipment. In a second response to the Harvard criteria, included in this section, Hans Jonas takes a much stronger line than the Hastings Institute task force. Professor Jonas draws into doubt any definition of death that does not include the death of the entire organism and not just some of its vital functions. He raises the unpleasant possibility of using the "brain-dead" body for research purposes, experimenting with various kinds of transplants, drugs, diseases, and so forth.

Since it is unlikely that Jonas and others of a similar mind will prevail when the medical skills in transplantation are becoming increasingly sophisticated, it is urgent that some orderly procedure be developed for the fair application of the technology in institutions of care. In a carefully argued essay, where he discusses the use of what he calls "exotic lifesaving therapy," Nicholas Rescher offers such a procedure. He, too, reminds the reader that while the decision must be made *by* medical personnel it is not a medical, but an ethical, decision. The subtlety of the issues involved appears when, in Rescher's closely argued proposal, large questions arise for which there are no unambiguous answers. When two persons are competing for the same organ or for the same lifesaving equipment, shall we decide between them on the basis of their intelligence, their moral rectitude, their importance to the community? Or should such factors be eliminated? If Rescher brings clarity to the discussion it is because he indicates which issues have yet to be dealt with along with those which can be resolved by careful reasoning.

The next selection for this section faces the character of the institutions of caring from another perspective: William May questions the societal need to isolate its sick and dying as it does. May explores the darker face we referred to above—the desire to remove the ailing from view—and finds that it is by no means a phenomenon of contemporary culture, and certainly not an accidental by-product of the technological revolution in health care. He traces the roots of this impulse to the mythic subsoil of the modern world, discovering that from the earliest awakening of his imagination man has reserved a role of devouring and hiding for the gods—a role that is repeated in the modern hospital. When this aspect of the caring institution is considered, however, it is not only the hospital, but also the asylum, the old age home, and the prison which are to be viewed as the modern "devouring" counterpart to the gods of the mythic imagination.

May's essay tackles the issue of death and society from a surprising direction and offers a solution which many readers will find provocative, if not disturbing, but it underscores the widespread conviction that the human attitude toward death, and strategies for dealing with it, arise from the deepest sources of humanity itself. In fact, whether one agrees with May or not, his essay invokes the ancient philosophic wisdom that the way persons approach death is a sure sign of the way they approach life.

Happily, there is a striking example of the kind of caring institution May implies is necessary; an institution founded and directed by persons who approach death quite as they do life: with affection, hope, and energy. This institution is usually referred to as a "hospice." The term "hospice," comes from the Middle Ages, and refers to the places of rest for travelers, particularly those setting off for the Crusades or returning from them.

As the term "hospice" was first used for St. Christopher's in London, it was meant to indicate a place of rest before the journey on into death. Founded and directed by Dr. Cecily Saunders, St. Christopher's is designed exclusively for the care of the terminally ill. So successful and appealing has this plan been that St. Christopher's is now but the first of many similar institutions being established through the world. Robert E. Neale's essay, "Between the Nipple and the Everlasting Arms," the concluding piece in this section, is a personal account of his experience on the staff of St. Christopher's during a leave from his position on the faculty at Union Theological Seminary in New York. Neale's article effectively shows the bold and humane character of the hospice, therewith containing a message that is appropriate for the final chapter of a book on death and society: there are ways we can act individually and collectively to counteract the terrible loss and suffering that death often brings; indeed, there are ways we can live with each other, however desperate our physical condition, that allow death to be a richly meaningful event.

A DEFINITION OF
IRREVERSIBLE COMA

Report of the Ad Hoc Committee of the Harvard
Medical School to Examine the Definition
of Brain Death, Henry K. Beecher, et al.

*There have been many attempts to offer a definiton of death,
but with the rise of sophisticated technological skills the definition
is no longer a matter of merely academic interest. The remarkable ability to transplant an organ from one body to another, and
the equally remarkable ability to keep seriously ill or injured bodies
alive longer, make the question of defining death an issue of
increasing urgency. Certainly the most famous attempt at such a
definition is this report, prepared by a body of specialists whose
names appear at the conclusion.*

This article is taken from the Journal of the American Medical
Association, *volume 205, August 1968.*

Our primary purpose is to define irreversible coma as a new criterion
for death. There are two reasons why there is need for a definition:
(1) Improvements in resuscitative and supportive measures have led
to increased efforts to save those who are desperately injured. Sometimes these efforts have only partial success so that the result is an
individual whose heart continues to beat but whose brain is irreversibly damaged. The burden is great on patients who suffer permanent
loss of intellect, on their families, on the hospitals, and on those in
need of hospital beds already occupied by these comatose patients.
(2) Obsolete criteria for the definition of death can lead to controversy in obtaining organs for transplantation.

Irreversible coma has many causes, but *we are concerned here
only with those comatose individuals who have no discernible central*

nervous system activity. If the characteristics can be defined in satisfactory terms, translatable into action—and we believe this is possible—then several problems will either disappear or will become more readily soluble.

More than medical problems are present. There are moral, ethical, religious, and legal issues. Adequate definition here will prepare the way for better insight into all of these matters as well as for better law than is currently applicable.

CHARACTERISTICS OF IRREVERSIBLE COMA

An organ, brain or other, that no longer functions and has no possibility of functioning again is for all practical purposes dead. Our first problem is to determine the characteristics of a *permanently* nonfunctioning brain.

A patient in this state appears to be in deep coma. The condition can be satisfactorily diagnosed by points 1, 2, and 3 to follow. The electroencephalogram (point 4) provides confirmatory data, and when available it should be utilized. In situations where for one reason or another electroencephalographic monitoring is not available, the absence of cerebral function has to be determined by purely clinical signs, to be described, or by absence of circulation as judged by standstill of blood in the retinal vessels, or by absence of cardiac activity.

1. *Unreceptivity and Unresponsivity.*—There is a total unawareness to externally applied stimuli and inner need and complete unresponsiveness—our definition of irreversible coma. Even the most intensely painful stimuli evoke no vocal or other response, not even a groan, withdrawal of a limb, or quickening of respiration.

2. *No Movements or Breathing.*—Observations covering a period of at least one hour by physicians is adequate to satisfy the criteria of no spontaneous muscular movements or spontaneous respiration or response to stimuli such as pain, touch, sound, or light. After the patient is on a mechanical respirator, the total absence of spontaneous breathing may be established by turning off the respirator for three minutes and observing whether there is any effort on the part of the subject to breathe spontaneously. (The respirator may be turned off for this time provided that at the start of the trial period the patient's carbon dioxide tension is within the normal

range, and provided also that the patient had been breathing room air for at least 10 minutes prior to the trial.)

3. *No reflexes.*—Irreversible coma with abolition of central nervous system activity is evidenced in part by the absence of elicitable reflexes. The pupil will be fixed and dilated and will not respond to a direct source of bright light. Since the establishment of a fixed, dilated pupil is clear-cut in clinical practice, there should be no uncertainty as to its presence. Ocular movement (to head turning and to irrigation of the ears with ice water) and blinking are absent. There is no evidence of postural activity (decerebrate or other). Swallowing, yawning, vocalization are in abeyance. Corneal and pharyngeal reflexes are absent.

As a rule the stretch of tendon reflexes cannot be elicited; i.e., tapping the tendons of the biceps, triceps, and pronator muscles, quadriceps and gastrocnemius muscles with the reflex hammer elicits no contraction of the respective muscles. Plantar or noxious stimulation gives no response.

4. *Flat Electroencephalogram.*—Of great confirmatory value is the flat or isoelectric EEG. We must assume that the electrodes have been properly applied, that the apparatus is functioning normally, and that the personnel in charge is competent. We consider is prudent to have one channel of the apparatus used for an electrocardiogram. This channel will monitor the ECG so that, if it appears in the electroencephalographic leads because of high resistance, it can be readily identified. It also establishes the presence of the active heart in the absence of the EEG. We recommend that another channel be used for a noncephalic lead. This will pick up space-borne or vibration-borne artifacts and identify them. The simplest form of such a monitoring noncephalic electrode has two leads over the dorsum of the hand, preferably the right hand, so the ECG will be minimal or absent. Since one of the requirements of this state is that there be no muscle activity, these two dorsal hand electrodes will not be bothered by muscle artifact. The apparatus should be run at standard gains $10\mu v/mm$, $50\mu v/5$ mm. Also it should be isoelectric at double this standard gain which is $5\mu v/mm$ or $25\mu v/5$ mm. At least ten full minutes of recording are desirable, but twice that would be better.

It is also suggested that the gains at some point be opened to their full amplitude for a brief period (5 to 100 seconds) to see what is going on. Usually in an intensive care unit artifacts will dominate the picture, but these are readily identifiable. There shall be no electroencephalographic response to noise or to pinch.

All of the above tests shall be repeated at least 24 hours later with no change.

The validity of such data as indications of irreversible cerebral damage depends on the exclusion of two conditions: hypothermia (temperature below 90 F [32.2 C]) or central nervous system depressants, such as barbiturates.

OTHER PROCEDURES

The patient's condition can be determined only by a physician. When the patient is hopelessly damaged as defined above, the family and all colleagues who have participated in major decisions concerning the patient, and all nurses involved, should be so informed. Death is to be declared and *then* the respirator turned off. The decision to do this and the responsibility for it are to be taken by the physician-in-charge, in consultation with one or more physicians who have been directly involved in the case. It is unsound and undesirable to force the family to make the decision.

LEGAL COMMENTARY

The legal system of the United States is greatly in need of the kind of analysis and recommendations for medical procedures in cases of irreversible brain damage as described. At present, the law of the United States, in all 50 states and in the federal courts, treats the question of human death as a question of fact to be decided in every case. When any doubt exists, the courts seek medical expert testimony concerning the time of death of the particular individual involved. However, the law makes the assumption that the medical criteria for determining death are settled and not in doubt among physicians. Furthermore, the law assumes that the traditional method among physicians for determination of death is to ascertain the absence of all vital signs. To this extent, *Black's Law Dictionary* (fourth edition, 1951) defines death as

The cessation of life; the ceasing to exist; *defined by physicians* as a total stoppage of the circulation of the blood, and a cessation of the animal and vital functions consequent thereupon, such as respiration, pulsation, etc. [italics added].

In the few modern court decisions involving a definition of death, the courts have used the concept of the total cessation of all vital signs. Two cases are worthy of examination. Both involved the issue of which one of two persons died first.

In *Thomas* v. *Anderson,* (96 Cal App 2d 371, 211 P 2d 478) a California District Court of Appeal in 1950 said, "In the instant case the question as to which of the two men died first was a question of fact for the determination of the trial court. . . ."

The appellate court cited and quoted in full the definition of death from *Black's Law Dictionary* and concluded, " . . . death occurs precisely when life ceases and does not occur until the heart stops beating and respiration ends. Death is not a continuous event and is an event that takes place at a precise time."

The other case is *Smith* v. *Smith* (229 Ark, 579, 317 SW 2d 275) decided in 1958 by the Supreme Court of Arkansas. In this case the two people were husband and wife involved in an auto accident. The husband was found dead at the scene of accident. The wife was taken to the hospital unconscious. It is alleged that she "remained in coma due to brain injury" and died at the hospital 17 days later. The petitioner in court tried to argue that the two people died simultaneously. The judge writing the opinion said the petition contained a "quite unusual and unique allegation." It was quoted as follows:

> That the said Hugh Smith and his wife, Lucy Coleman Smith, were in an automobile accident on the 19th day of April, 1957, said accident being instantly fatal to each of them at the same time, although the doctors maintained a vain hope of survival and made every effort to revive and resuscitate said Lucy Coleman Smith until May 6th, 1957, when it was finally determined by the attending physicians that their hope of resuscitation and possible restoration of human life to the said Lucy Coleman Smith was entirely vain, and that as a matter of modern medical science, your pettitioner alleges and states and will offer the Court competent proof that the said Hugh Smith, deceased, and said Lucy Coleman Smith, deceased, lost their power to will at the same instant, and that their demise as earthly human beings occurred at the same time in said automobile accident, neither of them ever regaining any consciousness whatsoever.

The court dismissed the petition as a *matter of law*. The court quoted *Black's* definition of death and concluded.

Admittedly, this condition did not exist, and as a matter of fact, it would be too much of a strain of credulity for us to believe any evidence offered to the effect that Mrs. Smith was dead, scientifically or otherwise, unless the conditions set out in the definition existed.

Later in the opinion the court said, "Likewise, we take judicial notice that one breathing, though unconscious, is not dead."

"Judicial notice" of this definition of death means that the court did not consider that definition open to serious controversy; it considered the question as settled in responsible scientific and medical circles. The judge thus makes proof of uncontroverted facts unnecessary so as to prevent prolonging the trial with unnecessary proof and also to prevent fraud being committed upon the court by quasi "scientists" being called into court to controvert settled scientific principles at a price. Here, the Arkansas Supreme Court considered the definition of death to be a settled, scientific, biological fact. It refused to consider the plaintiff's offer of evidence that "modern medical science" might say otherwise. In simplified form, the above is the state of the law in the United States concerning the definition of death.

In this report, however, we suggest that responsible medical opinion is ready to adopt new criteria for pronouncing death to have occurred in an individual sustaining irreversible coma as a result of permanent brain damage. If this position is adopted by the medical community, it can form the basis for change in the current legal concept of death. No statutory change in the law should be necessary once the law treats this question essentially as one of fact to be determined by physicians. The only circumstance in which it would be necessary that legislation be offered in the various states to define "death" by law would be in the event that great controversy were engendered surrounding the subject and physicians were unable to agree on the new medical criteria.

It is recommended as a part of these procedures that judgment of the existence of these criteria is solely a medical issue. It is suggested that the physician in charge of the patient consult with one or more other physicians directly involved in the case before the patient is declared dead on the basis of these criteria. In this way, the responsibility is shared over a wider range of medical opinion, thus providing an important degree of protection against later questions which might be raised about the particular case. It is further suggested that the decision to declare the person dead, and then to turn off the respirator, be made by physicians not involved in any later effort to transplant organs or tissue from the deceased individual. This is advisable in order to avoid any appearance of self-interest by the physicians involved.

It should be emphasized that we recommend the patient be declared dead before any effort is made to take him off a respirator, if he is then on a respirator. This declaration should not be delayed until he has been taken off the respirator and all artificially stimulated signs have ceased. The reason for this recommendation is that in our judgment it will provide a greater degree of legal protection to those involved. Otherwise, the physicians would be turning off the respirator on a person who is, under the present strict, technical application of law, still alive.

COMMENT

Irreversible coma can have various causes: cardiac arrest; asphyxia with respiratory arrest; massive brain damage; intracranial lesions, neoplastic or vascular. It can be produced by other encephalopathic states such as the metabolic derangements associated, for example, with uremia. Respiratory failure and impaired circulation underlie all of these conditions. They result in hypoxia and ischemia of the brain.

From ancient times down to the recent past it was clear that, when the respiration and heart stopped, the brain would die in a few minutes; so the obvious criterion of no heart beat as synonymous with death was sufficiently accurate. In those times the heart was considered to be the central organ of the body; it is not surprising that its failure marked the onset of death. This is no longer valid when modern resuscitative and supportive measures are used. These improved activities can now restore "life" as judged by the ancient standards of persistent respiration and continuing heart beat. This can be the case even when there is not the remotest possibility of an individual recovering consciousness following massive brain damage. In other situations "life" can be maintained only by means of artificial respiration and electrical stimulation of the heart beat, or in temporarily by-passing the heart, or, in conjunction with these things, reducing with cold the body's oxygen requirement.

In an address, "The Prolongation of Life," (1957),[1] Pope Pius XII raised many questions; some conclusions stand out: (1) In a deeply unconscious individual vital functions may be maintained over a prolonged period only by extraordinary means. Verification of the moment of death can be determined, if at all, only by a physician. Some have suggested that the moment of death is the moment when irreparable and overwhelming brain damage occurs. Pius XII acknowledged that it is not "within the competence of the Church" to determine this. (2) It is incumbent on the physician to take all reasonable, ordinary means of restoring the spontaneous vital functions and consciousness, and to employ such extraordinary means as are available to him to this end. It is not obligatory, however, to continue to use extraordinary means indefinitely in hopeless cases. "But normally one is held to use only ordinary means—according to circumstances of persons, places, times, and cultures—that is to say, means that do not involve any grave burden for oneself or another." It is the church's view that a time comes when resuscitative efforts should stop and death be unopposed.

SUMMARY

The neurological impairment to which the terms "brain death syndrome" and "irreversible coma" have become attached indicates diffuse disease. Function is abolished at cerebral, brain-stem, and often spinal levels. This should be evident in all cases from clinical examination alone. Cerebral, cortical, and thalamic involvement are indicated by a complete absence of receptivity of all forms of sensory stimulation and a lack of response to stimuli and to inner need. The term "coma" is used to designate this state of unreceptivity and unresponsivity. But there is always coincident paralysis of brain-stem and basal ganglionic mechanisms as manifested by an abolition of all postural reflexes, including induced decerebrate postures; a complete paralysis of respiration; widely dilated, fixed pupils; paralysis of ocular movements; swallowing; phonation; face and tongue muscles. Involvement of spinal cord, which is less constant, is reflected usually in loss of tendon reflex and all flexor withdrawal or nocifensive reflexes. Of the brain-stem-spinal mechanisms which are conserved for a time, the vasomotor reflexes are the most per-

[1] Pius XII: "The Prolongation of Life," *Pope Speaks* 4: 393–98 (No. 4) (1958).

sistent, and they are responsible in part for the paradoxical state of retained cardiovascular function, which is to some extent independent of nervous control, in the face of widespread disorder of cerebrum, brain stem, and spinal cord.

Neurological assessment gains in reliability if the aforementioned neurological signs persist over a period of time, with the additional safeguards that there is no accompanying hypothermia or evidence of drug intoxication. If either of the latter two conditions exist, interpretation of the neurological state should await the return of body temperature to normal level and elimination of the intoxicating agent. Under any other circumstances, repeated examinations over a period of 24 hours or longer should be required in order to obtain evidence of the irreversibility of the condition.

[The Ad Hoc Committee includes Henry K. Beecher, MD, *chairman;* Raymond D. Adams, MD; A. Clifford Barger, MD; William J. Curran, LLM, SMHyg; Derek Denny-Brown, MD; Dana L. Farnsworth, MD; Jordi Folch-Pi, MD; Everett I. Mendelsohn, PhD; John P. Merrill, MD; Joseph Murray, MD; Ralph Potter, PhD; Robert Schwab, MD; and William Sweet, MD.]

REFINEMENTS IN CRITERIA FOR THE DETERMINATION OF DEATH: AN APPRAISAL

A Report by the Task Force on Death and Dying
of the Institute of Society, Ethics, and the
Life Sciences, Mark Lappe, et al.

The famous "Harvard definition" of death left a number of questions unanswered—questions which both require answers under the pressure of developing technological abilities and resist simple answers under the complexity of the problems facing medical personnel. This essay, largely in response to the Harvard definition, offers a survey of the difficulties remaining.

This article is taken from the Journal of the American Medical Association, *volume 221, July 3, 1972.*

The growing powers of medicine to combat disease and to prolong life have brought longer, healthier lives to many people. They have also brought new and difficult problems, including some which are not only medical but also fundamentally moral and political. An important example is the problem of determining whether and when a person has died—a determination that is sometimes made difficult as a direct result of new technological powers to sustain the signs of life in the severely ill and injured.

Death was (and in the vast majority of cases still is) a phenomenon known to the ordinary observer through visible and palpable manifestations, such as the cessation of respiration and heartbeat. However, in a small but growing number of cases, technological intervention has rendered insufficient these traditional signs as signs of continuing life. The heartbeat can be stimulated electrically; the heart itself may soon be replaceable by a mechanical pump. Respiration can be sustained entirely artificially with a mechanical respirator. If the patient requiring these artificial supports of vital functions is also comatose (as is often the case), there is likely to be confusion about his status and about his proper disposition.

Such confusion and uncertainty can have far-reaching and distressing consequences. Many social institutions, arrangements, and practices depend upon a clear notion of whether a person is still alive or not. At stake are matters pertaining to homicide, burial, family relations, inheritance, and indeed, all the legal and moral rights possessed by and the duties owed to a living human being. Also at stake is the role of the physician as the agent of the community empowered to determine, pronounce, and certify death. Thus, the establishment of criteria and procedures to help the physician answer the question "Is the patient dead?" would seem to be both necessary and desirable, and in the interests of everyone—patients, physicians, families, and the community.

In an effort to clear up the confusion and to provide the necessary guidelines, various individuals and groups have set forth proposals offering specific procedures, criteria, and tests to help the physician determine whether his patient has died. These proposals have been widely discussed, both by physicians and by the public. While they have gained acceptance in some quarters, they have stimulated considerable controversy and criticism, and have given rise to some public disquiet. In an effort to clarify this state of affairs, an interdisciplinary task force of the Institute of Society, Ethics, and the Life Sciences has undertaken an appraisal of the proposed new criteria for determining death and of the sources of public disquiet. This article reports the results of our deliberations.

SOME BASIC QUESTIONS AND DISTINCTIONS

An exploration of the meaning and definition of death unavoidably entails an exploration of some profound and enduring questions. To ask "What is death?" is to ask simultaneously "What makes living things alive?" To understand death as the transition between something alive and that "same" something dead presupposes that one understands the difference between "alive" and "dead," that one understands what it is that dies. Some people point out that it is possible to speak of life and death on many levels: the life and death of civilizations, families, individuals, organs, cells. Both clinical medicine and the community (and hence, also our task force) are concerned primarily with the life and death of individual human beings. The boundary between living and dead that we are seeking is the boundary that marks the death of a human organism.

Yet, even with this clarification, difficulties persist. First, the terms "human" and "organism" are ambiguous. Their meaning has been and remains the subject of intense controversy among and within many disciplines. Second, in addition to the ambiguity of each of the terms taken separately, it may make a considerable difference which of the two terms—"human" or "organism"—is given priority. Emphasis on the former might mean that the concepts of life and death would be most linked to the higher human functions, and hence, to the functioning of the central nervous system (CNS), and ultimately, of the cerebral cortex. Emphasis on the latter might mean that the concepts of life and death would be most linked to mere vegetative existence, and hence, to the functioning of the circulatory system and the heart. Finally, the concept of a "boundary" itself invites questions. How "wide" is the line between living and dead? Is there any line at all, or are "living" and "dead" parts of a continuum? Is death a process or an event? The various answers to these last questions very much depend upon the various understandings of the more fundamental ideas of "living," "dead," "human," and "organism."

We have considered some of these philosophical questions about the concept of death. Not surprisingly, we have been unable to resolve many of the fundamental issues. We are convinced that some controversy concerning proper procedures for determining death is likely to persist so long as there is controversy concerning the proper concept of death. However, the present and persisting practical problems facing physicians, families, and the community need to be and can be addressed at a more practical level—by means of refinements in the criteria for determining whether death has already occurred. Hopefully, criteria can be developed that will be acceptable to persons holding various concepts of death. The rest of this report concerns itself with efforts to provide such refined criteria.

SOME CRITERIA FOR GOOD CRITERIA OF DEATH

When approaching the problem of setting down or evaluating criteria and procedures for determining death, it is worthwhile to keep in mind some formal characteristics that a set of criteria or procedures should share. We suggest that at least the following characteristics be considered.

1. The criteria should be clear and distinct, and the operational tests that are performed to see if the criteria are met should be expected to yield vivid and unambiguous results. Tests for presence or absence are to be preferred to tests for gradations of function.

2. The tests themselves should be simple, both easily and conveniently performed and interpreted by an ordinary physician (or nurse), and should depend as little as possible on the use of elaborate equipment and machinery. The determination of death should not require special consultation with specialized practitioners.

3. The procedure should include an evaluation of the permanence and irreversibility of the absence of functions and a determination of the absence of other conditions that may be mistaken for death (e.g., hypothermia, drug intoxication).

4. The determination of death should not rely exclusively on a single criterion or on the assessment of a single function. The more comprehensive the criteria, the less likely will be the occurrence of alleged or actual errors in the final determination.

5. The criteria should not undermine but should be compatible with the continued use of the traditional criteria (cessation of spontaneous heartbeat and respiration) in the vast majority of cases where artificial maintenance of vital functions has not been in use. The revised criteria should be seen as providing an alternative means for recognizing the *same* phenomenon of death.

6. The alternative criteria, when they are used, should determine the physician's actions in the same way as the traditional criteria; that is, all individuals who fulfill either set of criteria should be declared dead by the physician as soon as he discerns that they have been fulfilled.

7. The criteria and procedures should be easily communicable, both to relatives and other laymen as well as to physicians. They should be acceptable by the medical profession as a basis for uniform practice, so that a man determined to be dead in one clinic, hospital, or jurisdiction would not be held to be alive in a different clinic,

hospital, or jurisdiction, and so that all individuals who equally meet the same criteria would be treated equally, that is, declared dead. The criteria and procedures should be acceptable as appropriate by the general public, so as to provide the operational basis for handling the numerous social matters which depend upon whether a person is dead or alive, and so as to preserve the public trust in the ability of the medical profession to determine that death has occurred.

8. The reasonableness and adequacy of the criteria and procedures should be vindicated by experience in their use and by autopsy findings.

APPRAISING A SPECIFIC PROPOSAL

The most prominent proposal of new criteria and procedures for determining, in the difficult cases, that death has occurred has been offered in a Report of the Ad Hoc Committee of the Harvard Medical School to Examine the Definition of Brain Death. The following criteria were presented, and described in some detail: (1) unreceptivity and unresponsivity to externally applied stimuli and inner need; (2) no spontaneous muscular movements or spontaneous respiration; (3) no elicitable brain reflexes; and (4) flat electroencephalogram. In addition, the report suggests that the above findings again be verified on a repeat testing at least 24 hours later, and that the existence of hypothermia and CNS depressants be excluded. It is also recommended that, if the criteria are fulfilled, the patient be declared dead before any effort is made to disconnect a respirator. (The reason given for this recommendation was that this procedure would "provide a greater degree of legal protection to those involved. Otherwise," the report continues, "the physicians would be turning off a respirator on a person who is, under the present strict, technical application of the law, still alive.")

The criteria of the Harvard Committee Report meet the formal characteristics of "good" criteria, as outlined in this communication. The criteria are clear and distinct, the tests easily performed and interpreted by an ordinary physician, and the results of the tests generally unambiguous. Some question has been raised about the ease of obtaining an adequate electroencephalographic assessment, but the report does not consider the electroencephalographic examination mandatory. It holds that the EEG provides only confirmatory data for what is, in fact, a clinical diagnosis. Recognizing that electroencephalographic monitoring may be unavailable, the report states "when available it should be utilized."

On the score of comprehensiveness, the tests go beyond an assessment of higher brain function to include a measure of various lower brain-stem (vegetative) functions, and go beyond an assessment just of brain activity by including the vital function of spontaneous respiration. It is true that the circulatory system is not explicitly evaluated. However, because of the close link between circulation and respiration, a heartbeat in a patient on a mechanical respirator (i.e., in a patient who has permanently lost his spontaneous capacity to breathe) should not be regarded as a sign of continued life. The continued beating of the heart in such cases may be regarded as an "artifact," as sustained only by continued artificial respiration.

The new criteria are meant to be necessary for only that small percentage of cases where there is irreversible coma with permanent brain damage, and where the traditional signs of death are obscured because of the intervention of resuscitation machinery. The proposal is meant to complement, not to replace, the traditional criteria of determining death. Where the latter can be clearly established, they are still determinative.

The Harvard Committee Report does not explicitly require that the physician declare the patient dead when the criteria are fulfilled; because it was a novel and exploratory proposal, it was more concerned to permit, rather than to oblige him to do so. However, once the criteria are accepted as valid by the medical profession and the community, nothing in the report would oppose making the declaration of death mandatory on fulfillment of the criteria. Thus, the alternative criteria and the traditional criteria could be—and should be—used identically in determining the physician's actions.

Experience to date in the use of these criteria and procedures for determining death suggests them to be reasonable and appropriate. Support for their validity has come from postmortem studies of 128 individuals who fulfilled the Harvard criteria. On autopsy, the brains of all 128 subjects were found to be obviously destroyed (E. Richardson, unpublished results). The electroencephalographic criterion has received an independent evaluation. The largest single study, done with 2,642 comatose patients with isoelectric (i.e., flat) EEGs of 24-hours' duration, revealed that not one patient recovered (excepting three who had received anesthetic doses of CNS depressants, and who were, therefore, outside the class of patients covered by the report). Although further evidence is desirable and is now being accumulated (in studies by the American EEG Society and by the National Institute of Neurological Diseases and Stroke, among others), the criteria seem well-suited to the detection of whether the patient has indeed died.

We are not prepared to comment on the precise technical aspects of each of the criteria and procedures. Medical groups, and especially neurologists and neurosurgeons, may have some corrections and refinements to offer. Nevertheless, we can see no medical, logical, or moral objection to the criteria as set forth in the Harvard Committee Report. The criteria and procedures seem to provide the needed guidelines for the physician. If adopted, they will greatly diminish the present perplexity about the status of some "patients," and will thus put an end to needless, useless, costly, time-consuming, and upsetting ministrations on the part of physicians and relatives.

CAUSES OF CONCERN

Despite the obvious utility and advantages of the proposed criteria and procedures, the Report of the Ad Hoc Committee of the Harvard Medical School has met with opposition, both within and outside the medical profession. Some public disquiet is to be expected when matters of life and death are at stake. In fact, little concern has been generated by the criteria themselves. Rather, the concern which has been expressed is largely due to the ways in which some people have spoken about the new criteria, and especially about the reasons why they are needed. Four causes of concern have been identified: (1) problems with concepts and language; (2) reasons behind the new criteria and the relationship of organ transplantation; (3) problems concerning the role of the physician and the procedures for establishing the new criteria; and (4) fears concerning possible further updatings of the criteria.

Problems With Concepts and Language.—Some of the difficulties go back to the unresolved ambiguities surrounding the concept of death. The proliferation and indiscriminate use of terms such as clinical death, physiological death, biological death, spiritual death, mind death, brain death, cerebral death, neocortical death, body death, heart death, irreversible coma, irreversible loss of consciousness, and virtual death only add to the confusion. The multiplicity of these terms and the difficulties encountered in defining them and in relating them to one another and to the idea of death of a person testify to the need for greater clarity in our understanding of the concept of death. Pending the advent of such clarity, it should be remembered that what is needed are criteria and procedures for determining that a man has died. The various abstract terms listed above do not contribute to the devising of such criteria. They are, perhaps, best avoided. Even more to be avoided is the notion that the new criteria constitute a new or an alternative *definition* of death, rather than a refined and alternative means for detecting the same "old" phenomenon of death.

A second confusion concerns the relation of the "medical" and "legal" definitions of death. Some commentators have drawn a sharp distinction between these two definitions, and have even gone so far as to say that a given individual died medically on one day and legally on another. This is loose, misleading, and probably incorrect usage. It is true that the law offers its own various "definitions" of "death" to serve its own various purposes—for example, in deciding about inheritance or survivorship. But these so-called "definitions" of "death" are in fact only definitions of "who shall inherit." With regard to the actual biological phenomenon of death, the law generally treats the matter as a medical question of fact, to be determined according to criteria established by physicians. No statutory change in the law will be necessary once the medical profession itself adopts the new criteria—provided, of course, that the public does not object.

A third confusion concerns the use of the term "arbitrary" to describe the new criteria. It is the arbitrary (in the sense of "capricious," "without justification") conduct of physicians that the public fears in regard to the definition of death. To be sure, the criteria are man-made, the result of human decision and arbitrament, but they are in no sense capricious. The selection of 24 hours as the waiting period between examinations is, it is true, arbitrary in the sense that it could just as well have been 20 hours or 30 hours. But the selection of 24 hours was considered reasonable, i.e., sufficient to check for any reversibility in the signs of death. The criteria themselves, far from being arbitrary, have been selected as best suited to reveal the phenomenon of death.

A fourth confusion is especially serious, since it goes to the very heart of what is being done and why. Some have spoken of the criteria enunciated by the Harvard Committee Report as criteria for stopping the use of extraordinary means to keep a patient alive. (Actually, the report itself invokes the statement of Pope Pius XII to the effect that there is no obligation on the part of the physician to employ extraordinary means to prolong life.) This language serves to confuse the question of the determination of death with a second important question facing the physician, namely, "When is it desirable or permissible to withdraw or withhold treatment so that a patient (unquestionably still alive) may be allowed to die?" The only question being considered in this communication, and by the Ad Hoc Committee, is "When does the physician pronounce the (ex) patient dead?" The two questions need to be kept apart.

Reasons Behind the New Criteria: The Relation of Transplantation.—Following the first heart transplantation, there appeared in the medical literature and in the popular press a series of articles calling for clarification of the criteria for determining death. Some called for an "updating" of the criteria to facilitate the work of the transplant surgeons and the taking of organs. Others asked for the establishment of agreed-upon guidelines to protect the integrity of the donor against possible premature organ removal or to protect the physician against possible charges of malpractice, or even of homicide. The frequent mention of organ transplantation in connection with proposals offering new criteria of death has created an uneasiness on the part of many people—including some physicians and also a few members of this task force—that the need for organs for transplant has influenced, or might sometime in the future influence, the criteria and procedures actually proposed for determining that death has occurred.

While we cannot deny the fact that the growth of the practice of transplantation with cadaveric organs provided a powerful stimulus to reassess the criteria for determining death, the members of this task force are in full agreement that the need for organs is not and should not be a reason for changing these criteria, and especially for selecting any given criterion or procedure. Choice of the criteria for pronouncing a man dead ought to be completely independent of whether or not he is a potential donor of organs. The procedures, criteria, and the actual judgment in determining the death of one human being must not be contaminated with the needs of others, no matter how legitimate those needs may be. The medical profession cannot retain trust if it does otherwise, or if the public suspects (even wrongly) that it does otherwise.

There are ample reasons, both necessary and sufficient, and independent of the needs of potential transplant recipients of the patient's family and of society, for clarifying and refining the criteria and procedures for pronouncing a man dead. It is the opinion of the task force that the widespread adoption and use of the Harvard Committee's (or similar) clearly defined criteria will, in fact, allay public fears of possible arbitrary or mischievous practices on the part of some physicians. We also believe that if the criteria for determining death are set wholly independently of the need for organs, there need be no reticence or embarrassment in making use of any organs which may actually become more readily available if the criteria are clarified (provided, of course, that other requirements of ethical medical practice are met).

Problems Concerning the Role of the Physician and the Procedures for Establishing the New Criteria.—Even if it has been agreed that there is a need for a revision of the traditional definition or criteria of death, there remain questions of who is to make the revision, and how (i.e., according to what procedure) that revision is to be made. There are at least five levels where decisions are made with respect to the death of a human being: (1) establishing a concept of death; (2) selecting general criteria and procedures for determining that a patient has died; (3) determining in the particular case that the patient meets the criteria; (4) pronouncing him dead; and (5) certifying the death on a certificate of record. Until recently, because there was tacit agreement on the concept of death, our society was content to leave the last four matters solely in the hands of physicians. At the present time, opinion is divided on the proper role and authority of the physician, especially with respect to the first two decisions. Some have questioned the status and authority of the various groups who have proposed new criteria. Some have questioned whether the decision to move to a "brain centered" concept of life and death is a decision to be left to the medical profession, whereas others have questioned whether any other profession or group may be any more qualified. Some have called for the establishment of a definition of death by legal statute.

The state of Kansas has recently enacted a statute which establishes two alternative concepts of death (it refers to them as "definitions of death") : permanent absence of spontaneous respiratory and cardiac function, and permanent absence of spontaneous brain activity. The specific criteria are left to "ordinary standards of medical practice." Both the desirability of this law and its specific language have recently been attacked and defended. The controversy over the Kansas statute has illuminated some of the advantages and disadvantages of legislation in this area. We are sympathetic to the value of having any changes in the concept of death, or even major changes in criteria for determining death, ratified by the community, as a sign of public acceptance and for the legal protection of physicians. On the other hand, we are concerned about the possibility of confused, imprecisely drafted, or overly rigid statutes. Moreover, we do not believe that legislation is absolutely necessary in order to permit physicians to use the new criteria, once these receive the endorsement and support of the medical profession. Clearly, these matters of decision-making and the role of law need further and widespread discussion. The acceptability of any new concept or criteria of death will depend at least as much on the acceptability of the procedure by which they are adopted as on their actual content. The precedents now established are likely to be very important, given the likelihood that the increase of organ transplantation or the rising costs of caring for the terminally ill will produce renewed pressures to alter again concepts and criteria of death.

Fears Concerning Possible Further Updatings of the Criteria.— The fear of being pronounced dead prematurely is an understandable human fear, and, in some earlier ages, a justifiable fear based upon actual premature burials. A similar fear may be behind the concern that current revisions in criteria for determining death will serve as precedents for future updatings, with the result that persons who would be considered alive by today's criteria will be declared dead by tomorrow's criteria. In protest against this prospect, one commentary has put the matter succinctly and well: "A living body turns into a corpse by biological reasons only—not by declaration, or the signing of certificates."[1]

Recent proposals to place exclusive reliance on electroencephalography for the determination of death may be said to represent a current example of efforts to further update the criteria. In accord with other commentators, we view this prospect with some con-

[1] A. Rot, H. A. H. Van Till, "Neocortical death after cardiac arrest," *Lancet* 2 1099–1100 (1971).

cern. Leaving aside technical questions having to do with the reliability of the electroencephalographic evaluations, we wish to comment on some of the assumptions underlying the proposed shift away from the recommendation that the EEG be used as a *confirmatory* adjunct to the clinical determination of death, and not as a definitive criterion.

Most such proposals appear to rest on three assumptions: (1) that the existence of human life, no less than its essence, is defined in terms of activities normally associated with higher brain function; (2) that such activities are exclusively centered in the anatomical locus known as the neocortex; and (3) that the EEG provides a full and complete measure of neocortical function. From these assumptions, the following conclusion is drawn: In the absence of a functioning neocortex, as determined by an isoelectric EEG, human life has ceased.

These assumptions appear to be sufficiently questionable to rule out exclusive reliance on the EEG for determinations of death: the first on purely philosophical grounds, and the second and third on the strength of preliminary experimental findings. For example, the second assumption that activities like instrumental learning and cognition reside entirely in the neocortex has now been called into question by a recent report describing evidence for instrumental learning in neodecorticate rabbits.

The overall conclusion that an isoelectric EEG signifies the end of human life must be questioned in the light of a recent article reporting that patients with isoelectric EEGs (and subsequently verified anatomical death of their neocortices) continued to breathe spontaneously for up to six months. The authors of this study express uncertainty as to whether or not such decorticate patients should be declared dead. While they agree that the Harvard criteria pointed clearly to a diagnosis of "alive," they imply that they have some difficulty with this conclusion. While an isoelectric EEG may be grounds for interrupting all forms of treatment and allowing these patients to die, it cannot itself be the basis for declaring dead someone who is still spontaneously breathing and who still has intact cerebral reflexes. It is inconceivable that society or the medical profession would allow the preparation of such persons for burial. To prevent such confusion and the possible dangerous practices that might result from a shift to exclusive reliance on the EEG, we urge that the clinical and more comprehensive criteria of the Harvard

Report be adopted. We are supported in this conclusion by the report that a majority of neurologists have rejected the proposition that EEG determinations are sufficient as the sole basis for a determination of death.

[Members of the Task Force on Death and Dying include: Eric Cassell, MD, and Leon R. Kass, MD, PhD (*co-chairmen*); Marc Lappe, PhD (staff associate); Henry K. Beecher, MD; Daniel Callahan, PhD; Renee C. Fox, PhD; Michael Horowitz, LLB; Irving Ladimer, SJD; Robert Jay Lifton, MD; William F. May, PhD; Joseph A. Mazzeo, PhD; Robert S. Morison, MD; Paul Ramsey, PhD; Alfred Sadler, MD; Blair Sadler, LLB; Jane Schick, MD; Robert Stevenson, PhD; and Robert Veatch, PhD.

This study was supported in part by a grant from the New York Foundation.]

AGAINST THE STREAM: COMMENTS ON THE DEFINITION AND REDEFINITION OF DEATH

Hans Jonas

Certainly not all the difficulties with a definition of death are medical. Lying in the issue are questions which cannot be answered from the medical sciences themselves. These questions might be considered as philosophical, or personal, or even political. A distinguished philosopher, Hans Jonas turns his analytical, and critical, attention to the labors so far given to the task of settling on a workable definition.

Hans Jonas is a Professor at the New School for Social Research.

This article is taken from Philosophical Essays, *by Hans Jonas, Prentice Hall, Englewood Cliffs, 1974.*

[Editors's note: The citations in this essay are to the book from which it was taken.]

The by now famous "Report of the *Ad Hoc* Committee of the Harvard Medical School to Examine the Definition of Brain Death" advocates the adoption of "irreversible coma as a new definition of death." The report leaves no doubt of the practical reasons "why there is need for a definition," naming these two: relief of patient, kin, and medical resources from the burdens of indefinitely prolonged coma; and removal of controversy on obtaining organs for transplantation. On both counts, the new definition is designed to give the physician the right to terminate the treatment of a condition which not only cannot be improved by such treatment, but whose mere prolongation by it is utterly meaningless to the patient himself. The last consideration, of course, is ultimately the only valid rationale for termination (and for termination only!) and must support all the others. It does so with regard to the reasons mentioned under the first head, for the relief of the patient means automatically also that of his family, doctor, nurses, apparatus, hospital space, and so on. But the other reason—freedom for organ use—has possible implications that are not equally covered by the primary rationale, which is the patient himself. For with this primary rationale (the senselessness of mere vegetative function) the Report has strictly speaking defined not death, the ultimate state, itself, but a criterion for permitting it to take place unopposed—e.g., by turning off the respirator. The Report, however, purports by that criterion to have defined death itself, declaring it on its evidence as already given, not merely no longer to be opposed. But if "the patient is declared dead on the basis of these criteria," i.e., if the comatose individual is not a patient at all but a corpse, then the road to other uses of the definition, urged by the second reason, has been opened in principle and will be taken in practice, unless it is blocked in good time by a special barrier. What follows is meant to reinforce what I called "my feeble attempt" to help erect such a barrier on theoretical grounds.

My original comments of 1968 on the then newly proposed "redefinition of death" were marginal to the discussion of "experimentation on human subjects," which has to do with the living and not the dead. They have since, however, drawn fire from within the medical profession, and precisely in connection with the second of the reasons given by the Harvard Committee why a new definition is wanted, namely, the *transplant* interest, which my kind critics felt threatened by my layman's qualms and lack of understanding. Can I take this as corroborating my initial suspicion that this *interest,* in spite of its notably muted expression in the Committee Report, was and is the major motivation behind the definitional effort? I am confirmed in this suspicion when I hear Dr. Henry K. Beecher, author of the Committee's Report (and its Chairman), ask elsewhere: "Can society afford to discard the tissues and organs of the hopelessly unconscious patient when they could be used to restore the otherwise hopelessly ill, but still salvageable individual?" In any case, the tenor and passion of the discussion which my initial polemic provoked from my medical friends left no doubt where the surgeon's interest in the definition lies. I contend that, pure as this interest, viz., to save other lives, is in itself, its intrusion into the *theoretical* attempt to define death makes the attempt impure; and the Harvard

Committee should never have allowed itself to adulterate the purity of its scientific case by baiting it with the prospect of this *extraneous*—though extremely appealing—gain. But purity of theory is not my concern here. My concern is with certain practical consequences which under the urgings of that extraneous interest can be drawn from the definition and would enjoy its full sanction, once it has been officially accepted. Doctors would be less than human if certain formidable advantages of such possible consequences would not influence their judgment as to the theoretical adequacy of a definition that yields them—just as I freely admit that my shudder at one aspect of those consequences, and at the danger of others equally sanctioned by that definition, keeps my theoretical skepticism in a state of extreme alertness.

Since the private exchanges referred to (which were conducted in the most amicable spirit of shared concern) somewhat sharpened my theoretical case and in addition brought out some of the apprehensions that haunt me in this matter—and which, I think, should be in everyone's mind before final approval of the new definition takes matters out of our hands—I base the remainder of this paper on a statement titled "Against the Stream" which I circulated among the members of the informal group in question.[1]

I had to answer three charges made à propos of the pertinent part of my *Daedalus* essay: that my reasoning regarding "cadaver donors" counteracts sincere life-saving efforts of physicians; that I counter precise scientific facts with vague philosophical considerations; and that I overlook the difference between death of "the organism as a whole" and death of "the whole organism," with the related difference between spontaneous and externally induced respiratory and other movements.

I plead, of course, guilty to the first charge for the case where the cadaver status of the donor is in question, which is precisely what my argument is about. The use of the term "cadaver donor" here simply begs the question, to which only the third charge (see below) addresses itself.

As to the charge of vagueness, it might just be possible that it vaguely reflects the fact that mine is an argument—a precise argument, I believe—*about* vagueness, viz., the vagueness of a condition.

[1] Of its members I name the renal surgeon Dr. Samuel Kountz, specializing in kidney transplantation, and Drs. Harrison Sadler and Otto Guttentag, all of the Medical Center of the University of California in San Francisco.

Giving intrinsic vagueness its due is not being vague. Aristotle observed that it is the mark of a well-educated man not to insist on greater precision in knowledge than the subject admits, e.g., the same in politics as in mathematics. Reality of certain kinds—of which the life–death spectrum is perhaps one—may be imprecise in itself, or the knowledge obtainable of it may be. To acknowledge such a state of affairs is more adequate to it than a precise definition, which does violence to it. I am challenging the undue precision of a definition and of its practical application to an imprecise field.

The third point—which was made by Dr. Otto Guttentag—is highly relevant and I will deal with it step by step.

a. The difference between "organism as a whole" and "whole organism" which he has in mind is perhaps brought out more clearly if for "whole organism" we write "every and all parts of the organism." If this is the meaning, then I have been speaking throughout of "death of the organism as a whole," not of "death of the whole organism"; and any ambiguity in my formulations can be easily removed. Local subsystems—single cells or tissues—may well continue to function locally, i.e., to display biochemical activity for themselves (e.g., growth of hair and nails) for some time after death, without this affecting the definition of death by the larger criteria of the whole. But respiration and circulation do not fall into this class, since the effect of their functioning, though performed by subsystems, extends through the total system and insures the functional preservation of its other parts. Why else prolong them artificially in prospective "cadaveric" organ donors (e.g., "maintain renal circulation of cadaver kidneys in situ") except to keep those other parts "in good shape"—viz., alive—for eventual transplantation? The comprehensive system thus sustained is even capable of continued overall metabolism when intravenously fed, and then, presumably, of diverse other (e.g., glandular) functions as well—in fact, I suppose, of pretty much everything not involving neural control. There are stories of comatose patients lingering on for months with those aids; the metaphor of the "human vegetable" recurring in the debate (strangely enough, sometimes in support of redefining death—as if "vegetable" were not an instance of life!) say as much. In short, what is here kept going by various artifices must—with the caution due in this twilight zone—be equated with "the organism as a whole" named in the classical definition of death—much more so, at least, than with any mere, separable part of it.

b. Nor, to my knowledge, does that older definition specify that the functioning whose "irreversible cessation" constitutes death must be spontaneous and does not count for life when artificially induced and sustained (the implications for therapy would be devastating). Indeed, "irreversible" cessation can have a twofold reference: to the function itself or only to the spontaneity of it. A cessation can be irreversible with respect to spontaneity but still reversible with respect to the activity as such—in which case the reversing external agency must continuously substitute for the lost spontaneity. This is the case of the respiratory movements and heart contractions in the comatose. The distinction is not irrelevant, because if we could do for the disabled brain—let's say, the lower nerve centers only—what we can do for the heart and lungs, viz., *make* it work by the continuous input of some external agency (electrical, chemical, or whatever), we would surely do so and not be finicky about the resulting function lacking spontaneity: the functioning as such would matter. Respirator and stimulator could then be turned off, because the nerve center presiding over heart contractions (etc.) has again taken over and returned *them* to being "spontaneous"—just as systems presided over by circulation had enjoyed spontaneity of function when the circulation was only nonspontaneously active. The case is wholly hypothetical, but I doubt that a doctor would feel at liberty to pronounce the patient dead on the ground of the nonspontaneity at the cerebral source, when it can be *made* to function by an auxiliary device.

The purpose of the foregoing thought-experiment was to cast some doubt (a layman's, to be sure) on the seeming simplicity of the spontaneity criterion. With the stratification and interlocking of functions, it seems to me, organic spontaneity is distributed over many levels and loci—any superordinated level enabling its subordinates to be naturally spontaneous, be its own action natural or artificial.

c. The point with irreversible coma as defined by the Harvard group, of course, is precisely that it is a condition which precludes reactivation of any part of the brain is *every* sense. We then have an "organism as a whole" minus the brain, maintained in some partial state of life so long as the respirator and other artifices are at work. And here the question is not: has the patient died? but: how should he—still a patient—be dealt with? Now *this* question must be settled, surely not by a definition of death, but by a definition of man and of what life is human. That is to say, the question cannot be answered by decreeing that death has already occurred and the body is therefore in the domain of things; rather it is by holding, e.g., that it is humanly not justified—let alone, demanded—to artificially prolong the life of a brainless body. This is the answer I myself would advocate. On that philosophical ground, which few will contest, the physician can, indeed should, turn off the respirator and let the "definition of death" take care of itself by what then inevitably happens. (The later utilization of the corpse is a different matter I am not dealing with here, though it too resists the comfortable patness of merely utilitarian answers.) The decision to be made, I repeat, is an axiological one and not already made by clinical fact. It begins when the diagnosis of the condition has spoken: it is not diagnostic itself. Thus, as I have pointed out before, no redefinition of death is needed; only, perhaps, a redefinition of the physician's presumed duty to prolong life under all circumstances.

d. But, it might be asked, is not a definition of death made into law the simpler and more precise way than a definition of medical ethics (which is difficult to legislate) for sanctioning the same practical conclusion, while avoiding the twilight of value judgment and possible legal ambiguity? It would be, if it really sanctioned the same conclusion, and no more. But it sanctions indefinitely more: it opens the gate to a whole range of other possible conclusions, the extent of which cannot even be forseen, but some of which are disquietingly close at hand. The point is, if the comatose patient is by definition dead, he is a patient no more but a corpse, with which can be done whatever law or custom or the deceased's will or next of kin permit and sundry interests urge doing with a corpse. This includes—why not?—the protracting of the inbetween state, for which we must find a new name ("simulated life"?) since that of "life" has been preempted by the new definition of death, and extracting from it all the profit we can. There are many. So far the "redefiners" speak of no more than keeping the respirator going until the transplant organ is to be removed, then turning it off, then beginning to cut into the "cadaver," this being the end of it—which sounds innocent enough. But why must it be the end? Why turn the respirator off? Once we are assured that we are dealing with a cadaver, there are no logical reasons against (and strong pragmatic reasons for) going on with the artificial "animation" and keeping the "deceased's" body on call, as a bank for life-fresh organs, possibly also as a plant for manufacturing hormones or other biochemical compounds in demand. I have no doubts that methods exist or can be perfected which allow the natural powers for the healing of surgical wounds by new tissue growth to stay "alive" in such a body. Tempting also is the idea of a self-replenishing blood bank. And that is not all. Let us not forget research. Why shouldn't the most wonderful surgical and grafting experiments be conducted on the complaisant subject-nonsubject, with no limits set to daring? Why not immunological explorations, infection with diseases old and new, trying out of drugs? We have the active cooperation of a functional organism declared to be dead: we have, that is, the advantages of the living donor without the disadvantages imposed by his rights and interests (for a corpse has none). What a boon for medical instruction, for anatomical and physiological demonstration and practicing on so much better material than the inert cadavers otherwise serving in the dissection room! What a chance for the apprentice to learn *in vivo,* as it were, how to amputate a leg, without his mistakes mattering! And so on, into the wide open field. After all, what is advocated is "the full utilization of modern means to maximize the value of cadaver organs." Well, this is it.

Come, come, the members of the profession will say, nobody is thinking of this kind of thing. Perhaps not; but I have just shown that one *can* think of them. And the point is that the proposed definition of death has removed any reasons not to think of them and, once thought of, not to do them when found desirable (and the next of kin are agreeable). We must remember that what the Harvard group offered was not a definition of irreversible coma as a rationale for breaking off sustaining action, but a definition of death by the criterion of irreversible coma as a rationale for conceptually transposing the patient's body to the class of dead things, *regardless* of whether sustaining action is kept up or broken off. It would be hypocritical to deny that the redefinition amounts to an antedating of the accomplished fact of death (compared to conventional signs that may outlast it); that it was motivated not by exclusive concern with the patient but with certain extraneous interests in mind (organ donorship mostly named so far); and that the actual use of the general license it grants is implicity anticipated. But no matter what particular use is or is not anticipated at the moment, or even anathematized—it would be naive to think that a line can be drawn anywhere for such uses when strong enough interest urge them, seeing that the definition (which is absolute, not graded) negates the very principle for drawing a line. (Given the ingenuity of medical science, in which I have great faith, I am convinced that the "simulated life" can eventually be made to comprise practically every extraneural activity of the human body; and I would not even bet on its never comprising *some* artificially activated neural functions as well: which would be awkward for the argument of nonsensitivity, but still under the roof of that of nonspontaneity.)

e. Now my point is a very simple one. It is this. We do not know with certainty the borderline between life and death, and a definition cannot substitute for knowledge. Moreover, we have sufficient grounds for suspecting that the artificially supported condition of the comatose patient may still be one of life, however reduced— i.e., for doubting that, even with the brain function gone, he is completely dead. In this state of marginal ignorance and doubt the only course to take is to lean over backward toward the side of possible life. It follows that interventions as I described should be regarded on a par with vivisection and on no account be performed on a human body in that equivocal or threshold condition. And the definition that allows them, by stamping as unequivocal what at best is equivocal, must be rejected. But mere rejection in discourse is not enough. Given the pressure of the—very real and very worthy —medical interests, it can be predicted that the permission it implies in theory will be irresistible in practice, once in the definition is installed in official authority. Its becoming so installed must therefore be resisted at all cost. It is the only thing that still can be resisted; by the time the practical conclusions beckon, it will be too late. It is a clear case of *principiis obsta.*

The foregoing argumentation was strictly on the plane of common sense and ordinary logic. Let me add, somewhat conjecturally, two philosophical observations.

I see lurking behind the proposed definition of death, apart from its obvious pragmatic motivation, a curious revenant of the old soul-body dualism. Its new apparition is the dualism of brain and body. In a certain analogy to the former it holds that the true human person rests in (or is represented by) the brain, of which the rest of the body is a mere subservient tool. Thus, when the brain dies, it is as when the soul departed: what is left are "mortal remains." Now nobody will deny that the cerebral aspect is decisive for the human quality of the life of the organism that is man's. The position I advanced acknowledges just this by recommending that with the irrecoverable total loss of brain function one should not hold up the naturally ensuing death of the rest of the organism. But it is no less an exaggeration of the cerebral aspect as it was of the conscious soul, to deny the extracerebral body its essential share in the identity of the person. The body is as uniquely the body of this brain and no other, as the brain is uniquely the brain of this body and no other. What is under the brain's central control, the bodily total, is as individual, as much "myself," as singular to my identity (fingerprints), as noninterchangeable, as the controlling (and reciprocally controlled) brain itself. My identity is the identity of the whole organism, even if the higher functions of personhood are seated in the brain. How else could a man love a woman and not merely her brains? How else could we lose ourselves in the aspect of a face? Be touched by the delicacy of a frame? It's this person's, and no one else's. Therefore, the body of the comatose, so long as—even with the help of art—it still breathes, pulses, and functions otherwise, must still be considered a residual continuance of the subject that loved and was loved, and as such is still entitled to some of the sacrosanctity accorded to such a subject by the laws of God and men. That sacrosanctity decrees that it must not be used as a mere means.

My second observation concerns the morality of our time, to which our "redefiners" pay homage with the best of intentions, which have their own subtle sophistry. I mean the prevailing attitude toward death, whose faintheartedness they indulge in a curious blend with the toughmindedness of the scientist. The Catholic Church had the guts to say: under these circumstances let the patient die—speaking of the patient alone and not of outside interests (society's, medicine's, etc.). The cowardice of modern secular society which shrinks from death as an unmitigated evil needs the assurance (or fiction) that he is already dead when the decision is to be made. The responsibility of a value-laden decision is replaced by the mechanics of a value-free routine. Insofar as the redefiners of death—by saying "he is already dead"—seek to allay the scruples about turning the respirator off, they cater to this modern cowardice which has forgotten that death has its own fitness and dignity, and that a man has a right to be let die. Insofar as by saying so they seek to provide an even better conscience about keeping the respirator on and freely utilizing the body thus arrested on the threshold of life and death, they serve the ruling pragmatism of our time which will let no ancient fear and trembling interfere with the relentless expanding of the realm of sheer thinghood and unrestricted utility. The "splendor and misery" of our age dwells in that irresistible tide.

THE ALLOCATION OF EXOTIC MEDICAL LIFESAVING THERAPY

Nicholas Rescher

Anytime the actual need for lifesaving medical care is greater than the technological capacity to meet it, decisions will have to be made as to who lives and who dies. Professor Rescher proposes a way of approaching such decisions that guarantees maximum justice as well as maximum mercy.

Nicholas Rescher is a professor of philosophy at the University of Pittsburgh.

This article is taken from Ethics, *April 1969.*

I. THE PROBLEM

Technological progress has in recent years transformed the limits of the possible in medical therapy. However, the elevated state of sophistication of modern medical technology has brought the economists' classic problem of scarcity in its wake as an unfortunate side product. The enormously sophisticated and complex equipment and the highly trained teams of experts requisite for its utilization are scarce resources in relation to potential demand. The administrators of the great medical institutions that preside over these scarce resources thus come to be faced increasingly with the awesome choice: *Whose life to save?*

A (somewhat hypothetical) paradigm example of this problem may be sketched within the following set of definitive assumptions: We suppose that persons in some particular medically morbid condition are "mortally afflicted": It is virtually certain that they will die within a short time period (say ninety days). We assume that some very complex course of treatment (e.g., a heart transplant) represents a substantial probability of life prolongation for persons in this mortally afflicted condition. We assume that the facilities available in terms of human resources, mechanical instrumentalities, and requisite materials (e.g., hearts in the case of a heart transplant) make it possible to give a certain treatment—this "exotic (medical) lifesaving therapy," or ELT for short—to a certain, relatively small, number of people. And finally we assume that a substantially greater pool of people in the mortally afflicted condition is at hand. The problem then may be formulated as follows: How is one to select within the pool of afflicted patients the ones to be given the ELT treatment in question; how to select those "whose lives are to be saved"? Faced with many candidates for an ELT process that can be made available to only a few, doctors and medical administrators confront the decision of who is to be given a chance at survival and who is, in effect, to be condemned to die.

As has already been implied, the "heroic" variety of spare-part surgery can pretty well be assimilated to this paradigm. One can foresee the time when heart transplantation, for example, will have become pretty much a routine medical procedure, albeit on a very limited basis, since a cardiac surgeon with the technical competence to transplant hearts can operate at best a rather small number of times each week and the elaborate facilities for such operations will most probably exist on a modest scale. Moreover, in "spare-part" surgery there is always the problem of availability of the "spare parts" themselves. A report in one British newspaper gives the following picture: "Of the 150,000 who die of heart disease each year [in the U.K.], Mr. Donald Longmore, research surgeon at the National Heart Hospital [in London] estimates that 22,000 might be eligible for heart surgery. Another 30,000 would need heart and lung transplants. But there are probably only between 7,000 and 14,000 potential donors a year."[1] Envisaging this situation in which at the very most something like one in four heart-malfunction victims can be saved, we clearly confront a problem in ELT allocation.

A perhaps even more drastic case in point is afforded by long-term haemodialysis, an ongoing process by which a complex device —an "artificial kidney machine"—is used periodically in cases of chronic renal failure to substitute for a non-functional kidney in "cleaning" potential poisons from the blood. Only a few major in-

[1] Christine Doyle, "Spare-Part Heart Surgeons Worried by Their Success," *Observer* (May 12, 1968).

stitutions have chronic haemodialysis units, whose complex operation is an extremely expensive proposition. For the present and the
foreseeable future the situation is that "the number of places available for chronic haemodialysis is hopelessly inadequate."[2]

The traditional medical ethos has insulated the physician against
facing the very existence of this problem. When swearing the Hippocratic Oath, he commits himself to work for the benefit of the sick
in "whatsover house I enter." In taking this stance, the physician
substantially renounces the explicit choice of saving certain lives
rather than others. Of course, doctors have always in fact had to face
such choices on the battlefield or in times of disaster, but there the
issue had to be resolved hurriedly, under pressure, and in circumstances in which the very nature of the case effectively precluded
calm deliberation by the decision maker as well as criticism by
others. In sharp contrast, however, cases of the type we have postulated in the present discussion arise predictably, and represent
choices to be made deliberately and "in cold blood."

It is, to begin with, appropriate to remark that this problem is
not fundamentally a medical problem. For when there are sufficiently many afflicted candidates for ELT then—so we may assume
—there will also be more than enough for whom the purely medical
grounds for ELT allocation are decisively strong in any individual
case, and just about equally strong throughout the group. But in this
circumstance a selection of some afflicted patients over and against
others cannot *ex hypothesi* be made on the basis of purely medical
considerations.

[2] J. D. N. Nabarro, "Selection of Patients for Haemodialysis," *British
Medical Journal* (March 11, 1967), p. 623. Although several thousand patients die in the U.K. each year from renal failure—there are about thirty
new cases per million of population—only 10 per cent of these can for the
foreseeable future be accommodated with chronic haemodialysis. Kidney
transplantation—itself a very tricky procedure—cannot make a more than
minor contribution here. As this article goes to press, I learn that patients
can be maintained in home dialysis at an operating cost about half that of
maintaining them in a hospital dialysis unit (roughly an $8,000 minimum).
In the United States, around 7,000 patients with terminal uremia who
could benefit from haemodialysis evolve yearly. As of mid-1968, some 1,000
of these can be accommodated in existing hospital units. By June 1967, a
world-wide total of some 120 patients were in treatment by home dialysis.
(Data from a forthcoming paper, "Home Dialysis," by C. M. Conty and
H. V. Murdaugh. See also R. A. Baillod *et al.,* "Overnight Haemodialysis
in the Home," *Proceedings of the European Dialysis and Transplant Association,* VI [1965], 99 ff.).

The selection problem, as we have said, is in substantial measure not a medical one. It is a problem *for* medical men, which must somehow be solved by them, but that does not make it a medical issue—any more than the problem of hospital building is a medical issue. As a problem it belongs to the category of philosophical problems—specifically a problem of moral philosophy or ethics. Structurally, it bears a substantial kinship with those issues in this field that revolve about the notorious whom-to-save-on-the-lifeboat and whom-to-throw-to-the-wolves-pursuing-the-sled questions. But whereas questions of this just-indicated sort are artificial, hypothetical, and far-fetched, the ELT issue poses a *genuine* policy question for the responsible administrators in medical institutions, indeed a question that threatens to become commonplace in the foreseeable future.

Now what the medical administrator needs to have, and what the philosopher is presumably *ex officio* in a position to help in providing, is a body of *rational guidelines* for making choices in these literally life-or-death situations. This is an issue in which many interested parties have a substantial stake, including the responsible decision maker who wants to satisfy his conscience that he is acting in a reasonable way. Moreover, the family and associates of the man who is turned away—to say nothing of the man himself—have the right to an acceptable explanation. And indeed even the general public wants to know that what is being done is fitting and proper. All of these interested parties are entitled to insist that a reasonable code of operating principles provides a defensible rationale for making the life-and-death choices involved in ELT.

II. THE TWO TYPES OF CRITERIA

Two distinguishable types of criteria are bound up in the issue of making ELT choices. We shall call these *Criteria of Inclusion* and *Criteria of Comparison,* respectively. The distinction at issue here requires some explanation. We can think of the selection as being made by a two-stage process: (1) the selection from among all possible candidates (by a suitable screening process) of a group to be taken under serious consideration as candidates for therapy, and then (2) the actual singling out, within this group, of the particular individuals to whom therapy is to be given. Thus the first process narrows down the range of comparative choice by eliminating *en bloc* whole categories of potential candidates. The second process calls for a more refined, case-by-case comparison of those candidates that remain. By means of the first set of criteria one forms a selection group; by means of the second set, an actual selection is made within this group.

Thus what we shall call a "selection system" for the choice of patients to receive therapy of the ELT type will consist of criteria of these two kinds. Such a system will be acceptable only when the reasonableness of its component criteria can be established.

III. ESSENTIAL FEATURES OF AN ACCEPTABLE ELT SELECTION SYSTEM

To qualify as reasonable, an ELT selection must meet two important "regulative" requirements: it must be *simple* enough to be readily intelligible, and it must be *plausible,* that is, patently reasonable in a way that can be apprehended easily and without involving ramified subtleties. Those medical administrators responsible for ELT choices must follow a modus operandi that virtually all the people involved can readily understand to be acceptable (at a reasonable level of generality, at any rate). Appearances are critically important here. It is not enough that the choice be made in a *justifiable* way; it must be possible for people—*plain* people—to "see" (i.e., understand without elaborate teaching or indoctrination) that *it is justified,* insofar as any mode of procedure can be justified in cases of this sort.

One "constitutive" requirement is obviously an essential feature of a reasonable selection system: all of its component criteria—those of inclusion and those of comparison alike—must be reasonable in the sense of being *rationally defensible.* The ramifications of this requirement call for detailed consideration. But one of its aspects should be noted without further ado: it must be *fair*—it must treat relevantly like cases alike, leaving no room for "influence" or favoritism, etc.

IV. THE BASIC SCREENING STAGE: CRITERIA OF INCLUSION (AND EXCLUSION)

Three sorts of considerations are prominent among the plausible criteria of inclusion/exclusion at the basic screening stage: the constituency factor, the progress-of-science factor, and the prospect-of-success factor.

A. The Constituency Factor

It is a "fact of life" that ELT can be available only in the institutional setting of a hospital or medical institute or the like. Such institutions generally have normal clientele boundaries. A veterans' hospital will not concern itself primarily with treating nonveterans, a children's hospital cannot be expected to accommodate the "senior citizen," an army hospital can regard college professors as outside its sphere. Sometimes the boundaries are geographic—a state hospital may admit only residents of a certain state. (There are, of course, indefensible constituency principles—say race or religion, party membership, or ability to pay; and there are cases of borderline legitimacy, e.g., sex.) A medical institution is justified in considering for ELT only persons within its own constituency, provided this constituency is constituted upon a defensible basis. Thus the haemodialysis selection committee in Seattle "agreed to consider only those applications who were residents of the state of Washington. . . . They justified this stand on the grounds that since the basic research . . . had been done at . . . a state-supported institution—the people whose taxes had paid for the research should be its first beneficiaries."[3]

While thus insisting that constituency considerations represent a valid and legitimate factor in ELT selection, I do feel there is much to be said for minimizing their role in life-or-death cases. Indeed a refusal to recognize them at all is a significant part of medical tradition, going back to the very oath of Hippocrates. They represent a departure from the ideal arising with the institutionalization of medicine, moving it away from its original status as an art practiced by an individual practitioner.

B. The Progress-of-Science Factor

The needs of medical research can provide a second valid principle of inclusion. The research interests of the medical staff in relation to the specific nature of the cases at issue is a significant con-

[3] Shana Alexander, "They Decide Who Lives, Who Dies," *Life,* LIII (November 9, 1962), 102–25 (see p. 107).

sideration. It may be important for the progress of medical science—and thus of potential benefit to many persons in the future—to determine how effective the ELT at issue is with diabetics or persons over sixty or with a negative RH factor. Considerations of this sort represent another type of legitimate factor in ELT selection.

A very definitely *borderline* case under this head would revolve around the question of a patient's willingness to pay, not in monetary terms, but in offering himself as an experimental subject, say by contracting to return at designated times for a series of tests substantially unrelated to his own health, but yielding data of importance to medical knowledge in general.

C. The Prospect-of-Success Factor

It may be that while the ELT at issue is not without *some* effectiveness in general, it has been established to be highly effective only with patients in certain specific categories (e.g., females under forty of a specific blood type). This difference in effectiveness—in the absolute or in the probability of success—is (we assume) so marked as to constitute virtually a difference in kind rather than in degree. In this case, it would be perfectly legitimate to adopt the general rule of making the ELT at issue available only or primarily to persons in this substantial-promise-of-success category. (It is on grounds of this sort that young children and persons over fifty are generally ruled out as candidates for haemodialysis.)

* * *

We have maintained that the three factors of constituency, progress of science, and prospect of success represent legitimate criteria of inclusion for ELT selection. But it remains to examine the considerations which legitimate them. The legitimating factors are in the final analysis practical or pragmatic in nature. From the practical angle it is advantageous—indeed to some extent necessary—that the arrangements governing medical institutions should embody certain constituency principles. It makes good pragmatic and utilitarian sense that progress-of-science considerations should be operative here. And, finally, the practical aspect is reinforced by a whole host of other considerations—including moral ones—in supporting the prospect-of-success criterion. The workings of each of these factors are of course conditioned by the ever-present element of limited availability. They are operative only in this context, that is, prospect of success is a legitimate consideration at all only because we are dealing with a situation of scarcity.

V. THE FINAL SELECTION STAGE: CRITERIA OF SELECTION

Five sorts of elements must, as we see it, figure primarily among the plausible criteria of selection that are to be brought to bear in further screening the group constituted after application of the criteria of inclusion: the relative-likelihood-of-success factor, the life-expectancy factor, the family role factor, the potential-contributions factor, and the services-rendered factor. The first two represent the *biomedical* aspect, the second three the *social* aspect.

A. The Relative-Likelihood-of-Success Factor

It is clear that the relative likelihood of success is a legitimate and appropriate factor in making a selection within the group of qualified patients that are to receive ELT. This is obviously one of the considerations that must count very significantly in a reasonable selection procedure.

The present criterion is of course closely related to item C of the preceding section. There we were concerned with prospect-of-success considerations categorically and *en bloc*. Here at present they come into play in a particularized case-by-case comparison among individuals. If the therapy at issue is not a once-and-for-all proposition and requires ongoing treatment, cognate considerations must be brought in. Thus, for example, in the case of a chronic ELT procedure such as haemodialysis it would clearly make sense to give priority to patients with a potentially reversible condition (who would thus need treatment for only a fraction of their remaining lives).

B. The Life-Expectancy Factor

Even if the ELT is "successful" in the patient's case he may, considering his age and/or other aspects of his general medical condition, look forward to only a very short probable future life. This is obviously another factor that must be taken into account.

C. The Family Role Factor

A person's life is a thing of importance not only to himself but to others—friends, associates, neighbors, colleagues, etc. But his (or her) relationship to his immediate family is a thing of unique intimacy and significance. The nature of his relationship to his wife, children, and parents, and the issue of their financial and psychological dependence upon him, are obviously matters that deserve to be given weight in the ELT selection process. Other things being anything like equal, the mother of minor children must take priority over the middle-aged bachelor.

D. The Potential Future-Contributions Factor
(Prospective Service)

In "choosing to save" one life rather than another, "the society," through the mediation of the particular medical institution in question—which should certainly look upon itself as a trustee for the social interest—is clearly warranted in considering the likely pattern of future *services to be rendered* by the patient (adequate recovery assumed), considering his age, talent, training, and past record of performance. In its allocations of ELT, society "invests" a scarce resource in one person as against another and is thus entitled to look to the probable prospective "return" on its investment.

It may well be that a thoroughly egalitarian society is reluctant to put someone's social contribution into the scale in situations of the sort at issue. One popular article states that "the most difficult standard would be the candidate's value to society," and goes on to quote someone who said: "You can't just pick a brilliant painter over a laborer. The average citizen would be quickly eliminated."[4] But what if it were not a brilliant painter but a brilliant surgeon or medical researcher that was at issue? One wonders if the author of the *obiter dictum* that one "can't just pick" would still feel equally sure of his ground. In any case, the fact that the standard is difficult

---

[4] Lawrence Lader, "Who Has the Right To Live?" *Good Housekeeping* (January 1968), p. 144.

to apply is certainly no reason for not attempting to apply it. The problem of ELT selection is inevitably burdened with difficult standards.

Some might feel that in assessing a patient's value to society one should ask not only who if permitted to continue living can make the greatest contribution to society in some creative or constructive way, but also who by dying would leave behind the greatest burden on society in assuming the discharge of their residual responsibilities. Certainly the philosophical utilitarian would give equal weight to both these considerations. Just here is where I would part ways with orthodox utilitarianism. For—though this is not the place to do so—I should be prepared to argue that a civilized society has an obligation to promote the furtherance of positive achievements in cultural and related areas even if this means the assumption of certain added burdens.

E. The Past Services-Rendered Factor (Retrospective Service)

A person's services to another person or group have always been taken to constitute a valid basis for a claim upon this person or group—of course a moral and not necessarily a legal claim. Society's obligation for the recognition and reward of services rendered—an obligation whose discharge is also very possibly conducive to self-interest in the long run—is thus another factor to be taken into account. This should be viewed as a morally necessary correlative of the previously considered factor of *prospective* service. It would be morally indefensible of society in effect to say: "Never mind about services you rendered yesterday—it is only the services to be rendered tomorrow that will count with us today." We live in very future-oriented times, constantly preoccupied in a distinctly utilitarian way with future satisfactions. And this disinclines us to give much recognition to past services. But parity considerations of the sort just adduced indicate that such recognition should be given *on grounds of equity*. No doubt a justification for giving weight to services rendered can also be attempted along utilitarian lines. ("The reward of past services rendered spurs people on to greater future efforts and is thus socially advantageous in the long-run future.") In saying that past services should be counted "on grounds of equity"—rather than "on grounds of utility"—I take the view that even if this utilitarian defense could somehow be shown to be fallacious, I should still be prepared to maintain the propriety of taking services into account. The position does not rest on a utilitarian basis and so would not collapse with the removal of such a basis.

* * *

As we have said, these five factors fall into three groups: the biomedical factors *A* and *B,* the familial factor *C,* and the social factors *D* and *E.* With items *A* and *B* the need for a detailed analysis of the medical considerations comes to the fore. The age of the patient, his medical history, his physical and psychological condition, his specific disease, etc., will all need to be taken into exact account. These biomedical factors represent technical issues: they call for the physician's expert judgment and the medical statisticians' hard data. And they are ethically uncontroversial factors—their legitimacy and appropriateness are evident from the very nature of the case.

Greater problems arise with the familial and social factors. They involve intangibles that are difficult to judge. How is one to develop subcriteria for weighing the relative social contributions of (say) an architect or a librarian or a mother of young children? And they involve highly problematic issues. (For example, should good moral character be rated a plus and bad a minus in judging services rendered?) And there is something strikingly unpleasant in grappling with issues of this sort for people brought up in times greatly inclined towards maxims of the type "Judge not!" and "Live and let live!" All the same, in the situation that concerns us here such distasteful problems must be faced, since a failure to choose to save some is tantamount to sentencing all. Unpleasant choices are intrinsic to the problem of ELT selection; they are of the very essence of the matter.

* * *

But is reference to all these factors indeed inevitable? The justification for taking account of the medical factors is pretty obvious. But why should the social aspect of services rendered and to be rendered be taken into account at all? The answer is that they must be taken into account not from the *medical* but from the *ethical* point of view. Despite disagreement on many fundamental issues, moral philosophers of the present day are pretty well in consensus that the justification of human actions is to be sought largely and primarily—if not exclusively—in the principles of utility and of justice. But utility requires reference of services to be rendered and justice calls for a recognition of services that have been rendered. Moral considerations would thus demand recognition of these two factors. (This, of course, still leaves open the question of whether the point of view provides a valid basis of action: Why base one's actions upon moral principles?—or, to put it bluntly—Why be moral? The present paper is, however, hardly the place to grapple with so fundamental an issue, which has been canvassed in the literature of philosophical ethics since Plato.)

VI. MORE THAN MEDICAL ISSUES ARE INVOLVED

An active controversy has of late sprung up in medical circles over the question of whether non-physician laymen should be given a role in ELT selection (in the specific context of chronic haemo-dialysis). One physician writes: "I think that the assessment of the candidates should be made by a senior doctor on the [dialysis] unit, but I am sure that it would be helpful to him—both in sharing re-sponsibility and in avoiding personal pressure—if a small unnamed group of people [presumably including laymen] officially made the final decision. I visualize the doctor bringing the data to the group, explaining the points in relation to each case, and obtaining their approval of his order of priority.[5]

Essentially this procedure of a selection committee of laymen has for some years been in use in one of the most publicized chronic dialysis units, that of the Swedish Hospital of Seattle, Washington. Many physicians are apparently reluctant to see the choice of allo-cation of medical therapy pass out of strictly medical hands. Thus in a recent symposium on the "Selection of Patients for Haemo-dialysis,"[6] Dr. Ralph Shakman writes: "Who is to implement the selection? In my opinion it must ultimately be the responsibility of the consultants in charge of the renal units . . . I can see no reason for delegating this responsibility to lay persons. Surely the latter would be better employed if they could be persuaded to devote their time and energy to raise more and more money for us to spend on

[5] J. D. N. Nabarro, *op. cit.,* p. 622.
[6] *British Medical Journal* (March 11, 1967), pp. 622–24.

out patients."[7] Other contributors to this symposium strike much the same note. Dr. F. M. Parsons writes: "In an attempt to overcome . . . difficulties in selection some have advocated introducing certain specified lay people into the discussions. Is it wise? I doubt whether a committee of this type can adjudicate as satisfactorily as two medical colleagues, particularly as successful therapy involves close cooperation between doctor and patient."[8] And Dr. M. A. Wilson writes in the same symposium: "The suggestion has been made that lay panels should select individuals for dialysis from among a group who are medically suitable. Though this would relieve the doctor-in-charge of a heavy load of responsibility, it would place the burden on those who have no personal knowledge and have to base their judgments on medical or social reports. I do not believe this would result in better decisions for the group or improve the doctor-patient relationship in individual cases."[9]

But no amount of flag waving about the doctor's facing up to his responsibility—or prostrations before the idol of the doctor-patient relationship and reluctance to admit laymen into the sacred precincts of the conference chambers of medical consultations—can obscure the essential fact that ELT selection is not a wholly medical problem. When there are more than enough places in an ELT program to accommodate all who need it, then it will clearly be a medical question to decide who does have the need and which among these would successfully respond. But when an admitted gross insufficiency of places exists, when there are ten or fifty or one hundred highly eligible candidates for each place in the program, then it is unrealistic to take the view that purely medical criteria can furnish a sufficient basis for selection. The question of ELT selection becomes serious as a phenomenon of scale—because, as more candi-

[7] *Ibid.,* p. 624. Another contributor writes in the same symposium, "The selection of the few [to receive haemodialysis] is proving very difficult—a true 'Doctor's Dilemma'—for almost everybody would agree that this must be a medical decision, preferably reached by consultation among colleagues" (Dr. F. M. Parsons, *ibid.,* p. 623).

[8] "The Selection of Patients for Haemodialysis," *op. cit.* (n. 10 above), p. 623.

[9] Dr. Wilson's article concludes with the perplexing suggestion—wildly beside the point given the structure of the situation at issue—that "the final decision will be made by the patient." But this contention is only marginally more ludicrous than Parson's contention that in selecting patients for haemodialysis "gainful employment in a well chosen occupation is necessary to achieve the best results" since "only the minority wish to live on charity" (*ibid.*).

dates present themselves, strictly medical factors are increasingly less adequate as a selection criterion precisely because by numerical category-crowding there will be more and more cases whose "status is much the same" so far as purely medical considerations go.

The ELT selection problem clearly poses issues that transcend the medical sphere because—in the nature of the case—many residual issues remain to be dealt with once *all* of the medical questions have been faced. Because of this there is good reason why laymen as well as physicians should be involved in the selection process. Once the medical considerations have been brought to bear, fundamental social issues remain to be resolved. The instrumentalities of ELT have been created through the social investment of scarce resources, and the interests of the society deserve to play a role in their utilization. As representatives of their social interests, lay opinions should function to complement and supplement medical views once the proper arena of medical considerations is left behind. Those physicians who have urged the presence of lay members on selection panels can, from this point of view, be recognized as having seen the issue in proper perspective.

One physician has argued against lay representation on selection panels for haemodialysis as follows: "If the doctor advises dialysis and the lay panel refuses, the patient will regard this as a death sentence passed by an anonymous court from which he has no right of appeal."[10] But this drawback is not specific to the use of a lay panel. Rather, it is a feature inherent in every *selection* procedure, regardless of whether the selection is done by the head doctor of the unit, by a panel of physicians, etc. No matter who does the selecting among patients recommended for dialysis, the feelings of the patient who has been rejected (and knows it) can be expected to be much the same, provided that he recognizes the actual nature of the choice (and is not deceived by the possibly convenient but ultimately poisonous fiction that because the selection was made by physicians it was made entirely on medical grounds).

In summary, then, the question of ELT selection would appear to be one that is in its very nature heavily laden with issues of medical research, practice, and administration. But it will not be a question that can be resolved on solely medical grounds. Strictly social issues of justice and utility will invariably arise in this area—

[10] M. A. Wilson, "Selection of Patients for Haemodialysis," *op. cit.,* p. 624.

questions going outside the medical area in whose resolution medical laymen can and should play a substantial role.

VII.   THE INHERENT IMPERFECTION (NON-OPTIMALITY) OF ANY SELECTION SYSTEM

Our discussion to this point of the design of a selection system for ELT has left a gap that is a very fundamental and serious omission. We have argued that five factors must be taken into substantial and explicit account:

A. *Relative likelihood of success.*—Is the chance of the treatment's being "successful" to be rated as high, good, average, etc.?

B. *Expectancy of future life.*—Assuming the "success" of the treatment, how much longer does the patient stand a good chance (75 percent or better) of living—considering his age and general condition?

C. *Family role.*—To what extent does the patient have responsibilities to others in his immediate family?

D. *Social contributions rendered.*—Are the patient's past services to his society outstanding, substantial, average, etc.?

E. *Social contributions to be rendered.*—Considering his age, talents, training, and past record of performance, is there a substantial probability that the patient will—*adequate recovery being assumed*—render in the future services to his society that can be characterized as outstanding, substantial, average, etc.?

This list is clearly insufficient for the construction of a reasonable selection system, since that would require not only *that these factors be taken into account* (somehow or other), but—going beyond this—would specify *a specific set of procedures for taking account of them*. The specific procedures that would constitute such a system would have to take account of the interrelationship of these factors (e.g., B and E), and to set out exact guidelines as to the relevant weight that is to be given to each of them. This is something our discussion has not as yet considered.

In fact, I should want to maintain that there is no such thing here as a single rationally superior selection system. The position of affairs seems to me to be something like this: (1) It is necessary (for reasons already canvassed) to *have* a system, and to have a system that is rationally defensible, and (2) to be rationally defensible, this system must take the fatcors *A–E* into substantial and explicit account. But (3) the exact manner in which a rationally defensible system takes account of these factors cannot be fixed in any one specific way on the basis of general considerations. Any of the variety of ways that give *A–E* "their due" will be acceptable and viable. One cannot hope to find within this range of workable systems some one that is *optimal* in relation to the alternatives. There is no one system that does "the (uniquely) best"—only a variety of systems that do "as well as one can expect to do" in cases of this sort.

The situation is structurally very much akin to that of rules of partition of an estate among the relations of a decedent. It is important *that there be* such rules. And it is reasonable that spouse, children, parents, siblings, etc., be taken account of in these rules. But the question of the exact method of division—say that when the decedent has neither living spouse nor living children then his estate is to be divided, dividing 60 percent between parents, 40 percent between siblings versus dividing 90 percent between parents, 10 percent between siblings—cannot be settled on the basis of any general abstract considerations of reasonableness. Within broad limits, a *variety* of resolutions are all perfectly acceptable—so that no one procedure can justifiably be regarded as "the (uniquely) best" because it is superior to all others.

VIII.   A POSSIBLE BASIS FOR A REASONABLE SELECTION SYSTEM

Having said that there is no such thing as *the optimal* selection system for ELT, I want now to sketch out the broad features of what I would regard as *one acceptable* system.

The basis for the system would be a point rating. The scoring here at issue would give roughly equal weight to the medical considerations (*A* and *B*) in comparison with the extramedical considerations (*C* = family role, *D* = services rendered, and *E* = services to be rendered), also giving roughly equal weight to the three items involved here (*C, D,* and *E*). The result of such a scoring procedure would provide the essential *starting point* of our ELT selection mechanism. I deliberately say "starting point" because it seems to me that one should not follow the results of this scoring in an *automatic* way. I would propose that the actual selection should

only be guided but not actually be dictated by this scoring procedure, along lines now to be explained.

IX. THE DESIRABILITY OF INTRODUCING AN ELEMENT OF CHANCE

The detailed procedure I would propose—not of course as optimal (for reasons we have seen), but as eminently acceptable—
would combine the scoring procedure just discussed with an element
of chance. The resulting selection system would function as follows:

1. First the criteria of inclusion of Section IV above would be
applied to constitute a *first phase selection group*—which (we shall
suppose) is substantially larger than the number n of persons who
can actually be accommodated with ELT.

2. Next the criteria of selection of Section V are brought to
bear via a scoring procedure of the type described in Section VIII.
On this basis a *second phase selection group* is constituted which is
only *somewhat* larger—say by a third or a half—than the critical
number n at issue.

3. If this second phase selection group is relatively homogeneous as regards rating by the scoring procedure—that is, if there are
no really major disparities within this group (as would be likely if
the initial group was significantly larger than n)—then the final
selection is made by *random* selection of n persons from within this
group.

This introduction of the element of chance—in what could be
dramatized as a "lottery of life and death"—must be justified. The
fact is that such a procedure would bring with it three substantial
advantages.

First, as we have argued above (in Section VII), any acceptable selection system is inherently non-optimal. The introduction of
the element of chance prevents the results that life-and-death choices
are made by the automatic application of an admittedly imperfect
selection method.

Second, a recourse to chance would doubtless make matters
easier for the rejected patient and those who have a specific interest
in him. It would surely be quite hard for them to accept his exclusion by relatively mechanical application of objective criteria in
whose implementation subjective judgment is involved. But the cir-

cumstances of life have conditioned us to accept the workings of chance and to tolerate the element of luck (good or bad): human life is an inherently contingent process. Nobody, after all, has an absolute right to ELT—but most of us would feel that we have "every bit as much right" to it as anyone else in significantly similar circumstances. The introduction of the element of chance assures a like handling of like cases over the widest possible areas that seems reasonable in the circumstances.

Third (and perhaps least), such a recourse to random selection does much to relieve the administrators of the selection system of the awesome burden of ultimate and absolute responsibility.

These three considerations would seem to build up a substantial case for introducing the element of chance into the mechanism of the system for ELT selection in a way limited and circumscribed by other weightier considerations, along some such lines as those set forth above.

It should be recognized that this injection of *man-made* chance supplements the element of *natural* chance that is present inevitably and in any case (apart from the role of chance in singling out certain persons as victims for the affliction at issue). As F. M. Parsons has observed: "any vacancies [in an ELT program—specifically haemodialysis] will be filled immediately by the first suitable patients, even though their claims for therapy may subsequently prove less than those of other patients refused later."[11] Life is a chancy business and even the most rational of human arrangements can cover this over to a very limited extent at best.

---

[11] "Selection of Patients for Haemodialysis," *op. cit.,* p. 623. It seems plausible to take the (somewhat antiutilitarian) view that a patient should not be terminated simply because a "better qualified" patient comes along later on. It would seem that a quasi-contractual relationship has been created through established expectations and reciprocal understandings.

INSTITUTIONS AS SYMBOLS OF DEATH

William F. May

It is easy to assume that the rise of institutions of medical care was made necessary by the increasing technological sophistication of the medical profession. This assumption would be largely mistaken if Professor May's view is correct, that the caring institutions have their roots in the depths of the human psyche and the mythic past. In this forceful, even shocking, essay, May compels us to reflect on the fact that the caring institutions not only heal the sick; they also hide them, remove them from view.

William F. May is a professor of religion, Indiana State University, and former president of the American Academy of Religion.

This article, to be published in the Journal of the American Academy of Religion, *was delivered as a presidential address at the annual meeting of the Academy, October 31, 1975.*

Under this topic I do not propose to examine those institutions and movements that obviously traffic in killing—war machines, concentration camps, and revolutionary terrorism—but rather to attend to our health care institutions, which, though devoted to the fight against death, ironically become its instrument and symbol. Their symbolization of death would be impossible, however, if death itself were a wholly indeterminate abstraction, if it did not image itself forth in ways that our current institutions might reflect. My first step in this essay therefore will be to examine certain primordial images for death, prominent in folklore, literature, dream life and ritual behavior, that get articulated today in our institutional procedures. I have in mind the images of hiding and devouring.

I. THE HIDER-GODDESS AND DEVOURER

The name of the nymph "Calypso," who encounters Odysseus as the embodiment of death, means literally the one who hides. The death-demon in Indo-Germanic and even pre–Indo-Germanic times, according to Herman Güntert, is a Hider-Goddess. A "mysterious hiding and shrouding has been experienced as the first essential character-trait of the numinous, hidden power of death in early times."[1] According to belief in traditional societies, the soul of the dead man journeyed to a hidden realm. In Ganda to this day, the deceased king is referred to as "going away" or "disappearing."

Sickness also has been interpreted in many traditional societies as a departure from the human scene. The enfeebled condition of the sick man or woman suggested that the animating principle, that is, the soul, had obviously withdrawn from the body and retired to an invisible place, inaccessible to ordinary folk. Only the shaman could heal by tracking after and retrieving the soul, a feat which the therapist accomplished by going into a state of ecstasy. He left his own body to fetch back the soul of the afflicted.

On death, at length, when the soul departed for good, the body of the deceased became a shroud, a mask; that is, it now hid rather than revealed the soul that once animated it. Appropriately enough, then, it was important to shroud the shroud, that is, to wrap up the body, and hide it away permanently in the ground. So important was this final ritual of hiding that Antigone was horrified by Creon's refusal to let her bury her brother's body. It was wholly unfitting that Polyneices' corpse should remain exposed to view where it could be seen by men. It should be hidden from sight.

Death is equally associated with images of devouring. To this day certain diseases are explicitly associated with eating. Tuberculosis is "consumption;" the malignant tumor feeds off its host; high fever burns and consumes. In the natural world, wolves, vultures, and sharks are symbols of predatory death. Hollywood producers make a killing on the strength of the fact that the "shark has pretty teeth, dear"; and long before Peter Benchley, Erich Neumann noted the connection between death and devouring in archaic myth and contemporary dream life. "Eating, devouring, hunger, death, and

[1] Cited by Edgar Herzog, *Psyche and Death, Archaic Myths and Modern Dreams in Analytical Psychology,* (London, Hodder and Stroughton, 1966) p. 39.

maw go together; and we still speak, just like the primitive, of 'death's maw,' a 'devouring war,' a 'consuming disease.' "[2] The association appears in the symbol of the *Uroboros,* the dragon that consumes its own tail, and in mythic representations of the devouring mother.

In Hindu literature, the representation of death as devourer is a common theme. In one text, (identified by David Kinsley in his paper on "Dying to the World in Medieval Hinduism," A.A.R. paper, Chicago, 1973)[3] death (Mrtyu) complains to the gods that man will become immortal through sacred knowledge and ritual action and aggressively asks, "what share will be mine?" The gods reply that

> "from now on no man will reach immortality with the body. . . . body will be Death's portion but the spiritual part of man might become immortal either through sacred knowledge or ritual actions. Those who acquire this knowledge or perform [righteous] actions come to immortal life but those who do not, return again and again to serve as food (annam) for Death."

In another passage it is clear that destiny and death work together in a kind of restaurant for two. Destiny is cook and death the voracious patron.

> Kala (that is, Time-Destiny) "cooks all creatures," meaning that it ripens them with the passage of time in order to make them fit to be swallowed by death.[4]

Or again, in the Bhagavad Gita, Krsna announces,

> Kala am I, wreaker of the world's destruction, once matured—resolved (am I) to devour the worlds.[5]

Peasant culture in Europe, to this day, similarly links illness, death and devouring. A particularly trenchant image is used to describe the plight of the new born infant and the newly delivered mother in rural Greece. The Blums report in their study of health in rural Greece

[2] Erich Newmann, *The Origins and History of Consciousness* (Princeton: Bollingen Series, 1970), p. 28.
[3] To be published in a volume entitled *Religious Encounters With Death* (Pennsylvania State University Press, Spring 1975).
[4] Cited by Kinsley.
[5] Ibid.

> . . . for the lechoma [that is, the new mother] and the new born
> child the grave is open; for 40 days the earth is ready to receive
> them.[6]

This passage expresses vividly the special vulnerability of the new born and the newly delivered. The earth is about to devour them. No wonder that the word, "sarcophogous," is derived from Greek terms meaning "flesh-eating stones."

So far, we have tended to distinguish the two images of hiding and devouring as they define the fate of the body, but, understandably, the two images coincide. The corpse, which is hidden or buried in the ground is thereby swallowed up and absorbed. Conversely, the flesh devoured by the scavenger, by that very process, disappears; and the cremated body consumed by fire thereby vanishes into thin air. Thus the images of hiding and devouring reinforce one another.

The image of devouring can also have a social reference that prepares us directly for the subject of institutions as symbols of death. In Greek villages certain features of community life can be described by the image of devouring. The Blums write

> The villagers described their life together as an uneasy one,
> with each family feeling competitive and jealous toward any other
> that might achieve success or happiness. The phrases they use over
> and over were, "We eat each other," or "They eat the bride,"
> "They eat the newborn infant."[7]

Those afflicted with jealously and envy are ruthless in falling upon others favored with happiness or good fortune; they eat them up. The sin of betrayal in the Western medieval tradition is cannibalistic at its root. So Dante understood it when he placed Judas, Brutus, and Cassius in the innermost circles of hell with each gnawing on the other and Satan devouring them all. This medieval vision extends beyond social criticism. Its root is metaphysical-religious. Once Satan defected from God he descended from being to nonbeing. In this fateful descent, he suffered a loss of being, but not his appetite for being. Voraciously hungry, Satan can attempt to satisfy his appetite only by tempting others similarly to defect. The strategy, alas, is hopeless. For once a creature turns from God to Satan, he similarly falls from being to non-being. The juicy morsel

---

[6] Richard and Eva Blum, *Health and Healing in Rural Greece,* (Stanford University Press, 1965) p. 129.
[7] Ibid.

promptly loses its power to nourish. Whenever Satan wins, therefore, he loses. Satan's boundless appetite can never be satisfied, least of all by his successes. Thus his primary betrayal of God is followed by an inevitable, secondary betrayal of his minions. In becoming his, they become worthless. Restlessly he must move on to others. Satan is characterized by a limitless capacity for treason.

So much for the predatory features of hell. We turn now to modern institutions of health care and their link with these symbols of death.

II. THE HIDER-GODDESS AND HER CARE OF THE SICK, THE AGED, THE EMPRISONED, AND THE MENTALLY ILL

A striking feature of our management of the problems of old age, illness and mental disturbance is our segregation of the populations so afflicted from the society at large. The nursing home industry has grown huge in recent decades and special regions of the country have been set aside where we hide away the aged. It used to be said that children should be seen but not heard. Now we reapply that stricture to the aged, suggesting to them that they should be neither seen nor heard. Long before their death we have consigned them over to the Hider-Goddess.

Similarly, hospitals, mental hospitals, and penal institutions have acquired certain subliminal associations with the oblivion of death. " 'The prisoner,' a Sing Sing chaplain observed, 'was taught to consider himself dead to all without the prison walls.' "[8] A warden of that era prohibited contacts with the outside world saying, " . . . while confined here . . . you are to be literally buried from the world."[9] Such strictures on communication with the outside world have been lessened today, but, still, prisoners call themselves the forgotten men. The thick walls of prisons and other institutions have been constructed not only to keep inmates in but also to keep the world out. The walls say two things to an inmate: do not expect to *escape* from here, but also do not really expect others to visit you here. The same message gets through to the mentally disturbed and

[8] David J. Rothman, *The Discovery of the Asylum* (Boston: Little, Brown and Co., 1971) p. 95.
[9] Cited by Professor Rothman, Ibid.

the chronically ill who are dumped into institutional bins where they receive minimal, custodial care until their final disappearance.

This colonization of the distressed goes on for all the understandable reasons that obtain in a highly differentiated society and its specialization of functions and services. The nuclear family is overloaded, often isolated, and unable to cope with the problems of total care for the seriously distressed or disabled. Institutions meanwhile are equipped to deliver certain technical services that could not be offered except through their mobilization of professional resources.

But these stated philanthropic reasons for institutionalization do not reckon with the darker, somewhat more ruthless, compulsions at work within the society that lead us to segregate. This ruthlessness is apparent, both procedurally and substantively. Procedurally, we are inclined to ride roughshod over rights, as we hustle off various classes of the distressed to their respective institutions. And once we get them there we are slow to review their cases. Sensitive lawyers have taken note of our lack of adequate safeguards for the rights of the mentally ill, both on matters of commitment and later review of commitment. The rights of the criminally insane are even more attenuated, falling short of those available to criminals, particularly with respect to the review of cases.

Nor are we conscientious in monitoring the quality of services offered to the institutionalized. Nursing home care has been particularly cynical, and even scandalous, in recent years; the treatment of the physical ailments of the mentally disturbed is notoriously poor. On the latter subject, one harrassed hospital administrator in New York City spoke with particular bitterness. Apparently, he said, the emotionally disturbed are miraculously endowed with total immunity to disease once committed to a mental hospital. For, in the New York City hospitals with which he is familiar, the insane never seem to come down with cases of cancer, gall bladder trouble, pulmonary or heart conditions serious enough to treat.[10]

---

[10] More recently, it would appear that the impulse to segregate has diminished with the development of local community health programs, out-patient services, early parole procedures, and half-way houses for criminals. Some of these efforts have been salutary, but others have produced only new and subtler forms of janitorial treatment. The emotionally disturbed today may be shipped out of the huge custodial institutions where they were formerly incarcerated, but only to be reassigned to high rise hotels where therapeutic services are even more minimal.

Even more serious than the low quality of technical services delivered to inmates is the loss of community that their special location in the social order imposes on them. The existentialists used to define being human as "being present" to others and letting others be present to oneself. Institutionalization not only deprives the inmate of the opportunity to be present to the community but also relieves the larger society of the need to be present to the aged and distressed.

Although one would not want to do without the technical services that our health bureaucracies offer, they exact a high price by imposing upon inmates a kind of premature burial. The institutionalized have forced upon them a loss of name, identity, companionship and acclaim—an extremity of deprivation of which the ordinary citizen has a foretaste in his complaints about the anonymous and impersonal conditions of modern life. The nursing home, prison, and chronic care hospital function as destination and symbol for a society at large that operates as a kind of Hider-Goddess depriving its citizens of significance.

III. THE HOSPITAL AND DEATH AS DEVOURER

While disease wracks his body, the acutely ill patient often has a more general sense of being exhausted and burned out by a world that has consumed all his personal resources. In the recent western past, such a breakdown in health for a member of the middle class meant that he sought respite from a devouring world in the sanctuary of the home where the doctor visited him. This at least was the pattern of care for the middle and upper classes through the nineteenth and early twentieth centuries. Treatment for the poor was different; it was hospital-based. They went to the teaching hospitals where, in exchange for medical services, they sometimes consigned over to the staff their cadavers for research purposes. Thus the hospital acquired for the poor associations with an institution that not only serves, but appropriates the body.

Today, care for the middle class has been moved to the hospitals thus giving the middle class a taste of the earlier plight of the indigent. Despite its indisputable technological advantages over the home, the hospital exacts a high price both psychologically and financially. Psychologically, it assaults—with its alien machines, rhythms, language, and routines—that identity which a person previously maintained in the outside world. The patient's customary *control* of his world must be surrendered not only to the disease but to those who fight against it. His capacity for *savoring* his world is also numbed, once again, not only by the disease, but by those procedures imposed upon him in the fight against it—diet, drugs, X-rays, surgery, nausea-inducing therapy, and sleeping potions. Finally, his capacity for *communicating* with his world is unsettled by his loss of social role. Just at the moment that disease rips him out of his usual place in the community and makes him feel least secure in his dealings with fellows, the procedures of the hospital remind him acutely of this loss, by placing him in the hands of professionals—the nurse and the doctor—precisely those who seem unassailably secure in their own indentities.

The financial trauma in all this should not be overlooked. Today at fees of over $100 per day it is difficult to think of the hospital as sanctuary. One is eaten up not only by disease but by medical expenses. The family as well as the patient feels savaged by the illness. Current systems of national health care, while distributing costs somewhat, have caused the total social expense of medicine to skyrocket to a figure estimated by some at $120 billion a year without increasing commensurately the quality of health care. Nothing quite matches inflation for producing a sense that one is being consumed by one's world; and no item, except energy, matches health care in the inventory of rising costs.

Chronic, even more than acute, care centers have acquired associations with death as devourer. This theme has been worked out best by Erving Goffman, in his long essay on *Asylums*. Goffman included prisons, mental hospitals, monasteries and the like, among total institutions. He defines them as places of

> residence and work where a large number of like-situated individuals, cut off from the wider society for an appreciable period of time, together lead an enclosed, formally administered round of life.[11]

Such an institution is devouring in the sense that it deprives systematically the sick, the deviant, and the aged of their former identities.

> The recruit comes into the establishment with a conception of himself made possible by certain stable social arrangements in his home

[11] Erving Goffman, *Asylums* (Garden City, New York: Anchor Books, 1961, XIII).

world. Upon entrance, he is immediately stripped of the support provided by these arrangements. In the accurate language of some of our oldest total institutions, he begins a series of abasements, degradations, humiliations, and profanations of self. His self is systematically, if often unintentionally, mortified . . .[12]

Goffman gives particular attention as a sociologist to admission rites and procedures. The act of taking off one's old clothes and donning new garments impresses symbolically upon the inmate the price he is about to pay for entrance into the total institution: the surrender of his old personal identity and autonomy and the aquisition of a new identity oriented to the authority of the professional staff and to the aims and purposes and the smooth operation of the institution. (The metaphor of changing clothes, of course, dates all the way back to the Benedictine Rule, and behind that to the letters of the Apostle Paul, and, still earlier to rites of passage in primitive societies. It tells the prospective candidate that the condition of his new life is a death and devouring of the old, though in the case of the asylum inmate the new identity itself often leads to nothing more than the oblivion of death.)

The word "total" refers not simply to the comprehensive ways in which the institution organizes all activities—eating, sleeping, working, leisure and therapy sessions—but also to the strategies by which the institution invades the interior life of its inmates. In civilian life, Goffman observes, institutions usually make a claim on one's overt behavior alone, releasing to the individual the question of his private attitude toward the organization. But in total institutions, one's interior reactions to authority are also the legitimate business of the staff through a process that Goffman calls "looping." The individual finds to his dismay that his protective response to an assault upon his dignity itself collapses back into the situation; "he cannot defend himself in the usual way by establishing distance between the mortifying situation and himself."[13] Both his inner and outer life are looped into the all monitoring eye of the supervisor, to be subjected to further professional manipulation. Although Goffman's book was written nearly twenty years ago the practice clearly has not abated; indeed, it may even have been perfected—in T groups one is tempted to say—and most rigorously at the Patuxent Prison in Maryland where the device of indeterminate sentences justifies total control of the inmate-patient. His inner life, as well as

[12] Ibid., p. 14.
[13] Ibid., p. 36.

his outer behavior, belongs to his keepers. He is not sentenced once for his crimes by a judge, but rather judged daily and relentlessly as he seeks to reshape himself to please his guardians and to secure release from the prison of his therapy.

IV. THE MOTIVES FOR INSTITUTIONALIZATION

If we are given to structural ruthlessness in our patterns of institutionalization, and impose on the segregated the evils of banishment and deprivation, what explanations can we offer for our behavior?

Philip Slater blamed it on the peculiarities of the American experience and the American populace. He argued that Americans are tempted to solve their problems by resorting to what he called the toilet assumption. We behave as though the most efficient and sanitary way of solving a problem is to avoid it by voiding it. To argue the depth of this tendency in the American character, Slater had to resort to some revisionist writing in the *Pursuit of Loneliness* on the motives of immigrants who settled this country. Americans were not the most heroic of Europe's millions, as our history books suggest. Rather they were self-selectively those who were most inclined to solve the problems of an ancient continent and aging relatives by escaping from them. This strategy of abandonment has been repeated over and over again in American life; as an immigrant people became a migratory people, moving from the East across the plains to the West; and then as a migratory people, became a mobile people, leaving small towns in order to "make it" in the city, and (after making our cities uninhabitable) fleeing from the city to the suburbs, and, finally, retreating from the tedium of the suburbs to the weekend retreat in the country. Slater sees in all this the work of the toilet assumption—the instinctive tendency to dispose of problems by flushing them.

His summary historical analysis lends itself to a certain obvious application to the matter at hand, particularly in the treatment of the aged. One generation voided their parents by leaving them in Europe, another left them behind in small American towns, still another, in the cities, and now in our own generation, they are exported to specially segregated institutions, care centers for the aged, or specially designated parts of the country where we offer to them in their old age a parting gift of loneliness. Inevitably guilt feelings stir up about all this and so we atone for our acts of abandonment through the good offices of Hallmark Cards and the Bell Telephone.

But why are we so drawn to what Slater calls the toilet assumption? His attempt to explain it as a special character defect of those who migrated to America seems historically dubious. Most immigrants did not come to the United States in order to flush the problems of their native countries. Certainly not the blacks, and probably not, most of the whites. In his essay on *Going to America,* Terry Colman notes that English absentee landlords in the late 1840s sought to get rid of huge numbers of Irish peasants on their estates by shipping them off to America. The practice was commonly known as "shovelling out."[14] It would appear that some of our forefathers were not the flushers as much as the flushed.

Furthermore, historically, if Michel Foucault's *Madness and Civilization* can be credited, the tendency to solve problems by banishing a defiled population to a special institution or place was already a major impulse in European life, particularly powerful in the Classical Period of the seventeenth and eighteenth century.

Medieval society, according to Foucault, except for its treatment of lepers, was much less inclined to incarcerate its own members for reasons of deviancy. Renaissance society was also reasonably indulgent in letting the mad and the indigent mingle in the society at large. But by the seventeenth and eighteenth centuries, the idle, the poor, the insane, and the criminal were incarcerated without distinction in the former Lazar Houses. Foucault believes that the religious ritual of confession may have been symbolically important in shaping the earlier medieval attitude toward deviancy. Confession is predicated on the fact of human imperfection, but it also implies some confidence that evil can be let out into the open without engulfing those who pray. But Classicism and Rationalism "felt a shame in the presence of the inhuman"[15] that the earlier ages did not experience. After the seventeenth century, Western society increasingly assumed that one could handle evil only by banishing it. Put another way: an age that aspires to total autonomy finds it more difficult to admit as part of its life the dependent, the defective, and

---

[14] Terry Colman, *Going to America* (New York City: Random House, 1972) p. 216.
[15] Michel Foucault, *Madness and Civilization* (New York: Random House, 1968).

the irrational. They represent a negativity so threatening and absolute that they can only be put out of sight.

Foucault was aware that this impulse to banish is not a simple
expression of brutality. He recognized the philanthropic element in
the move to sequester: "Interest in cure and expulsion coincide."[16]
But it took David Rothman's recent Bancroft Book Award winner,
The Discovery of the Asylum, to show the intimate historical connection between the impulse to rehabilitate and the compulsion to
segregate. Rothman has documented the drastic change that occurred in the 1820s and afterward in the U.S. in the handling of
crime, madness, and indigency. Until the early nineteenth century,
criminals were either whipped, pilloried, driven out of town, or
hung. Jails were no more than temporary lock-ups until decisions
about punishment could be reached. Not until the 1820s did this
country hit upon the strategy of incarcerating, and then isolating
criminals within huge penitentiaries.

Similar changes occurred about the same time in the handling
of the indigent and the insane. Until the 1820s, welfare funds were
directed to families or substitute families to take care of the poor.
But increasingly the nineteenth century saw the construction of great
work-houses where the poor were institutionalized. Likewise the
mad were moved from the attic and the hovel at the edge of town
to the insane asylum.

Reformers made these changes for the philanthropic purpose of
removing stricken populations from the evil influences of the society
at large to the protected environment of the penitentiary or the
asylum, where, under carefully controlled conditions (including isolation, work, discipline, and obedience under the authority of the
professional), the distressed had a chance for rehabilitation. By the
end of the Civil War, however, these massive, standardized facilities
became the institutional bins we are familiar with to this day,
manned by professionals and subprofessional staff and filled with
racial minorities.

In the medieval church, as a priest and his assistants dragged a
leper out of the church with backward step and committed him to
the Lazar House, they would say to him: "And howsoever thou
mayest be apart from the church and the company of the Sound,
yet art thou not apart from the grace of God."[17]

[16] Ibid., p. 7.
[17] Ibid., p. 6.

In the last one hundred years, our implied ritual address to the mad, the aged, and the criminal has been: "And howsoever thou mayest be apart from the community and the company of the Sound, yet art thou not apart from the ministrations of the Professional."

Thus rationalism, philanthropy and professionalism are linked to the evils of banishment and ultimate deprivation.

In my judgment, however, Slater's attempt to locate the toilet assumption uniquely in the American immigrant experience and Foucault's effort to blame the impulse to banish exclusively on classical rationalism are equally dubious. Solving problems by dodging them is as old as the parable of the Good Samaritan. "Passing by on the other side" was simply an early version of achieving some distance from the distressed. The impulses both to sequester and to devour are within humankind and not just an idiosyncracy of the American experience or the Enlightenment.

The real power, moreover, of these impulses within us would be underestimated if we adopted too moralistic a view of their origin —if we assumed that they issue from a gratuitous ruthlessness or complacency. Our neglect of the indigent does not result solely from the fact that we are too smug, too complacent, too engrossed in our own riches, to bother with them. If we examine our excuses for neglect, including our reasons for institutionalization, we discover not so much smugness but anxiety, not self-assurance but a sense of harrassment, not riches but a feeling of bankruptcy. The statement, "I am too busy to care for her now," is often but a way of saying in anxiety, "I am riddled with concern about my own affairs. I can't break free from the grip of my own needs. They hold me in a vise. Maybe next year will be different. But this year is impossible."

Or again, the question, "What can I do?" is often but a way of saying in despair, "I have nothing for the real needs of another because what I have doesn't satisfy my own. What help could I possibly be to him? It is better to avoid him. To have to face him would be too depressing. He would remind me of the emptiness of my own fate." Many a man avoids a visit to the bed of a dying friend for reason of the latter dread. He knows he has nothing to say that will help. He feels resourceless before his friend's imminent death and his own. He himself is in need, and a face-to-face meeting with his friend would remind him of his own exigency.

Thus, not all expediency in our treatment of the distressed is gross callousness; we are busily engaged in obscuring from view our own poverty. We consign to oblivion the maimed, the disfigured, and the decrepit, because we have already condemned to oblivion a portion of ourselves. To address them in their needs would require us to permit ourselves to be addressed in our needs. But we are disinclined to want to accept the depths of our own neediness. The hidden away are a threat to us because of what we have already hidden away from ourselves. For some such reason, it is preferable, even at great expense, to have them removed from sight. And what better way to place them in the shadows and to obscure our own neediness, than to put them in the hands of professionals whose metier it is to make a show of strength, experience, and competence in handling a given subdivision of the distressed? Thus the exigent are converted into an occasion in and through which the community seeks to exhibit its precedence and power over them.

V.   A CONCLUDING COMMENT

I have tried to bring into view the institutional activities of hiding and devouring and to expose some of the reasons why we are complicit in these predatory ways of handling others and ourselves. In closing I will attempt to provide a context for interpreting the two major political responses to the problems we have raised and to do so in the light of the religious tradition that engages me as a theologian. The two basic and opposing political positions to which reference must be made are the conservative and the utopian reformist and/or revolutionary.

The modern pragmatic conservative would find in David Rothman's account of the emergence and decline of the asylum a confirmation of his skepticism about reform. It is but another sad tale of reform gone to seed. In the brief period of forty years, institutions with utopian aspirations deteriorated into dumping grounds for the desperate. Why bother, Mr. Reformer? Spare me your plans and save me some change.

Hobbes and his latter-day descendants would deepen this historical skepticism into a categorical pessimism. Our institutions are miserable and necessarily miserable because of the murderous appetites to which human beings are subject. The impulses to sequester and devour are rooted in humankind and not just a cultural idiosyncracy. Hobbes provide the anthropological foundations for this claim by observing: animals are *hungry* only with the hunger of the moment but man spontaneously desires *infinitely*. His infinite, devouring hunger makes man "the most predatory, the most cunning, the strongest, and the most dangerous animal."[18] Moreover, Hobbes proceeded, by implication, to link this activity of devouring with the further impulse to sequester when he argued that "the characteristic difference between man and animal" is "the striving after honor and positions of honor, after precedence over others and recognition of this precedence by others, ambition, pride, and the passion for fame."[19] One man's glory is another man's eclipse. When we aspire to step forward into the light and take precedence over others, the underside of this aspiration is a readiness to see others overshadowed by our presence. Man's boundless craving, and specifically his appetite for honor and precedence, generates that enmity among humankind which justifies, in Hobbes' estimate, his characterization of the state of nature as "solitary, poor, nasty, brutish, and short." Thus devouring and overshadowing are interconnected activities and these murderous impulses, in turn, are reinforced by our fears that we will be devoured and surpassed by others. For Hobbes, the only solution is to accept the state and its agencies, which, albeit oppressive, exercise a monopoly over the power of death and thereby keep terror within limits.

In brief, both conservative skepticism and Hobbesian pessimism end up justifying the *status quo* or the *status quo ante,* with respect to those institutions in a society that consume, consign to oblivion or oppress. The message then is to leave well enough alone. Things are bad, but they could be worse.

At the opposite end of the political spectrum, utopian reformers and revolutionaries tend to locate death in our institutional life alone. Individuals and groups are relatively innocent victims of an oppressive social order. They believe moreover that institutional murder is not merely discrete and episodic, but systemic. The specter of overtaxed clinics in ghetto neighborhoods, of rotting vegetable wards, of bad blood, and foul jails are instances of evils that are symptomatic of the entire social and political structure. It serves

[18] Leo Strauss, *The Political Philosophy of Hobbes* (Oxford: The Clarendon Press, 1936) p. 9.
[19] Ibid., p. 11.

the excellors and the devourers rather than the failed and the deprived. Since, moreover, individuals and groups are relatively innocent vicitms of the system, revolutionaries believe that humankind possesses the moral resources for the global displacement of the current system by one superior to it.

(Utopians and revolutionaries may be in a small minority in this country, but, I believe, their pessimism about current institutions has been widely and persistently shared across three decades. If there has been one thread of continuity in mood since the 1950s, it is a rather consistent pessimism about the whole network of outer forms and institutions: a belief that our institutions are basically predatory. Most interpreters have drawn a sharp line through the middle of the sixties. They have assumed that before that time Americans believed in their institutions while thereafter the student left, the black militants, and the peace movement massively repudiated them. It is my own judgment that the pessimistic assessment of our institutions in the late sixties was not too far removed from the perception of the fifties. The overriding diagnostic slogan for the fifties, after all, was "conformity." The phrase, along with associate metaphors of the period, the "windmill," the "grind," and the "ratrace," betrays a very low estimate of institutional life.)

What response can one make theologically to the contending social theories and moods of our time concerning the status of institutions? Surely the most influential response during the period under review was provided by Reinhold Niebuhr. His criticisms were essentially anthropological. Niebuhr faulted the Hobbesian pessimists for locating destructiveness exclusively within the murderous impulses of humankind and for dealing too kindly with its institutional manifestations. He also criticized the reformers and the revolutionary optimists, however, for locating oppression exclusively in the social system and exculpating individuals and groups as their relatively innocent victims. He himself was committed to a balanced, more complex, anthropological statement that sought to do justice both to the human and institutional capacity for good and the individual and social capacity for destructiveness.

Niebuhr's theological response was altogether salutary, but it did not, in my judgment, address the more metaphysical question that underlies the social debates of our time. Both parties to the political debate, despite their differences, share in common a somewhat gloomy metaphysical vision. They both tend to define their politics by the experience of death and destruction alone. They justify institutions in the one case or justify their overthrowal in the other case on the basis of reaction to a negativity rather than to the experience of some positive nurturant power which is authorizing ground for their action. The fear of death and destruction keeps the conservative defensive of his institutions; the hatred of death provokes the utopian reformer and the revolutionary to his attack upon them.

Fear is the pneumatic that makes the system work for the conservative. Inasmuch as institutions derive their power from the fear of death, they cannot be expected to dispense with this fear. Leviathan—and all its attendant institutions—is granted a monopoly over the power of death for fear of that even more murderous state of affairs that would be ours in a state of nature without its ministrations. Correspondingly, the hatred of death usually provides the utopian reformer and the revolutionary with a sense of their life's meaning and work. Such activists are right, in my judgment, in their perception of evils in the system, but wrong in their definition of their vocation by that perception alone. Evil has become for them that absolute by which their activities are authorized and their plans for a new society are shaped. They seek relentlessly to eliminate the negative from human life. This is their passion and calling.

Perhaps the lesson to be learned, however, from the eighteenth-century European and nineteenth-century American experiments with total institutions is that an ethic defined by resistance alone usually imposes on others what it seeks to depose. The total institution failed and failed brutally because it operated reflexively against negativities, the absolute negativities of madness, crime, dependency, and decrepitude. Society proceeded on the assumption that the negative absolutely had to be eliminated (through the ministrations of the professional) and when it could not be eliminated it had to be sequestered or eliminated by being sequestered.

It may be a good deal healthier to begin with the assumption that the negative is not absolute and therefore that its elimination is not the pre-condition of a truly human existence. Once the negativities of suffering and death are not treated as absolutes, then one may be less tempted to lay upon professionals the fatal charge to eliminate negativity or to banish ruthlessly its host. This deflation of evil moreover need not lead to quietism or complacency. It may not be necessary to inflate evil to an absolute level in order to justify action against it.

Where, however, does one find theological warrant for this alternative vision of the metaphysical context in which social action takes place? In my own efforts to puzzle over this problem as a Christian theologian, I have found myself drawn to the passages about the so-called "suffering servant" in Isaiah. Remarkably enough, the text locates the servant in the very arena of death that we have been exploring. He exposed himself to deprivation and oblivion. "He was despised and rejected by men; a man of sorrows and acquainted with grief, and as one from whom men hide their faces, he was despised, and we esteemed him not." Furthermore, the passage does not suggest that he is engulfed by this move into the site of deprivation and death. Though "he was cut off from the land of the living" and though he "poured out his soul to death," his resources are not thereby depleted or thinned out. Quite the contrary: in and through his outpouring of service, the will of the Lord actually prospers in his hand. The passage thus suggests a peculiarly intimate connection between prosperity and his own dying. The assertion of any such link contrasts starkly with our ordinary conception of social action. In traditional social action, we assume some kind of dualistic battle in which either we gradually prevail over death (in which case death diminishes) or we find our resources gradually thinned out by death (in which case we diminish). But this passage suggests that he makes his own dying, that is, his own laying down of his life, an essential ingredient in that life which he shares with the community.[20] By his stripes we are healed.

The conventional implication of this passage for Christians is moral. A community that professes such a servant as savior cannot avoid going into places marked by rejection, pain, and oblivion. In failing to do so it would defect from its own being in a God from whom no secret places are hid.

Concretely, for the churches, this means that in our time they cannot leave health care exclusively in the hands of the bureaucracies and their professional staffs which are the current chief instruments of sequestering. The churches must find to open themselves up to

---

[20] The best theological expansion I have seen of this theme is to be found in some of the recent work of Professor Arthur C. McGill of Harvard Divinity School in a paper, as yet unpublished, on Identity and Death.

the needy: 1) to provide supplemental services above and beyond those that bureaucracies can provide; 2) to criticize bureaucracies for their failure to provide what they ought to provide; 3) to encourage the development of alternative delivery systems where appropriate; and 4) to provide the community at large with sufficient contact with the plight of the deprived and the forlorn so as to effect a more favorable ethos in the society toward them and their problems.

But a moralistic reading of the passage from Isaiah does not cut through to the nerve of the problem before us. The problem, we suggested, is not simply other people's suffering but our own. We avoid the failures of others because we cannot bear to see our own failures reflected in their faces; we deprive the needy because we are absorbed in the task of overcoming our own limitless sense of deprivation; and never are we so tempted to impose pain on others as when we are hellbent on relieving it, convinced of the absolute righteousness of our cause and the indispensability of our contribution in promoting that cause.

Thus the final word spoken in Isaiah 53 must be in the order of a metaphysical statement.

If the annointed of God has exposed himself to deprivation and oblivion, then men and women need fear no longer that the death and failure that they know in themselves can separate them from God. Those powers they fear to be absolute have been rendered of no account either as they appear in them or in their fellow creatures.

This position of metaphysical optimism is far removed from the vision of the conservative who elevates the powers of darkness and disorder into a divine figure in the person of Tiamat; or, from the pessimism of the revolutionary whose cause derives its inspiration from the melodramatic negativity that he seeks to overcome. The art of dying for others penetrates, rather than sidesteps or merely reacts to, the negative. Death is one of the principalities and powers, to be sure, but a creature for all of that, incapable of separating human beings from the substance of self-expending love.

The final question remains as to whether this position undercuts the motive for works of mercy and relief among people and the reformation of defective institutions. I think not. Quite the contrary, it is an enabling act. The negative has been deprived of its ultimacy. Hence men and women have been relieved of the burden of messianism. They need no longer repress the negative in themselves, or impose it on others, or be obsessed with it in their enemies, or protect themselves from it through the shield of the professional. They are free therefore to perform whatever acts of kindness they can and even to receive them from others, as a limited sign of a huge mercy which their own works have not produced.

BETWEEN THE NIPPLE AND
THE EVERLASTING ARMS

Robert E. Neale

*Not all institutions deserve the attack made by William May in
the previous essay. There is one kind of institution that has come
into existence in recent years almost, it seems, in response to the
very issues May has raised. Called a "hospice," it is devoted exclusively to the care of the terminally ill. This personal account
of St. Christopher's Hospice in England, the first of such institutions, gives a vivid idea of the kind of personal care that can be
given the dying—and their families.*

*Robert E. Neale is a professor of psychiatry and religion at
Union Theological Seminary in New York City.*

This article is taken from the Union Seminary Quarterly Review,
Vol. XXVII, No. 2, 1972.

After the Fall, what happened when the first man died from disease?
At St. Christopher's Hospice, outside London, the people know. It
was one thing for God to demand obedience, proclaim judgment,
and institute suffering and death. It was quite another for Him to
witness a dying human being. When it happened, God was struck
dumb. No Word. Then God wept. He picked up the man, pressed
him to His breast, and cradled him in His arms. And on the Lord
God's face there appeared a wistful look that remains to this day. It
can be seen on the faces of the patients and staff at the Hospice. To
be there is to live between the nipple and the everlasting arms.

This is how Mr. A. lived and died. I met him on the first day
of my six-month visit as volunteer chaplain. Like the vast majority
of patients at the Hospice, he was suffering from the last stages of
cancer and no further active treatment was deemed possible. He

was quiet, shy, kind, sad, and lonely. His brother lived in another country and his other two relatives were elderly, unable to visit, and uninformed as to the seriousness of his condition. When he had been feeling better, he had had frequent conversations with another patient. He often asked about his friend. Mr. A. and I met many times during the week. We talked about opera.

On the Thursday of my second week, Mr. A.'s condition deteriorated. I sat with him for most of the day. He said that he knew death was close and that he wanted company. Somewhat to my surprise, I found I enjoyed "just" sitting with him. By Friday, he had pneumonia. I sat with him for the morning. He was very uncomfortable. When he was coherent, he was embarrassed about his wandering mind. His head hurt. He couldn't urinate when he felt he had to. He was often thirsty. His hand would reach out, appear to hold a glass, move to his lips, and then drop to his lap as if he discovered that there was no glass there. Sometimes he just closed his hand into a fist and put his thumb in his mouth. At these times, I would ask if he wanted a drink, he would respond, and I would bring a glass to his lips for a sip. He talked all the time, but was difficult to understand. Sometimes he wanted me to do something and I could not fathom his request. He gave me advice on the current opera and ballet schedules. He asked about his friend. And he asked about whether he should stop fighting death. He said he was tired of fighting. I told him that I thought it would be all right to stop fighting if he wanted to. I did want him to die then. He was suffering enough and should allow himself to stop living.

When I returned from lunch, I discovered that the nurse had cleaned out his bladder and bowels to ease discomfort and was in the process of giving an additional dose of diamorphine. After about ten minutes, he became unconscious from the effect of the drug and never awoke. I remained with Mr. A., with my hand on his shoulder and my mind on him, on death, on the Hospice, and on many unrelated matters. It occurred to me that he was really going to die. As I looked at him, I was struck over and over by the fact that he was a good man. What I meant was that he was good, regardless of what I did not know about him. Really, he was beyond any concern for good and bad. It occurred to me that I was just saying to myself, to him, and to God, that Mr. A. was a human being. What more can be said? That was what I meant by "good."

As I was thinking these things, I noticed that his breathing changed. He was going to die now. My loving thoughts disappeared. The pit of my stomach gave a clear signal. Panic. He was actually going to die, now, and I would be touching him while he died and when he was dead. I wanted to remove my hand from his shoulder. I looked at him and my hand. I knew that I could leave. Someone from the staff would replace me. I would not be disgraced. The staff would understand my beginner's flight and support me. But Mr. A. was a human being. The panic passed. The hand remained. And I remained. I was comfortable and it seemed that Mr. A. was comfortable. He looked and sounded at ease. Five or six minutes passed and I knew that any breath might be the last. This was fine with me and I hoped it was fine with him. I decided that it was fine with him. What had I been so anxious about? Then Mr. A. stopped breathing. I looked and listened. Sure enough, he was dead. I thought that it was easily done by him. He still looked good to me. I gave his shoulder a final squeeze and told him that he was good. Everything was all right. And that was the beginning. Mr. A. and I have been living between the nipple and the everylasting arms.

I have said something about Mr. A., more about myself, and implied something about St. Christopher's Hospice. The dictionary defines a hospice as a house of refuge for travelers. St. Christopher's is just this. In order to suggest the atmosphere of the Hospice, I shall discuss it as a house, a place of refuge, and a way station for travelers.

Polly Adler once said that "A house is not a home." Well, there is more than one kind of prostitution. Not all hospitals are homes. St. Christopher's is a home. Even to speak of its people—patients and staff—as a community is not sufficient. This home is occupied by a family. It is not always a wise family, not always a happy family; but, nevertheless, it is a family.

The staff side of the family is large for a fifty-four bed hospital. This means that people have time to talk with each other. I felt at home within a few days. When Mr. A. died, I knew that the staff was supporting me just as I was trying to support Mr. A. After he died, I wandered into a nurse's station and happened onto the deputy medical director, and she stayed with me while I responded to the death of Mr. A. After about a month, when all the dying and deaths began to get to me, my tired step and wan look was noted and I was encouraged to take some days off. They put it very nicely, saying that my reactions were typical and that I was right on schedule. People were always there when I needed them. And the staff has time for meetings that are not always devoted to the technical care of patients. There was a discussion group that met on Friday after lunch. One afternoon a doctor from Boston was our guest. He was dumbfounded! Why? Because the group included the medical director, deputy medical director, a head nurse, a psychiatrist, a chaplain, and a switchboard operator. Because members of the group were Jewish, Roman Catholic, Anglican, Protestant, Greek Orthodox, and atheist with Zen Buddhist flavoring. Because we were just listening to a Bach chorale. Because it was during working hours. Because this discussion group was defined as part of and necessary to our work. I was dumbfounded that he was dumbfounded. Work at the Hospice is defined in such a way that members of the staff have time and interest in knowing and being with each other.

The patients are the center of this family. No one could talk about the Hospice without mentioning one or more patients. When the medical director, Cecily Saunders, is asked to speak about the institution, frequently she talks about some patients she has known and says nothing more. These patients are what I call her saints. The Hospice has its local saints, and members of the staff have their saints. Mr. A. is one of mine. The patients are at the center. They live in a new, spacious house located in the suburbs. There are only a few single rooms, for they are encouraged to live together. They have a social club. They are encouraged to keep their possessions with them, even to the extent of putting their own pictures on the wall. They do help each other, often being more effective than the staff. Mr. A. was very concerned about his fellow patient.

But the clearest evidence for patients being the center of the family is the amount and quality of time spent with them by staff. Only some of this time is technical time, a time for doctoring or nursing in the narrow sense. Indeed, it takes a while for some nurses to become accustomed just to sitting and listening and talking with a patient. The theme of the Hospice is "being present." This presence begins outside the building. Mr. D. said to me: "When I came here in the ambulance, a doctor, and a nurse were right there. Usually, when I enter a hospital, they ask me my name, age, and so forth. You know what they said here? 'Hello, Mr. D. welcome to St. Christopher's.' I felt at home before I entered the building!" There is always time for staff to go outside the building to greet a patient.

Once inside, very rarely is a patient passed by because a member of the staff is too busy. And this permanent welcome is extended to relatives. The visiting hours are generous, freely abused, and there is no age limit. Children come to play in the presence of their parents or grandparents. Relatives help nurse and sometimes stay overnight. One patient and his wife used Dr. Saunders' apartment several times. After the patient dies, there is no rush to get rid of relatives. A nurse doesn't just have them leave the ward, but has tea with them, helps with information about funeral services, and finally, walks with them to the lobby of the building. The goodbye is a courteous and concerned one. Some relatives maintain their relationship to the Hospice after the patient dies. This welcome is truly genuine. I do not recall ever feeling that a relative was in the way. Relatives are a part of the family.

So, St. Christopher's Hospice is a house, a house that is a home for a family. Mr. A. and I knew that we were members of this family.

To be more specific about this family, we can consider the house as a place of refuge. A refuge is a shelter from danger. The Hospice defines the danger as abandonment. Dying means separation from and possible abandonment by the living. Death means the same. Mr. A. did not want to be alone. After he died, I did not want to be alone. What kind of a refuge is the Hospice? Three elements in its theme of being present seem pertinent: touching, feeding, loving.

Of course, touching is an inevitable part of medical and nursing care. But such touching is not inevitably a sign of being present to a patient. At the Hospice, it is the extra touch that really counts. At the beginning of my stay, I was surprised to learn that it was permissible for staff to sit on a patient's bed. Chairs were always available, but use of the bed could be more intimate. Touching occurs commonly when medical and nursing care was not taking place. My hand was on Mr. A.'s shoulder for hours. I was embraced by relatives and I embraced them. For six months, I was engaged in holding hands. Other members of the staff did the same. There were patients who would not let go of me. And there were times when I would not let go of them. First of all, then, being present means touching.

Being present also means feeding. Surely the patients are fed in innumerable ways, but I single out the feeding of food, alcohol, and heroin.

Food is to be enjoyed. The welcome of gifts of food to patients from relatives, the variety and options of menus presented by the Hospice, the large staff which makes serving of hot food possible, and the presence of staff to feed those who cannot feed themselves, makes eating a possible enjoyment. The Hospice has a pronounced dislike of apparatus. There is no use of either nasal tubes or intravenous feeding. The feeding is all by hand, by the patient, relative, or staff. A patient with amyatrophic lateral sclerosis takes a long time to feed. This is a most inefficient use of staff time and the patient may still not get enough nourishment. But he does receive the intimate presence of another human being for several hours each day.

The consumption of alcohol is possible at every evening meal. Mr. A. had his choice of beer, wine, or hard liquor. I recall one mobile gentleman who walked to the local pub every morning and returned for the afternoon to sleep it off. I observed Dr. Saunders taking a bottle with her to visit a patient. And I had sherry with various members of the staff quite consistently, and groups of staff had frequent celebrations. All this is not to imply that dying at the Hospice is participation in a drunken brawl, but that alcohol is perceived as a physiological, psychological, and social support. Families do enjoy a drink together.

Perhaps the most pertinent feeding is the serving of morphine and diamorphine. The staff is expert on elimination of pain. The principle of anticipating pain and preventing rather than alleviating it leads to use of low and frequent dosages. The basic drug is heroin. It does induce euphoria, but the understanding of the staff is that the patient in pain is way below the normal level and that the drug raises this up to and not exceeding the normal. Research is being done to test the conviction that heroin is more effective than morphine.

So, a second aspect of being present is feeding with food, alcohol, and heroin. It provides relief from pain and anticipated pain, physical enjoyment, and social contact. Feeding the patient is a fundamental element in the family life.

Being present means touching, feeding, and loving. It means, "I love you, we all love you, God loves you." Two consequences of this understanding can be noted. First, staff roles are diffuse. Anybody can love. In this family, not only doctors, nurses, psychotherapists, and social workers serve patients. Switchboard operators, receptionists, domestics, maintenance men, over a hundred volunteers

—all have contact with and purpose in meeting patients. Frequently, for a casual observer, it would have been difficult to pigeon hole me as a nurse, social worker, psychotherapist, or clergyman when I met with Mr. A. The right person at the right time does what is needed. Loving cuts across categories.

Love also challenges professional distance. I told some patients that my brother was dying. When he did die, I flew to the States. On my return, I found that the patients knew about this death. One patient with the identical disease wanted to know all the details —the reactions of the children, the wife, and my reactions. I gave them. He was comforted. I was comforted. Who was serving whom? There was little professional distance here. I recall one nurse who was very experienced, competent, and wise. She had a photograph of a current patient in her living room. This is not a typical sign of professional distance. I told Mr. A. that he was a good man. That was a euphemism. What I meant and should have said was: "I love you, we all love you, and God loves you."

Being present is loving. Love at the Hospice cuts across categories within the helping professions and across the category of professional and patient. So presence as touching, feeding, and loving is the dynamic which makes the Hospice a house of refuge from the danger of abandonment.

Any house that is a home is a place of refuge. But not all homes are for travelers. The Hospice is for pilgrims. Where are they going? They are going into death and into God's everlasting arms.

The first thing to say about these travelers is that they are traveling into death. The Hospice exists to help them die. The vast majority of patients have not been told that they are dying. Some know it. Some know it and speak of it to staff, as Mr. A. did to me. Others are determined not to know it despite all signs to the contrary. The rule of the staff is to respond as the patient indicates. Ideally, there is no problem about what to tell the patient. The task is to listen to him and discover how he desires to handle the issue. I did not find it difficult to make this discovery. I did find it difficult sometimes to behave accordingly. It was easy to encourage Mr. A. to stop fighting, and equally easy to encourage another patient to continue fighting. It was relatively easy to hope with the hopeful. It was difficult to respond to cheerful denial.

The staff has a genuine ability to listen, perceive, and follow the various approaches of patients to their dying. I believe that this ability is related to the fact that the whole purpose of the Hospice is to help the patients die. The purpose is not to cure. Nor is it to prolong. No extraordinary measures are taken to prolong life. Indeed, I believe some would claim that not even many normal measures are taken to prolong life. For example, I do not recall penicillin being used for cure of pneumonia in a dying patient. Rather, morphine or diamorphine is used to relieve discomfort. If a drug used for this purpose also causes death, that is not of primary concern. Patients are expected to die and the staff is expected to help them die in comfort. This focus came home to me when a staff conference was called on the topic of the patient who does not die. If there is a typical problem patient for the Hospice, it is the one who goes against expectations and does not die. Clearly, the staff will rejoice, but such a patient does present a problem—administratively and psychologically. So the expectation is that these patients are truly travelers who are going into death.

They are also traveling into God's everlasting arms. Both patients and staff include all of the varieties of believers and nonbelievers in God. There are no blatant attempts to convert the latter. Yet this is *St. Christopher's* Hospice. Dr. Saunders is a devout Christian who has been strongly influenced by religious communities. There is a chapel and much religious art scattered throughout the house. There are daily services for staff and patients in the chapel and evening prayers on the ward. There is a chaplain, and many local clergymen are about. There is a Bible study group and several religious discussion groups. So the atmosphere of the institution is religious. Indeed, I found it to appear far more religious in spirit than the one other institution I know—a Christian seminary. What the patients and staff catch from this atmosphere is not Bible stories, creeds, or beliefs. What they catch is the gentle persuasion that, somehow, everything is ALL RIGHT. This message comes out of strong faith and is presented in many different ways, even to those who have nothing to do with traditional faiths in God. What it means is that to die is not to be abandoned but to be remembered by the living and taken up into God's arms. These arms are invisible, and often presented indirectly, but they are there and received by those who have little to do with God. I did talk with patients about their faith and my faith very directly at times. But frequently, I responded to them with the simple conviction that they will never be alone and that it will be ALL RIGHT.

Perhaps the theme of traveling is best stated by the phrase, "Watch with me." This classical approach of being with the dying until they die and afterward sums up the attitude of the Hospice. I found the experience of watching to be strange and profound. At best, they were moments of truly being in someone's presence and being present to that person, moments of prayer (which are quite infrequent in my life), and moments of meditation on many things. This happened to me when I watched with Mr. A. I discovered also that watching with the dying becomes, eventually, a welcoming of death. To watch and to wait is to become ready for death. By the time death occurs, it does seem natural and right. I was glad when Mr. A. died and glad when others died. When I was not glad, it was when people I knew well died in my absence. Indeed, I was a little bit put out with them for being rather inconsiderate in their time of dying. In the same way, a corpse of a person I had not watched with appeared totally foreign and horrible to me. But the corpse of Mr. A. and others I had been with was quite natural and right. Finally, I began to discover that to watch with is to die with. To watch is to initiate a process in which part of the staff person dies with the patient and part of the patient lives in the staff person. To be a traveler's guide is to accompany him. And to accompany him is to receive a part of him. John Gunther said to Charles Wertenbaker: "You will live in us always." This is the situation for me with Mr. A. The Hospice serves the living. Yet it is a monument to the dead. It exists for all the saints who from their labors rest. Perhaps this is precisely why it serves the living. This family is truly an extended one.

It should be obvious that I have made no attempt to give an objective picture of St. Christopher's Hospice. Nor have I tried to share all of my impressions and offer a balanced response to my experience. I have taken only one theme out of many and suggested some of its elements. The Hospice is a house of refuge for travelers. It is a family in which the staff is present to patients by touching, feeding, and loving, helping them die by watching with them into death. To live in the Hospice as a patient or as a member of the staff is to live between the nipple and the everlasting arms.

My general reaction to the Hospice is very positive. If seminaries are abolished by students, I would be eager to work at the Hospice. If I am to die, which I diligently doubt, I would be eager to die at the Hospice. It is the best place to die that I know about.

But I do not suggest that is the best possible place. There are many questions to be raised, even on the one theme I have selected.

Philip Wylie, in reflecting on my experiences, might simply shout, "Momism." He would have reason for suspicion. It took me several months to realize fully that I was surrounded by women for the first time in my life. Not only are the nurses female, but so also are the doctors and the director of the Hospice. There were and are two male psychiatrists and a male chaplain, but members of these professions are hardly noted for possession of masculine traits and concerns. It is not enough to note that these women are dedicated and competent. It is to be noted also that they are, by and large, middle-aged, buxom, and single.

Freudians might put the issues more usefully. The orthodox would wonder about regression, dependency, orality, identification, transference and counter-transference, and idealization. Ernst Kris might apply his concept of "regression in service of the ego," and Erik Erikson might remind us of basic trust *versus* basic mistrust and of integrity *versus* despair. All these categories are neutral in the abstract and could be positive or negative or both in analytical application to the atmosphere of the Hospice. Is the patient's regression in the service of the ego? If so, in what ways? Does counter-transference occur? How is it handled? As far as I know, the Hospice has not carefully explored such questions. It might be to its advantage to do so.

My own conclusion is a religious one. The god of the Hospice is a god with everlasting arms and overflowing breasts. It is a god of powerful comfort. This image contrasts with one presented in a ballet of the prodigal son. At the end of the story, the son finds his way home. The father stands at one corner of the stage. He is large, stern, immobile. The son crawls across the stage to his father. The passage seems interminable. He reaches his father's feet. He looks up. The father remains large, stern, immobile. The son takes another eternity to pull himself up into his father's folded arms. When he finally reaches the arms, his father cradles him and effortlessly carries him home. This god is a father and lord, concerned about obedience, sin, guilt, confession, judgment. Yet, this god also touches, feeds, and loves his children. The God of the Judaic-Christian tradition is both these gods. Because of my experience at the Hospice, my God now has breasts. But the hair on His chest remains. And the everlasting arms are sometimes vehicles for fists. Even so, this God weeps.

Although the Hospice might well examine the possible analyses from Freudians and others, I am convinced that it has begun at the beginning. What contemporary man tends to forget is that any healing requires a return to the beginning. Primitive man knew this. An ancient cure for healing a toothache begins with an account of the first toothache and how it was healed. Healing of the terminally ill requires their return to a basic trust in another. This is the necessary first stage in the development of those about to die. But it is only the first stage in dying as it is in living. For regression to be in service of the ego, there must be a return to other stages. For integrity, there must be movement from this renewed basic trust to autonomy, initiative, industry, identity, intimacy, and generativity. That such things can be is attested to by patients at the Hospice who do move forward beyond regression and basic trust. It is welcomed when it occurs. It is encouraged by staff in many explicit ways. But the atmosphere of the Hospice is not always conducive to this movement. The powerful comfort which rules the house may implicitly inhibit the patient's growth. I conclude that the Hospice has created an ideal situation for movement into the first stage for the dying. That it has achieved this so well is what makes the need for a second stage so clear.

At St. Christopher's Hospice, all live between the nipple and the everlasting arms. Fundamentally, no one could live in any other way. A second stage builds onto the first, but does not replace it. When Goethe was about to die, he cried, "Light, the world needs more light." Many years later, the philosopher Unamuno heard this and wrote: "No, Goethe was wrong, what he should have said was 'Warmth, the world needs more warmth.' We shall not die from the dark, but from the cold." Because of this warmth, the dying at St. Christopher's Hospice are living.

APPENDIX

Monroe Lerner's careful and extensive study of mortality statistics, "When, Where, and Why People Die," is offered as an concluding essay. There is no doubt that the arithmetic of death can be so treated that it conceals altogether the range of human suffering and loss, not to mention courage and dignity, that lie behind the numbers. But in the kind of study Lerner has done there are suggestive, and even alarming, patterns that bring into view aspects of dying and death that do not appear in individual instances. The curious shift in the causes of death over the past several decades, the variations in mortality rates according to economic class and racial background, and the increasing role of institutions come into sight only when we survey death from a distance, but without such knowledge we are likely to continue the social policies that lead to costly injustices. Lerner provides few reasons for the statistical patterns he describes, but for the thoughtful person there is much here that commends further investigation and a sharpened sensitivity to many of the societal issues in dying and death.

WHEN, WHY, AND WHERE
PEOPLE DIE

Monroe Lerner

In a broad survey of mortality statistics Professor Lerner offers a careful profile of the patterns of dying in the United States and notes the changes in these patterns that invite speculation on the social causes of death.

Monroe Lerner is a professor in the Department of Medical Care and Hospitals and the Department of Behavioral Sciences, School of Hygiene and Public Health, Johns Hopkins University.

This article is from The Dying Patient, *Orville Brim, Jr., Howard E. Freeman, Sol Levine, and Norman A. Scotch, editors, Russell Sage Foundation, New York, 1970, pp. 5–29.*

Perhaps one of man's greatest achievements in his endless quest to extend the limits of his control over nature has been his success in increasing the average duration of his lifetime. This success has been particularly substantial in the modern era, beginning with the mid-seventeenth century, and during the second third of the twentieth century it extended even to the far corners of the globe. During this period, and possibly for the first time in human history, the lifetimes of a substantial proportion of the world's population have been extended well beyond even the economically productive years, so that most people can now reasonably expect to survive at least into their retirement period.

The ability to do this has always been highly valued, at least as an ideal, and perhaps especially in those societies able at best to struggle along only at the subsistence margin and with almost no economic surplus to support life during the barren years. But even in other circumstances, more than one conception of the "good society" has had a component notion that survival beyond the productive years could be within the realm of possibility for all. Nevertheless, only in the technologically advanced Western nations of today does the *average* duration of life reach, and even in some instances exceed, the famous Biblical standard of threescore and ten. If the average duration of life—life expectancy, to use the technical term of statisticians and actuaries—is conceived of as an important indicator of man's control over nature and at the same time also as a crucial element in the moral evaluation of society, then surely man's difficult journey down the long paths of history may be described as social progress rather than merely as evolution.

In any case, whether progress or evolution, man certainly has extended his average lifetime. This chapter first traces that process, as much as it is possible to do so from the inadequate historical data, and only in the most general terms, from prehistory down to the present situation in the United States. Life expectancy, however, is in one sense simply a refined measure of mortality, and for some purposes it is more useful to deal with mortality rates rather than with life expectancy. Mortality, then, becomes the focus of the remainder of the present discussion.

Later, mortality trends in the United States are traced from 1900 to the present, for the total population and separately by age and sex. Young people—infants, children, and young adults—and females at all ages have clearly been the chief beneficiaries of this process, although other segments of the population have also gained substantially. The major communicable diseases—tuberculosis, influenza and pneumonia, gastritis and duodenitis, the communicable diseases of childhood, and so on—have declined as leading causes of death, to be replaced by the "degenerative" diseases, that is, diseases associated with the aging process—heart disease, cancer, and stroke —and by accidental injury.

Populations may be perceived not only as consisting of sex and age groups, but also as individuals and families ranged along a multidimensional, socioeconomic continuum. The problem then becomes: How do people at various points or in various sections of this continuum fare with regard to mortality risk or, in a more literal meaning of the term than was intended by the German sociologist Max Weber who coined it, what are their life-chances?

Perhaps the most meaningful way of dealing with this question, if the objective is to identify large groups or strata in the population who actually do experience gross or at least identifiable differences in mortality risk, is to assume the existence of three major socio-economic strata in this country, each characterized by a distinctive and unique life-style—the white-collar middle class, the blue-collar working class, and the poverty population. Various structural factors in the life-styles of these populations are conducive to different outcomes in mortality risk. In general, the poverty population experiences relatively high mortality rates at the younger ages and from the communicable diseases, while the white-collar middle class, especially its male members, experiences relatively high mortality rates at mid-life and in the older ages, from the "degenerative" diseases. The blue-collar working class, to the extent that it avoids both types of disabilities, appears for the moment at least to be experiencing the lowest mortality rates among the three strata.

Finally, the place where death occurs—that is, in an institution, at home, or elsewhere—has long been a neglected area of mortality statistics. From national data presented later in this chapter, it seems clear that the proportion of all deaths in this country occurring in institutions has been rising steadily, at least for the last two decades and probably for much longer than that. It may now be as high as, or higher than, two-thirds of all deaths. Almost 50 percent of all deaths occurring outside an institution in 1958 were due to heart disease, and especially to the major component of this cause-of-death category, arteriosclerotic heart disease, including coronary disease, which accounted for 37 percent of the total. Cancer, stroke, and accidents comprised the remaining major components of the total, accounting for another 30 percent of the out-of-institution deaths.

HISTORY AND THE DURATION OF HUMAN LIFE

Scholars can only estimate, in the absence of direct date, what the average duration of life must have been during prehistory. Such estimates have been made, however, and they appear to be roughly consistent with the fragmentary data available from the few surviving contemporary primitive groups, in Africa and elsewhere, whose conditions of life resemble those of our remote ancestors at least in some of their major relevant aspects. Prehistoric man lived, according to these estimates, on the average about 18 years (Dublin, 1951:386–405); life during prehistory was, in the Hobbesian sense, indeed nasty, short, and brutish. Violence was the usual cause of death, at least judging from the many skulls found with marks of blows, and man's major preoccupation was clearly with satisfying his elemental need for survival in the face of a hostile environment including wild beasts and other men perhaps just as wild. Survivorship in those days was very seldom beyond the age of 40. Persons who reached their mid-20s and more rarely their early 30s were *ipso facto* considered to have demonstrated their wisdom and were, as a result, often treated as sages.

With the rise of the early civilizations and the consequent improvements in living conditions, longevity must surely have risen, reaching perhaps 20 years in ancient Greece and perhaps 22 in ancient Rome. Life expectancy is estimated to have been about 33 years in England during the Middle Ages, about 35 in the Massachusetts Bay Colony of North America, about 41 in England and Wales during the nineteenth century, and 47.3 in the death-registration states of the United States in 1900.[1] Thus a definite upward progression in life expectancy has been evident in the Western world throughout its history, and this progression is, furthermore, one in which the pace has clearly accelerated with the passage of time.

The upward progression has continued during the twentieth century and, at least in the United States, its rate of increase has accelerated even further. Thus, life expectancy continued to rise in this country after 1900, even if somewhat erratically; by 1915 it had reached a temporary peak at 54.5 years. The 1918 influenza epidemic caused a sharp drop in life expectancy, to just below 40 years, a level probably typical of "normal" conditions in the United States during the first half of the nineteenth century (Lerner and Anderson, 1963:317–326). But thereafter the upward trend in life expectancy resumed and, between 1937 and 1945 and following the devel-

[1] All life expectancy and mortality figures presented in this chapter pertaining to the U.S. in 1900 or subsequent years, unless otherwise specified, are based on various published reports of the National Vital Statistics Division of the National Center for Health Statistics (formerly the National Office of Vital Statistics), U.S. Public Health Service. The reports themselves are not specifically cited here, but the source for each figure is available upon request. Rates for years prior to 1933 are based on the "death-registration states" only. In 1900 this group consisted of ten states, primarily in the northeastern part of the country, and the District of Columbia. However, the number of states included in this registration area gradually increased over the years, and by 1933 all states in the continental U.S. were part of it. For comparison purposes, figures for the death-registration states are customarily considered as satisfactorily representing the experience of the entire country, and this practice is followed in the present discussion.

opment of the sulfa drugs and the introduction of penicillin during World War II, its increase was extraordinarily rapid. From 1946 to 1954, however, although life expectancy in this country continued upward, the *rate* of increase tapered off. And from 1954, when life expectancy was 69.6 years, to 1967[2] when it had reached only to 70.2, the gain was at a snail's pace compared to what it had been during the earlier period.

In broader perspective, that is, during the first two-thirds of the twentieth century that we have now experienced, life expectancy rose by almost twenty-three years, an average annual gain of about one-third of a year. This is a breathtaking pace compared to any period of human history prior to this century, and it clearly could not be sustained over a long period of time without enormous social disruption. In line with this, however, life expectancy in the country may now have reached a plateau at, or just above, 70 years.

Where does the United States stand in life expectancy compared with other nations, and what can we anticipate as the reasonable upper limit, or goal, that this country *should* be able to attain in the present state of the arts? Although international comparisons of this type appear to be a hazardous undertaking, in large part because of the substantial obstacles to comparability, a number of other nations clearly have higher life expectancies than we do, and at least in some instances the differences are fairly substantial. Even cursory observation of a recent international compendium of demographic statistics (United Nations, 1967: 562–583) reveals, for example, that in Australia, Denmark, The Netherlands, New Zealand, Norway, and Sweden life expectancy may be as much as two to three years higher than the comparable figure in the United States. Countries such as Belgium, France, East Germany, the Federal Republic of Germany, Switzerland, England and Wales, and many others, also exceed us in life expectancy, but not by so wide a margin. Surely this country should at least be able to reach the level of those listed above, if not to exceed them. It is possible that these countries may be nearing an upper limit, however, one that may persist unless some major medical breakthrough occurs. Returning to our own country, future projections of life expectancy and mortality made prior to 1954 now appear to have been much too conservative (Dorn, 1952); on the other hand, those made subsequent to 1954

---

[2] All 1966 and 1967 figures shown in this chapter are provisional. Based on past experience, however, the provisional rates are likely to be identical, or nearly so, to the final rates.

were clearly too optimistic. Tarver (1959), for example, projected a life expectancy of about 73.5 years in 1970, but it now appears that we may be a long time in reaching this goal.

Life expectancy by definition is equivalent to the average duration of life. But how are the numbers obtained for this measure? Starting with a hypothetical cohort of one hundred thousand persons at birth, the mortality rates by age and by sex of a given population in a given year are applied to this cohort as it ages and moves through its life cycle, reducing it in number until no survivors of the original cohort remain (Spiegelman, 1968:293). The number of years lived by the *average* person in this cohort is termed the given population's life expectancy. Clearly then, the life-expectancy figure thus obtained is simply the inverse of mortality experience; it depends entirely upon age-and-sex-specific mortality rates. Employment of the measure "life expectancy" as an indicator of the mortality experience of a population is useful for comparison purposes both currently and across time. This is especially true because this measure eliminates the disturbing influence on the mortality rate of variation in the age-and-sex composition of populations. It is precisely because of this characteristic that life expectancy was used in the preceding discussion to make comparisons across the long span of history. For discussion of the immediate past and current situations, however, it is perhaps best to shift the locus of the discussion from life expectancy to mortality.

MORTALITY IN THE UNITED STATES, 1900 TO 1967: TRENDS AND DIFFERENTIALS, OVERALL AND BY AGE AND SEX

Paralleling inversely the increase in life expectancy from 1900 to the present, the mortality rate (deaths per 1,000 population) of the United States population has declined sharply during this century. Thus in 1900 the mortality rate was 17.2 per 1,000 population, but by 1954 it had dropped to 9.2 per 1,000, the lowest ever recorded in the United States. Since that time it has fluctuated between 9.3 and 9.6, and in 1967 the rate was 9.4, representing a decline of about 45 percent since 1900. These figures understate the extent of the "true" decline, however, primarily because the age composition of the United States population has changed drastically since 1900. This change has generally been in the direction of increasing the high-mortality-risk age segments of the population as a proportion of the total and at the expense of the low. With age composition held constant, that is, using the 1940 age composition of the United States population as a standard, the hypothetical "age-adjusted" death rate in this country declined between 1900 and 1967 from 17.8 to 7.2 per 1,000, a drop of about 60 percent.

Age and Sex

The pattern of mortality rates by age in this country during 1900 was generally similar to that prevailing today (see Table 1).

TABLE 1

Mortality Rates per 1,000 Population by Age and Sex, United States, 1900 and 1966

Age (in years)	1900			1966		
	Both Sexes	Males	Females	Both Sexes	Males	Females
All ages	17.2	17.9	16.5	9.5	11.0	8.1
Under 1	162.4	179.1	145.4	23.1	25.7	20.4
1–4	19.8	20.5	19.1	1.0	1.0	0.9
5–14	3.9	3.8	3.9	0.4	0.5	0.4
15–24	5.9	5.9	5.8	1.2	1.7	0.6
25–34	8.2	8.2	8.2	1.5	2.0	1.0
35–44	10.2	10.7	9.8	3.1	3.9	2.3
45–54	15.0	15.7	14.2	7.3	9.7	5.1
55–64	27.2	28.7	25.8	17.2	23.6	11.2
65–74	56.4	59.3	53.6	38.8	52.0	28.1
75–84	123.3	128.3	118.8	81.6	98.5	69.5
85 and over	260.9	268.8	255.2	202.0	213.6	194.9

Thus in 1900 the mortality rate was high during infancy, 162.4 per 1,000, in comparison to the rates at other ages; it dropped to the lowest point for the entire life cycle, 3.9, at ages 5–14; but thereafter it rose steadily with increasing age until at ages 85 and over the mortality rate was 260.9 per 1,000 population. In 1966 the comparable rate was only 23.1 per 1,000 during infancy; the low point was 0.4 at ages 5–14; and again the rates rose steadily with increasing age, to 202 per 1,000 at ages 85 and over. Between 1900 and 1966 the largest *relative* declines in the mortality rates took place at the younger ages, especially during infancy and childhood. Although the declines at the older ages are less impressive percentages, they are, nevertheless, very substantial in absolute numbers. For example, at ages 85 and over the mortality rate dropped by about 59 deaths per 1,000 population, that is, from 261 to 202 per 1,000.

Although the mortality rates for both males and females in the United States population declined substantially since 1900, the *rate* of decline was much sharper for females. Thus the mortality rate for females dropped from 16.5 in 1900 to 8.1 in 1966, a decline of 51 percent. For males the corresponding drop was from 17.9 to 11.0, or by 39 percent. The male death rate has been significantly higher than the female death rate in this country throughout the twentieth century, but the relative excess of male over female rates has increased over the years, from 8.5 percent in 1900 to 36 percent in 1966. When these rates are age-adjusted to a standard population, the excess of male over female rates in 1966 is considerably larger, about 70 percent.

In 1900, the relative excess of male over female mortality rates by age was largest during infancy, at 23 percent. At ages 5–14, the mortality rates for males were actually slightly lower than the comparable rates for females; at ages 15–34, rates were about the same for each sex; and in each of the age groups at 35 and over, the mortality rates for males exceeded the comparable rates for females only by a relatively slight amount, that is, by from 5 to 11 percent. By 1966, however, although the mortality rates at each age were lower for each sex than the comparable rates in 1900, the decline in almost all cases was larger for females. As a result, the percentage excess of male mortality rates over female rates was larger in most age groups during 1966 than it had been during 1900. It was largest (an excess of almost 200 percent in 1966), at ages 15–24.

MORTALITY IN THE UNITED STATES, 1900 TO 1967: TRENDS AND DIFFERENTIALS BY CAUSE OF DEATH

One of the most significant changes in the mortality experience of this country since 1900 has been the decline in the major communicable diseases as leading causes of death[3] and the consequent in-

[3] Cause of death in U.S. mortality statistics is currently determined in ac-

crease *in relative importance* of the so-called chronic degenerative diseases, that is, diseases occurring mainly later in life and generally thought to be associated in some way with the aging process. Accidents, especially motor vehicle accidents, have also risen in relative importance as causes of death during this period, but mortality during infancy and maternal mortality, that is, mortality associated with childbearing, have declined sharply.

THE COMMUNICABLE DISEASES

The leading cause of death [4] in 1900 was the category: "influenza and pneumonia, except pneumonia of the newborn." This major communicable disease category was listed as the cause of 202.2 deaths per 100,000 population in 1900 (see Table 2), and it accounted for 11.8 percent of all deaths in that year. By 1966, however, the mortality rate for this category was down to 32.8, it ranked fifth among the leading causes of death, and it now accounted for only 3.4 percent of all deaths during the year.

Tuberculosis (all forms) and the gastritis grouping,[5] second and third leading causes of death, respectively, in 1900, were both re-

cordance with World Health Organization Regulations, which specify that member nations classify causes of death according to the International Statistical Classification of Diseases, Injuries and Causes of Death, 1955. Besides specifying the classification, World Health Organization Regulations outline the form of medical certification and the coding procedures to be used. In general, when more than one cause of death is reported, the cause designated by the certifying physician as the underlying cause of death is the cause tabulated (cf. World Health Organization, 1957).

[4] The method of ranking causes of death used here follows the procedure recommended by the *Public Health Conference on Records and Statistics* at its 1951 meeting. Only those causes specified in the "List of 60 Selected Causes of Death" were included in the ranking, and the following categories specified in that list were omitted: the two group titles, "major cardiovascular-renal diseases" and "diseases of the cardiovascular system"; the single title, "symptoms, senility, and ill-defined conditions"; the residual titles, "other infective and parasitic diseases," "other bronchopulmonic diseases," "other diseases of the circulatory system," and "all other diseases"; and all subtitles represented within a broader title. Causes of death are ranked on the basis of rates unadjusted for age or to a specific Revision of the International List of Diseases and Causes of Death, and the above discussion is based on these "crude" rates. But the *titles* used, and the 1966 rates, are those of the Seventh Revision.

[5] The full title of this cause-of-death grouping, in the nomenclature of the Seventh Revision of the International List of Diseases and Causes of Death, is: gastritis, duodenitis, enteritis, and colitis, except diarrhea of the newborn.

TABLE 2

The Ten Leading Causes of Death, by Rank, United States, 1900 and 1966

		1900	
Rank	Cause of Death	Deaths per 100,000 Population	Percent of All Deaths
	All causes	1,719.1	100.0
1	Influenza and pneumonia	202.2	11.8
2	Tuberculosis (all forms)	194.4	11.3
3	Gastritis, duodenitis, enteritis, etc.	142.7	8.3
4	Diseases of the heart	137.4	8.0
5	Vascular lesions affecting the central nervous system	106.9	6.2
6	Chronic nephritis	81.0	4.7
7	All accidents	72.3	4.2
8	Malignant neoplasms (cancer)	64.0	3.7
9	Certain diseases of early infancy	62.6	3.6
10	Diphtheria	40.3	2.3
		1966	
	All causes	954.2	100.0
1	Diseases of the heart	375.1	39.3
2	Malignant neoplasms (cancer)	154.8	16.2
3	Vascular lesions affecting the central nervous system	104.6	11.0
4	All accidents	57.3	6.0
5	Influenza and pneumonia	32.8	3.4
6	Certain diseases of early infancy	26.1	2.7
7	General arteriosclerosis	19.5	2.0
8	Diabetes mellitus	18.1	1.9
9	Cirrhosis of the liver	13.5	1.4
10	Suicide	10.3	1.1

duced so significantly and to such low rates during the course of this with 40.3 deaths per 100,000 population. In 1966 this condition accounted for only forty deaths all told in this country, that is, considering the entire United States population as at risk, so that the death rate was about one death per five million persons. Other major communicable diseases with impressive declines in mortality were some of the other communicable diseases of childhood, such as whooping cough, measles, scarlet fever, and streptococcal sore throat, and syphilis, typhoid and paratyphoid fevers, rheumatic fever, and typhus.

Hillery *et al.* (1968), comparing recent mortality data from forty-one countries, have shown that the communicable diseases ("infectious diseases" in their terminology) as causes of death decline significantly as a proportion of all deaths in each country as these countries move "up" in the demographic transition, that is, as their birth and death rates decline, and as they concomitantly become at least presumably more "advanced" technologically and socially. Thus, in the "transitional" countries (low death rates but high birth rates), communicable diseases account for about one-third of all deaths on the average, while in the demographically "mature" countries (both death rates and birth rates low), the comparable proportion is about one in twelve of all deaths. This finding is generally in conformity with past experience in this country and elsewhere.

THE DEGENERATIVE DISEASES

"Diseases of the heart" ranked fourth among the leading causes of death in this country during 1900; this category caused 137.4 deaths per 100,000 and accounted for 8.0 percent of all deaths. By 1966, however, it had risen so far in importance that it had become the leading cause of death, far outranking all others. Its mortality rate had risen to 375.1 deaths per 100,000 population, and it accounted for nearly 40 percent of all deaths in that year. Between 1900 and 1966 the unadjusted death rate from this disease rose by 173 percent; the rise was much less if the age-adjusted rates for these two years are compared, but even this rise was very substantial.

The pattern of increase for malignant neoplasms (cancer) as a cause of death was generally quite similar. This disease ranked eighth among the leading causes of death in 1900. It accounted for 64 deaths per 100,000 population and less than 4 percent of all deaths. By 1966, however, its rank among the leading causes had risen to second, its rate per 100,000 to 154.8, and its proportion of the total of all deaths exceeded 16 percent. Vascular lesions of the central nervous system, although remaining relatively stable in number of deaths per 100,000 (106.9 in 1900 and 104.6 in 1966), nevertheless rose in rank (fifth to third) and as a proportion of all deaths (6 to 11 percent).

How can we account for the increases, in both absolute and

relative terms, in these "degenerative" diseases as causes of death? As the classification implies, these are diseases occurring later in life and closely associated with the aging process. Whereas formerly people died on the average much earlier in life, victims primarily of the communicable diseases, they survive today to a much later age, only to succumb in due time to the degenerative conditions. Hillery and his associates (1968) in their interesting study have generalized this trend also. Thus in their demographically transitional countries (low death rates but high birth rates) the degenerative diseases account for less than one-third of all deaths, whereas in their demographically mature countries (both death rates and birth dates low) these diseases account for just under two-thirds of the total. The net overall gain has clearly been an extension of life by many years.

MORTALITY AND SOCIOECONOMIC STATUS

There appears to be a good deal of confusion in this country today, and perhaps especially among social scientists, demographers, and health statisticians, as to the precise nature of the relationship between mortality and socioeconomic status. This confusion has existed, and perhaps will continue to exist for some time, despite the fact that quite a few studies in the past, and a number of ongoing studies, have attempted to clarify the relationship. Part of this confusion may be occasioned by what is perhaps the changing nature of that relationship, a change which in turn may have been brought about by the tremendous improvements in medical technology and therapies during the past century and by the increasing general affluence of the American population. But part of it results also from the lack of a generally accepted method for the construction of an overall index of socioeconomic status (Lerner, 1968).

In turn, the failure of social scientists to develop a generally accepted method for the construction of an overall index reflects their lack of general agreement on the number or composition of social classes or social strata in the United States, especially when this entire culturally diverse country is considered as the unit of analysis. Different numbers of classes or strata have been identified, depending on definitions and operational purposes, but none of these is a real entity. Various measures of socioeconomic status have been related to mortality, and the results of one very large study along these lines are now beginning to appear (Kitagawa, 1968). Nevertheless, the overall pattern continues to remain quite unclear at this writing.

For present purposes—to relate socioeconomic status to mortality—it appears that the most meaningful division of the United States population from a conceptual, rather than an operational, standpoint is into three socioeconomic strata. These strata are set apart from one another, in the most general terms, by a distinctive and unique life-style, even though the boundaries between these strata are not sharp, and there may be a considerable movement of individuals and families among them. The life-styles of these strata, in turn, are dependent upon or associated with income, wealth, occupation and occupational prestige, dwelling, ethnic origin, educational attainment, and many other factors, all of which, in some as yet unspecified way, add up to the total. The life-styles, in turn, are directly relevant to the health level, and more specifically the mortality experience of each stratum. The structural factors in each of the three major life-styles through which the relationship to mortality operates include at least these four: the level of living (food, housing, transportation, or other factors); degree of access to medical care within the private medical care system; occupation of the family head (sedentary or involving physical activity); and the nature of the social milieu for that stratum (that is, its degree of economic or social security).

The highest stratum consists of those who are usually designated as the middle- and upper-class white-collar business executives at all levels and professionals, and all those who are above this category. It even includes the highest echelons of skilled blue-collar workers (tool-and-die makers), foremen, supervisors, or the like. Although the range of variation *within* this stratum is great, the group as a whole shares the essential elements of a "middle-class" way of life, that is, residence in "better" neighborhoods and suburbs, general affluence, and so on. This group will subsequently be designated in the present discussion as the middle class.

The second stratum consists of this country's blue-collar working class—mainly the semi-skilled and unskilled workers in the mass-production and service industries, but also small farmers and possibly even farm laborers, and lower level white-collar workers. These people are also relatively affluent, but not to the same extent as the middle class. Again, although the range of variation *within* this stratum is great, they also share a unique style of life distinctively different from that of the higher stratum. This group will subsequently be designated in the present discussion as the working class.

The lowest of the three strata includes those who are generally designated as the poverty population. By definition, these people generally do not share in the affluence characteristic of this country. It consists of the poor in large-city ghettos and the rural poor (residents of Appalachia or the Deep South, as well as others); the Negro, Puerto Rican, Mexican, and French-Canadian populations, and the other relatively poor ethnic minorities in this country; Indians on reservations; the aged; migratory laborers; and the dependent poor.

Although, as stated above, this mode of classification or socioeconomic status appears to be the most meaningful from a conceptual standpoint in terms of relating it to mortality, it clearly lacks merit from the operational point of view. This is because there would appear to be no ready way of segregating these groups from one another in the available national statistical data, relating either to population data or health statistics, and especially to study their respective mortality experiences. Nevertheless, here and there some attempts have been made; and some studies, mostly local and regional in character and particularly of the poverty population, have been carried out (cf. Chicago Board of Health, 1965; and Lerner, 1968). What follows, therefore, is to be understood as more of an overall gross impression and prediction, rather than anything else, and one based on a general familiarity with the literature of what would be found if the data were available in the form required by the present framework.

The poverty populations generally are likely to have the highest death rates of the three strata on an overall basis, but especially from the communicable diseases. This has been true historically between rich and poor nations in the modern era and still represents the situation in the world today at various levels of wealth and technological advancement (Pond, 1961; Anderson and Rosen, 1960). Within this country, a considerable amount of evidence exists to show that mortality rates among the poverty population are likely to be highest during infancy, childhood, and the younger adult ages. The communicable diseases of childhood, gastrointestinal diseases, and influenza and pneumonia are still a relatively serious health problem among this population, even where public health facilities and services are relatively adequate, as, for example, in the slums of large cities in this country today. What this population lacks most, perhaps, is adequate access to personal health services within the private medical care system. Although these services are to some degree available under other auspices (Strauss, 1967), they may be relatively ineffective and not oriented to the life-style of their recipients, while the cultural impediments to their use appear to be substantial.

In contrast, the white-collar middle class does enjoy relatively adequate access to personal health services under the private medical care system, and their mortality rates during infancy, childhood, and even young adulthood are substantially lower than that of the poverty population. This is especially true for mortality from the communicable diseases, but appears to extend almost to the entire spectrum of causes of death. The higher levels of living enjoyed by this stratum in general buttress its advantage during the younger years. During mid-life and especially during the later years, however, its mortality rates appear to become substantially higher than those of the rest of the population, primarily for the "degenerative" diseases, especially heart disease, cancer, and stroke.

One possible hypothesis that has been offered in explanation of this phenomenon merits comment here. It may be that, because of improved survival by members of this stratum at the younger ages, many persons are carried into mid-life with a lower "general resistance" factor than that which characterizes persons in the poverty stratum, and that these individuals are perhaps therefore more vulnerable to the diseases and hazards most prevalent at mid-life and beyond. At the moment, at least, there seems to be no possible way of testing this hypothesis.

Another hypothesis is that this excess mortality at mid-life is a concomitant of the general affluence characterizing the life-styles of the middle class and of their sedentary occupations (executive and white-collar). Both of these, in turn, may result in obesity, excessive strains and tensions, excessive cigarette smoking, and perhaps ultimately premature death. Men aged 45–64 (mid-life), especially white men, appear to be particularly vulnerable to coronary artery disease and respiratory cancer. Middle-class women, on the other hand, appear to be less affected by these affluence-related forms of ill health than middle-class men, perhaps because of innate resistance, social pressures to avoid obesity, cigarette smoking without inhalation, and generally less stressful lives, or perhaps some combination of these factors. In any case, women in this stratum appear to have the best of all possible worlds, that is, they have none of the health disabilities associated with the sedentary occupations characteristic of their spouses while at the same time enjoying adequate medical care.

The blue-collar working class appears to have the best overall mortality record. This group appears to have relatively low mortality during the younger ages and from the communicable diseases, especially because they do have access to good medical care in the private medical care system. At mid-life, moreover, they appear to suffer from relatively few of the disabilities associated with middle-class affluence.

WHERE DEATH OCCURS

Where people die—in a hospital or other institution, at home, or in a public place—has been a relatively neglected aspect of mortality statistics in this country during the past few years. Although this information is contained on each death certificate and relatively little additional effort or expense would be required to code and tabulate it, this has not been done, perhaps because it has not been at all clear that the returns would be commensurate to the additional expense. As a result, the last national tabulation of these data based on the regular vital statistics data-collection system relates to 1958, and these data were far from complete; many of the cross-tabulations that could have been made were not, in fact, carried out. Some of the states and cities here and there have published tabulations since that time, however.

Recently, some new interest has been expressed in this question among public health circles, possibly stimulated by the coming into being of Regional Medical Programs throughout the country. These in turn were set up under the Heart Disease, Cancer, and Stroke Amendments of 1965 (P.L. 89–239), which provided for the establishment of regional cooperative arrangements for improvement of the quality of medical care through research and training, including continuing education, among medical schools, research institutions, and hospitals, and in related demonstrations of patient care. The new legislation was aimed generally at improving the health, manpower, and facilities available, but one specific purpose was to make new medical knowledge available, as rapidly as possible, for the treatment of patients (Yordy and Fullarton, 1965). The assumption in public health circles was that the place of occurrence of some death, and the circumstances, may have been related to an inability to obtain proper medical care either at the moment of death or immediately preceding it, as in cases of sudden death, or at some point during the illness or condition leading to death in other cases. The extent to which this assumption is true is, of course, difficult to test given the present paucity of relevant data.

In 1958, according to the most recent *national* data available (see Table 3), 60.9 percent of all deaths in this country occurred in

TABLE 3

Number and Percent of Deaths Occurring in Institutions by Type of Service of Institution, United States, 1949 and 1958

Type of Service of Institution	1958		1949	
	Number	Per-cent	Number	Per-cent
Total deaths	1,647,886	100.0	1,443,607	100.0
Not in institution	644,548	39.1	728,797	50.5
In institution	1,003,338	60.9	714,810	49.5
Type of service of institution				
General hospital	784,360	47.6	569,867	39.5
Maternity hospital	1,862	0.1	2,249	0.2
Tuberculosis hospital	9,097	0.6	13,627	0.9
Chronic disease, convalescent and other special hospitals	24,180	1.5	12,402	0.9
Nervous and mental hospitals	57,675	3.5	45,637	3.2
Convalescent and nursing homes, homes for the aged, etc.	98,444	6.0	22,783	1.6
Hospital department of institutions, and other domiciliary institutions	3,646	0.2	41,841	2.9
Type of service not specified	24,074	1.5	6,404	0.4

institutions, that is, in hospitals, convalescent and nursing homes, and in hospital departments of institutions or in other domiciliary institutions. This figure represented a considerable rise over the comparable 49.5 percent recorded in 1949, the most recent preceding year for which a national tabulation was made. On the basis of these data it appeared that the proportion was rising by an average of better than 1 percent annually.

National data to test whether the trend continued beyond that year are unavailable, but state and local data appear to indicate that this, in fact, may have been the case. In New York City, for example, the proportion of deaths occurring in institutions rose steadily, with only one very slight fluctuation, from 65.9 percent in 1955 to 73.1 percent century that neither category was listed among the ten leading causes of death in 1966. Tuberculosis had caused 194.4 deaths per 100,000 in 1900, or 11.3 percent of all deaths, while the gastritis grouping, with 142.7 deaths per 100,000, had accounted for 8.3 percent of the total. By 1966 the comparable rates for these two categories were 3.9 and 3.3, respectively, with each accounting for substantially less than one-half of 1 percent of all deaths in that year. The percentage declines for each from 1900 to 1966 were by 98 percent.

Diphtheria had been listed as tenth leading cause of death in 1900, in 1967 (see Table 4). These same data indicate that the proportion of deaths occurring at home dropped commensurately during these years, from 31.4 percent to 24.2 percent. The proportion of deaths occurring elsewhere, primarily in public places, remained relatively constant. Data from the Maryland State Department of Health also indicate a substantial upward progression in the proportion of all deaths occurring in institutions, from 64.4 percent in 1957 to 71.8 percent in 1966 (Maryland State Department of Health, 1967).

Most of the deaths occurring in "institutions," as the data of Table 3 indicate, occurred in hospitals, the vast majority of which were general hospitals. Nervous and mental hospitals during each of the two years to which the table relates, however, accounted for somewhat more than 3 percent of all deaths. The proportion occurring in convalescent and nursing homes, homes for the aged, and similar establishments increased substantially between 1949 and 1958, from 1.6 percent to 6.0 percent.[6]

Table 5 shows the percent of deaths, by color, that occurred in institutions in 1949 and 1958, for the entire country and for each geographic division. In both years the proportion of deaths occur-

---

[6] However, there is some lack of comparability between these two figures, and this increase, although undoubtedly substantial, may not be quite as large as these figures indicate.

TABLE 4

Number and Percent of Deaths by Place of Death,
New York City, 1955–1967

	Number of Deaths				Percentage			
	Total	In Insti-tution	At Home	Other	Total	In Insti-tution	At Home	Other
1955	81,612	53,746	25,598	2,268	100.0	65.9	31.4	2.8
1956	81,118	54,716	24,193	2,209	100.0	67.5	29.8	2.7
1957	84,141	57,141	24,609	2,391	100.0	67.9	29.2	2.8
1958	84,586	57,946	24,230	2,410	100.0	68.5	28.6	2.8
1959	85,352	58,859	24,127	2,366	100.0	69.0	28.3	2.8
1960	86,252	59,413	24,341	2,498	100.0	68.9	28.2	2.9
1961	86,855	60,061	24,524	2,270	100.0	69.2	28.2	2.6
1962	87,089	60,409	24,315	2,365	100.0	69.4	27.9	2.7
1963	88,621	61,588	24,677	2,356	100.0	69.5	27.8	2.7
1964	88,026	62,391	23,602	2,033	100.0	70.9	26.8	2.3
1965	87,395	62,308	22,879	2,208	100.0	71.3	26.2	2.5
1966	88,418	63,599	22,576	2,243	100.0	71.9	25.5	2.5
1967	87,610	64,083	21,222	2,305	100.0	73.1	24.2	2.6

Source of basic data: Personal communication from Mr. Louis Weiner, New York City Department of Health.

ring in institutions was substantially lower for the nonwhite population than for the white when the country as a whole is considered as the unit. However, for the New England, Middle Atlantic, and East North Central states in both years and the West North Central states in 1949 the reverse pattern was true, that is, the proportion of deaths occurring in institutions was higher for the nonwhite population than for the white. In general, the proportions in both years for the East South Central, West South Central, and South Atlantic states, and especially for their nonwhite populations, were very low in comparison to the rest of the country. In Mississippi, even as late as 1958, only 31.0 percent of the nonwhite deaths occured in institutions. (These data are not shown in Table 5.)

By cause of death, as Table 6 indicates, the most important categories in which the proportion of deaths occurring in institutions was relatively small were the external causes of death (accidents, suicide, and homicide), diseases of the heart, influenza, and the catchall category, "symptoms, senility, and ill-defined conditions." Less than one-half of all deaths following accidents occurred in the

TABLE 5

Percent of Deaths Occurring in Institutions by Color and
Geographic Division, United States, 1949 and 1958

Geographic Division	1958			1949		
	Total	White	Non-White	Total	White	Non-White
United States	60.9	61.9	53.2	49.5	50.4	43.2
New England	64.2	64.0	72.4	52.2	52.0	67.1
Middle Atlantic	62.8	62.3	68.9	53.2	52.2	69.0
East North Central	63.6	63.2	67.9	51.5	50.9	59.7
West North Central	63.8	63.9	61.5	50.7	50.6	54.4
South Atlantic	55.8	58.6	48.4	42.5	45.3	36.3
East South Central	47.6	51.8	37.3	34.6	37.8	27.6
West South Central	54.9	57.7	44.2	42.8	45.3	34.3
Mountain	63.5	63.4	64.1	55.2	54.9	61.0
Pacific	66.5	66.3	68.8	58.5	58.1	65.5

hospital, and the comparable figure was only 44 percent for motor vehicle deaths. Only about one-half of all deaths from diseases of the heart occurred in an institution, and somewhat less than that figure for arteriosclerotic heart disease, including coronary disease. In the case of each of these conditions, as well as for suicide and homicide, it seems likely that the short time-interval between onset of the condition and death is probably a major reason for the relatively small proportions occurring in hospitals. Finally, only about one-fourth of all deaths for which a cause could not clearly be delineated (deaths attributed to symptoms, senility, and ill-defined conditions) occurred in hospitals.

Considering the almost 645,000 deaths that occurred outside an institution in 1958, almost one-half (49 percent) were accounted for by diseases of the heart (see Table 7). (Within this category, arteriosclerotic heart disease, including coronary disease, accounted for about 37 percent of the total.) The next three most important causes of death in accounting for all deaths outside of institutions were malignant neoplasms, 13.1 percent; vascular lesions, 10.1 percent; and accidents, 7.4 percent. These first four categories combined accounted for about 80 percent of all deaths occurring outside institutions, but other causes of death—for example, influenza and pneumonia, suicide, general arteriosclerosis, and so on—were also important in the total.

TABLE 6

Total Deaths and Percent Occurring in Institutions by Cause,
for Selected Causes of Death, United States, 1958

	Total Deaths, Number	Percent in Institutions
Tuberculosis, all forms	12,361	80.0
Syphilis and its sequelae	3,469	71.7
Dysentery, all forms	407	62.4
Scarlet fever and streptococcal sore throat	139	57.6
Whooping cough	177	60.5
Meningococcal infections	746	87.9
Acute poliomyelitis	255	91.8
Measles	552	63.8
Malignant neoplasms, including neoplasms of lymphatic and hematopoietic tissues	254,426	67.7
Benign neoplasms	4,961	82.5
Asthma	5,035	55.4
Diabetes mellitus	27,501	68.6
Anemias	3,195	72.4
Malignant neoplasms, including neoplasms tuberculous	2,247	91.8
Vascular lesions affecting central nervous system	190,758	65.8
Diseases of heart	637,246	50.4
Arteriosclerotic heart disease, including coronary disease	461,373	48.5
Other hypertensive disease	13,798	68.5
General arteriosclerosis	34,483	61.8
Other diseases of circulatory system	17,204	79.5
Chronic and unspecified nephritis, etc.	13,827	67.6
Influenza and pneumonia	57,439	68.6
Influenza	4,442	43.1
Pneumonia, except pneumonia of newborn	52,997	70.7
Bronchitis	3,973	61.7
Ulcer of stomach and duodenum	10,801	88.2
Appendicitis	1,845	94.5
Hernia and intestinal obstruction	8,853	90.5
Gastritis, duodenitis, enteritis, etc.	7,838	78.7
Cirrhosis of liver	18,638	79.3
Cholelithiasis, cholecystitis, and cholangitis	4,720	90.0

TABLE 6 (Cont.)

	Total Deaths, Number	Percent in Institutions
Acute nephritis, and nephritis with edema, etc.	2,203	76.0
Infections of kidney	6,889	85.5
Hyperplasia of prostate	4,627	81.1
Deliveries and complications of pregnancy, childbirth, and the puerperium	1,581	85.5
Congenital malformations	21,411	86.5
Certain diseases of early infancy	68,960	94.5
Symptoms, senility, and ill-defined conditions	19,729	25.2
Accidents	90,604	47.6
Motor vehicle accidents	36,981	44.0
Other accidents	53,623	50.0
Suicide	18,519	18.5
Homicide	7,815	34.1

CONCLUSIONS AND IMPLICATIONS

It would appear, at least from the point of view and focus of the preceding discussion, that the implicit goal of the health establishment in this country, to "assure for everyone the highest degree of health attainable in the present state of the arts" has been far from realized. For example, with regard to mortality and its derivative, life expectancy, other nations have clearly outdistanced us, and by a substantial margin. It is true that most of these countries are smaller and more homogeneous, and the environmental hazards plaguing them may not be operative in the same manner and to the same degree as they are among us. Nevertheless, we do appear to have fallen short of what has been achieved elsewhere, and it is therefore appropriate to raise questions about the reasons for this apparent failure.

Three broad lines of inquiry have been suggested as possible approaches in this chapter, and a fourth influencing and possibly underlying the others will be mentioned. When one considers the entire spectrum of causes of death and their "places of occurrence," it is not unreasonable to assume *as a working hypothesis* that many deaths are occurring from causes—disease conditions—that are

TABLE 7

Deaths Occurring Outside Institutions by Cause, for
Selected Causes of Death, United States, 1958

Cause of Death	Percent	Number
All Causes	644,548	100.0
1. Diseases of the heart	316,074	49.0
Arteriosclerotic heart disease, including coronary disease	237,607	36.9
2. Maligant neoplasms, including neoplasms of the lymphatic and hematopoietic tissues	84,724	13.1
3. Vascular lesions affecting the central nervous system	65,239	10.1
4. Accidents, all forms	47,476	7.4
Motor-vehicle accidents	20,709	3.2
Other	26,767	4.2
5. Influenza and pneumonia	18,036	2.8
Pneumonia	15,528	2.4
Influenza	2,508	0.4
6. Suicide	15,093	2.3
7. General arteriosclerosis	13,173	2.0
8. Diabetes mellitus	8,635	1.3
9. Homicide	5,150	0.7

amenable, at least under optimum conditions in the present state of the arts, to medical management and control. Of course, the sex and age of the patient, the general state of health and degree of "resistance" of the organism, and many other factors should be considered in the evaluation of each case before any death is characterized as needless or preventable. Furthermore, it may be very difficult to refrain from setting up, as working standards, ideal conditions that are unattainable anywhere, given the realities and the imperatives of social organization, the relatively low priority of health in the hierarchy of human values and "needs," the "mass" nature of society, and the vagaries and irrational elements in what is colloquially described as "human nature." Nevertheless, the social and economic differentials in mortality discussed in this chapter would appear to argue that there is much room for improvement, that the low mortality rates now attained by some could be attained, theoretically at least, by all.

If this is true, and if our goal is indeed to assure the highest degree of health attainable *for everyone,* then we must ask ourselves whether the social organization of the provision of health services to the population in some degree shares responsibility for the discrepancy between goal and reality. If responsible inquiry is directed toward this problem, the unknowns in this vital area of public policy may be reduced, and we may begin to reexamine the place of health in our presently implicit hierarchy of values as opposed, for example, to education, other forms of welfare, space exploration, urban crowding, rural poverty, national security, and the myriad national concerns to which we allocate community resources. We may even be able to move toward calm and rational discussion of some alternative forms of social organization of the health care system, including their economic and perhaps social costs, hopefully with the result that we ultimately arrive at intelligent decisions.

SELECTED BIBLIOGRAPHY OF RECENT BOOKS
ON DEATH AND DYING

General

Aries, Phillippe, *Western Attitudes Toward Death*. Baltimore: Johns Hopkins University Press, 1975.

Becker, Ernest, *The Denial of Death*. New York: Free Press, 1974.

Boase, T. S., *Death in the Middle Ages*. New York: McGraw-Hill, 1972.

Cook, Sarah Sheets, et al., *Children and Dying: An Exploration and Selective Bibliographies*. New York: Health Sciences Pub. Corp., 1974.

Dempsey, David, *The Way We Die*. New York: Macmillan, 1975.

Hendin, David, *Death as a Fact of Life*. New York: W. W. Norton, 1973.

Holck, Frederick H., ed., *Death and Eastern Thought*. Nashville: Abingdon Press, 1974.

Kastenbaum, Robert, and Aisenberg, Ruth, *The Psychology of Death*. New York: Springer Publishing Co., 1972.

Kübler-Ross, Elisabeth, ed., *Death: The Final Stage of Growth*. Englewood Cliffs, N.J.: Prentice-Hall, 1975.

——, *On Death and Dying*. New York: Macmillan, 1969.

——, *Questions and Answers on Death and Dying*. New York: Macmillan, 1974.

Lifton, Robert J., and Olson, Eric, *Living and Dying*. New York: Praeger Publishers, Inc., 1974.

Mack, Adrien, ed., *Death in American Experience*. New York: Schocken Books, 1973.

Mills, Liston O., *Perspectives on Death*. Nashville: Abingdon Press, 1969.

Neale, Robert, *The Art of Dying*. New York: Harper & Row, 1973.

Rahner, Karl, *On the Theology of Death*. New York: Seabury Press, 1961.

Riemer, Jack, ed., *Jewish Reflections on Death*. New York: Schocken Books, 1974.

Euthanasia

Kluge, Eike-Henner W., *The Practice of Death*. New Haven: Yale University Press, 1975.

Maguire, Daniel C., *Death by Choice*. New York: Schocken Books, 1975.

Mannes, Marya, *Last Rights*. New York: William Morrow & Co., 1974.

Russell, O. Ruth, *Freedom to Die: Moral and Legal Aspects of Euthanasia*. New York: Human Sciences Press, 1975.

Wilson, Jerry B., *Death by Decision: The Medical, Moral, and Legal Dilemmas of Euthanasia*. Philadelphia: Westminster Press, 1975.

Suicide

Alvarez, A., *The Savage God*. New York: Random House, 1972.

Haim, Andre, *Adolescent Suicide*. New York: International Universities Press, 1974.

Handke, Peter, *A Sorrow Beyond Dreams, a Life Story*. Farrar, Straus & Giroux, Inc., 1974.

Sexton, Anne, *The Awful Rowing Toward God*. Boston: Houghton Mifflin, 1975.

Aging

Abernathy, Jean B., *Old is NOT a Four Letter Word*. Nashville: Abingdon Press, 1975.

Britton, Joseph H. and Jean O., *Personality Changes in Aging*. New York: Basic Books, 1972.

Butler, Robert N., *Why Survive? Being Old in America*. New York: Harper & Row, 1975.

Curtin, Sharon R., *Nobody Ever Died of Old Age*. Boston: Little, Brown and Co., 1973.

Galton, Lawrence, *Don't Give Up On an Aging Parent*. New York: Crown Publishers, 1974.

Hiltner, Stewart, ed., *Toward a Theology of Aging*. New York: Human Sciences Press, 1975.

Jury, Mark and Dan, *Gramp: A Man Ages and Dies*. New York: Grosset and Dunlap, Inc., 1975.

Weissman, Avery D., and Kastenbaum, R., *The Psychological Autopsy: A Study of the Terminal Phase of Life*. New York: Human Sciences Press, 1972.

Terminal Illness

Alsop, Stewart, *Stay of Execution*. Philadelphia: J. B. Lippincott Co., 1973.

Beauvoir, Simone De, *A Very Easy Death*. New York: Warner Books, 1973.

Crane, Diana, *Sanctity of Social Life: Physicians' Treatment of Critically Ill Patients*. New York: Basic Books, 1975.

Eissler, K. R., *The Psychiatrist and the Dying Patient*. New York: International Universities Press, 1968.

Gunther, John, *Death Be Not Proud* (new edition). New York: Harper & Row, 1971.

Kelly, Orville E., with Becker, Randall, *Make Today Count*. New York: Delacorte Press, 1975.

Kutscher, Austin H., and Goldberg, M. R., eds., *Caring for the Dying Patient and His Family*. New York: Health Sciences, 1973.

Lund, Doris, *Eric*. Philadelphia: J. B. Lippincott Co., 1974.

Rosenbaum, Ernest H., *Living With Cancer*. New York: Praeger Publications, 1975.

Schoenberg, Bernard, et al., *Psychosocial Aspects of Terminal Care*. New York: Columbia University Press, 1972.

Shepard, Martin, *Someone You Love Is Dying*. New York: Crown Publishers, 1975.

Weisman, Avery D., *The Realization of Death*. New York: Jason Aronson, Inc., 1974.

Wolitzer, Hilma, *Ending*. New York: Macmillan, 1975.

Wright, H. T., *The Matthew Tree*. New York: Pantheon Books, 1975.

The Funeral

Arvio, Raymond P., *The Cost of Dying, And What You Can Do About It*. New York: Harper & Row, 1974.

Habenstein, Robert W., and Lamers, W. M., *Funeral Customs the World Over*. Milwaukee: The National Funeral Directors Association, 1963.

Lamm, Maurice, *The Jewish Way in Death and Mourning*. Flushing, N.Y.: Jonathan David Publishers, 1969.

Mitford, Jessica, *The American Way of Death*. New York: Simon and Schuster, 1963.

Morgan, Ernest, *A Manual of Death Education and Simple Burial*. Burnsville, N.C.: Celo Press, 1975.

Bereavement

Greenberg, Sidney, ed., *A Treasury of Comfort*. Los Angeles: Wilshire Blvd. Book Co., 1954.

Kutscher, Austin, ed., *But Not to Lose: A Book of Comfort for Those Bereaved*. New York: Frederick Fell Publishers, 1969.

——, et al., *Death and Bereavement*. Springfield, Ill.: Charles C. Thomas, 1969.

——, and Kutscher, L. G., eds., *Religion and Bereavement*. New York: Health Sciences, 1972.

Lewis, C. S., *A Grief Observed.* New York: Seabury Press, 1961.

Pincus, Lily, *Death and the Family: The Importance of Mourning.* New York: Pantheon Books, 1974.

Schoenberg, Bernard, Carr, Arthur, et al., *Anticipatory Grief.* New York: Columbia University Press, 1974.

Schoenberg, Bernard, Carr, Arthur, et al., *Grief: Selected Readings.* New York: Health Sciences, 1975.

Schoenberg, Bernard, Gerber, I., et al., *Bereavement: Its Psychosocial Aspects.* New York: Columbia University Press, 1975.

Spiro, Jack D., *A Time to Mourn: Judaism and the Psychology of Bereavement.* New York: Health Sciences, 1972.

Readers desiring more bibliographical information may consult the following sources:

Halpern, Roberta, *The Thanatology Library,* an up-to-date list of books on death and dying currently in print, available for one dollar from Highly Specialized Promotions, 20 Schermerhorn Street, Brooklyn, New York, 11201.

Kutscher, Austin H., and Kutscher, A. H., Jr., *A Bibliography of Books on Death, Bereavement, Loss and Grief.* New York: Foundation of Thanatology, 1969.

——, *Supplement I.* New York: Health Sciences, 1974.

CREDITS AND ACKNOWLEDGMENTS

For permission to reprint material used in this book, the editors would like to thank the following:

AMERICAN MEDICAL ASSOCIATION   For "A Definition of Irreversible Coma" by Henry K. Beecher, et al., from the *Journal of the American Medical Association,* August 5, 1968, vol. 205, pp. 337–40. Copyright 1968, American Medical Association. Reprinted by permission of the publisher and the author. For "Refinements in Criteria for the Determination of Death: An Appraisal" by Marc Lappe, et al., from the *Journal of the American Medical Association,* July 3, 1972, vol. 221, pp. 48–53. Copyright 1972, American Medical Association. Reprinted by permission of the publisher and the author. For "The Uniform Anatomical Gift Act" by Alfred M. Sadler, et al., from the *Journal of the American Medical Association,* December 9, 1968, vol. 206. Copyright 1968, American Medical Association. Reprinted by permission of the publisher.

AMERICAN PSYCHIATRIC ASSOCIATION   For "Observations on Suicidal Behavior Among American Indians" by H. L. P. Resnik and Larry D. Dizmang from the *American Journal of Psychiatry,* vol. 127, pp. 882–87, 1970. For "Murder of the Newborn: A Psychiatric Review of Neonaticide" by Phillip J. Resnick from the *American Journal of Psychiatry,* vol. 127, pp. 1414–20, 1970. Copyright, 1970, the American Psychiatric Association. Reprinted by permission.

ANNUAL SURVEY OF AMERICAN LAW   For "Capital Punishment Since *Furman*." Reprinted from the 1973/74 *Annual Survey of American Law* with permission of New York University.

BEHAVIORAL PUBLICATIONS, INC.   For "The Right to Suicide: A Psychiatrist's View" by Jerome A. Motto, M.D., from *Life-Threatening Behavior,* vol. 2, no. 3, Fall 1972, pp. 183–88. Published by Behavioral Publications, 72 Fifth Ave., New York. Copyright 1972.

BASIC BOOKS, INC.   For "When, Why, and Where People Die" by Monroe Lerner from *The Dying Patient,* edited by Orville G. Brim, Jr., Howard E. Freeman, Sol Levine, and Norman A. Scotch. © 1970 Russell Sage Foundation.

THE CATHOLIC LAWYER   For "Individual Liberty and the Common Good" by Brendan F. Brown from *The Catholic Lawyer,* Summer 1974, pp. 213–25. For "The Humanity of the Unborn Child" by Eugene F. Diamond from *The Catholic Lawyer,* Spring 1971, pp. 174–80.

COLUMBIA UNIVERSITY PRESS   For "A Liberal Catholic's View" by J. F. Donceel from *Abortion in a Changing World,* edited by R. E. Hall, vol. 1, copyright © 1970 Association for the Study of Abortion, Inc., published in New York by the Columbia University Press, 1970. Reprinted by permission of the publisher, the Association for the Study of Abortion, Inc., and Professor Donceel.

THE CONTEMPORARY REVIEW COMPANY LTD.   For "The Case for Voluntary Euthanasia" by Eliot Slater from the *Contemporary Review,* August 1971, pp. 84–88. Reprinted by permission of the publisher and the author.

THE HASTINGS CENTER   For "The Indignity of 'Death With Dignity' " by Paul Ramsey (*Hastings Center Studies,* vol. 2, no. 2, May 1974). Reprinted by permission of the publisher and the author.

JAMES HILLMAN   For the excerpt from *Suicide and the Soul* by James Hillman, published in Zürich and New York by Spring Publications.

HUMANITIES PRESS, INC.   For "The Principle of Euthanasia" by Anthony Flew from *Euthanasia and the Right to Death,* edited by A. B. Downing. New Jersey: Humanities Press, Inc.

JOURNAL OF THE AMERICAN ACADEMY OF RELIGION   For "Institutions as Symbols of Death" by William F. May from the *Journal of the American Academy of Religion,* vol. 44, no. 2, June 1976, pp. 211–23. Reprinted by permission of the publisher and the author.

JOURNAL OF BIOSOCIAL SCIENCE   For "Aspects of Old Age in Age-Specific Mortality Rates" by W. R. Bytheway from the *Journal of Biosocial Science,* vol. 2, 1970. Reprinted by permission of the publisher and the author.

JOURNAL OF CRIMINAL LAW AND CRIMINOLOGY   For "Euthanasia: None Dare Call It Murder" by Joseph Sanders from the *Journal of Criminal Law,*

Criminology & Police Science, vol. 60, no. 3. Reprinted by special permission. Copyright © 1969 by Northwestern University School of Law.

JOURNAL OF SOCIAL ISSUES   For "The Aged and the Dying Process: The Inevitable Decisions" by Richard A. Kalish from the *Journal of Social Issues,* vol. 21, no. 4, 1965, pp. 87–96. Reprinted by permission of the publisher and the author.

LITTLE, BROWN AND COMPANY   For the excerpt from *Nobody Ever Died of Old Age* by Sharon R. Curtin, by permission of Little, Brown and Co. in association with the Atlantic Monthly Press. Copyright © 1972 by Sharon R. Curtin.

METROPOLITAN LIFE   For "Suicide—International Comparisons" from *The Metropolitan Life Statistical Bulletin,* vol. 53, August 1972. Courtesy, Metropolitan Life Insurance Company.

ROBERT E. NEALE   For "Between the Nipple and the Everlasting Arms" by Robert E. Neale from the *Union Seminary Quarterly Review,* vol. 27, no. 2, Winter 1972.

THE NEW ENGLAND JOURNAL OF MEDICINE   For "Active and Passive Euthanasia" by James Rachels from *The New England Journal of Medicine,* vol. 292, Jan. 9, 1975, pp. 78ff. For "Dilemmas of 'Informed Consent' in Children" by Anthony Shaw, M.D., from *The New England Journal of Medicine,* vol. 289, Oct. 25, 1973. Reprinted by permission of the publisher.

NOTRE DAME LAWYER   For the excerpts from "The Death Penalty after *Furman*" by Carol S. Vance from the *Notre Dame Lawyer,* vol. 48, 1973, p. 850. Reprinted with permission. © by the *Notre Dame Lawyer,* University of Notre Dame.

PHYSICIANS POSTGRADUATE PRESS   For "Suicide Among Physicians" by Mathew Ross from *Diseases of the Nervous System,* vol. 34, no. 3, March 1973, pp. 145–50. Reprinted by permission of the publisher and the author.

PRENTICE-HALL, INC.   For the excerpt from *Philosophical Essays: From Ancient Creed to Technological Man* by Hans Jonas. © 1974. Reprinted by permission of Prentice-Hall, Inc., Englewood Cliffs, New Jersey.

PRINCETON UNIVERSITY PRESS   For the excerpt from "A Defense of Abortion" by Judith Jarvis Thomson from *Philosophy and Public Affairs,* vol. 1, no. 1, pp. 47–66. Copyright © 1971 by Princeton University Press. For "Abortion and Infanticide" by Michael Tooley from *Philosophy and Public Affairs,* vol. 2, no. 1, pp. 55–65. Copyright © 1972 by Princeton University Press. Reprinted by permission of Princeton University Press.

PUBLIC HEALTH REPORTS   For "On Aging, Dying, and Denying: Delivering Care to Older Dying Patients" by James O. Carpenter and Charles M. Wylie from *Public Health Reports,* vol. 89, no. 5, pp. 403–07. Reprinted by permission of the publisher and the authors.

SPRINGER-VERLAG NEW YORK   For "Ethics and Euthanasia" by Joseph Fletcher from *To Live and To Die: When, Why, and How,* edited by Dr. R. H. Williams, published in New York by Springer-Verlag, 1973.

UNIVERSITY OF CHICAGO PRESS   For "Abortion: Parameters for Decision" by R. J. Gerber from *Ethics,* vol. 82, no. 2, January 1972, pp. 137–54. Copyright © 1972, University of Chicago Press. Reprinted by permission of University of Chicago Press. For "The Allocation of Exotic Medical Life-saving Therapy" by Nicholas Rescher from *Ethics,* vol. 79, no. 3, April 1969, pp. 173–86. Copyright © 1969, University of Chicago Press. Reprinted by permission of University of Chicago Press and the author.

UNIVERSITY OF PENNSYLVANIA LAW REVIEW   For the excerpt from "Statutory Definition of the Standards for Determining Human Death" by A. M. Capron and L. R. Kass from the *University of Pennsylvania Law Review,* vol. 121, pp. 87–118. Reprinted by permission of the publisher and Fred B. Rothman & Co.

THE WILLIAM ALANSON WHITE PSYCHIATRIC FOUNDATION, INC.   For the excerpts from "Suicide Notes Reconsidered" by Edwin S. Shneidman from *Psychiatry,* vol. 36, 1973, pp. 379–94. Copyright The William Alanson White Psychiatric Foundation, Inc. Reprinted by special permission of The William Alanson White Psychiatric Foundation, Inc., and the author.